PROMISE OF DEVELOPMENT

*Theories of Change
in Latin America*

Also of Interest

†*Latin America: Capitalist and Socialist Perspectives of Development and Underdevelopment,* Ronald H. Chilcote and Joel C. Edelstein

†*The Gap Between Rich and Poor: Contending Perspectives on the Political Economy of Development,* edited by Mitchell A. Seligson

†*Latin American Politics and Development,* edited by Howard J. Wiarda and Harvey F. Kline

†*Latin American Political Economy: Financial Crisis and Political Change,* edited by Jonathan Hartlyn and Samuel A. Morley

†*From Dependency to Development: Strategies to Overcome Underdevelopment and Inequality,* edited by Heraldo Muñoz

†*The Fitful Republic: Economy, Society, and Politics in Argentina,* Juan E. Corradi

†*New Directions in Comparative Politics,* edited by Howard J. Wiarda

†*Latin America, Its Problems and Its Promise: A Multidisciplinary Introduction,* edited by Jan Knippers Black

†*Theories of Development and Underdevelopment,* Ronald H. Chilcote

A Bias for Hope: Essays on Development and Latin America, Albert O. Hirschman

Limits to Capitalist Development: The Industrialization of Peru, 1950–1980, John Weeks

Regional Integration: The Latin American Experience, edited by Altaf Gauhar

Politics and Economics of External Debt Crisis: The Latin American Experience, edited by Miguel S. Wionczek, in collaboration with Luciano Tomassini

Brazil's Economic and Political Future, Julian Chacel, Pamela S. Falk, and David V. Fleischer

†Available in hardcover and paperback.

About the Book and Editors

In recent years Latin Americanists have been among the most innovative and productive theorists of the uneven process of development. This collection of substantial selections from some of the most prominent theorists in the field represents a scholarly consolidation and reassessment of the controversies concerning the development of Latin America.

Beginning with a historiographic overview, the editors emphasize the origins, evolution, and historical context of the development of each theoretical school (modernization, dependency and Marxism, corporatism, and bureaucratic authoritarianism) and then present key selections drawn from the writings of major theorists, organized by school. Each selection is prefaced with a short editorial introduction that highlights the central themes. A concluding section outlines the main debates surrounding each school and suggests new directions in theoretical development that might arise from criticism of the theories of authoritarianism and the search for democratic processes of development. The book's usefulness as a text is further enhanced by selected bibliographies that contain additional readings on each development theory.

Here is a single source for Latin Americanists who hope to interest and instruct their students in the rich theoretical traditions and debates in Latin American studies. This book can also be a strong core volume for courses on other developing areas.

Peter F. Klarén is a professor of Latin American history at The George Washington University and a professorial lecturer on Andean history and politics at the School of Advanced International Studies, The Johns Hopkins University. He is the author of *Modernization, Dislocation and Aprismo* (1973) and a contributor to *The Cambridge History of Latin America* (1986). **Thomas J. Bossert** is a professor of political science at Sarah Lawrence College and lectures on politics at the Harvard School of Public Health. His studies of development issues in Latin America have appeared in the *Latin American Research Review*, *Comparative Politics*, the *Political Science Quarterly*, *Latin American Perspectives*, and several edited works.

PROMISE
OF DEVELOPMENT
*Theories of Change
in Latin America*

*edited by Peter F. Klarén
and Thomas J. Bossert*

Westview Press / Boulder and London

Copyright © 1986 by Westview Press, Inc.

Published in 1986 in the United States of America by Westview Press, Inc.; Frederick A. Praeger, Publisher; 5500 Central Avenue, Boulder, Colorado 80301

Library of Congress Cataloging-in-Publication Data
Main entry under title:
Promise of development.
  Bibliography: p.
  Includes index.
    1. Latin America—Politics and government—
1945–   —Addresses, essays, lectures. 2. Authori-
tarianism—Latin America—Addresses, essays, lectures.
3. Latin America—Economic conditions—1945–   —Ad-
dresses, essays, lectures. 4. Latin America—Dependency
on foreign countries—Addresses, essays, lectures.
5. Corporate state—Latin America—Addresses, essays,
lectures. I. Klarén, Peter F., 1938–   .
II. Bossert, Thomas J.
JL966.P75 1986   303.4′098   85-26425
ISBN 0-8133-0006-1
ISBN 0-8133-0007-X (pbk.)

Printed and bound in the United States of America

The paper used in this publication meets the minimum requirements of the American National Standard for Permanence of Paper for Printed Library Materials Z39.48-1984.

10   9   8   7   6   5   4   3   2   1

For Alexandra
whose delightful companionship
ever enlivened this intellectual endeavor

P.F.K.

For Claudia
who constantly fulfills and renews
her own promise and who must, by now,
know how much I love her

T.J.B.

Contents

Preface

This is a particularly appropriate time in the field of Latin American studies to undertake a volume of readings that gathers together representative selections of works by key theorists and places them in comparative perspective. In recent years Latin Americanists have been the most innovative and productive theorists of the uneven process of development. They have contributed mightily to the elaboration of dependency and Marxist theory and to the model of bureaucratic authoritarianism as well as to the application of the theories of modernization and corporatism to Latin America. After an intense two-decade period of creative activity, theoretical model building by Latin Americanists has now, in the mid-1980s, reached a momentary plateau. We believe that a comparative reader can, at this moment of scholarly consolidation and reassessment, uniquely serve to focus on the debates surrounding the development of Latin America, in both its historical and contemporary dimensions.

The idea for this reader also emerged from our dissatisfaction, as teachers of Latin American history and politics, with existing texts on Latin America. Although a number of works focus on particular theoretical schools, there are none that comparatively and comprehensively embrace all the different schools, particularly in a single volume. In the classroom, therefore, we were forced to use our own compilation of class readings—often a haphazard collection of reserved readings—or to treat theory in a more isolated fashion, primarily in lectures. We have tried to make *Promise of Development* the single source for Latin Americanists who hope to interest and instruct their students in the rich theoretical traditions and debates in Latin American studies.

We used several criteria in selecting the articles for this book. First, we endeavored to include the principal theorists in each school represented. For instance, Fernando Henrique Cardoso is one of the central figures in dependency theory, and Guillermo O'Donnell is the originator of bureaucratic authoritarianism. Second, we selected authors whose writings have a specific empirical reference to Latin America. This is the case, for example, with Seymour Martin Lipset, who applied the more general modernization theory to an exploration of value change in Latin America. Third, we included authors whose works develop crucial distinctions within a broader theoretical perspective and whose clarity of expression uniquely contributes to the reader's understanding. Both John J. Johnson and Jacques Lambert, who explore, respectively, the middle classes and the landed estate, develop concrete issues in modernization theory. Finally, we sought to avoid the fragmentation often found in anthologies by including substantial, in-depth selections rather than short excerpts. In our view this approach is more intellectually and pedagogically sound. With this method the reader acquires a more accurate and thorough knowledge of the theory while being forced to grapple intensively with the material.

We were, of course, unable to include the works of many important theorists. We do not mean to suggest by these omissions that their contributions are less significant than those we did include. Selections were made in part by how well each work fit together with the other works in the volume as well as by how clear and self-explanatory the work's necessarily shortened arguments might be. We tried to retain a sense of historical progression in the development of theory, selecting passages that specified the important differences among theorists and at the same time showed the richness and complexity of each approach.

We begin our reader with a historiographic overview, emphasizing the origins, evolution, and historical context for the development of each theoretical school and outlining the main criticisms and ensuing debates that have sprung up around each school. The core of the book, key selections drawn from the writings of the major theorists, is organized by schools. Each section is, in turn, prefaced with a short introduction that highlights the central themes. The concluding chapter suggests new directions in theoretical development that might arise from criticism of the theory of bureaucratic authoritarianism and from the renewed search for democratic processes of development.

We edited the selections when we felt a need to clarify a particular point or passage. We also deleted some purely descriptive, out-of-date, or repetitive passages. For example, we deleted multiple examples used to illustrate a point when we felt a single example would suffice.

There are, of course, many people who directly or indirectly contributed to this book. We would like to thank those who first taught us Latin American history and politics: Robert Burr, Stanley Stein, Paul Sigmund, Charles Anderson, Alex Wilde, and William Glade. Their interests and inspirations deeply influenced the logic of this book. Our colleagues who offered insights and encouragement include Nancy Bermeo, Arturo

Valenzuela, Peter Smith, Joyce Reigelhaupt, Howard Wiarda, Guillermo O'Donnell, and Riordan Roett. Special acknowledgments are due to Ian Roxborough, whose own analysis of Latin American development theory and freely given advice helped to inspire our introduction and conclusion; to Ken Sharpe, whose observations, logic, and penetrating questions helped clarify our arguments; and to James Kurth, whose sparkling and imaginative approach to these issues is embedded in our concluding analysis. While these colleagues have shaped our thinking, they should not be held accountable for our mistakes. We are solely responsible for the original material in this book.

We must also thank our students, some of whom worked through the early photocopies of this book, for teaching us what was important to include and refreshing our interest in the promise of development. Our patient editors, first Lynne Rienner and then Miriam Gilbert, courageously waited through the long gestation of this book and offered useful advice and encouragement. Thanks, too, go to the authors and publishers who kindly granted permission for their works to appear here. Finally, because a work like this inevitably draws on family resources, we must thank our families for their patience, understanding, and support.

Peter F. Klarén
Washington, D.C.

Thomas J. Bossert
Bronxville, N.Y.

INTRODUCTION

1 / Lost Promise: Explaining Latin American Underdevelopment

Peter F. Klarén

"The development of underdevelopment" is the way one observer, the controversial economist Andre Gunder Frank, characterized Latin America's evolution since the Iberian invasion of the late fifteenth century. Although many reject Frank's theory of causality, few dispute the stark reality of Latin America's profound underdevelopment in today's world. Once imagined by its Iberian conquerors as a land of "El Dorado," Latin America stands five centuries later at the precipice of economic and social disaster. It is a region wracked by the possibility of collective bankruptcy and the reality that most of its people, to borrow from Franklin D. Roosevelt's famous description of the United States in the depths of the depression, are ill housed, ill clothed, and ill fed. Crowded into the sprawling urban slums that surround Latin America's primary cities or locked into a "feudalized" hinterland, prisoners of a decaying economic and social system, Latin America's masses confront an uncertain, increasingly desperate material future.

Explanations for this dismal state of affairs abound. The historiography of the problem reveals numerous interpretations that at best are replete with oversimplification and overgeneralization and at worst are infused with racial stereotype and cultural bias. Prior to this century, for example, Anglo-American writers such as Willam H. Prescott (1796–1859) viewed the Iberian world through a "glass darkly" and described a world distorted by international rivalry and a collective mythology that stressed religious, cultural, and racial superiority. The image presented by these writers conjured up a "black legend" that attributed Latin American underdevelopment to a brutal Iberian colonialism that mercilessly enslaved and exploited the native peoples of Latin America for metropolitan

3

gain. The object of such hyperbole was, as often as not, wholly self-serving, meant to glorify the emerging democratic experiment of the North by contrasting it to some dark, despotic, Catholic-Latin world in the South.

Another widely held interpretation of Latin American backwardness was the product of nineteenth-century European racist thought that was assimilated by the Creole (Spanish American) elite after their independence from Spain. A strong sense of racial superiority helped them justify their claim as the new, legitimate rulers of the region. Although implicitly extolling white superiority, they blamed Latin America's lack of progress (defined in European terms) on the Indian, Black-African, or mestizo masses who were judged inferior and inherently incapable of self-improvement.

In more recent times, these and other equally shallow or warped explanations have given way to more complex, sophisticated interpretations of what many consider to be the paramount issue of our time. Since the end of World War II, the West has become increasingly aware of the dilemmas of the Third World. This awareness was spurred by three factors: first, the process of postwar decolonization and recurrent wars of national liberation around the world; second, the technological revolution that drew the world closer together and made it more interdependent; and third, the bipolarization of global politics and the rise of the cold war between East and West, each side with contrasting ideologies competing for influence in every corner of the world. By converging when they did and heightening awareness in the West of the human condition of Third World people, these factors worked in the postwar era, particularly within the emerging social sciences, to focus intellectual resources on finding solutions to the development conundrum.

As a result, four distinct and often opposing theories of Latin American development—modernization, dependency and Marxism, corporatism, and bureaucratic authoritarianism—gradually emerged during the past few decades. Theorists from each school explained and interpreted Latin American underdevelopment while proposing their own formula for promoting development in the region. Since no theory is produced in an intellectual vacuum and without certain "precursors," let us briefly turn back to the great transformation that forged the European industrial revolution and the rise of modern Western society. Each of the Latin American development theories in one way or another traces its philosophical roots back to that period of complex change and intellectual ferment that occurred in Europe from the sixteenth through the nineteenth centuries.

Classical Sociological Theory:
Marx, Weber, Durkheim

Between the sixteenth and nineteenth centuries, a series of developments culminated in modern industrial capitalism, which was to transform not only the West but much of the entire world, including Latin America, by the end of the twentieth century. Fascination with the nature of this vast transition—when, why, and how it occurred—first emerged in the nineteenth century with a corpus of social thought that came to be known as classical sociological theory. The scions of this theory, although by no means its only elaborators, were three towering nineteenth-century thinkers—Marx, Weber, and Durkheim. Thus, the discourse on the problem of modern underdevelopment in the southern hemisphere begins with this triumvirate of European intellectual giants.

Karl Marx (1818–1883)—the great German economist, philosopher, and sociologist—presented an evolutionary view of the development of man and society. According to Marx, society had passed through several stages—tribal (communal); slave (Greece, Rome); and feudal (Europe in the Middle Ages)—and had arrived at modern capitalism, whose industrial phase he personally observed in England (primarily Manchester) in the mid-nineteenth century. For Marx, who regarded the material, economic conditions of life as the basis of societal organization, the central feature of society's great transformation was the emergence of capitalism.

According to Marx, capitalism had several defining characteristics. These included

- A ruling class
- the bourgeoisie or capitalists who owned the means of production
- a production system based on the exploitation of labor
- the expropriation of labor's "surplus value" by the bourgeoisie to form the "accumulated" capital necessary to drive the system
- the alienation of the worker from the product of his work
- the tendency of capital to concentrate in ever-fewer hands, thereby polarizing society into two hostile classes—the propertied or bourgeois class and the propertyless working class or proletariat.

Marx further believed that this polarization would culminate in a final class struggle in which the proletariat would be victorious and capitalism destroyed. The victorious proletariat would then proceed to construct socialism and communism (terms Marx used interchangeably), which Marx viewed as the final or highest stage of society's evolution.

Like other philosophers of his era Marx believed that his theory of society had established the existence of universal laws of evolution and that each stage was a prerequisite for the next. Thus, although societies might evolve at different rates, none could avoid passing through these stages. Capitalism, according to Marx, was a crucial, if transitory, stage in the evolution of Western society. Marx believed that it was primarily a sixteenth-century phenomenon with roots in the medieval cities of feudal Europe. The discovery of America in 1492 and its subsequent colonization, along with the opening of trade to China and India, provided enormous, expanding markets that stimulated Europe's budding industry and commerce.

For Max Weber (1864–1920), the renowned German sociologist and political economist, capitalism was also an important feature of the great transformation. However, Weber was more interested in explaining the uniqueness of modern Western society, which he saw as radically different from the premodern world. For him the core of this distinctiveness lay in modern society's rationality, epitomized by the development of science and the empirical method. This rationalism permeated the entire fabric of Western society, particularly its religious structure (Protestantism and its stress on doctrine and ethics as opposed to ritual and ceremony), polity (the growing importance of bureaucracy with its division of labor and impersonal rules), and economy (the rise of capitalism).

Weber observed in European history a rationalist tendency in the political sphere marked by the slow rise of bureaucratic organizations. Lacking direction, however, bureaucratic rule was periodically eclipsed by the emergence of charismatic leaders who sprang from the masses to seize power from traditional leaders. After periods of unrestrained and unpredictable rule by such leaders, the forces of routinization would reassert themselves. A successor to the charismatic leader would be selected and would reimpose a rationalized and routinized form of rule on society.

As Weber saw it Western society had alternated dialectically between periods of bureaucratic routine and irrational outbreaks of charismatic rule. In general, however, the tendency toward increasing bureaucratic rationalization of the polity was slow in developing, as was the economy, until the forces of capitalism transformed the organization of production and rationalized the economy.

For Weber capitalism was but one further expression of the process of rationalizing Western society. Unlike Marx, however, who saw the essence of capitalism in the expropriation of surplus value from labor, or the neo-classical economists, who saw capitalism in the pursuit of profit, Weber emphasized what he called the new capitalist spirit among entrepreneurs and workers, which he linked to the advent of the Reformation. Weber made this unique theoretical contribution in his seminal work *The Protestant Ethic and the Spirit of Capitalism,* which stressed the importance of values and ideas as well as strictly economic factors (upon which Marx's theory was based) in the rise of capitalism.[1]

While Weber asserted that the uniqueness of the West derived from the increasing rationalization of society, Emile Durkheim (1858–1917), a French sociologist and philosopher, focused on what he perceived as the breakdown of community that occurred during the transition from a traditional society to a modern society. Under the impact of rapid social change brought about by the increasing capitalization of the economy, the ties of mechanical solidarity that traditionally had bound people in tightly knit communities rapidly unraveled. Urbanization, in particular, had brought about a depersonalization of life, and the traditional authority of the church, the family, and other institutions had eroded, leaving the masses directionless and suspended in a spiritual void. The result of this increasingly soulless individualism was, in Durkheim's view, widespread "anomie," a sense of isolation and alienation from others.

To counteract this tendency Durkheim, using an analogy from biology, advocated the creation of an organic solidarity, composed of new institutions such as the state that would replace older sources of moral authority. Community could be re-formed, for example, at the workplace, where the corporate guild could serve as a new harmonious, if hierarchical, institution anchoring people's lives. Durkheim thus became an advocate of corporatist theory whose idea of the organic state goes back to the political philosophies of Aristotle (384–322 B.C.) and St. Thomas Aquinas (1225?–1274).

Despite their obvious theoretical differences and emphases, these three nineteenth-century thinkers agreed on one essential point. The West had experienced in their view a profound transition from a traditional to a modern society. Moreover, this transformation had produced a breakdown in community life and the emergence of a more universal and impersonal social structure. It remained for social scientists in the next century to elaborate further this dichotomous view of world development (i.e., the transition from traditional to modern society) in their attempts to analyze the problem of underdevelopment in the Third World.

Reconceptualization of Development
After World War II

The preoccupation of the nineteenth-century philosophers with explaining the development of the West shifted in the twentieth century to understanding the lag or lack of development in most of the non-Western, or Third World, countries. The Russian Revolution of 1917 did much to precipitate this intellectual reorientation. Here was a revolution of monumental significance, which, contrary to Marx's prediction, did not occur as a result of capitalist development in Europe, but rather in a backward, noncapitalist, largely agrarian, non-Western country that saw only the beginnings of European capitalist growth. Why had the Third World remained seemingly impervious to the developmental evolution that had been experienced in the West? It was not until the end of World War II that social scientists, particularly in the United States, became preoccupied with this question in response to the fundamental changes taking place in world affairs during the postwar period.

First, the defeat of the Axis powers in 1945 marked the rise of both the United States and the Soviet Union as world powers and the subsequent polarization between East and West. Second, the postwar period inaugurated a trend toward self-determination, which led to the breakup of the vast colonial empires in Asia and Africa carved out by the West in the nineteenth century. As a myriad of independent nation states emerged from this breakup, their leaders were confronted with two problems. One was how to relate, in a bipolar world, to the two great powers that were intensively competing for influence. The other problem was how to foster development of their backward economies. Most of these leaders shared the nearly universal aspiration for modernity and a better standard of living for their citizens, which they felt could be achieved through rapid economic growth and social transformation.

In this context, U.S. policymakers searched for arguments to counter Soviet claims that Marxism represented a better alternative for development in the Third World than did Western capitalism. At the same time U.S. scholars began to study in earnest the causes of underdevelopment. In particular scholars asked why the West had developed and most of the rest of the world had not.

Whether there was a direct relationship between U.S. national interests and the formulation of modernization theory is not altogether clear. However, critics of modernization suggest that it was no coincidence that as the political and economic power of the United States expanded in the postwar period, so too did the preeminence of liberal, developmental thought in the form of modernization theory. These critics argue that U.S. social science, overtly or subtly as the product of a collective cold war mentality prone to defend liberal, Western, capitalist values, was put to the service of U.S. policymakers makers and U.S. national interest. The critics further contend that this use of U.S. social science explains the substantial investment that was made by U.S. foundations and the U.S. government in building a sophisticated social science establishment in the United States during the postwar years as well as the strongly ethnocentric and self-serving world view that they perceive as infusing modernization theory.

Modernization Theory

In any case, modernization theory evolved directly from two ideas about social change that were developed by the nineteenth-century fathers of sociology. One idea was Weber's polar conception of traditional versus modern, which was given a Third World dimension in this century by anthropologist Robert Redfield in his theory of a folk-urban dichotomy. The other idea was the theory of evolution developed by Auguste Comte (1798–1857), the French founder of the philosophical system of Positivism, who also based his thinking on the polar conception. Comte conceived of a theory of social evolution in which modern ("industrial" and "scientific") society was the culmination of a series of stages in human development from a traditional ("theological" and "military") society.[2] The idea that human society had evolved in a series of evermore complex stages, a theory further elaborated by English philopher Herbert Spencer (1820–1903), came to form an important part of mainstream nineteenth-century thought.

These two strands were combined into a theory of the "stages of growth," which came to form the core of modernization theory in the mid-twentieth century. This theory held that all societies were alike at the "traditional" stage and that eventually they would pass through the same set of changes that had led the West to the "modern" stage.

This polar conception is particularly evident in the work of economist Walt W. Rostow (1960) who elaborated a theory of economic "take-off" in which self-sustained growth involved five stages of development from traditional to modern. Modeled on the experience of the British industrial revolution, Rostow's theory assumed that Third World societies could replicate this experience by developing policies to increase capital accumulation and investment as well as to foster entrepreneurial values or entrepreneurship. For Rostow and other economists who held similar beliefs, modernization for the Third World meant primarily the application of technology to the control of nature as a means of increasing per capita growth.

Dualism, as formulated in the work of economist W. A. Lewis (1955), likewise reflected a polar conception. Lewis distinguished between a dynamic "capitalist" sector and a stagnant "subsistence" sector within the economy. The latter lagged far behind the former in capital, income, and rate of growth. Moreover, interaction between the two sectors was reduced to the unlimited amount of labor supplied by the subsistence sector to the capitalist sector.

The same polar concept of modernization appeared in the work of sociologist Talcott Parsons (1951), a founder of the structural-functionalist approach to social change. A neo-evolutionist, Parsons drew from Weber but particularly from the *Gemeinschaft* to *Gesellschaft* (community to association) dichotomy developed by German sociologist Ferdinand Tönnies (1855–1936). Like other sociologists and social anthropologists, Parsons was primarily concerned with the process of differentiation that characterized modern societies.

Parsons believed that forces such as the increasing division of labor were working steadily to divide society. To counteract this tendency toward social disintegration, these new forces had to be accompanied by other forces, pulling society back together again. Here Parsons sought to define the way society reintegrates itself. Differentiation occurred in the economic system and in the social, particularly status, elements of that system. Modernization occurred when economic and technological change made the traditional social and status structures obsolete.

Parsons also suggested that specific characteristics, which he called "pattern variables," distinguished traditional societies from modern societies. He argued that traditional societies contained values often associated with small, local communities: little division of labor and all-encompassing interpersonal relationships. By contrast modern societies were larger and more complex, with greater division of labor and increased mobility. Individual achievements were more important than family background or other inherent factors. In addition the hierarchical, personalistic sources of authority that permeated all aspects of traditional societies were replaced in modern societies by separate political insitutions with rational, legal, and impersonal bases of authority.

Parsons viewed the process of modernization as requiring changes in social values toward those associated with the modern "ideal." In particular, diffuse, multifaceted relationships that tied people together in a community had to be replaced by more specific, segmented relationships associated with distinct roles representing separate functions in the new, more complex division of labor. "Collective" traditional values had to be replaced by "individual" modern values. The tendency to treat others according to personal ties—what Parsons called "particularism"—had to be replaced by universally valid, objective, and impersonal criteria.

This typology was based on the assumption that a society's value system, as well as its institutional configuration, was paramount in determining its potential for development. The attainment of self-sustaining growth involved far more than purely economic processes of production, investment, and consumption, as the developmental economists would have it. Rather the values, institutions, and patterns of a society had to be considered. In the case of traditional society, these elements were both a cause and an effect of underdevelopment and constituted obstacles to modernization. For modernizationists the norms and structures of traditional society had to be changed. Traditional society had to give way to sweeping innovations. New ideas, values, techniques, and organizations had to be introduced into the old social order.

There was, however, disagreement over the specific nature of this change. Modernizationists such as Neil Smelser (1963), a sociologist at Berkeley, and Parsons himself affirmed that modernization derived from increasing societal and institutional differentiation and from the rise of new sources of integration (i.e., nationalism, political parties, bureaucracies). Others such as sociologists Everett Hagen (1962) and David McClelland (1962), based on their studies of attitudes in traditional societies, emphasized the assimilation of modern values by individuals.

How this innovation would occur in the Third World was clarified by, among others, political scientist Daniel Lerner (1958) in his in-depth study of the Middle East. Lerner argued that although the West had modernized because of endogenous cultural and institutional changes, non-Western development would be exogenous, brought about by the mechanism of diffusion. Progress was to be diffused from the West—the United States and Europe—to the rest of the world, which would adopt and adapt Western technology, assimilate Western values and patterns of action, and import Western institutions. In short, Third World countries would be able to adopt already established social and economic patterns and would move quickly on the path to development already followed by the West.

The political implications of modernization in Third World countries were drawn by Harvard sociologist Seymour Martin Lipset (1967) and political scientist James Coleman (1960). Westernization, industrialization, and economic growth would generate the preconditions for the evolution of greater social equality and hence, it was assumed, the rise of stable, democratic institutions. Progress, as defined by the West, would in the end transform the underdeveloped world and propel it headlong into the twentieth century and modernity.

As the main lines of modernization theory unfolded, however, such unbounded initial optimism was soon tempered by a troubling question. Was the presumed beneficial impact on Third World societies all that substantial or clear cut? Political scientist Dankwart Rustow (1967), for example, warned that the effects of modernization were morally ambiguous and that, together with the unprecedented benefits, modernization also brought inevitable hazards and deprivations. Others, such as Harvard political scientist Samuel Huntington (1968) and Princeton historian Cyril Black (1966), saw modernization as disruptive, the source of discontent and social and political conflict. Huntington in particular challenged the idea that modernization led to the emergence of greater equality and democracy in developing areas. Pointing to the growing evidence of revolution, violence, and coups, Huntington suggested instead that rapid development often triggered sociopolitical tensions that led to the breakdown of stable regimes and a form of "praetorian politics." In this scenario the military, not democratic parties, stabilized the polity and created the necessary preconditions for sustained economic growth.

Modernization Theory Applied to Latin America

Despite these and other questions, many writers on Latin America, particularly in the United States, applied modernization theory to explain the region's developmental problems. These writers argued that traditional values and institutions that originated in the Iberian colonization of the region in the sixteenth century blocked efforts toward economic and sociopolitical development. They singled out in particular the attitudes of Catholicism, of the large Indian populations, and of the aristocratic landed elite as inimical to the process of modernization and development in the region.

One of the first Latin Americans to apply modernization theory to the problem of Latin American development was Gino Germani. A pioneer of modern sociological analysis in his native Argentina, Germani later came to the United States where he taught for many years at Harvard with Talcott Parsons and Seymour Martin Lipset. Focusing on the impact of rapid industrialization and urbanization on Argentine society, Germani's most important work, published in 1963, was entitled *Política y Sociedad en una Epoca de Transición* (Politics and Society in an Epoch of Transition).

Germani envisioned Latin America as passing through a series of stages from a traditional to a "mass" or modern society. This was a decidedly disjointed, often accelerated, process punctuated by serious social dislocations that, for Germani, explained the unstable nature of politics. In Parsonian terms the transition in Latin America had produced a rapid process of structural differentiation but not the necessary reintegration to solidify the modern social organism. To a large extent Germani viewed the process as disruptive and negative in its effect on Third World "latecomers" to the process of modernization, industrialization, and development, such as Latin America.

In the United States perhaps the foremost modernizationist writing on Latin American development was Seymour Martin Lipset. His essay "Values, Education and Entrepreneurship" introduced the widely read and influential work *Elites in Latin America,* published in 1967. Lipset was strongly influenced by the ideas of Weber and drew directly on the theories of both Parsons and McClelland in arguing the centrality of differing value systems to explain the disparity between the development of North America and that of South America. For Lipset, echoing Weber, the lack of an entrepreneurial ethic, which he attributed to Hispanic feudalism, was crucial in explaining Latin American underdevelopment. Underdevelopment could be overcome, however, with the spread of a westernized educational system throughout the region. Unlike Germani, Lipset viewed modernization as beneficial to Latin America, something to be pursued vigorously by the policymakers of both North and South.

Political scientist Kalman Silvert followed a similar line of reasoning in arguing that a "Mediterranean ethos" explained Latin America's historic underdevelopment. "Modernizers," however, were increasingly emerging from the middle- and upper-classes to challenge this ethos, a fact that gave promise to the future of a more democratic, pluralistic polity. That idea was echoed by Stanford University historian John J. Johnson whose historical analysis of what he called the "middle sectors" in early twentieth-century society suggested a trend toward greater democracy and modernization. French sociologist Jacques Lambert, on the other hand, took a different analytical tact. Lambert conceived of a dual society in which modernization, diffusing from the urban areas, was impeded by the large landed estates—latifundia—that dominated the rural areas. Only through agrarian reform could structural change unleash the forces of modernity.

Despite the clarity and cogency of the modernization paradigm, it was not long before a number of telling criticisms were leveled against it. One problem involved its use of evolutionary theory and the assumption by modernizationists that all societies moved on a linear, developmental continuum from traditional to modern, as had allegedly happened in the West, passing through a series of universal stages of growth. One difficulty with this idea was that contact between two cultures, Parson's "diffusion" and Lerner's optimistic "exogenous" influences, might well modify such a sequence of stages. More importantly, with respect to the dichotomy between traditional and modern, not all preindustrial societies were or are alike. Social structures vary greatly around the world, and there was no reason to assume that feudal, tribal, or bureaucratic societies would all change in the same way. Furthermore, the word traditional conveyed a false image of a wholly static equilibrium, which was simply not the case in many non-Western societies.

Finally, modernizationists, assuming that the Western transition could be mechanically replicated anywhere, insisted on imposing their culturally based model of development somewhat indiscriminately on the rest of the world. Moreover, they emphasized that endogenous more than exogenous factors would stimulate the value changes in traditional Latin American society that would lead to the rise, as in the West, of an entrepreneurial elite that would spearhead development. However, such a view of change largely ignored the powerful economic effects of international trade. As more scholarly attention was focused on the processes of change in the Third World, the modernization viewpoint was vigorously disputed, particularly by proponents of a new perspective that came to be known as dependency.

Dependency and Marxism

The dependency theory or approach began as a serious challenge to modernization theory in the 1960s.[3] The theory originated in the extensive Latin American debate over the problem of underdevelopment, and as such it became a distinctly Latin American contribution to modern social science. Two factors converged to form the dependency school: discussions of underdevelopment that coalesced in the work of the United Nations Economic Commission for Latin America (ECLA) and the revision of orthodox Marxism, which came to be known as "neo-Marxism."

Early discussion of underdevelopment in Latin America was characterized by intense self-criticism and a nearly universal tendency on the part of *pensadores* ("thinkers") to apply European thought (eighteenth-century evolutionism, Comtean Positivism, and social Darwinism) to Latin American conditions. It was not until the era of World War I, which saw the Mexican and Russian revolutions as well as a continuation of interventions in Latin America by the United States, that Latin Americans began to attribute their problems to the world at large. The Great Depression of the 1930s intensified this tendency to externalize the causes of Latin American underdevelopment and formed the background for the peripheral theory of economic development. Pioneered by Raúl Prebisch, an Argentine economist and director of ECLA in the 1950s, this theory attributed the causes for Latin America's underdevelopment to the system of international free trade.

To understand why Latin American underdevelopment persisted, ECLA economists focused on the region's relationship with the world economy, which they portrayed as divided into a developed "center" and an underdeveloped "periphery." Departing from the conventional approach of modernizationists, ECLA economists argued that Latin America was adversely affected by its trade relationship with the industrialized countries of the West. In the nineteenth and early twentieth centuries the Latin American periphery increasingly specialized in the production of raw materials (cotton, wool, various minerals) and foodstuffs (wheat, sugar, cattle products) for the industrial center, receiving in return manufactured goods. ECLA argued that instead of benefiting both trading partners equally, according to laws of comparative advantage of neo-classical economics, the terms of trade had turned against Latin America: the prices (hence profits) on exports from the periphery steadily declined, while the prices of manufactured goods from the center conversely increased. Only when trade was cut off between the center and the periphery because of the world wars or depression did Latin America experience a surge of industrial development and thus a more balanced cycle of growth. Whenever trade ties were reestablished between the two regions, Latin American "outward" development resumed, and industrial development again languished.

To reverse this structural imbalance between the center and the periphery, ECLA proposed policies to foster import-substitution industrialization (ISI) and thereby turn Latin America from an outward to an inward pattern of development. A series of measures would be undertaken at the initiative of the state to accomplish this goal. Domestic industries were to be protected from foreign competition by tariffs and stimulated by various government subsidies and a controlled exchange rate. Structural reforms, such as land reform, and income redistribution policies would be pursued in order to expand the internal market for local industry by increasing the purchasing power of peasants and workers.

Initial acceptance of the ECLA strategy, particularly its emphasis on land reform, was slow in unfolding, but by the mid-1950s several Latin American countries had adopted import substitution industrialization programs based on ECLA proposals. After a short period of success, however, ISI expansion came to a halt during the 1960s as the domestic market reached new limits and became saturated. In addition, to avoid tariff barriers to their products U.S. multinational corporations simply established manufacturing subsidiaries in many Latin American countries. In its analysis of underdevelopment, ECLA had never questioned the role of foreign capital, which it found salutory in the developmental process; nor had it explored the role of imperialism in this process.

This exploration would now be done by a growing number of critics within ECLA who drew upon Marxist theories of imperialism to alter and expand upon ECLA's idea of the center's exploitation of the periphery.

Marxism and the New Left

As with the main nineteenth-century theories seeking to explain the great transformation in the West, early theories of imperialism focused upon its causes in the metropolis rather than its effects on the periphery. Political economist J. A. Hobson (1858–1940) theorized that because of waning demand in the metropolis Western capitalists sought overseas markets for their goods. The great Communist theorist V. I. Lenin (1870–1924), expanding on Hobson's argument, believed that declining profits at home pushed capitalists to find more profitable investments abroad. Lenin also envisioned imperialism as a distinct stage in the world development of capitalism and not as a relationship between two nations or economies. Indeed, Lenin claimed, erroneously as it turned out, that imperialism was the highest stage of capitalism. His predictions were belied by the post–World War II process of decolonization, which did not bring about the collapse of capitalism.

ECLA critics now studied imperialism as part of their analysis of why the ECLA strategy of ISI had gone awry in the 1960s. However, they concentrated their view of imperialism not from the center countries, as Lenin had done, but from the periphery. Contrary to the optimism of some modernizationists, these critics found the effects of exogenous Western influence to be decidedly deleterious to developing nations.

At this point neo-Marxism began to make its imprint on the genesis of dependency. The political context nourishing the neo-Marxist critique of orthodox Marxism was provided by the rise of the New Left in Latin America during the 1960s. Representing the challenge of a new generation to orthodox Marxism, the New Left was particularly critical of the Stalinist tradition adopted by most of the Communist parties on the continent.

According to the Stalinist tradition, Latin America was still in the grip of feudal economic and political relationships. The first stage of what has been labeled the Communist party's two-stage revolutionary strategy called for an alliance with the national bourgeoisie in order to overthrow the remnant powers of the feudal oligarchy. Once capitalism was brought to full bloom under the aegis of the bourgeoisie, the Communist party would undertake the second stage—the proletarian revolution that would lead to the overthrow of capitalism and the establishment of socialism.

The success of the Cuban Revolution of 1959 galvanized the New Left throughout the continent. The revolution illuminated a powerful new path in which the peasants were more inclined to revolt than the workers and mobilizing rural guerrillas appeared to be a viable alternative to organizing urban laborers. The revolution also led the New Left to question the Communist Party's historic two-stage strategy. It grew increasingly impatient with the failure of the "objective conditions" for revolution to materialize, as predicted by orthodox Marxist doctrine (e.g., the capitalist stage to be fully developed, enabling the proletariat to be mobilized). As a result, the New Left adopted the ideas of Che Guevara (1928–1967), Latin American revolutionary and leader of the Cuban Revolution, about the ability of the human will to overcome such objective limitations—the so-called voluntarist revolutionary strategy. Boldly proclaiming that the duty of a revolutionary was to make revolution, this new generation set off seismic reverberations in Marxist political and intellectual circles.

A major challenge to orthodox Marxist views on development had already appeared in a work by political economist Paul Baran entitled *The Political Economy of Growth,* published in 1957. In it Baran argued that Western imperialism, rather than initiating the global transition from feudalism to capitalism according to Marxist-Leninist theory, had actually stunted the growth of capitalism in the Third World by draining off capital and killing native industry through unequal competition. Here was a derailment of Marx's evolutionary theory of development. Baran concluded that the Third World had stagnated somewhere between feudalism and capitalism. Imperialism did not represent the highest stage of capitalism in its inexorable march toward proletarian revolution and worldwide socialism. Rather, according to Baran, it had produced a chronic condition of perpetual underdevelopment in the Third World.

Later dubbed the "development of underdevelopment" by economist Andre Gunder Frank in his analysis of Latin America (1967), Baran's ideas seemed to validate the New Left's revolutionary tactics. Why wait patiently for the "objective conditions" to appear when in fact the Latin American bourgeoisie seemed incapable of bringing about total national capitalist development? If Latin America was indeed doomed to perpetual underdevelopment, the only way to break out of this condition was to mount an immediate revolution with the resources at hand.

Genesis of the Dependency School

At this point these neo-Marxist currents were stirring within a small group of economists and social scientists located in and around ECLA in Santiago who were increasingly dissatisfied with, and critical of, some aspects of ECLA's analysis of underdevelopment. What emerged from their intense debate on the development issue was the new dependency school.

The dependency analysts rejected the modernizationists' contention that certain Latin American cultural and institutional features were the major reasons for the region's underdevelopment. While not totally discounting these factors, these analysts broadened the narrow national focus of modernization to a more global interpretation that linked internal and external factors in a more holistic fashion. For the dependency analysts, Latin America's insertion into the developing world economy during the Age of Imperialism (the sixteenth to the nineteenth centuries) was central to the region's economic stagnation. This global politico-economic system was characterized by the unequal development of its component parts. In this configuration the center, drawing first upon its own resources, began to industrialize and later colonized the periphery to provide the primary goods (mainly agricultural and mineral) that would sustain the process of metropolitan development. This international division of labor imposed by the West did not lead, as the neo-classical economists predicted, to comparative advantage. Rather, the center gained at the expense of the periphery by relegating the Third World to an inferior position in the global system as solely a producer of primary goods. This imposed division of labor constrained the economic potential of the Third World and contributed to its underdevelopment.

Theotonio dos Santos (1970), an important Brazilian dependency analyst, succinctly captured the essence of this condition:

By dependence we mean a situation in which the economy of certain countries is conditioned by the development and expansion of another economy to which the former is subjected. The relation of interdependence between two or more economies, and between these and world trade, assumes the form of dependence when some countries (the dominant ones) can expand and can be self-sustaining, while other countries (the dependent ones) can do this only as a reflection of that expansion, which can have either a positive or a negative effect on their immediate development.[4]

It was not only the peripheral economies, however, that were conditioned by the dominant center. The internal social and political structures of Latin America were also shaped so as to reinforce the primary nature of the export economy. In this sense, internal and external structural elements were connected to form an elaborate pattern of structural underdevelopment.

Thus, for dependency analysts it was not so much the cultural or institutional factors that blocked entrepreneurship and therefore development. Latin American entrepreneurs operated in a perfectly rational, profit-oriented manner. However, the structures of dependency caused them to behave in a way that preserved and rearticulated dependency to their benefit—hence the enduring and reinforcing nature of the primary export economy throughout the region. Given all of this, it was therefore quite impossible for Latin America, locked into this asymmetrical, interdependent structure, to replicate, as the modernizationists would have it, the evolutionary experience of the West.

In developing what was primarily a historical rather than theoretical model, dependency analysts noted that the pattern of primary exports (gold, silver, dyewoods, sugar, tobacco) established by Spain and Portugal during the colonial period continued in Latin America although the composition of the commodities changed. Even when Spanish America became independent of Spain in the 1820s, "outward development" persisted with export production, which was now directed not toward Spain, but to England and northern Europe. In return for primary products Latin America imported manufactured goods from Europe that flooded the domestic market, often destroying noncompetitive domestic manufacturing.

The Change in Export Structures Within Latin America

Toward the end of the nineteenth century, however, an important difference in the nature of the export structure emerged between various regions of Latin America. In some areas the local elite lost control of export production and were displaced by foreign enclaves. For example, British and U.S. firms moved into nitrate and copper mining in Chile, and U.S. investors began to dominate the Cuban sugar industry. At the same time the state began to regulate and tax these foreign enclaves and became an intermediary between the local economy and the enclaves. Unfortunately, little if any direct stimulation of the local economy occurred since the enclaves remained isolated from the economy at large. Other regional differences developed at this time because of different export products or natural resources, the importance of incipient manufacturing, and the size of the middle and working classes.

The two world wars and the depression of the 1930s produced a succession of crises for the export economy by cutting off foreign markets and throwing Latin America back onto its own resources. To pick up the slack left by falling imports, internal manufacturing was stimulated. The state encouraged this trend by adopting policies (e.g., import substitution) to foment incipient industrialization in industries such as food processing and manufacturing of textiles and other light consumer goods.

Depending on the success in forging multiclass alliances, various countries, such as Argentina, Brazil, and Mexico, were able to attain a considerable level of industrial growth during this period. However, the limits to such growth became evident by mid-century, symbolized by the fall from power of national, populist regimes in Argentina (Juan Perón) and Brazil (Getulio Vargas).[5]

While these tendencies unfolded at the periphery of the world economy, a major development occurred at the center that gave a new dimension to dependency. The postwar rise of the multinational corporation (MNC) created what Oswaldo Sunkel (1970), a Chilean economist, called a new "transnational system." Drawing upon large capital, marketing, and technological resources in the West, MNCs established subsidiaries throughout Latin America with the aim of distributing and/or producing products for local consumption, thereby avoiding tariff barriers. For dependency analysts this trend, in effect, undermined (denationalized) the older import-substitution industries within Latin America and created what Fernando Henrique Cardoso (1969), a Brazilian sociologist, and Enzo Faletto (1963), a Chilean historian, called the internationalization of the internal market.

Several individuals made important contributions to the elaboration of the dependency model. Celso Furtado, a Brazilian economist and historian who was associated with ECLA, had become increasingly critical of ECLA's analysis. The inability of ISI to sustain economic growth led Furtado to "radicalize" ECLA's analysis by incorporating elements of Marxism and Keynesian theory.[6] Furtado advocated a greater effort in bringing about structural reforms together with a larger state role in restructuring the entire economy to improve production and income distribution. His main work *Economic Development of Latin America* (1969), like that of the work by Andre Gunder Frank, helped the dependency perspective gain an international audience.

Less widely known outside Latin America but equally important in radicalizing the ECLA perspective was Oswaldo Sunkel. Although not rejecting Marxism, Sunkel worked in a more eclectic fashion within the structuralist tradition of ECLA. He worked with ECLA during the early 1960s, but unlike Prebisch, Sunkel emphasized the internal factors in the peripheral model. "The possibilities of carrying out a national development policy," he wrote, "basically depend on the domestic situation,"[7] in other words they depend on effecting radical structural reforms. This was something that ECLA, as an international agency, had been reluctant, for diplomatic reasons, to advocate. ECLA did not want to offend the conservative governments in power in Latin America during the 1950s.

Dependency and Development

If Furtado and Sunkel radicalized ECLA's analysis of Latin American underdevelopment, Fernando Henrique Cardoso approached the problem explicitly from a Marxist perspective. Cardoso, who took up residence in Santiago after the 1964 coup in Brazil drove him into exile, collaborated with Enzo Faletto on a book entitled *Dependencia y Desarrollo en América Latina* (Dependency and Development in Latin America, 1979) that has become one of the classics on dependency theory. The work was enriched by the lively debate on development taking place at the time within and outside ECLA in Santiago.

Cardoso accepted as a given that Third World countries were conditioned by the global economic system centered in the West. What was crucial to him was how and under what circumstances each dependent economy was linked to the world market. In other words, the key question was one of political power—how class alliances were formed and political decisions taken in each country in a given historical circumstance. Thus, Cardoso's principal contribution to dependency theory was to add an important sociopolitical dimension to ECLA's predominantly economic analysis. The result, which he called a "historical-structural approach," was at once a more sophisticated and complex analysis than ECLA's and captured the interplay of international economic forces and internal political forces.

Although generally acknowledged as a principal formulator of dependency theory, Cardoso himself takes a more modest credit for the intellectual origins of the theory. He declared that dependency

> did not represent new methodological propositions. What happened was that a current which was already old in Latin American thought managed to make itself heard in the discussions that were taking place in institutions normally closed to it: ECLA, the universities, some government planning agencies, and—last but not least—the North American academic community.

He goes on to say that a critique arose both inside and outside of ECLA that presented "alternatives both to orthodox analyses [modernization] and to what we might call the ECLA-Keynesian analysis." Referring to his own role in this process, Cardoso declared that "a few groups of intellectuals in Santiago in the mid-1960s took up the ECLA problematic and tried to redefine it radically, while seeking to avoid 'vulgar Marxism.'"[8]

Frank and the Development of Underdevelopment

If Cardoso deepened and enriched the dependency analysis, Andre Gunder Frank popularized it beyond the small circle of intellectuals clustered in Santiago, particularly in the English-speaking world. His *Capitalism and Underdevelopment* (1967), according to one commentator, "flashed across the Latin American intellectual horizon like a dazzling, fleeting comet."[9] It was written at a time when Latin America was convulsed in crisis and turmoil. The Castro revolution had triumphed in Cuba in 1959, unleashing a revolutionary storm elsewhere on the continent, only to culminate in a backlash of reaction first in Brazil in 1964 and finally a decade later in Chile in 1973.

Frank's work closely reflected the mood and temper of the times, representing a defiant alternative to both the existing social order in Latin America and the traditional theories and practices of the socialist world. Indeed, according to Frank's publisher, the book's economic and political analysis complemented the political conclusions reached by Régis Debray (1967), the flamboyant French theoretician of the left who had embraced the Castro revolution of 1959. Frank himself stated that the fall of the populist government of Goulart in Brazil in 1964 influenced much of the way he treated Brazilian history. Searching the past for clues to the fall of the Brazilian regime, Frank concluded that any attempt to change the socioeconomic order in Brazil or elsewhere must begin by breaking away from the capitalist order.

This was a conclusion that many on the Latin American left, both at home and abroad, were more than ready to accept. The early Cuban experience with socialism and revolutionary change had provided the left with an alternative to the reformism of earlier populist models as well as the moderate, gradualist tactics and goals long adopted by the Communist parties in Latin America. At the same time social scientists, disillusioned with the linear interpretations founded on a Marxist understanding of the transition from feudalism to capitalism as well as the modernizationist view of society moving from a traditional to a modern order, were also ready to consider Frank's alternative model of dependency theory.

On another level Frank's book as well as the favorable reception (Cardoso called it "consumption") in the United States for dependency theory was the distinct product of the U.S. intellectual climate of the times. Just as modernization might be said to have offered a model of capitalist development that dovetailed with the anti-Communist thrust of American foreign policy during the cold war era, Frank's work and dependency generally emerged as an alternative, counter model to a new generation in the United States (1960s) that reacted against and rejected that older model. During this period Marxism had, with considerable help from McCarthyism,[10] been virtually eliminated from the U.S. intellectual horizon. The tumultuous decade of the 1960s, culminating in the civil rights movement and the drive to end U.S. intervention in Vietnam led to a general critique of U.S. society and foreign policy and made radical ideas, as during the 1930s, more acceptable to broader sectors of the intelligentsia. It was in this context that dependency theory and Frank's book were readily assimilated into the

American political awakening of the 1960s by a public that was "eager to get from the past a confirmation of the lessons the present was apparently offering."[11]

Although closely linked with the Latin American structuralist approach associated with ECLA, Frank's *Capitalism and Underdevelopment* was more than just a recapitulation of dependency theory. While roundly criticized from all sides, Frank's work, nevertheless, made an important contribution to a new formulation of dependency theory. As one scholar put it, "he fused the separate strands of U.S. neo-Marxist and Latin American structuralist thought in a powerful synthesis."[12]

Frank boldly argued that capitalism, by its penetration of Latin America, had caused the region's underdevelopment, rather than it being caused by "traditional" or "backward" structures, as modernizationists maintained. This penetration, which succeeded in incorporating Latin America into the capitalist world system, was characterized by a series of metropolitan-satellite relationships, both on an international and a national level. These relationships worked to drain surplus capital from the region toward the center. Furthermore, Frank rejected the notion of a dualist structure, one traditional and the other modern. Rather he envisioned a linkage between the two systems by way of capitalism, which worked from the modern sector to exploit and expropriate surplus from the traditional sector. Finally, since underdevelopment resulted from close ties to the metropolitan West, Frank reasoned that in order for development to occur those ties should logically be severed.

In one of his more controversial assertions Frank maintained that capitalism had been in force in Latin America since the Iberian conquest. The national bourgeoisie, he argued, had become hopelessly tied to the external economy, which undermined the potential for national development. His conclusion was to promote a nationalist alliance of the peasantry and proletariat and to forsake the national bourgeoisie in the revolutionary process of establishing socialism. Much of his argument drew significant inspiration from the success of the Cuban Revolution and posed a direct challenge to the two-stage revolutionary strategy of the Latin American Communist parties.

Renewing the Debate Within Marxism

Frank's argument raised an old debate within Marxism, now brought up to date by the revolutionary fervor of the 1960s. This debate, which surrounded the Russian Revolution (an event unimagined by Marx himself), raised questions about how to define Russia's position in Marx's theory of historical stages: was Russia feudal and therefore in need of a capitalist revolution, or was it already capitalist and therefore able to begin the process toward socialism? Lenin, building on the theory of "permanent revolution" developed by Leon Trotsky (1879–1940), argued strongly and persuasively for most subsequent Marxists that capitalism, though weak, was sufficiently in evidence in Russia for the proletariat to carry out the revolution. Lenin's argument, however, was specific to Russia in the early twentieth century. Stalin was able to establish a new orthodoxy that defined the national conditions in most of the Third World in terms not unlike those of the modernizationists: the Third World was not sufficiently capitalist to achieve socialism without an alliance with the bourgeoisie.

This debate within Marxism emerged again after dependency analysis had gained a significant following in Latin America. The debate focused on both the conceptual issue of how to define the historical stage in the Marxist typology and the strategic issues of whether to ally with the national bourgeoisie or to push directly for socialist revolution. The conceptual issue became defined as how to determine the "mode of production" in Latin America.

Frank had defined the mode of production as capitalist because Latin America was so firmly entrenched in a world economic system that was based on merchant capitalism. The new Marxist criticism of this view was first expressed by Ernesto Laclau (1971), an Argentine political scientist at the University of Essex. Laclau found that Frank's definition of capitalism was not based on Marx's own emphasis on the mode of production but rather on the exchange of goods (commodities) that occurred under many modes of production, such as slavery, feudalism, and capitalism. Laclau and others who followed this "modes of production analysis" argued that pre-capitalist modes of production persisted in Latin America and that there was no a priori way of determining the dominant mode of production without carefully examining each nation. In particular, the class structures and the relations between workers and owners in specific production environments needed to be scrutinized. It was likely, Laclau and his colleagues argued, that several different modes of production existed at the same time and that in some cases they were reinforced by each other. For instance, merchant capitalism seemed to reinforce feudal production on latifundia that produced for the world market.

The task for analysis then became one of defining the class and economic relationships within a "mixed mode of production." This focus, while not denying the importance of external factors for the economic structure in Latin American nations, suggested that the dominance of the world economy by merchant capitalism did not necessarily imply the complete penetration of capitalism within each nation and that the central focus of analysis should still be the internal class and productive relationships. This more orthodox Marxist approach returned analysis to the dynamics within the nations and suggested that a greater variety of social, economic, and political situations existed in Latin American nations.

The implications of this more complex approach for the strategic issues of revolutionary practice were unclear. It was obvious that such analysis raised serious questions about the optimistic predictions and prescriptions of Frank and others who argued for more daring revolutionary paths. However, the implications of this analysis were that each nation's productive force had to be examined on its own terms. No blanket recommendations for strategy were likely to be valid. Unfortunately, these analysts were not able to develop specific guidelines for strategies in mixed modes of production, leaving the implications of their analysis for political practice open to question.

The debate raised by modes of production analysis was widely reflected in several important articles in the *New Left Review,* an influential English Marxist journal. It was also adopted by several Latin American scholars, including Agustín Cueva (1977) and Roger Bartra (1975).[13] It soon became clear that the modes of production analysis, although shifting the dynamics of change within Latin America to the internal productive and class forces, had not sufficiently developed an analytic framework that could prioritize the relationships and define the political implications of these more complex relationships. In addition, the modes of production analysis, while suggesting that more sophisticated dependency analysts like Cardoso did not give sufficient attention to the internal economic and class issues, really did not challenge the general thrust of these more complex uses of the dependency perspective. Modes of production analysis remains a general approach that has presented a major critique of dependency, without developing a clear direction of its own.

As the foregoing discussion might suggest, the literature on dependency is far from homogeneous. Indeed, numerous debates and disagreements have occurred among its adherents as to what constitutes the main features of the approach. Moreover, whereas the original thrust of dependency addressed the problem of underdevelopment, recent studies,[14] particularly in the United States, have been more interested in explaining international relations than in resolving the problem of underdevelopment. For these scholars, dependency is viewed principally as an asymmetry or imbalance in the international structure of power that exists between two sovereign nation states. These scholars' solution to the problem is the necessary dialogue and negotiation between center and periphery, North and South, over the redistribution of global resources.

In another direction a group of dependency analysts from the United States chose to underscore the role played by U.S. imperialism in forming Latin American dependency and underdevelopment. According to this view the United States not only came to dominate Latin American trade and its financial flow but also exercised political and military hegemony over the region. For example, political scientist James Petras (1974) and sociologist Dale Johnson (1972) focused special attention on the U.S. role in Chile before, during, and after the Marxist government of Salvadore Allende Gossens (1970–1973).[15] Those who see dependency in terms of U.S. imperialism usually advocate its replacement by various forms of socialism.

Corporatism

Let us now turn to a third major approach to the problem of development, one heralded by both Comte and Durkheim. Corporatism is a very old concept of community and of the state. In contrast to modernization and dependency, it traces its origins back to Aristotle. Its particular Iberian form derives from the Roman occupation that lasted over four centuries and imposed a degree of unity and political organization never before experienced. Superceded by the long Moorish occupation, Roman law and imperial achievements were rediscovered, fused, and blended with the Christian, Thomistic-Suarezian[16] conception of the state that supported Iberian society from the sixteenth century onward. It then passed, at least in its essential features, to post-conquest Ibero-America where it took root and endured. There it formed a unique blend of Roman and Thomistic values, an authoritarian political heritage, and a corporatist economic and social organization.[17]

According to modern corporatist theorists Latin American under-development is a product of this unique and enduring corporatist tradition, which not only stood apart from but rejected the revolutionary spirit that animated the West in the age of capitalism and modernity after 1500. Both anticapitalist and anti-Marxist, corporatists reject what they see as the imposition of foreign, alien developmental models on Latin America. Modernity and development, if it is to come to the region, must be filtered through and adapted to what they see as a uniquely Latin American structure and tradition. For many the core of this distinctiveness is to be found in the authority of the state and the central role it has played in shaping the society and the economy. Some corporatists have thus envisioned a third, noncapitalist, non-Marxist path to modernity and development. This move is directed by a powerful, activist, and interventionist state, but one that is within the essentially

Catholic cultural and philosophical framework of Latin American tradition.

The core of corporatist theory lies in what one commentator calls the organic-state tradition.[18] This tradition originated with Aristotle and ran through Roman law, medieval natural law, and contemporary Catholic social philosophy. Organic statism stresses the political community, a specific theory of functional associations called "the concession theory of association," and the central role of the state in achieving the common good.

The starting point for organic statism is the idea that the preferred form of political life is an association of individuals as members of a community. (By contrast liberalism emphasizes the rationale of individual self-interest, and Marxism stresses the dominant mode of production and class struggle.) Since people are, by nature, political beings, political institutions are a natural, organic element of society. But in order to fulfill their proper role, these institutions must be infused with order and power—authority. In this conception the state is viewed as the most perfect form of political community. However, its component parts (individual, family, and private associations such as churches, clubs, and interest groups) all have a proper function, a natural sphere of action within the organic whole (i.e., the state) to which they are intimately connected.

The role of the state then is central in the organic-state tradition of corporatism. Equally important is the notion that the state has a moral end, a moral *telos,* which, as defined by Aristotle, is to govern with a view to the common interest and general welfare of the entire community. This view of the common good, together with the organic political community, became crucial to Catholic social philosophy in the nineteenth and the early twentieth centuries. On the one hand, it could challenge the Marxist notion of class conflict, which violated the organic-state ideal of the harmonious community (as, of course, did liberalism's emphasis on the sanctity of the individual). On the other hand, it criticized liberalism, together with modern capitalism, which led to the abuse and antagonism between classes. Also the corporatist idea of an activist state intervening in society to promote the common good contradicted the liberal notion of a weak state. Over the years the idea that the state should play a relatively autonomous, architectural role in the polity had become another central precept of the organic-state tradition.

Finally, the concession theory of association played an important role in organic statism. This theory was derived from the Greeks who believed that the public common interest was dominant and that private interests should be allowed only the freedom consistent with the organic functioning of society. When transferred from the city state to the bureaucratic state of the Roman Empire, this concession theory took on new significance. According to Roman law, interest groups had to be chartered by the state, thereby reinforcing the idea of the organic state. The interest group, in exchange for the privilege of official recognition, accepted the obligation that in effect made it an integral part of the state. For example, guilds were licensed and granted monopolies in return for maintaining high-quality output and paying taxes to the crown.

The New Corporatism

The "new corporatism" represents a revival of this older, time-honored theoretical model of the state. Political scientist Philippe Schmitter has provided the following "ideal-type" definition of the concept:

> Corporatism can be defined as a system of interest representation in which the constituent units are organized into a limited number of singular, compulsory, noncompetitive, hierarchically ordered and functionally differentiated categories, recognized or licensed (if not created) by the state and granted a deliberate representational monopoly within their respective categories in exchange for observing certain controls on their selection of leaders and articulation of demands and supporters.[19]

Corporatism provides an indigenous (Iberian) alternative to Western liberal capitalism and Marxist socialism, both of which are viewed by certain Latin American elites as inherently disruptive and as alien threats to the traditional fabric of Latin American society. For its practitioners, who reject both modernization and dependency theory, corporatism provides a model of development that is genuinely Latin American. It is also a means of providing social solidarity and avoiding unrestrained individualism or class conflict in the face of the dislocations of modernity. At the same time corporatism seeks to integrate the masses by providing opportunities for popular participation in local, regional, and functional groups. Above all it stands as a nationalist bulwark to prevent a revolution from below (popular) by initiating a process of controlled development from above (the state) that is at once nationalist and consistent with Latin America's monistic and authoritarian traditions.

Numerous criticisms have been leveled at corporatist theory. Some critics see it primarily as an apology for fascism, designed to repress conflict, tensions, and the general sociopolitical crisis unleashed by modernization. Others with Marxist inclinations reject the corporatists' rigid denial of class conflict, even in supposedly harmonious corporatist settings. Schmitter challenges the notion that corporatism is a uniquely

Mediterranean phenomenon and argues that corporatist variants can be found in Northern Europe and even the United States. Finally, social scientists Samuel and Arturo Valenzuela (1978) question the idea that corporatism represents a significant departure from modernization theory. They suggest similarities in the two theories' stress on cultural values and note the implicit acceptance by at least one corporatist (Wiarda) of the modern versus traditional dichotomy proposed by modernizationists.[20]

Bureaucratic Authoritarianism

Our final development theory, bureaucratic authoritarianism (BA), grew out of attempts to understand the emergence of authoritarian and military governments in Brazil in 1964 and Argentina in 1966. Both regimes inaugurated periods of rule by the military as an institution, with the intention of promoting accelerated industrial growth based on massive new foreign investment. In the process they eliminated or drastically controlled elections, restricted the freedom of labor unions, and adopted economic austerity programs that imposed wage controls on the urban popular sector, which was composed of the working and lower middle classes.

The principal architect of BA, who explained these regimes, was the Argentine political scientist Guillermo O'Donnell (1973) who drew, albeit critically, on all three theories: modernization, dependency and Marxism, and corporatism. To O'Donnell and others, early developmental analysis, which suggested a positive connection between socioeconomic modernization and democracy, hardly seemed appropriate for explaining the rise of this new authoritarianism. On the contrary, as O'Donnell saw it, quite the opposite seemed to have happened. He developed a hypothesis that suggested that in late-developing countries more advanced levels of industrialization might actually coincide with the collapse of democracy and an increase in inequality.

O'Donnell argued that economic stagnation, coupled with increasing political demands, led to the breakdown of the progressive populist coalitions of the 1930s and 1940s. At this point sectors of the bourgeoisie (new industrialists and managers), together with new technocratic elements (high-level civil and military bureaucrats and technocrats), that in a Weberian sense emerged from an era of economic expansion, seized power through the military. They then moved to rationalize the economic and social systems by excluding the popular sectors and encouraging economic growth by way of broadened links with foreign capital and technology. Rather than modernization producing a tendency toward democratization and greater social equality, O'Donnell saw it as moving in the opposite direction toward BA.

O'Donnell's work in effect synthesized several intellectual traditions that had tended to remain disparate. This was particularly the case with his uses of modernization, dependency, and corporatist models. O'Donnell recast modernization theory by arguing that "the processes set in motion by high-level modernization tend to generate authoritarianism."[21] Moreover, O'Donnell's key concept of BA owed much to Weber's theory of bureaucracy and politics, especially Weber's concern with values and roles (reflected in O'Donnell's emphasis on "technocratic roles"). At the same time, as political scientists Karen Remmer and Gilbert Merkx of the University of New Mexico point out, "his [O'Donnell's] analysis had an historical-materialist character because of its focus on the manner in which social and economic contingencies structure political development."[22] Finally, O'Donnell's description of the mechanisms of control in BA regimes drew on corporatist conceptions of authority and functional groups.

The fact that BA, as a hypothesis to explain political change, was limited to the Southern Cone (first, Argentina and Brazil and later Chile and Uruguay as well) raised certain questions. Could it be extended to embrace other Latin American countries so as to constitute a more global model? Was the political-economic model pursued in these four countries as consistent and coherent as O'Donnell argued, particularly when the levels of industrialization in these countries did not appear comparable? Critics suggested that BA appeared to be simply a restoration of the type of authoritarianism that existed in the 1930s and 1940s. Finally, some critics questioned the economic arguments used in explaining the emergence of BA.[23]

O'Donnell's work on BA marks a good stopping point for our overview of Latin American theories of development. While his analysis has come under considerable criticism, no major theoretical approach has yet emerged to take its place. Moreover, since O'Donnell's theory represents something of a synthesis of the previous theories, O'Donnell charts a path toward a convergence of theoretical concerns that might, as we suggest in our concluding chapter, represent the most fruitful direction for future theory building.

In the following sections the theories that form the building blocks of our understanding of Latin American development are presented in the terms of their original authors. These theories present a rich heritage that is too often forgotten in the heat of immediate debate. We hope that our readers will find the merits as well as the faults in each of the sections and move on, as the historiography of theory evolves, to construct new interpretations.

Notes

1. For Weber this new capitalist spirit emphasized ascetic, achievement-oriented values among entrepreneurs. These values extolled hard work and saving as opposed to more moderate living and working habits. Thus, for Weber, capital accumulation, the key to the emergence of capitalism, was derived not from the expropriation of the peasant-worker, as Marx asserted, but rather through the dedication and self-denial of entrepreneurs and workers. This new capitalist spirit, according to Weber, grew out of the rise of Protestantism, particularly the doctrines of sixteenth-century Calvinism in which worldly success became a sign for being one of the "elect," those who were predestined for eternal salvation. Driven by their anxiety to ensure salvation, seventeenth-century Puritans, therefore, dedicated themselves to hard work and the acquisition and saving of wealth, which became the moving force in the development of modern capitalism. For Weber this explained why the Protestant countries—England, the Netherlands, and the United States (New England)—developed to a greater extent than did the Catholic countries—Spain, Portugal, and Italy.

2. Comte believed that the development of man's capacity to think, which grew from fetishism to what he called "positivism," mirrored this transition. Positivism, marked by observation and accuracy, was elaborated by the natural sciences and later the social sciences, particularly sociology. For Comte the task of sociology was to identify the stage reached by society, thereby facilitating the creation of the modern order.

3. Fernando Henrique Cardoso, one of the founders of the dependency school, prefers to use the term approach rather than theory, which he believes others have incorrectly attributed to dependency. See his "The Consumption of Dependency Theory in the United States," *Latin American Research Review* 12:3 (1977), pp. 15–17.

4. Theotonio dos Santos, "The Structure of Dependence," *The American Economic Review* 60:2 (May 1970), pp. 231–236.

5. The period of national populism was from 1930 to roughly 1950 when an alliance of the new bourgeoisie, the middle classes, and the working classes succeeded in wresting control of the state away from the export-oriented oligarchy. This state then pursued interventionist economic policies designed to stimulate national industries as well as to incorporate the lower classes into the economy and into society.

6. Economist John Maynard Keynes (1883–1946) reformulated liberal economic theory in his influential *The General Theory of Employment, Interest and Money,* published in 1936. According to Keynes's theory, correct government policies could smooth out the economic cycle. When the economy lags the government should lower the interest rates charged to borrowers, especially businesses, to encourage production. They should also spend money on public works and social welfare to put more money into circulation and thus to stimulate

consumption. As the economy expands the opposite policies should be followed to check inflation and excessive speculation. Keynes's theory formed the theoretical foundation for Franklin D. Roosevelt's New Deal program of social and economic reform and is still dominant in the academic and business worlds.

7. Quoted in Magnus Blomstrom and Bjorn Hettne, *Development Theory in Transition, The Dependency Debate and Beyond: Third World Responses* (London: Zed Books, 1984), p. 59.

8. Cardoso, "The Consumption of Dependency Theory," pp. 9–10.

9. Tulio Halperin-Donghi, "'Dependency Theory' and Latin American Historiography," *Latin American Research Review* 17:1 (1982), p. 116.

10. Senator Joseph McCarthy (1909–1957) campaigned to root out alleged Communist influence in government during the 1950s. His indiscriminate, often unfounded, accusations, inquisitorial investigative methods and sensationalism, ostensibly in the suppression of communism, were widely condemned at the time.

11. Halperin-Donghi, "'Dependency Theory' and Latin American Historiography," p. 418.

12. Charles W. Bergquist, *Alternative Approaches to the Problem of Development: A Selected and Annotated Bibliography* (Durham, N.C.: Carolina Academic Press, 1979), item #118.

13. See Colin Henfrey, "Dependency, Modes of Production, and Class Analysis of Latin America," *Latin American Perspectives* 8:3–4 (1981), pp. 17–54.

14. See, for example, Robert A. Packenham, *Latin American Dependency Theories,* mimeo (Stanford, Calif.: Stanford University, July 1974); and David Ray, "The Dependency Model of Latin American Underdevelopment: Three Basic Fallacies," *Journal of Inter-American Studies and World Affairs* 15 (February 1973), pp. 4–20.

15. See Marcelo J. Cavarozzi and James F. Petras, "Chile," in *Latin America: The Struggle with Dependency and Beyond,* edited by Ronald H. Chilcote and Joel C. Edelstein (New York: John Wiley & Sons, 1974), pp. 495–578; and James Cockcroft, Andre Gunder Frank, and Dale Johnson, *Dependency and Underdevelopment: Latin America's Political Economy* (Garden City, N.Y.: Doubleday, 1972).

16. Thomism refers to the theological and philosophical system of Saint Thomas Aquinas (1225?–1274), the Italian scholastic philosopher and a major theologian of the Roman Catholic church. Francisco Suárez (1548–1617) was a Spanish theologian and philosopher.

17. The classic example of a corporatist institution is the Roman Catholic church, which is organically and hierarchically organized with some residual autonomy at the level of the individual priest.

18. Alfred Stepan, *The State and Society: Peru in Comparative Perspective* (Princeton, N.J.: Princeton University Press, 1978), pp. 26–40.

19. "Still the Century of Corporatism?" *The New Corporatism: Socio-Political Structures in the Iberian World,* edited by Fredrick B. Pike and Thomas Stritch (Notre Dame, Ind.: University of Notre Dame Press, 1974), pp. 93–94. For a discussion of the modern roots of corporatism see below Chapter 11 by Ronald

C. Newton. Another important book on the new corporatism is *Politics and Social Change in Latin America: The Distinct Tradition,* edited by Howard J. Wiarda (Amherst: University of Massachusetts Press, 1974).

20. J. Samuel Valenzuela and Arturo Valenzuela, "Modernization and Dependency: Alternative Perspectives in the Study of Latin American Underdevelopment," *Comparative Politics* 10:4 (July 1978), pp. 542–543.

21. Guillermo A. O'Donnell, *Modernization and Bureaucratic Authoritarianism: Studies in South American Politics.* 2d ed. (Berkeley, Calif.: Institute of International Studies, 1979), p. 206n.

22. Karen L. Remmer and Gilbert W. Merkx, "Bureaucratic-Authoritarianism Revisited," *Latin American Research Review* 17:2 (1982), p. 5.

23. See *The New Authoritarianism in Latin America,* edited by David Collier (Princeton, N.J.: Princeton University Press, 1979), pp. 7–9 passim.

Selected Bibliography

Bergquist, Charles W. *Alternative Approaches to the Problem of Development: A Selected and Annotated Bibliography.* Durham, N.C.: Carolina Academic Press, 1979.

Bill, James A., and Robert L. Hardgrave, Jr. *Comparative Politics: The Quest for Theory.* Columbus, Ohio: Merrill, 1973.

Blomstrom, Magnus, and Bjorn Hettne. *Development Theory in Transition, The Dependency Debate and Beyond: Third World Responses.* London: Zed Books, 1984.

Cardoso, Fernando Henrique. "The Consumption of Dependency Theory in the United States," *Latin American Research Review* 12:3 (1977), pp. 7–24.

Chilcote, Ronald H., and Joel C. Edelstein (eds.). *Latin America: The Struggle with Dependency and Beyond.* New York: John Wiley & Sons, 1974.

Collier, David (ed.). *The New Authoritarianism in Latin America.* Princeton, N.J.: Princeton University Press, 1979.

Debray, Regis. *Revolution in the Revolution?* New York: Monthly Review Press, 1967.

Etzioni-Halevy, Eva. *Social Change: The Advent and Maturation of Modern Society.* London: Routledge & Kegan Paul, 1981.

Etzioni-Halevy, Eva, and Amitai Etzioni (eds.). *Social Change: Sources, Patterns, and Consequences.* 2d ed. New York: Basic Books, 1973.

Halperin-Donghi, Tulio. "'Dependency Theory' and Latin American Historiography," *Latin American Research Review* 17:1 (1982), pp. 115–130.

Hirschman, Albert O. "Ideologies of Economic Development in Latin America," in Hirschman, Albert O. *Latin American Issues: Essays and Comments.* New York: Twentieth Century Fund, 1961, pp. 3–42.

Kahl, Joseph A. *Modernization, Exploitation and Dependency in Latin America.* New Brunswick, N.J.: Transaction Books, 1976.

Love, Joseph L. "Raul Prebisch and the Origins of the Doctrine of Unequal Exchange," *Latin American Research Review* 15:1 (1980), pp. 45–72.

Malloy, James M. *Authoritarianism and Corporatism in Latin America.* Pittsburgh, Penn.: University of Pittsburgh Press, 1977.

O'Donnell, Guillermo. "Reply to Remmer and Merkx," *Latin American Research Review* 17:2 (1982), pp. 41–50.

Pike, Fredrick B., and Thomas Stritch (eds.). *The New Corporatism: Social-Political Structures in the Iberian World.* Notre Dame, Ind.: University of Notre Dame Press, 1974.

Remmer, Karen L., and Gilbert W. Merkx. "Bureaucratic-Authoritarianism Revisited," *Latin American Research Review* 17:2 (1982), pp. 3–40.

Roxborough, Ian. *Theories of Underdevelopment.* London: Macmillan, 1979.

Stepan, Alfred. *The State and Society: Peru in Comparative Perspective.* Princeton, N.J.: Princeton University Press, 1978.

Valenzuela, J. Samuel, and Arturo Valenzuela. "Modernization and Dependency: Alternative Perspectives in the Study of Latin American Underdevelopment," *Comparative Politics* 10:4 (July 1978), pp. 535–557.

Weiner, Myron (ed.). *Modernization: The Dynamics of Growth.* New York: Basic Books, 1966.

Wiarda, Howard J. (ed.). *Politics and Social Change in Latin America: The Distinct Tradition.* Amherst: University of Massachusetts Press, 1974.

PART 1
MODERNIZATION

The authors we have chosen to exemplify the "modernization" perspective are part of a broad tradition in development theory that explicitly followed the concepts of Max Weber and Talcott Parsons. This philosophical perspective envisioned value changes and social mobility in historical processes as more important than the emphasis on economic and class conflict made by Marxist analysts. Some authors, such as Kalman Silvert, openly recognized the "liberal bias" that this perspective entails, as well as its central underlying assumption that modern Western Europe and the United States provide the model not only for what the "less developed countries" would and should become but also for the likely transition they would make from feudal nations to industrialized capitalist economies. The modernization authors searched for those "feudal" values and structures in Latin America that had delayed progress along the path (they implicitly assumed that path to be fairly straight) toward modernity.

Most of the writers saw the middle classes—or as John Johnson calls them, "middle sectors"—as crucial to the process of modernization. The middle classes were most likely to be the bearers of "modern"—more specifically entrepreneurial—values, and, because they made up the greater percentage of the population of modern societies, they were seen as a stabilizing force. Stable and expanding middle classes could provide opportunities of upward social mobility for the lower classes, and eventually could create a democratic polity, historically blocked by the rigid two-class polarity between the few rich and the many poor in feudal societies. A central anomaly for the modernizationists was, as Johnson and Lipset suggest, the enduring adherence of the emerging Latin American middle classes to traditional values coupled with their surprising willingness to expand state economic activities. This willingness was contrary to that of the European middle classes, which sought a liberal laissez-faire economy. As Lipset so clearly shows, for modernizationists, education in modern values and technology was often seen as the crucial factor for actively promoting a move toward modernity. Others authors, such as Jacques Lambert, were more structurally oriented and saw the emergence of a dual society in which the feudal rural areas dominated by the large landed estates—latifundia—were holding back the modernization processes in urban areas. The solution these writers saw was to promote agrarian reform. Most modernizationists thought that foreign investment by the modern world would also hasten the process of development. With considerable optimism the modernizationists thought that the modern countries could help the less developed countries move rapidly toward the type of society and the economic and political systems the modern countries exemplified.

2 / Values, Education, and Entrepreneurship

Seymour Martin Lipset

Perhaps the foremost U.S. writer of Latin American modernization theory was Harvard sociologist Seymour Martin Lipset. His essay "Values, Education, and Entrepreneurship," which opens our section on modernization, introduced the widely read and influential work *Elites in Latin America*. In this essay Lipset argues that contemporary underdeveloped countries "preserve values which foster behavior antithetical to the systematic accumulation of capital." Drawing from Weber, he contrasts the prevailing value systems of North and South America to explain the lag in Latin American development:

> The overseas offspring of Great Britain seemingly had the advantage of values derivative in part from the Protestant Ethic and from the formation of "New Societies" in which feudal ascriptive elements were missing. Since Latin America, on the other hand, is Catholic, it has been dominated for long centuries by ruling elites who created a social structure congruent with feudal social values.

According to Lipset, the origins of this feudal value system are derived from fifteenth- and sixteenth-century Iberian values and institutions that were transferred to and took root in Latin America with its conquest and subsequent colonization by the Iberians. Lipset views these values as having worked against the formation of an entrepreneurial spirit. This lack of spirit was, for Lipset, a crucial reason for Latin America's underdevelopment and lack of progress. In specifying these values Lipset draws on Talcott Parson's "pattern variables." Latin Americans were imbued with the values of a traditional social order and followed particularistic and ascriptive patterns of behavior. They learned to emphasize diffuseness and elitism; to profess a weak achievement orientation; and to hold a general scorn for pragmatism, manual labor, materialism, and hard work. These behavioral traits prevented Latin Americans from developing modern, rational business enterprises that engaged in competition, took calculated risks, and developed bureaucratic structures. In this essay Lipset is particularly concerned with showing how the educational system continued to perpetuate such detrimental cultural values.

Discussions of the requisites of economic development have been concerned with the relative importance of the appropriate economic conditions, rather than the presumed effects on varying rates of economic growth of diverse value systems. Much of the analysis which stems from economic thought has tended to see value orientations as derivative from economic factors. Most sociological analysts, on the other hand, following in the tradition of Max Weber, have placed a major independent role on the effect of values in fostering economic development.

Although the evaluation of the causal significance of economic factors and value orientations has often taken the form of a debate pitting one against the other, increasingly more people have come to accept the premise that both sets of variables are relevant. Many economists now discuss the role of "non-economic" factors in economic growth, and some have attempted to include concepts developed in sociology and psychology into their overall frame of analysis. Sociologists, from Weber on, have rarely argued that value analysis could account for economic growth. Rather the thesis suggested by Weber is that, given the economic conditions for the emergence of a system of rational capital accumulation, whether or not such growth occurred in a systematic fashion would be determined by the values present. Structural conditions make development possible; cultural factors determine whether the possibility becomes an actuality. And Weber sought to prove that capitalism and industrialization emerged in Western Europe and North America because value elements inherent in or derivative from the "Protestant Ethic" fostered the necessary kinds of behavior by those who had access to capital; while conversely during other periods in other cultures, the

Reprinted with permission from *Elites in Latin America*, by Seymour Lipset and Aldo Solari, pp. 3–60. New York: Oxford University Press, 1967. Copyright © 1967 by Oxford University Press, Inc. (Ed. note: For reasons of economy and space the text has been edited to remove some nonessential passages. Similarly some nonsubstantive footnotes have been deleted.)

social and religious "ethics" inhibited a systematic rational emphasis on growth.[1]

The general Weberian approach has been applied to many of the contemporary underdeveloped countries. It has been argued that these countries not only lack the economic prerequisites for growth, but that many of them preserve values which foster behavior antithetical to the systematic accumulation of capital. The relative failure of Latin American countries to develop on a scale comparable to those of North America or Australasia has been seen as, in some part, a consequence of variations in value systems dominating these two areas. The overseas offspring of Great Britain seemingly had the advantage of values derivative in part from the Protestant Ethic and from the formation of "New Societies" in which feudal ascriptive elements were missing. Since Latin America, on the other hand, is Catholic, it has been dominated for long centuries by ruling elites who created a social structure congruent with feudal social values. . . .

On a theoretical level, the systematic analysis of the relations of value systems to the conditions for economic development requires concepts which permit one to contrast the relative strength of different values. Thus far, the most useful concepts for this purpose are Talcott Parsons' "pattern-variables." These refer to basic orientations toward human action and are sufficiently comprehensive to encompass the norms affecting behavior within all social systems, both total societies and their subsystems, such as the family or the university.[2]

Distinctions which seem particularly useful for analyzing the relation between values and the conditions for development are achievement-ascription, universalism-particularism, specificity-diffuseness, and equal-itarianism-elitism. (The latter is not one of Parson's distinctions, but rather one which I have added.) A society's value system may emphasize that a person in his orientation to others treats them in terms of their abilities and performances (achievement) or in terms of inherited qualities (ascription); applies a general standard (universalism) or responds to some personal attribute or relationship (particularism); deals with them in terms of the specific positions which they happen to occupy (specificity) or in general terms as individual members of the collectivity (diffuseness).

Concepts such as these are most appropriately used in a comparative context. Thus the claim that the United States is achievement-oriented, or that it is equalitarian, obviously does not refer to these characteristics in any absolute sense. The statement that a national value system is equalitarian clearly does not imply the absence of great differences in power, income, wealth, or status. It means rather that from a comparative perspective nations defined as equalitarian tend to place more emphasis than elitist nations on universalistic criteria in interpersonal judgments, and that they tend to de-emphasize behavior patterns which stress hierarchical differences. No society is equalitarian, ascriptive, or universalistic in any total sense; all systems about which we have knowledge are characterized by values and behavior which reflect both ends of any given polarity, e.g., all systems have some mobility and some inheritance of position.

In his original presentation of the pattern-variables, Parsons linked combinations of two of them—achievement-ascription and universalism-particularism—to different forms of existing societies. Thus the combination of universalism-achievement may be exemplified by the United States. It is the combination most favorable to the emergence of an industrial society since it encourages respect or deference toward others on the basis of merit and places an emphasis on achievement. It is typically linked with a stress on specificity, the judging of individuals and institutions in terms of their individual roles, rather than generally.[3] The Soviet system expresses many of the same values as the United States in its ideals. One important difference, of course, is in the position of the Communist party. Membership in the party conveys particularistic rights and obligations. Otherwise both systems resemble each other in "value" terms with reference to the original pattern-variables. Both denigrate extended kinship ties, view ethnic subdivisions as a strain, emphasize individual success, but at the same time insist that inequality should be reduced and that the norms inherent in equalitarianism should govern social relationships. The two systems, North American and Communist, diverge, however, with respect to another key pattern-variable polarity, self-orientation vs. collectivity-orientation—the emphasis that a collectivity has a claim on its individual units to conform to the defined interests of the larger group, as opposed to the legitimacy of actions reflecting the perceived needs of the individual unit.

Conceptualization at such an abstract level is not very useful unless it serves to specify hypotheses about the differences in norms and behavior inherent in different value emphases. Such work would clearly have utility for the effort to understand the varying relationships between levels of economic development and social values.

The Latin-American system has been identified by Parsons as an example of the particularistic-ascriptive pattern. Such a system tends to be focused around kinship and local community and to de-emphasize the need for powerful and legitimate larger centers of authority such as the state. Given a weak achievement orientation, such systems see work as a necessary evil. Morality converges around the traditionalistic acceptance of received standards and arrangements. There is an emphasis on expressive rather than instrumental behvior. There is little concern with the behavior of external authority so long as it does not interfere with expressive freedom. Such systems also tend to emphasize diffuseness and elitism. The status conferred by one position tends to be accorded in all situations. Thus if one plays one elite role, he is respected generally.[4]

Although the various Latin American countries obviously differ considerably—a point which will be elaborated later—it is interesting to note that a recent analysis of the social structure of the most developed nation, Uruguay, describes the contemporary situation there in much the same terms as Parsons does for the area as a whole. Aldo Solari has summed up some of his findings about his own country:

It is clear that particularism is a very important phenomenon in Uruguayan society and it prevails over universalism. A great number of facts support this. It is well known that the prevailing sytem of selection for government employees is based on kinship, on membership in a certain club or political faction, on friendship, etc. These are all particularistic criteria. A similar phenomenon is present in private enterprise where selection of personnel on the basis of particularistic relations is very common. The use of universalistic criteria, such as the use of standardized examinations, is exceptional. Quite frequently when such universalistic criteria seem operative, they are applied to candidates who have been previously selected on the basis of personal relationships.[5]

Ascriptive ties are also quite strong in Uruguay, linked in large part to the importance of the family in the system. Concern with fulfilling family obligations and maintaining family prestige leads propertied Uruguayans to avoid risking the economic base of the family position. The concerns of the middle class which tend to affect the expectations and norms of the whole society are for "security, moderation, lack of risk, and prestige."[6]

The sources of Latin American values have been generally credited to the institutions and norms of the Iberian nations, as practiced by an Iberian-born elite during the three centuries of colonial rule. Those sent over from Spain or Portugal held the predominant positions, and in the colonies "ostentatiously proclaimed their lack of association with manual, productive labor or any kind of vile employment."[7] And Spain and Portugal, prior to colonizing the Americas, had been engaged for eight centuries in conflict with the Moors, resulting in the glorification of the roles of soldier and priest and in the denigation of commercial and banking activities, often in the hands of Jews and Moslems. Iberian values and institutions were transferred to the American continent. To establish them securely, there were constant efforts by the "Church militant" to Christianize heathen population[s], the need to justify morally Spanish and Portuguese rule over "inferior" peoples, Indians, and imported Africans, and the fostering of a "get rich quick mentality" introduced by the *conquistadores* but reinforced by efforts to locate valuable minerals or mine the land and, most significantly, by the establishment of the *latifundia* (large-scale plantations) as the predominant form of economic, social, and political organization. Almost everywhere in Latin America, the original upper class was composed of the owners of *latifundia,* and these set the model for elite behavior to which lesser classes, including the businessmen of the towns, sought to adapt.

And as Ronald Dore points out, in *arielismo,* the Latin American scorn for pragmatism and materialism now usually identified with the United States, "there is an element that can only be explained by the existence of a traditional, landed upper class."[8] The period of the predominance of *latifundia* social structure is far from over. In most Latin American nations (Mexico, Bolivia, and Cuba are perhaps the major exceptions), agriculture is still dominated by *latifundia.* Thus farms of 1,000 hectares or more, which constitute 1.5 percent of all farms in Latin America, possess 65 percent of the total farm acreage. *Minifundias* (small farms of under 20 hectares) constitute 73 percent of all farms, but less than 4 percent of the acreage.[9] The high-status social clubs of most major cities are still controlled or highly influenced by men whose families derived their original wealth and status from *latifundia.* In spite of repeated demands for land reform, little has been done to reduce the economic source of the influence of *latifundia* families. [Ed. note: This was written before moderate land reform of the 1960s and 1970s.] Hence the continuation of pre-industrial values in much of Latin America can be linked in large part to the persistence of the rural social structure which originally fostered these values. Even in Uruguay, which has long been dominated by the metropolis of Montevideo, one finds that much of the upper social class of the city is composed of members of powerful old land-owning families. Many of those involved in commercial and banking activities have close kinship ties with the large cattle-raisers and *estancieros.* And the upper rural class maintains considerable influence on the society as a whole through its control over the main agricultural organizations, and the continued strength of a widespread ideology which states that the wealth of the country depends on land and on the activities of those who farm it.[10] . . .

The stress on values as a key source of differences in the rate of development of economic and political institutions has been countered by some students of Latin America; they will point to the southern states of the American union as an example of a sub-culture which has been relatively underdeveloped economically, which has lacked a stable democratic political system, and which has placed a greater emphasis on violence and law-violation to attain political ends than the rest of the country. And as these scholars point out, the white South is the most purely Anglo-Saxon and Protestant part of the United States.

The American South resembles much of Latin America, including Brazil, in having an institutional structure and value system erected around a plantation (or *latifundia*) economy, which employed large numbers of slaves and which, after the abolition of slavery, developed a stratification hierarchy correlated with variations in racial background. From this point of view, the clue to understanding the economic backwardness and political instability of Brazil and much of Spanish America lies in their structural similarities with the American South, rather than in those values which stem from Iberian or Catholic origins. This argument is strengthened by analyses of the differences between southern and northern Brazil. The southern part of the country, which was much less involved in large-scale slave labor agriculture, can be compared with the north, in much the same way as the United States North varies from its South. Southern Brazil and northern United States are much more developed economically, and they place more emphasis on the "modern" value system—achievement, universalism, and the like—than the warmer regions of their countries.

There are certain similarities in another American country, Canada, and its internal cultural and economic differentiation. French Canada, historically, has been less developed than English Canada. Much of its economic development has been dominated by entrepreneurs from English-speaking backgrounds. A recent analysis of French-Canadian businessmen, based on interviews, reports their economic value orientations in terms very reminiscent of the studies of Latin American entrepreneurs. Though not as unstable politically as the southern United States or most of Latin America, Quebec has long exhibited symptoms of political instability (an opposition party system is perhaps less institutionalized there than in any other populous province); charges of political corruption, illegal tactics in campaigns, violations of civil liberties, and the like seem much more common in Quebec than in the English-speaking provinces.[11] Quebec is certainly Latin and Catholic (if these terms have any general analytic or descriptive meaning), but it obviously has had no plantation culture, nor a significant racial minority, though it could be argued that the English-French relationships resemble those of white-Negro, or white-Indian, in other countries of the Americas.

Various analyses of the weakness of democracy in Quebec do argue that religious-linked factors are relevant. As Pierre Trudeau has put it: "French Canadians are Catholics; and Catholic nations have not always been ardent supporters of democracy. They are authoritarian in spiritual matters; and since the dividing line between the spiritual and the temporal may be very fine or even confused, they are often disinclined to seek solutions in temporal affairs through the mere counting of heads."[12] And many have pointed to the differences in the economic development of the two Canadas as evidence that Catholic values and social organization are much less favorable to economic development than Protestant ones have been. As S. D. Clark has reasoned, "in nineteenth-century Quebec religion was organized in terms of a hierarchy of social classes which had little relation to the much more fluid class system of capitalism, and sharp separation from the outside capitalist world was maintained through an emphasis upon ethnic and religious differences and through geographic isolation."[13]

These comparisons between the United States North and South, and English and French Canada, show that structure and values are clearly interrelated. Structure such as a plantation system combined with a racially based hierarchy is functionally tied to a given set of "aristocratic" values and antipathetic to an emphasis on achievement, universalism, and hard work. But any value system derived from given sets of historical experience institutionalized in religious systems, family structures, class relations, and education will affect the pace and even direction and content of social and economic change.

If we turn now to studies focusing directly on the relationship between values and entrepreneurial behavior, the available materials from many Latin American countries seem to agree that the predominant values which continue to inform the behavior of the elite stem from the continued and combined strength of ascription, particularism, and diffuseness. Thomas Cochran has examined the literature from various American cultures, as well as from his own empirical research, and has conjectured that Latin American businessmen differ from North American ones in being

(1) more interested in inner worth and justification by standards of personal feeling than they are in the opinion of peer groups; (2) disinclined to sacrifice personal authority to group decisions; (3) disliking impersonal as opposed to personal arrangements and generally preferring family relations to those with outsiders; (4) inclined to prefer social prestige to money; and (5) somewhat aloof from and disinterested in science and technology.[14]

Somewhat similar conclusions are reported in various surveys of managerial attitudes in various Latin American countries. These indicate that role specificity, i.e., separation of managerial from other activities, is relatively less common there than in more developed areas. A Latin American manager "is quite likely to devote part of his office hours to politics or family affairs."[15] Bureaucratic and competitive norms are comparatively weak. Personal characteristics are valued more than technical or organizational ability.

Family particularism is much more common among Latin American business executives than among their counterparts in more developed nations. "Managers are frequently selected on the basis of family links, rather than specialized training." The entire managerial group often came from one family, and the "great majority of managers interviewed either considered this to be an appropriate arrangement under the conditions of their country, or had not thought of alternatives."[16] In Brazil, even the growth of large industries and corporate forms of ownership has not drastically changed the pattern. In many companies the model pattern seems to involve an adjustment between family control and the rational demands of running a big business. Either the children or the in-laws of the old patriarch are technically trained, or the company involves a mixed system of family members working closely with technically educated non-family executives. However, the . . . managers employed by family groups are known as *hombres de confianza* (men who can be trusted), and have been selected more for this quality than for their expertise.[17]

Most analysts of Latin American business behavior agree that a principal concern of the typical entrepreneur is to maintain family prestige; thus he is reluctant to give up the family-owned and -managed type of corporation. Outsiders are distrusted, for the entrepreneur "is acutely aware that any advantage that may be given to somebody outside his family is necessarily at the expense of himself and his own family."[18] From this evolves an unwillingness to co-operate with others outside of one's firm and a defensiveness toward subordinates as well as toward creditors, distributors, and others. Such assumptions about the behavior of others are, of course, self-maintaining, since people tend to behave as significant others define them, thus reinforcing a mutual state of distrust. In the family-dominated firms which constitute such a large personnel will often be untrustworthy and inefficient [workers], since they will lack identification with firms in which "the 'road upward' is blocked by family barriers," and they are given limited responsibility.[19] This fear of dealing with outsiders even extends to reluctance to permit investment in the firm. For many Brazilian "industrialists, the sale of stocks to the public seems to involve . . . a loss of property." A Brazilian market research survey reported that 93 percent of entrepreneurs interviewed stated "that they had never thought of selling stock in their enterprise."[20] As Emilio Willems points out, "such a typically modern institution as the stock-market in large metropolitan centers failed to develop because the most important joint-stock companies are owned by kin-groups which handle transfer of stock as a purely domestic matter."[21] . . .

The managers of foreign-owned companies, whether Brazilian or foreign, are different in their behavior. They tend to emphasize a high degree of rationalization and bureaucratic practice in running their firms. Although they are interested in securing personal loyalty from subordinates, it is not the basic requirement for employment. The executive personnel are ambitious and competent employees, concerned with their personal success and valuing ambition in themselves and others.

The lack of a concern with national interests or institutional development among Latin American entrepreneurs has been related by Albert Hirschman to what he calls an "ego-focussed image of change," characteristic of badly integrated under-developed societies. Individuals in nations dominated by such an image, "not identifying with society," will view new developments or experiences simply as opportunities for self-aggrandizement. Although seemingly reflecting a desire to get ahead, this orientation, which inhibits efforts to advance by co-operation with others "is inimical to economic development, [since] . . . success is conceived not as a result of systematic application of effort and creative energy, combined perhaps with a 'little bit of luck,' but as due either to sheer luck or to the outwitting of others through careful scheming." And Hirschman, like other analysts of Latin America, sees the inability to trust and work with others as antithetical to effective entrepreneurship.[22]

Attitudes to money similar to those frequently reported as characteristic of a nonindustrial, traditional population have been reported in studies of Latin American business leaders. A short-range rather than a long-range orientation is common: make money now "and then to live happily—that is, idly—ever after."[23] This means that entrepreneurs frequently prefer to make a high profit quickly, often by charging a high price to a small market, rather than to maximize long-range profits by seeking to cut costs and prices, which would take more effort. Although the concept of immediate profit "in industrial enterprises usually meant within one year or else after paying back initial loans," this does not reflect a Schumpeterian assumption about the reward or encouragement necessary to entrepreneurial risk-taking. Rather, the overwhelming majority of the Latin American businessmen interviewed argued that risk is to be avoided, and that "when there is risk there will not be new investment," that investment risk is a luxury which only those in wealthy countries can afford.[24] Reluctance to take risks may be related to the strong concern with family integrity, with viewing business property much like a family estate. "Where bankruptcy might disgrace one's family, managers will be more cautious than where it is regarded impersonally as expedient corporate strategy."[25]

It is important to note that these generalizations about the attitudes and behavior of Latin American entrepreneurs are all made in a comparative context. Those who stress their commitment to particularistic and diffuse values are generally comparing them to North Americans or to a model of rational, bureaucratic, competitive enterprise. However, as contrasted with other groups within their societies, Latin American entrepreneurs, particularly those involved in large-scale enterprise, tend to be the carriers of "modern" values. Thus one analysis of Colombian businessmen points out: "They are urban people in a rural country. In a relatively traditionally oriented society, their values are rational and modern."[26]

The impact of Latin American orientations to entrepreneurial behavior has been summed up in the following terms:

Comparatively the Latin American complex: (1) sacrifices rigorous economically directed effort, or profit maximization, to family interests; (2) places social and personal emotional interests ahead of business obligations; (3) impedes mergers and other changes in ownership desirable for higher levels of technological efficiency and better adjustments to markets; (4) fosters nepotism to a degree harmful to continuously able top-management; (5) hinders the building up of a supply of competent and cooperative middle managers; (6) makes managers and workers less amenable to constructive criticism; (7) creates barriers of disinterest in the flow of technological communication; and (8) lessens the urge for expansion and risk-taking.[27]

The emphases on the value orientations of entrepreneurs as a major factor in limiting economic development in Latin America may be criticized for de-emphasizing the extent to which the values themselves are a product of, or sustained by, so-called structural or economic factors. Thus, it has been suggested that the unwillingness to delegate responsibility to non-family members reflects the objective dangers of operating in unstable political and economic environments. Such conditions dictate extreme caution and the need to be certain that one can quickly change company policy so as to avoid major losses or bankruptcy as a result of government policy changes, change in foreign exchange rates, and the like. An "outsider" presumably will not have as much interest in the finances of the firm, or the authority to react quickly. Rapid inflation, high interest rates, and other instability factors would all seem to inhibit long-range planning and encourage a quick and high profit. There can be little doubt that such structural factors help to preserve many of the traditionalistic practices. And such a conclusion would imply the need for deliberate government policies to create a stable environment, such as planned investment policies, regulation of inflation, and restrictions on the export of capital.

But if the existence of interacting supportive mechanisms, which will inhibit economic support, is admitted, the fact remains that similar generalizations have been made about the effect of values on attitudes and behavior of other groups and institutions. For example, an analysis of Argentine politics points to the effect of these values in preventing stable political life. "Argentina's class-bound politics assume that no public measure can be good for almost everybody, that the benefit of one group is the automatic loss of all others."[28] Although Argentina is, after Uruguay, socially the most developed nation in Latin America, highly literate and urbanized, its citizens still do not accept the notion of, nor do they show loyalty to, a national state which acts universalistically. Argentina is instead characterized by the "survival or localistic, sub-national views and loyalties archetypical of the traditional society."[29] . . .

Efforts to "modernize" values and behavior are not solely, or even primarily, located in the economic or political spheres. Rather, those professionally concerned with ideas and values, the intellectuals, may play a decisive role in resisting or facilitating social change. As John Friedmann has pointed out, the intellectual in developing countries has three essential tasks to fulfill, "each of which is essential to the process of cultural transformation: he mediates new values, he formulates an effective ideology, and he creates an adequate, collective (national) self-image."[30] In Latin America, however, the large body of literature concerning the values of the extremely prestigious *pensadores* or intellectuals, whether creative artists or academics, agrees that they continue to reject the values of industrial society, which they often identify with the United States. A survey of the writings of Latin American intellectuals points up this conclusion: "There is no school of literature in Latin America which argues that technology and technological change represent values which should be adopted, cherished, and used as a means to a more meaningful life."[31] Even when modern technology is accepted as a necessary precondition for social betterment, it is often described as a threat to the traditional values of the society.

Some of the factors which sustain these attitudes, even in the face of the recognized need of the nations of Latin America to change to get out of the "humiliating" status of being considered "underdeveloped" or even backward, have been suggested in an interesting comparison of the different ways in which Japan and Latin America reacted to similar concerns:

When seeking to define a national self-image in a nationalistic frame of mind, one is most likely to seize on those features which supposedly differentiate one from one's major international antagonist. For Japan this point of counter-reference, the thou [for] which one has to feel more holy, has been the West generally and in the twentieth century America more particularly. For Latin America, since the beginning of this century at least, it has been almost exclusively America. But in differentiating themselves from Americans, the Japanese could point to the beauties of their tight family system; their patriotic loyalty to the Emperor contrasting with American selfish individualism; the pacific subtleties of Buddhism contrasting with the turbulent stridency of Christianity; and so on. But it was not as easy for a Latin American to establish the Latin American differentiae in terms of family, political, or legal institutions. He had to fall back on "spirit" and attitudes; and since the most visible American was the businessman, he tended—*vide arielismo* as Ellison describes it— to make his dimension of difference the materialist-spiritual one. Thus by scorning American devotion to technology and profit, he made something of a virtue out of the stark fact of economic backwardness. For their part the Japanese had enough superior arguments with which to fortify their uncertain sense of their superior Japaneseness without resorting to this one, with its inhibiting effect on indigenous economic growth.[32]

While much of the anti–United States sentiment is presented in the context of left-wing critiques, *pensadores* of the right—those who uphold the virtues of tradition, Catholicism, and social hierarchy—also are aggressively opposed to North American culture, which they see as "lacking culture, grace, beauty, as well as widespread appreciation of aesthetic and spiritual values."[33]

The values fostered by the *pensadores* continue to be found as well in much of Latin American education. Most analysts of Latin American education agree that, at both university and secondary school level, the content of education still reflects the values of a landed upper class. Even in the second most developed Latin American country, Argentina, a study of national values points out that the traditional landed aristocratic disdain for manual work, industry, and trading continues to affect the educational orientations of many students. When an Argentine seeks to move up, "he will usually try to do so, not by developing his manual skills or by accomplishing business or industrial feats, but by developing his *intellectual* skills. He will follow an academic career typically in a field which is not 'directly productive' from an economic point of view— medicine, law, social sciences, etc."[34]

As Jacques Lambert has put it, "A ruling class deriving its resources from landed property looks to education for a means not of increasing its income but rather of cultivating the mind. The whole public education system has been organized as a preparation for higher education, and more particularly for the type of education provided in the faculties of law, which gave instruction not only in law but also in political and social science for a class of political leaders."[35] . . .

These generalizations about the strength of the traditional humanist bias in Latin America may be bolstered by reference to comparative educational statistics. Latin America as an area lags behind every other part of the world in the proportion of its students taking courses in engineering or the sciences. As of 1958-59, 34 percent of all West European undergraduates were studying science or engineering, in contrast to 23 percent in Asia (excluding Communist China and India), 19 percent in Africa, and 16 percent in Latin America.[36] The comparable figure for the major Communist countries including the Soviet Union and China is 46 percent.[37] China now trains more engineers per year than any country except the Soviet Union and the United States. And 90 percent of all China's scientists and engineers have been trained since 1949.[38] In Uruguay, on the other hand, slightly over half the students in higher education have been enrolled in faculties of humanities, fine arts, and law, about ten times as many as in the scientific and technical faculties. In Chile, in 1957, less than one-sixth of the students were studying science or engineering, and the increase in the numbers in these faculties between 1940 and 1959 was less than the growth in total university enrollment. "In Communist countries, of course, the proportions are almost exactly reversed; Czechoslovakia had 46 percent in scientific and technical faculties and only 6.4 percent in humanities, arts, and law."[39] Among Third World nations, only Israel with 42 percent of its students in science and engineering, and Nigeria with 40 percent, approached the Communist nations in degree of dedication of higher education to development training objectives."[40] . . .

Economic Growth and the Role of the "Deviant" in Anti-Entrepreneurial Cultures

The argument that Latin American values are antithetical to economic development can of course be pitted against the fact that a considerable amount of economic growth has occurred in many of these countries. Clearly, in the presence of opportunity, an entrepreneurial elite has emerged. The logic of value analysis would imply that the creation or expansion of roles which are not socially approved in terms of the traditional values should be introduced by social "deviants." This hypothesis is basic to much of the literature dealing with the rise of the businessman in different traditional societies.

In his classic analysis of economic development, Joseph Schumpeter pointed out that the key aspect of entrepreneurship, as distinct from being a manager, is the capacity for leadership in innovation, for breaking through the routine and the traditional.[41] From this perspective the analysis of the factors which resulted in the rise of an entrepreneurial group leading to economic growth under capitalism is comparable to the study of the conditions which brought about anticapitalist revolutionary modernizing elites of various countries in recent decades. The approach which emphasizes the theory of deviance assumes that those who introduce change must be deviants, since they reject the traditional elite's ways of doing things.[42] As Hoselitz puts it, "a deviant always engages in behavior which constitutes in a certain sense a breach of the existing order and is contrary to, or at least not positively weighted in, the hierarchy of existing social values."[43] In societies in which the values of the dominant culture are "not supportive of entrepreneurial activity, someone who is relatively outside of the social system may have a particular advantage in entering an entrepreneurial activity. The restraints upon entrepreneurial activity imposed by the network [of social restraints] would be less effective against such a person. Thus, an immigrant may be outside of many of the networks of the nation and freer to engage in entrepreneurial activity"—in other words, freer socially to deviate.[44]

If we assume, in following up such generalizations, that within the Americas the value system of Latin America has discouraged entrepreneurial activity, while that of the English-speaking Protestant world of the United States and Canada has fostered it, then a comparative study of the backgrounds of entrepreneurs in these countries should reveal that those of Latin America are recruited disproportionately from sociological "deviants," while those of North America should come largely from groups which possess traits placing them inside the central structures of the society. An examination of the research data bearing on this hypothesis indicates that it is valid.

In many countries of Latin America, members of minority groups, often recent immigrants, have formed a considerable section of the emerging business elite. "In general it appears that immigrants took the lead in establishing modern manufacturing before World War I [in Latin America]."[45] Recent studies in various countries reveal comparable patterns. Frequently, these new entrepreneurs come from groups not known for their entrepreneurial prowess at home, such as the Arabs and the Italians, although Germans and Jews are also among those who are to be found in disproportionate numbers in business leadership. . . . Analysis of the backgrounds of 286 "prestigious" entrepreneurs, taken from the Argentine *Who's Who,* indicates that 45.5 percent were foreign born.[46] However, many of those born in Argentina are "among the first generation born in the country."[47] Classifying the sample by origins, Imaz reports that only 10 percent came from the traditional upper class, and they, as in many other Latin American countries, are concentrated in industries which processed agricultural products, so that their role in industry is an extension of their position as a landed class. Among the rest, almost all are of relatively recent foreign origin.[48] . . .

The various studies of the backgrounds of the Latin American entrepreneurial elite indicate that on the whole they are a well-educated group, the majority of them in most countries are university graduates. And a study of the origins of students at the University of São Paulo suggests that much of the separation in career orientations between those of native background and others takes place while in school. Thus, the proportion of students of non-Brazilian background is higher among the students than in the population of the city; only 22 percent are of purely Brazilian descent. Even more significant is the fact that students with a higher proportion of foreign-born ancestors tend to enroll in the "modern" faculties, such as economics, engineering, pharmacy, and the like. Those with preponderantly Brazilian family backgrounds are more likely to be found in the more traditional high prestige schools such as law and medicine. And the author of this study comments:

> The children of foreign-born parents . . . are more inclined to take advantage of the new opportunities in occupations which have emerged from the economic development of the city of São Paulo. One should consider the fact that in Brazil the schools of Law and Medicine convey special social prestige to their students. It is easier for a not completely assimilated adolescent of foreign descent to ignore that prestige than for a "pure" Brazilian.[49]

The creative role of the deviant, or the outsider, has in part been conceptualized by the term "marginal man," those who for various reasons are partially outside the culture in which they are living, are less socially integrated in the structures which maintain conformity, and are therefore not as committed to the established values of the larger order. Hence they are more likely to be receptive to possibilities for change.[50] An analysis of those who successfully took advantage of the opportunity to shift the use of land in the vicinity of São Paulo from subsistence agriculture to lucrative commercial crops (mainly the growth of eucalyptus for firewood) points up this process. Over 90 percent of those who become small-scale, relatively well-to-do entrepreneurs were recent settlers in the area, "immigrants or children of immigrants . . . or members of a small but flourishing Protestant sect (the *Evangelistas*)." . . .

Almost all of the recent settlers were as poor as the *caboclos* [the native, lowest status rural dwellers] when they arrived. They managed to see new alternatives when they arose, to buy up small plots of land and gradually increase their holdings, mostly at the expense of the *caboclos*. . . . It is worth testing . . . the proposition that *participation in newly valued activities among members of low economic and prestige classes varies inversely with length of residence in a locality.* Old settlers at depressed levels have inherited habits of belief, a morality and expectation of role rights and obligations associated with their statuses . . . that they are only slowly adaptable in the presences of altered opportunities. One of the most striking occurrences in the changing situation within the *municipio* under consideration is the fact that several *caboclos* sold or were seeking to sell their properties of prospective entrepreneurs, and then turned around and hired their labor out for wages.[51]

The traits which are often associated with economic innovation lead their bearers to be frowned upon or even hated by those who adhere to the conventional traditions of the society or who resent the success of others. Thus in Brazil, Gilberto Freyre reports that many of non-Portuguese descent have

shown a lack of finer moral scruples which has given many of them the reputation of being morally or ethically inferior. . . . [Their actions which lead to success in politics and business] are given as an example of the fact that the sons of "immigrants" are morally inferior to the sons of old Brazilian families as political leaders, businessmen, and industrial pioneers. Of course, sons of immigrants who follow such careers are freer than the members of old and well-known families from certain moral controls that act upon men deeply rooted in their towns or countries or regions.[52] . . .

The logic of the analysis suggested here, however, does not agree with the thesis that innovating entrepreneurs in developing societies must be recruited disproportionately from the ranks of social "deviants," as some have interpreted data such as these. Rather it points with Weber to the fact that many minority groups have not shown such propensities. Clearly the Catholic minorities in England, or other Protestant countries, were much less likely than the general population to engage in entrepreneurial activity. In his analysis of the divergent consequences for economic behavior of Protestantism and Catholicism, Max Weber pointed to the greater business accomplishments of the Protestant *majority* as compared to the Catholic minority in Germany.[53] The key issue, as Weber has indicated, is the value system of the various groups involved. Latin America and some other less developed traditional societies are so vulnerable to economic cultural "deviants" because the predominant values of the host culture are in large measure antithetical to rational entrepreneurial orientations. Where national values support economic development, the Weberian emphasis on value would suggest that the innovating business elite would be drawn not from deviants but rather from the "in-group," from persons with socially privileged backgrounds.

An examination of the social characteristics of North American business leaders in both Canada and the United States bears out these assumptions. Compared to most other nations in the world, the United States and English-speaking Canada have been among the most hospitable cultures to economic development. The Protestant ethic as fostered by denominations spawned of Calvinist and Arminian origins strongly influenced all classes in these societies, the United States somewhat more than Canada. And a study of the business leaders of the United States in 1870, the period of its take-off into industrial development, indicates that 86 percent of them came from "colonial families" settled in the country before 1777. Only 10 percent were foreign born or the children of foreign born.[54] Over 98 percent of the post–Civil War business elite were Protestants. Although the proportions of those of non-Anglo-Saxon, non-Protestant, and foreign-born parentage have increased over the years, they have always remained considerably lower than their proportion in the population as a whole.[55] Canadian data are available only for the post–World War II period, but it should be noted that Canada's emergence as a major industrial society largely dates from the war. Previously its economy somewhat resembled that of Argentina, being largely dependent on agricultural exports. The Canadian case is extremely interesting since the country is composed of two separate cultures—English Protestant and Latin Catholic. And a comprehensive report on the Canadian elite shows a clear-cut picture: where cultural values congruent with entrepreneurship are ascendant, the business elite will be recruited largely from the dominant culture group, not from minorities. Thus those of Anglo-Saxon Protestant background are over-represented, while those of Latin, Catholic, and minority origins are under-represented.

> An examination of the social origins of the economic elite shows that economic power belongs almost exclusively to those of British origin, even though this ethnic group made up less than half of the population in 1951. The fact that economic development in Canada has been in the hands of British Canadians has long been recognized by historians. Of the 760 people in the economic elite, only 51 (6.7 percent) could be classified as French Canadians although the French made up about one-third of the population in 1951. . . . There were no more than a handful who . . . could be classified as top-ranking industrialists in their own province.

Ethnic groups of neither British nor French origin, which made up about one-fifth of the general population, were hardly represented at all. There were six Jews (.78 percent of the sample as opposed to 1.4 percent of the general population). . . . [O]nly 78 (about 10 percent) were Catholic. . . . 43 percent of the population in 1951 was Catholic.[56]

In seeking to account for the low representation of French Canadians in the economic elite, even within Quebec, John Porter points out that the evidence does not fit the assumption that it is largely a result of the greater power of the British Canadians. For French Canadians do quite well in other power structures, e.g., politics, the intellectual world, and religion. French weakness in industry seems related to elements in their culture comparable to those in much of Latin America.

The varying origins of the business elites of the American nations clearly indicate that "out" groups, such as ethnic-religious minorities are given the opportunity to innovate economically when the values of the dominant culture are antithetical to such activities. Thus, the comparative evidence from the various nations of the Americas sustains the generalization that cultural values are among the major factors which affect the potentiality for economic development.

Although I have focused on the direct effects of value orientations on the entrepreneurial behavior of certain groups, it should be clear that any given individual or group supports the values of their effective social environment. Although national values may discourage entrepreneurial activities, ethnic or religious sub-groups, or links to foreign cultures may encourage them for those involved. One explanation of the comparative success of members of some minority groups in Latin America, such as the Anglo-Argentines, is that they continue to respect their ancestral national culture more than that of their host society. The fact that many ethnic minorities in some Latin American nations continue to send their children to schools conducted in their ancestral language and to speak it at home attests to their lack of acceptance of national culture and values.

The key question basically is whether one is involved in a network of social relations which sustain or negate a particular activity. Viscount Mauá, Brazil's great nineteenth-century economic innovator, though a native Brazilian, was adopted while in his early teens by an English merchant in Rio de Janeiro; his biography clearly indicates that he became an "alien" within his native culture, that English became his "native" language, the one in which he thought and wrote his private thoughts.[57] Conversely, as we have seen, many successful entrepreneurs are drawn away from total commitment to their business life by an involvement in social networks and reference groups which supply more

prestige than their vocation. One of Argentina's most successful entrepreneurs, who was an immigrant, built up a complex network of industrial
companies, took the time to study at the university, accepted an
appointment as an associate professor of Economics and Industrial
Organization at the University of Buenos Aires when he was fifty years
of age, sought to secure a regular chair three years later, and bought a
6,600-acre *estancia,* on which he spent much time.[58] To facilitate the
emergence of a given new role in a society, it is necessary to help create
social recognition for it within meaningful sub-groups. The leaders of
Meiji Japan have provided an example of the way in which one nation
did this. To raise the prestige of the business class,

> social distinctions [were] granted to the presidents and main shareholders
> of the new companies. The presidents were given the privilege of the
> sword and family name. They were appointed by the government, as
> officials were. A president could walk directly into the room of a government
> official while common people had to wait and squat outside the building.
> Many other minor privileges were granted.[59]

It is important to recognize that the introduction of new activities
by those linked to "foreign" cultures or minority religions is not simply
one of the various ways to modernize a society. Innovations which are
associated with socially marginal groups are extremely vulnerable to
political attack from those who would maintain traditional values.
Consequently efforts at economic modernization, changes in the educational system, or social customs which are introduced by "outsiders"
may have much less effect in modifying the central value system than
when they are fostered by individuals who are members of the core
group, as occurred in Meiji Japan.

Although much of the discussion thus far has involved the presentation
of evidence concerning *the* Latin American value system, it is obvious
that there is considerable variation *among* Latin American nations, as
there is among the English-speaking countries. Thus, many of the
distinctions which have been drawn between Argentina and Uruguay
on the one hand and Brazil on the other refer to the greater equalitarianism
and universalism in the former two. Or the earlier and greater degree
of working-class consciousness in Chile (indicated by the strength of
Marxist parties) as contrasted with Uruguay and Argentina may be a
consequence of the greater elitism, ascription, and particularism of
Chile, which was a major center of population concentration under
colonial rule, while the values of the latter two were modified by their
later formation as immigrant cultures.

Uruguay (and to a somewhat lesser extent Argentina) differs from the rest of Latin America in being relatively committed to a historically rooted equalitarian ideology. This value orientation stems from the effects of widespread immigration, which helped provide a mass urban base for reformist political movements. As Gino Germani indicates, immigration "played a great part in the destruction of the traditional pattern of social stratification."[60]

The emphasis on equalitarianism in both Argentina and Uruguay is perhaps best reflected in the extension of their educational systems, which have long led all other Latin American nations in the proportions attending school, from primary to university. This commitment to education may have played a major role in facilitating economic growth during the late nineteenth century and the first three decades of the twentieth. However, when equalitarianism is associated with particularistic and ascriptive orientations, it seemingly serves to strengthen the concern with security mentioned earlier, and early successful pressures (more in Uruguay than Argentina) for welfare state measures. Both countries, today, face a major economic crisis, brought about in large measure because governments responsive to popular pressures have dedicated a large share of national revenues to welfare. . . .

Changes in Value Orientations

The evidence presented thus far would seem to indicate that, regardless of the causal pattern one prefers to credit for Latin American values, they are, as described, antithetic to the basic logic of a large-scale industrial system. However, as noted earlier, it should be recognized that these descriptions are all made in a relative or comparative context, that Latin American economic behavior is evaluated either in comparison with that in the United States, or other developed nations, or against some ideal model of entrepreneurship. The value system of much of Latin America, like Quebec, has, in fact, been changing in the direction of a more achievement-oriented, universalistic, and equalitarian value system, and its industrial development both reflects and determines such changes. Many Latin American entrepreneurs are hiring non-family members as executives, and in various ways have acted contrary to the supposed norms. To some extent this may reflect the fact that a large segment of the creative and successful entrepreneurs are members of minority ethnic groups. More important perhaps is the fact that bureaucratic corporate enterprise has an inherent logic of its own; those who build such organizations, or rise within them in once-traditional societies, are either "deviants" who have the necessary new orientations, or men who develop them. Paternalistic feudal attitudes toward workers are characteristically more common in the less developed Latin American countries than in the more industrialized ones, a finding which parallels the situation within Spain.[61] There, the more developed an area, the more "modern" the attitudes of its entrepreneurs.

Such developments have been analyzed by Fernando Cardoso in his study of the industrial entrepreneur in Brazil. The shift from the values of the *patron* to those of the modern professional entrepreneur occurred with the emergence of large-scale industries, such as automobile manufacturing or ship building. He points out that the rapidity of the adjustment to modern orientations depends on the attitudes of the entrepreneurs involved. And the same individuals and companies often react in what appear to be contradictory ways. These dual orientations, modern and traditional, reflect in part the mixed character of the Brazilian economy, which may still be characterized as incipient industrial capitalism.[62] The heterogeneity of entrepreneurial environments and orientations has, as yet, prevented the emergence of a consistent ideology to which most adhere. Hence, Cardoso points to changes in values with growing industrialization, although he does not challenge the general description of Latin American economic behavior, as still applying to much of the Brazilian present.

Values clearly change as societies become economically more developed. Many of the generalizations made about Latin American or other relatively underdeveloped societies, in contrast to the United States or northern Europe, were made, and are still being made, about such countries as Spain, France, or Italy, when they are compared with more economically developed countries.

Only a short time ago, economic "stagnation" in these European Latin countries was interpreted as the consequence of values incongruent with enterprising behavior. That breakthroughs in development occur for a variety of reasons in different countries is obvious. Values dysfunctional to economic growth may inhibit but not prevent growth, if other factors are favorable. As the history of various nations has suggested, processes or conflict about values may foster the emergence of groups motivated to achieve economically. But conclusions such as these do not offer any prospect for change, other than to suggest the need for detailed careful study of the relevant factors suggested by social science theory in each country, or to simply add to the amount of investment capital available in a given country. I would like, therefore, to turn to a discussion of the various ways which seem open to those who deliberately seek to change values so as to foster the emergence of entrepreneurial elites.

The experience of Japan, the one non-Western nation which has successfully industrialized, suggests that the key question may not be the creation of new values so much as the way in which cultural ideals supporting tradition can give rise to those supporting modernity, that the shift from tradition to modernity need not involve a total rejection of a nation's basic values.

In discussing this problem, Reinhard Bendix notes that in Weber's *The Protestant Ethic and the Spirit of Capitalism,* a study of the resolution of the contradiction between the coexisting traditional and modern within a developing society, western Europe, the author observes that Reformers continued to be concerned with their salvation and accepted the traditional, Christian devaluation of worldly pursuits. The emergence of the "spirit of Capitalism" represented a direct outgrowth of this early antimaterialistic tradition of Christianity, a growth which occurred without replacing this tradition. Linking Weber's approach to the various analyses of the preconditions for Japanese development, Bendix points out that the Samurai under the Tokugawa regime became a demilitarized aristocracy loyal to the traditional Samurai ethic of militancy, even though the Tokugawa regime pursued a public policy of disciplined pacification, of the avoidance of conflict or competitive struggles to change a status or power relationship among the feudal lords. After the Meiji Restoration of 1868, the virtues of achievement were socially accepted. The traditional Samurai ethic applied to a competitive world now meant that any self-respecting Samurai was obliged to show his ability and desire to win. Thus in nineteenth-century Japan, as in Reformation Europe, "modern" economic orientations emerged through the application of traditional values and sources of individual motivation to new structural conditions, rather than the supplanting of one set of values by another. Since Japan and western Europe are the only two non-Communist cultural areas which have developed successfully on their own, the finding that achievement values seemingly emerged out of a redefinition of traditional values, rather than the adoption of new ones, has obvious implications for those contemporary underdeveloped cultures which seek to industrialize.

In seeking for culturally accepted orientations which will lead a section of the elite to "split off" and endorse "modern" values, Talcott Parsons suggests that nationalism, concern for the international status of one's society, can motivate those who are most oriented to foreign opinion to press for new attitudes toward industrialization. And within the existing elites such people are most likely to be found among intellectuals, especially "those who have had direct contacts with the West, particularly through education abroad or under Western auspices at home."[63] In the name of fostering the national welfare, major changes may be introduced, which would be more strongly resisted if they were perceived as serving the interests of a sub-group within the society, such as the businessmen.

In Uruguay, governmental actions which are justified by a nonrevolutionary national development ideology are seen by the workers as another rationalization of the ruling class to consolidate its power.

If the source of new development concerns is to be nationalism rather than self-interest, then the means are more likely to be perceived in the political rather than in an autonomous economic arena. And within the political arena, it is necessary to disassociate the policies advocated from any identification with possible foreign control. In Latin America today, support of "socialism" as opposed to "capitalism" becomes a way in which intellectuals may advocate industrialization without being accused of seeking to foster foreign "materialistic" values which are destructive of the spiritual values of the society.

A "socialist" ideology of economic development may be conceived of as a functional alternative to the Meiji elite's use of loyalty to the Emperor, Shinto, and the nation, when seeking to industrialize Japan. "To an important degree, socialism and communism are strong because they are symbolically associated with the ideology of independence, rapid economic development, social modernization, and ultimate equality. Capitalism is perceived as being linked to foreign influences, traditionalism, and slow growth."[64]

The problem which can best be met by a revolutionary nationalist ideology justifying the rejection of the past has been well put by Gerschenkron:

> In a backward country the great and sudden industrialization effort calls for a New Deal in emotions. Those carrying out the great transformation as well as those on whom it imposes burdens must feel, in the words of Matthew Arnold, that
>
> . . . Clearing a stage
> Scattering the past about
> Comes the new age.
>
> Capitalist industrialization under the auspices of socialist ideologies may be, after all, less surprising a phenomenon than would appear at first sight.[65]

In formulating such ideologies, Latin America is at a disadvantage compared with the "new nations" of Asia and Africa. Most of the latter have recently attained independence under the leadership of mass parties whose revolutionary ideology subsumes the values of equalitarianism, achievement, universalism, and collectivity-orientation. Traditional practices may be attacked as antithetical to the national interest and self-image. In much of Latin America, however, many traditional values and practices are regarded as proper parts of the national identity. Supporters of these traditional practices cannot be challenged as being anti-nationalist. Conversely the initial steps toward attaining a national economic system in the United States were facilitated by its being "in many senses an underdeveloped country when it was transformed into a new nation-state by a revolution led by a new elite." The new United States faced the need to break down the particularistic loyalties and values of the "indigenous aristocracy" of each little colony. And under the aegis of the ideology proclaimed in the Declaration of Independence, the revolutionary elite modified "the social institutions inherited from the British to the needs of a continental political economy."[66] Latin America, however, did not use its revolutionary struggle for independence to legitimate major social and economic changes; rather, independence often confirmed the control of the traditional landed class in power. Hence, as segments of the elite have awoken in recent decades to the need for such changes, they find it difficult to create the political institutions and national consensus needed to foster new values.

Perhaps Mexico is the best example of a systematic effort at value change in Latin America. The Mexican Revolution transformed the image and legitimate political emphases of the nation. It sought to destroy the sense of superiority felt by those of pure Spanish descent by stressing the concept of *Mexicanidad* and by a glorification of its Indian past. There are almost no monuments to Spaniards from Cortés to independence in 1814. Emphases on white racial descent are socially illegitimate. The values of the Mexican Revolution are similar to those of the other Western revolutions—the American, French, and Russian. Though Mexico clearly retains major elements of the traditional Latin American system, it is the one country which has identified its national ethos with that of equality and an open society. And with the sense of a collective revolutionary commitment to growth and equalitarianism, one finds that business activities, which are sanctioned by government approval, are presented as ways of fulfilling national objectives. A detailed account of the way in which the Revolution affected value change concludes:

> [T]he Revolution fostered a shift from ascription to achievement as the basis for distributing income, and from particularistic to universalistic standards as the basis for distributing political and economically-relevant tasks among performers. . . .
>
> Finally, it is evident that the nationalistic character of the Revolutionary movement together with the broad area of congruence between politically significant new class interests and social goals has assisted the shift from

self-orientation to collectivity-orientation in the performance by the new elite of its social role.[67]

Many of the conclusions about the impact of the Revolution on Mexican society which have been drawn from institutional and anthropological research have recently been reiterated in an opinion survey focusing on the effect of the Revolution on political attitudes and behavior. The authors compared Mexican responses on a number of items to those of Italians, choosing the latter nation as another Latin, Catholic, semi-developed state which does not have a commitment to revolutionary ideals. Among their findings are:

> In Mexico, 30 percent of the respondents express pride in some political aspect of their nation—ten times the proportion of respondents in Italy, where only 3 percent expressed such pride. A large proportion in Mexico also express pride in its economic system—in particular, they talk of economic potential and growth. In contrast, few Italians express pride either in the political aspects of their nation or in the economic system. . . .
>
> There is some evidence . . . that the continuing impact of the Revolution explains part of the attachment to their political system that Mexican respondents manifest. Respondents in Mexico were asked if they could name some of the ideals and goals of the Mexican Revolution. Thirty-five percent could name none, while the remaining 65 percent listed democracy, political liberty and equality, economic welfare, agrarian reform, social equality, and national freedom. . . . Those respondents who mentioned goals of the Revolution were then asked if they thought those goals had been realized, had been forgotten, or were still actively being sought. Twenty-five percent of the 614 respondents in this category think the goals have been realized, 61 percent think that they are still being sought, and only 14 percent think they have been forgotten.[68]

The Mexican Revolution, of course, did not involve simply a symbolic transfer of power, as has occurred in a number of other Latin American countries. Rather it is the one major Latin American revolution in which genuine land reform has occurred. The old dominant class of large landowners has been eliminated. "The large landholders disappeared at the pinnacle of the social order, together with their luxury consumption, no-work value system, and the belief in the innate inequality of social segments."[69] The rapid economic growth rate of Mexico in recent decades has been credited by many to the consequences of this revolution in changing the value system, in making possible the rise of a middle class that is self-assured about its own role. It "is fairly abstemious and frugal; it is devoted to modernization and education and recognizes economic achievement as a worthwhile end." Conversely, its neighbor,

Guatemala, provides a case for "good comparative control" with a nation of similar social structure and history, but which has not changed its basic agricultural system and consequent class structure and value system, and shows little economic progress; the term retrogression would be more apt.[70]

The positive example of Mexico and the negative one of Guatemala, and many other countries as well, suggest that those concerned with Latin American economic development and social modernization might best devote themselves to an analysis of the conditions for revolutionary transformation of class relationships, particularly at the current stage of development in the rural areas. Presumably the quickest way to initiate major changes in values is through social revolutions which remove those dominant strata which seek to maintain their position and traditional values. A recent study of sociological changes in Mexico concludes that in the new middle class, "there is evidence that the Revolution, by reducing the level of affluence and power of *cacique* families and by redistributing hacienda lands, has had a considerable psychological impact on the population in the direction of strengthening attitudes of independence and initiative and, conversely, reducing those of submissiveness."[71] . . .

Education and the Motivation for Innovating Entrepreneurial Elites

Although revolution may be the most dramatic and certainly the most drastic method to change values and institutions which appear to be inhibiting modernization, the available evidence would suggest that reforms in the educational system which can be initiated with a minimum of political resistance may have some positive consequences. Changes in the educational system may affect values directly through the incorporation of modern values to which students are exposed; indirectly they may help to modify the occupational structure by both increasing the numbers trained for various "modern" professions and helping to increase the status of positions needed in a developing economy. Clearly the way in which nations conceive of elite status may affect the supply of talent available for leadership in economic development. Thus, a high evaluation of occupations associated with traditional sources of status—the land, the military, humanistic intellectual occupations, and the free professions—tends to direct talent into occupations which do not contribute much to industrial development. And in cultures with such occupational values, the children of the successful entrepreneurs of lowly, often foreign, origin frequently go to university to find means of entering the learned professions, politics, the arts, or similar occupations. Such behavior is likely to reduce both the talent and capital available for entrepreneurial expansion. . . .

There is, of course, no simple relationship between the values of modern science and the way universities or even industrial concerns and government agencies operate in different countries. The Japanese system illustrates a formula whereby a "modern" nation may maintain particularistic and ascriptive traits while also developing rigidly universalistic and competitive patterns which guarantee the recruitment of talent into elite positions.

Members of various Japanese organizations, business, academic, or governmental, are given particularistic protection once they are admitted to membership. There is little competition for promotion or salary increases; men move up largely by seniority. Similarly, within the school and university system, little competitive grading occurs; almost everyone is promoted and graduated. And the graduates of various elite institutions are accorded almost "ascriptive" rights by others; e.g., leading business firms and government bureaus tend to hire most of their executive trainees from a few select universities, much as they have done for decades.

Universalism enters into the Japanese educational and business systems at two stages, first at admission to university, and second at entrance into the lower rungs of business or government executive ladders. The entrance examinations for Japanese universities are completely competitive; admission is solely a function of how well the students do on them, and many children of university professors, politicians, and the wealthy do not qualify for admission to the prestigious universities. Before admission, no one has any special claim to be accepted. Once admitted, however, grades do not serve as an important basis for future selection. While a prospective employer may not learn much about a student from his grades, he can be fairly certain that almost any graduate of Tokyo, Kyoto, Waseda, and other high-quality universities will be among the very top group in the country in general intelligence and in ability to benefit from higher education. And as a further guarantee of quality there is another impersonal level of competititon: job applicants must often take examinations as a pre-condition for civil service or business employment.

The Japanese system therefore permits particularism to operate in every personal relationship, while recruiting in a manner designed to ensure that the elite will be both highly motivated in achievement terms and well qualified. A teacher will not fail a student—i.e., someone with whom he has a personal relationship—nor will an employer or supervisor subject a subordinate to a humiliating lack of confidence. But the competitive entrance examinations, in which the examiners judge people with whom they have no personal relationship or obligation, meet the requirements of both particularistic and universalistic values. . . .

Conversely, it may be pointed out that a society which strongly emphasizes universalism and achievement in its values may permit a great deal of particularism and ascription. Political patronage has continued in America to a greater degree than in many more particularistic European nations; nepotism may be found in industry; influence and family background may affect admission policies to universities, e.g., the children of alumni and faculty are often given preference over those with better records even in some of the best universities. It may be suggested that where a society has strong norms which fulfill certain basic requirements of the system, it does not need explicit rules. North Americans will yield to particularistic obligations, but within self-imposed limits, to avoid harming the institution by helping incompetents. Hence the very emphasis on achievement and universalism in the North American value system would seem to reduce the need for the kind of rigidly universalistic examination system which exists in Japan, where all the normative pressure is in the direction of particularism. And North American institutions are much less inhibited about dismissing students or employees for lack of ability.

Thus it would appear that modernizing societies require either strong values or rules sustaining achievement and universalism. *They need not reject their traditional value system if they can work out mechanisms to guarantee that a large section of the elite will be composed of men who are highly motivated and able to achieve.* However, much of Latin America and some other nations in the less developed parts of the world have not succeeded in doing either. Men from privileged backgrounds may be admitted to university, take courses in which it is easy to pass and get a degree, and then secure a high position on the basis of whom they know, or through family ties. These countries have not yet found mechanisms to associate talent with elite status. And those reformist student movements which resist making admission and examination standards more rigorous are, in effect, helping to maintain the traditional order.

There is, of course, considerable pressure on many Latin American state universities to change because of the increasing numbers of applicants. Today, in some countries, large numbers fail to qualify for university entrance. However, the entrance examinations have been subject to severe criticism in many countries for being biased in favor of those educated traditionally in private schools.

An admissions system which is biased against the children of the less well-to-do also discourages enrollment in courses leading to "modern" vocations as distinct from the traditional elite ones. Studies of occupational choices of university students indicate that the career aspirations of the less well-to-do resemble those of youth from minority ethnic backgrounds. They are both more likely to seek to achieve through studying subjects like business, engineering, or practical sciences. The source of the class bias in recruitment to Latin American universities is not solely, or even primarily, in the preference given to those whose pre-university training is in traditional subjects. Rather it lies in the fact that the road to university graduation requires a relatively high family income. And in poor countries, where most families have no possible economic reserve, they will not be able to sustain their children through the higher levels of schooling. In Latin America, about two-thirds of all secondary school students attend private schools which charge fees, a factor which undoubtedly operates to increase class discrimination. As compared even to other underdeveloped regions, Latin America has done little to "identify and encourage able students . . . to provide programmes for part-time students, although it is known that a sizeable proportion of the students in higher education support themselves through employment, and there is no programme for external or correspondence students. Perhaps most important of all, the number of students who receive financial assistance must be discounted as negligible."[72] This situation, of course, means that the overwhelming majority of students at Latin American universities are from quite privileged backgrounds. The distribution of class backgrounds may become more rather than less discriminatory in the future, if higher education does not expand rapidly. For greater selectivity brought about by a more rapid increase in demand than in places available will increase the relative advantage of those from well-to-do, culturally privileged homes, who can prepare for admission examinations after having attended good private schools or [with the help of] private examination tutors.

Evidence that a deliberate policy to encourage students to take modern rather than traditional subjects can work in Latin America has been presented by Risieri Frondizi, former rector of the University of Buenos Aires, who reports that the initiation of "a program of fellowships, offered only in fields like science and technology" cut the number studying law in half within three years, while the modern subjects gained greatly.[73] . . .

Another major problem of Latin American universities is the curricula and status orientations of students which encourage vast numbers to work for degrees in subjects which are not needed in large quantity. Educational policy often encourages such maladjustments by making it much easier to secure a degree in subjects such as law or the humanities rather than the sciences or engineering. Clearly it is an implicit policy decision to pass students in the former fields for less and easier work than in the latter, a decision which says, in effect, "We will over-train and over-encourage a section of our youth to aspire to occupational roles which are overcrowded and which do not contribute to social and economic modernization." . . .

These comments are clearly relevant to judging how education, particularly higher education, supports the elite in contributing to political stability and economic growth. First, as Arthur Lewis has suggested, there is some reason to suspect that the status concomitants linked to education *per se* should vary with the proportion and absolute size of the population that is educated. A relatively small higher educational establishment will encourage the retention, or even development, of diffuse elitist values among university graduates, while if a large proportion of the university-age population attends school, the pressures should be in the opposite direction. In much of Latin America, university students almost automatically "become part of the elite. It matters little whether a student is the son of a minister or the son of a workman. His mere enrollment at the university makes him one of the two per thousand most privileged in the land."[74] Conversely in the United States, with its mass educational system, few university graduates may expect to attain high status; many of them will hold relatively low positions in non-manual work; and a certain number will even be employed in manual occupations. . . .

A related consequence of increase in the numbers who attain higher levels of education should be an increase in the amount of high achievement orientation in a nation. Studies of the occupational goals of college students in nations with tiny systems of higher education suggest that the large majority of them expect positions in government work. Since some form of white-collar employment must be the goal of college and secondary students, a sharp increase in their numbers should make talent available for a variety of technical and entrepreneurial roles. As Tumin and Feldman have indicated: "From the point of view of a theory of stratification, education is the main dissolver of barriers to social mobility. Education opens up the class structure and keeps it fluid, permitting considerably more circulation through class positions than would otherwise be possible. Education, further, yields attitudes and skills relevant to economic development and such development, in turn, allows further opportunity for persons at lower ranks."[75] The thesis that sees positive effects from the expansion of universities has been countered by these arguments: a transfer of educational techniques from developed to underdeveloped societies sometimes results in dysfunctional efforts at innovation; and "over-expansion" of educational resources may create a frustrated, and hence politically dangerous, stratum whose political activities undermine the conditions for growth; the "educated" often develop diffuse elitist status and cultural sustenance demands so they refuse to work in the rural or otherwise "backward" parts of their country; the educated often resist doing anything which resembles manual employment; and rapid educational expansion results in many being poorly educated, while reducing the opportunities available to the small minority of really bright students.

There is no doubt, of course, that the rapid expansion of an educational system may result in an over-supply of persons with relatively high expectations of employment, salary, and status. The increase in the numbers of educated people in a developing economy necessarily means that as education becomes less scarce it should command less status and income. The process of adjusting expanded levels of higher education to reduced rewards is obviously a difficult one, and often results in political unrest. And as W. Arthur Lewis has pointed out, "upper classes based on land or capital have always favoured restricting the supply of education to absorptive capacity, because they know the political dangers of having a surplus of educated persons."[76] One must, however, separate the problem of the possible political consequences of educational expansion from the economic ones. As Lewis indicates, "as the premium for education falls, the market for the educated may widen enormously. . . . The educated lower their sights, and employers raise their requirements. . . . As a result of this process an economy can ultimately absorb any number of educated persons. . . . One ought to produce more educated people than can be absorbed at current prices, because the alteration in current prices which this forces is a necessary part of the process of economic development."[77] The argument against expansion is largely political rather than economic, and calls for a detailed examination of the sociological consequences. Mexico affords an example of the way in which economic growth and emphases on new values may reduce the tensions inherent in rapid educational expansion. William Glade contends that though the educated were often frustrated in pre-revolutionary Mexico, "the more or less steady expansion of the private sector activity since the mid-1920s" has meant a continuing demand for trained persons. "Secondly, . . . with the over-all expansion of the social, economic, and political structure there came a widening range of socially approved channels for the realization of achievement."[78]

To sum up the discussion of universities, the expansion of the educational system is of unquestioned benefit in providing the requisite skills, aspirations, and values essential to modern occupational roles. Not only expansion is required but also the content of education should be broadened. Specifically, education should be directed toward inculcating innovative orientations and teaching problem-solving techniques in all fields of knowledge. This would mean emphasizing and rewarding creative and independent effort on the part of students. The problem suggested earlier of the potentially disruptive political consequences of overproduction of university graduates would presumably be reduced if expansion is accompanied by a modernizing of the educational system. Underemployed graduates with modern, innovative orientations, are perhaps less likely to seek traditional political solutions to their plight, and more prone to look for other possible avenues toward achievement.

Proposals such as expansion and curricula change are easy to make but difficult to put into practice. Proposals to transform radically and to expand the educational system would meet, first of all, the opposition of present elites who are identified to some extent with the present system and see such changes as a threat. Considerable innovative skill may have to be applied to overcome such opposition.

The conclusion to this section on education also brings us full circle to a recognition of the need to change class relationships in order to foster a change in values. Governments and parties which are deliberately concerned with the need to change values must also seek for ways to foster the rise of new occupational strata to status and power and [to foster] the reduction of the privileged position of old power groups, such as the land-linked traditional oligarchies who have little interest in economic growth, social modernization, expanded opportunities for talent, or democracy and equality.

Notes

1. Max Weber, *The Protestant Ethic and the Spirit of Capitalism* (New York: Scribner's, 1935).

2. See Talcott Parsons, *The Social System* (Glencoe: The Free Press, 1951), pp. 58–67 passim; "Pattern Variables Revisited," *American Sociological Review*, 25 (1960), pp. 58–67; and "The Point of View of the Author," in Max Black (ed.), *The Social Theories of Talcott Parsons* (Englewood Cliffs, N.J.: Prentice-Hall, 1961), pp. 319–320, 329–336. I have discussed the pattern-variables and attempted to use them in an analysis of differences among the four major English-speaking nations. See S. M. Lipset, *The First New Nation* (New York: Basic Books, 1963), pp. 207–273.

3. See Parsons, *The Social System*, pp. 182–191.

4. Ibid., pp. 198–200.

5. Aldo E. Solari, *Estudios sobre la Sociedad Uruguaya* (Montevideo: Arca, 1964), p. 162.

6. Ibid., p. 171.

7. Frederick B. Pike, *Chile and the United States, 1880–1962* (Notre Dame: University of Notre Dame Press, 1962), p. 78. The strength of these values may be seen in the fact that for much of the colonial period, at the University of San Gregorio in Quito, "Applicants for entrance had to establish by a detailed

legal process 'the purity of their blood' and *prove that none of their ancestors had engaged in trade.*" Harold Benjamin, *Higher Education in the American Republics* (New York: McGraw-Hill, 1965), p. 16 (my italics).

8. R. P. Dore, "Latin America and Japan Compared," in John J. Johnson (ed.), *Continuity and Change in Latin America* (Stanford: Stanford University Press, 1964), p. 245.

9. United Nations Economic and Social Council. Economic Commission for Latin America, *Provisional Report on the Conference on Education and Economic and Social Development in Latin America* (Mar del Plata, Argentina: 1963. E/CN.12/639), p. 250.

10. Solari, pp. 127–129, 113–122.

11. Norman W. Taylor, "The French-Canadian Industrial Entrepreneur and His Social Environment," in Marcel Rioux and Yves Martin (eds.), *French-Canadian Society,* Vol. I (Toronto: McClelland and Stewart, 1964), pp. 271–295.

12. Pierre Elliot Trudeau, "Some Obstacles to Democracy in Quebec," in Mason Wade (ed.), *Canadian Dualism* (Toronto: University of Toronto Press, 1960), p. 245; see also Herbert Quinn, *The Union Nationale* (Toronto: University of Toronto Press, 1963), pp. 17–18.

13. S. D. Clark, *The Canadian Community* (Toronto: University of Toronto Press, 1962), p. 161.

14. Thomas C. Cochran, *The Puerto Rican Businessman* (Philadelphia: University of Pennsylvania Press, 1959), p. 131; see also pp. 151–154 and Cochran, "Cultural Factors in Economic Growth," *Journal of Economic History,* 20 (1960), pp. 515–530.

15. Albert Lauterbach, "Managerial Attitudes and Economic Growth," *Kyklos,* 15 (1962), p. 384.

16. Albert Lauterbach, "Government and Development: Managerial Attitudes in Latin America," *Journal of Inter-American Studies,* 7 (1965), pp. 202–203; see also L. C. Bresser Pereira, "The Rise of Middle Class and Middle Management in Brazil," *Journal of Inter-American Studies,* 4 (1962), pp. 322–323.

17. Fernando H. Cardoso, *El empresario industrial en América Latina: Brasil* (Mar del Plata, Argentina: Naciones Unidas Comisión Económica para América Latina, 1963. E/CN/12/642/Add. 2), pp. 25–26.

18. Tomás Roberto Fillol, *Social Factors in Economic Development. The Argentine Case* (Cambridge: M.I.T. Press, 1961), pp. 13–14.

19. Ibid., p. 61.

20. Cardoso, *El empresario industrial en América Latina: Brasil,* p. 31; Siegel, "Social Structure and Economic Change in Brazil," pp. 405–408. Robert J. Alexander, *Labor Relations in Argentina, Brazil, Chile* (New York: McGraw-Hill, 1962), pp. 48–49.

21. Emilio Willems, "The Structure of the Brazilian Family," *Social Forces,* 31 (1953), p. 343.

22. Albert Hirschman, *The Strategy of Economic Development* (New Haven: Yale University Press, 1958), pp. 14–19.

23. Lauterbach, "Managerial Attitudes and Economic Growth," p. 379; Fillol, pp. 13–14.

24. Lauterbach, "Government and Development," pp. 209–210. J. Richard Powell, "Notes on Latin American Industrialization," *Inter-American Economic Affairs*, 6 (Winter 1952), pp. 82–83.

25. W. Paul Strassman, "The Industrialist," in Johnson (ed.), *Continuity and Change in Latin America*, p. 173.

26. Aarón Lipman, *El empresario industrial en América Latina: Colombia* (Mar del Plata, Argentina: Naciones Unidas Comisión Económica para América Latina, 1963. E/CN/12/642/Add. 4), p. 30.

27. Cochran, "Cultural Factors in Economic Growth," pp. 529–530.

28. Kalman H. Silvert, "The Costs of Anti-Nationalism: Argentina," in Silvert (ed.), *Expectant Peoples: Nationalism and Development* (New York: Random House, 1963), p. 350.

29. Ibid., p. 353.

30. John Friedmann, "Intellectuals in Developing Countries," *Kyklos*, 13 (1964), p. 524.

31. William S. Stokes, "The Drag of the *Pensadores*," in James W. Wiggins and Helmut Schoeck (eds.), *Foreign Aid Reexamined* (Washington: Public Affairs Press, 1958), p. 63.

32. Dore, "Latin America and Japan Compared," p. 245.

33. Pike, p. 251.

34. Fillol, pp. 17–18.

35. Jacques Lambert, "Requirements for Rapid Economic and Social Development: The View of the Historian and Sociologist," in De Vries and Echavarría (eds.), p. 64.

36. J. Tinbergen and H. C. Bos, "The Global Demand for Higher and Secondary Education in the Underdeveloped Countries in the Next Decade," O.E.C.D., *Policy Conference on Economic Growth and Investment in Education, III, The Challenge of Aid to Newly Developing Countries* (Paris: O.E.C.D., 1962), p. 73.

37. Frederick Harbison and Charles A. Myers, *Education, Manpower and Economic Growth* (New York: McGraw-Hill, 1964), p. 179.

38. Ibid., p. 88.

39. Ibid., pp. 115–119.

40. James S. Coleman, "Introduction to Part IV," in J. S. Coleman (ed.), *Education and Political Development* (Princeton University Press, 1965), p. 530.

41. Joseph Schumpeter, *The Theory of Economic Development* (New York: Oxford University Press, 1961), pp. 74–94.

42. Bert Hoselitz, "Main Concepts in the Analysis of the Social Implications of Technical Change," in Hoselitz and Moore (eds.), *Industrialization and Society*, pp. 22–28.

43. Hoselitz, *Sociological Aspects*, p. 62; Peter T. Bauer and Basil S. Yamey, *The Economics of Underdeveloped Countries* (Chicago: University of Chicago Press, 1957), pp. 106–112.

44. Louis Kriesberg, "Entrepreneurs in Latin America and the Role of Cultural and Situational Processes," *International Social Science Journal*, 15 (1963), p. 591.

45. Strassmann, p. 164.

46. José Luis de Imaz, *Los que mandan* (Buenos Aires: Editorial Universitaria de Buenos Aires, 1964), p. 136.

47. Ibid.; see also Gino Germani, "The Strategy of Fostering Social Mobility," in Egbert De Vries and José Medina Echavarría (eds.), *Social Aspects of Economic Development in Latin America,* Vol. I (Paris: UNESCO, 1963), pp. 223–226; and Eduardo A. Zalduendo, *El empresario industrial en América Latina: Argentina* (Mar del Plata, Argentina: Naciones Unidas Comisión Económica para América Latina, 1963. E/CN/12/642/Add. 1), p. 10. The census of 1895 reported that 84 percent of the 18,000 business establishments were owned by foreign-born individuals. Thomas C. Cochran and Ruben E. Reina, *Entrepreneurship in Argentine Culture. Torcuato Di Tella and S.I.A.M.* (Philadelphia: University of Pennsylvania Press, 1962), p. 8.

48. Imaz, pp. 138–139.

49. Bertram Hutchinson, "A origem sócio-econômica dos estudantes universitários," in Hutchinson (ed.), *Mobilidade e Trabalho* (Rio de Janeiro: Centro Brasiliero de Pesquisas Educacionais Ministério de Educação e Cultura, 1960), p. 145.

50. See Robert Park, *Race and Culture* (Glencoe: Free Press, 1950), pp. 345–392; Everett Stonequist, *The Marginal Man* (New York: Russell and Russell, 1961).

51. Bernard J. Siegel, "Social Structure and Economic Change in Brazil," in Kuznets, Moore, and Spengler (eds.), pp. 399–400 (emphases in the original).

52. Gilberto Freyre, *New World in the Tropics. The Culture of Modern Brazil* (New York: Vintage Books, 1963), p. 161.

53. Max Weber, pp. 38–46.

54. Suzanne Keller, *The Social Origins and Career Lines of Three Generations of American Business Leaders* (Ph.D. Dissertation, Columbia University, 1953), pp. 37–41.

55. See S. M. Lipset and Reinhard Bendix, *Social Mobility in Industrial Society* (Berkeley: University of California Press, 1959), pp. 137–138.

56. John Porter, *The Vertical Mosaic: An Analysis of Social Class and Power in Canada* (Toronto: University of Toronto Press, 1965), pp. 286–289.

57. Anyda Marchant, *Viscount Mauá and the Empire of Brazil* (Berkeley: University of California Press, 1965), pp. 81, 83, 208–209, 241.

58. Cochran and Reina, pp. 147–151.

59. Johannes Hirschmeier, *The Origins of Entrepreneurship in Meiji Japan* (Cambridge: Harvard University Press, 1964), p. 35.

60. Germani, "The Strategy of Fostering Social Mobility," p. 226.

61. Amando do Miguel and Juan J. Linz, "Movilidad Social del Empresario Español," *Revista de Fomento Social,* 75–76 (July–December 1964).

62. Fernando H. Cardoso, *Empresário Industrial e Desenvolvimento Econômico no Brasil,* p. 157 passim.

63. Talcott Parsons, *Structure and Process in Modern Society* (New York: The Free Press, 1960), pp. 116–129.

64. S. M. Lipset, "Political Cleavages in 'Developed' and 'Emerging' Polities," in Erik Allardt and Yrjo Littunen (eds.), *Cleavages, Ideologies and Party Systems* (Helsinki: The Westermarck Society, 1964), p. 44.

65. Alexander Gerschenkron, *Economic Backwardness in Historical Perspective* (Cambridge: Harvard University Press, 1962), pp. 28, 59–62.

66. Robert Lamb, "Political Elites and the Process of Economic Development," in Bert Hoselitz (ed.), *The Progress of Underdeveloped Areas* (Chicago: University of Chicago Press, 1952), pp. 30, 38.

67. William P. Glade, Jr., "Revolution and Economic Development: A Mexican Reprise," in Glade and Charles W. Anderson, *The Political Economy of Mexico. Two Studies* (Madison: University of Wisconsin Press, 1963), pp. 50–52.

68. Sidney Verba and Gabriel A. Almond, "National Revolutions and Political Commitment," in Harry Eckstein (ed.), *Internal War* (New York: The Free Press, 1964), pp. 221–222, 229.

69. Manning Nash, "Social Prerequisites to Economic Growth in Latin America and Southeast Asia," *Economic Development and Cultural Change,* 12 (1964), p. 230.

70. Ibid., pp. 231–233.

71. Glade, "Revolution and Economic Development," p. 43.

72. Frank Bowles, *Access to Higher Education,* Vol. I (Paris: UNESCO, 1963), p. 148.

73. Risieri Frondizi, "Presentation," in Council on Higher Education in the Americas, *National Development and the University* (New York: Institute of International Education, 1965), p. 30.

74. Rudolph P. Atcon, "The Latin American University," *Die Deutsche Universitätszeitung,* 17 (February 1962), p. 16.

75. Melvin Tumin with Arnold S. Feldman, *Social Class and Social Change in Puerto Rico* (Princeton, N.J.: Princeton University Press, 1961), p. 7.

76. W. Arthur Lewis, "Priorities for Educational Expansion," O.E.C.D., p. 37.

77. Ibid., pp. 37–38.

78. Glade, pp. 44–46.

3 / The Politics of Social and Economic Change in Latin America

Kalman H. Silvert

In Chapter 3 political scientist Kalman Silvert recognizes the liberal bias of the modernizationists in assuming that Latin America had to follow the Western model of development. "What else is one to do," he asks, "other than define development by the selection of certain characteristics of the already developed states?" Echoing Lipset's cultural interpretation, Silvert argues that "there is something in the quality of the Latin American man in his culture which has made it difficult for him to become truly modern . . . which has made this part of the Western world so prone to excesses of scoundrels, so politically irrational in seeking economic growth, and so ready to reach for gimmicks."

If some Latin Americans were kept tradition-bound by a strong "Mediterranean ethos," however, they coexisted with other Latin Americans of a modernist bent. While reflecting the traditional-modern dichotomy in his analysis, Silvert is upbeat in his belief that the modernizers, particularly among the expanding middle classes, were in the forefront of the political, social, and economic changes that were rapidly transforming Latin American society. For Silvert these changes—particularly evident since World War II—were leading Latin America "to the antechamber of the truly modern state."

No society—regardless of how far it may have advanced toward self-sustaining rates of economic growth—can claim more than a partial and insecure resolution of such basic problems as the attainment of peace, plenty, freedom, full modernity. Whatever the form of economic or political organization or level of industrial advance, both substantial poverty and non-functional inequalities persist. Most men everywhere continue to accept and even embrace stifling discipline, taxing work, degrading status, and the short end of consumption while yielding to others the right to make decisions, control resources, consume the major share of what is collectively produced, and monopolize access to favored positions. No sociological evidence points in the direction of a withering away of stratification or other forms of social control, whatever the ideological guidelines or revolutionary capacity or intent of those who lead the process of change. The modern society now universally pursued will, under whatever guise it takes, for a long time accommodate and sustain extreme inequalities, and the process of transition may create wider social gulfs than existed before the drive for modernism began. The study of development, then, cannot be approached as simply the examination of strategies and mechanisms of change through which ancient oppression and inequality will be made to disappear. The modern "developed" nation is a new arena in which the classic struggle between individual autonomy and social commitment, personal realization and social solidarity, freedom and participation will be played out. The question then becomes what kinds of freedom do development or modernization really provide? What new forms of discipline or submission do they impose? The option that Latin Americans have open to them is thus not one of total salvation by embracing one or another version of the "finished" society, but rather between drift and the self-conscious effort to expand freedom and national capacity in determinate directions.[1]

Latin America offers great difficulties in analysis precisely because it sits between the developed countries of European culture and the underdeveloped world. The diversity within the area, too, is a fierce challenge to generalization. From the backwater of Haiti to the urban sophistication of São Paulo and Buenos Aires is a leap much greater than the cultural jump from Rio de Janeiro or Mexico City to New York. These problems of analysis make the Latin American case all the more useful for the general comparative politics of development. The

Reprinted with permission from *Sociological Review Monographs*, no. 11 (Latin American Sociological Studies, University of Keele, edited by Paul Halmos), pp. 47–58. London: Routledge & Kegan Paul PLC, Feb., 1967.

construction of a framework to build order into the Latin American situation is now appropriate.

The first task may well be to see what it is that we might mean by a "modern person," and then relate this individual and the attitudes and behavior by which we define him as modern to the social institutions whose power he creates by his consensual acceptance. This developed person may be defined in rather standard fashion as follows: he is a relativist in the sense that he does not seek absolute truth in public affairs; thus, he is willing to accept compromise solutions to social matters; in consequence of this relativism, he is also a secularist in his public beliefs, for otherwise he would seek to apply the necessary absolutes of theology to his political and economic choices; social affairs remain conceptually limited for him, then, and his acceptance of this limited system assumes that within it he will accept the rule of law as absolute. This statement contains a liberal bias, which means that development is being defined with reference to the experience of Western Europe and its cultural spawn. What else is one to do, other than define development by the selection of certain characteristics of the already developed states? After all, the term is a relative one, and the only way in which the swirling of ideas can be stopped long enough to put the cases on a scale is to draw a baseline. And what realistic baseline of development can be drawn into existence other than one founded on the experience of the already developed world?

If the institutions within which the Latin American modern man expresses himself must bear some resemblance to developed models, this resemblance need not be only a cheap replica of propagandistic descriptions of countries like France or the United States. I certainly do not hold that Latin American governments must attempt a carbon copy of the United States, say, if they are to succeed, but rather that certain functions and relationships must somehow be achieved if those societies are to reach self-sustaining levels of industrial civilization. The most sensitive illustration of this thesis that can be taken concerns the disagreement between those who would have Latin America adopt "free enterprise" economic policies and those who hold that the Latin American republics have no choice but to employ the state as the guide and regulator of the economic machine. The latter view would seem the more reasonable—that the Latin American states must take an active rôle in the development process as promoter, regulator, and even in some cases (such as utilities) as partner. But it is logically needless to take the other step and say that such state interventionism is in itself desirable. Instead, the more valid construction would be that private ownership as such does not guarantee responsible free enterprise, and that state interventionism as such does not guarantee the institutional conditions for modern development. Both systems must serve another common function if they are to be conducive to the elaboration of modern societies.

If the political thought of the post-Machiavellian period is looked at for its "modernization" content, so to speak, some suggestions still valid for today may be found. For example, what classical Liberalism espoused as ideology was the access of middle- and upper-class persons to an economic "market" in conditions of relative equality of opportunity. We know that the apposite real system was by no means perfect, but it probably at least partially rationalized the economic structure, ordered the participation of middle-class groups in the economic machine, spread ownership not universally but more widely than before, and permitted power to a new entrepreneurial group. This move in the economic realm had a concomitant political side. Equality before the economic market-place translated itself for some groups into equality before the laws in the political sphere. The joining of middle-class to upper-class persons in politico-economic fashions created supra-class identifications and served to channel class conflict between them in such ways as to promote the cohesion of all persons participant in the polity despite other secondary divisive factors, and in part precisely to keep others alienated. This set of supra-class, of truly national identifications, is what belied the predictions of Marxist theorists who saw not only a grinding away of the middle by the millstones of upper and lower strata, but also an identification among the proletariat across national and cultural lines. Exactly the opposite has occurred in the developed world, as certain strong identifications have become vertical inside national groupings, and not horizontal across them. The primary political community has been defined by those vertical identifications.

In familiar language, the political structure within which industrial development has taken place historically has been the nation-state. The economic system has never been classically *laissez-faire,* but always a combination of private and public power in both clash and co-operation used to maintain a system allowing for some degree of openness—labor mobility, the search for advantage, the success of the abler person, and so forth.

To use the word nation-state is dangerous. For many it conjures up the evil images of nationalism, super-nationalism, Fascism, Nazism, the emotional excesses of the leaders of new states, and so forth. Any discussion of the subject which failed to take these negative connotations into account would be most partial. The positive function of the nation-state in development, however, is to provide the political theater within which power can be distributed, absolutes contained by the play of plural interests, compromise decisions reached—in short, in which the secular, pragmatic relativism of the modern scientific society can begin to take shape. That the ideologies of the nation can become perverted, that the nation should be revered as a mystical entity for its sake alone, is of course totally destructive of the positive developmental functions which supra-class identification with the national community has discharged in the mature developed countries. Under those negative conditions, then, the course of development is arrested, growth is no longer self-sustaining, and the monstrous and wasteful indulgences of racism, genocide, and war stunt continued accommodation to the ever-present necessities for institutional change.

No country has as yet concluded the task of building fully, absolutely national communities in the sense of those words as used here. As has been said, everywhere men are partially alienated, a result not only of the nature and capacities of individual men, but also of the rigidities and systems of exclusion built into every society. The United States is still struggling with a racial problem obviously involving the ancient and fundamental question of equality before the laws and the economic marketplace for all men. Great Britain has a much milder problem with its West Indian immigrants, but still has not managed to open its educational system, especially at the higher levels, so that personal style and even accent no longer serve to distinguish among the social classes. The Germans have as yet to prove that the first label they attach to their neighbors is that of "fellow citizen," and not some other category which might be used to read that neighbor out of the human race at some future time. But in all the developed countries great masses of persons indeed do "belong," do find themselves participant in the national community, can at least partially transcend their social positions for certain political, social, and economic purposes. Most public decisions in these lands are compromises among power groups, they reveal some pragmatism and relativism, and are subject to some impersonal application.

By this time it must be clear that everything said boils down to the view that there is something in the quality of the Latin American man in his culture which has made it difficult for him to become truly modern. Of course that is the case. If country X in Central America, say, were emptied of its inhabitants, and a similar number of Swedes substituted for them, there can be no doubt that in a very short time country X would be fundamentally changed—and obviously in the direction of greater modernization. But this kind of statement only begs the case—it does not tell us what there is in the Latin American value systems which has made this part of the Western world so prone to the excesses of scoundrels, so politically irrational in seeking economic growth, and so ready to reach for gimmicks.

The Mediterranean ethos is dedicated to hierarchy and order and absolutes. This attitude of mind still drives men to the view that every single human action must be simultaneously weighed by universal moral as well as secular precepts; instead of assuming an entire system to be identified with ethical values so that individual acts can conform to the play of the structure within at least a partially relativistic and human context, traditionalists subsume system, individual act, social behavior and thought to immediate and absolute universal judgment. This stance— which serves to divide man from his neighbor, to make all conflict go up through the hierarchy before it can come down to local decision— serves to explain many antidevelopmental political patterns in Latin America.

For example, when labor disputes arise in most Latin countries it is an automatic procedure to avoid the face-to-face collective bargaining process and, as a matter of normal practice, to have recourse to government for their settlement. The best way to win a strike or to prevent one is then of course to control the government. The strong urge in the Mediterranean world toward corporative organization is another manifestation of this ethos. To identify man by his occupation, to keep him in the kennel of his job for all purposes of political representation, actualizes the neat order and the love for hierarchy and organization, which also serve to contain class conflict and to prevent individuals from attaining a social level in accord with their abilities. It is the way in which the hated individualism of the Liberal order, with its partial freeing of man for certain economic, social, and political purposes, can be avoided while at the same time adding sufficient structural complication to society to answer some of the institutional demands of industrial urbanization. Franco Spain and Salazar Portugal are, of course, syndicalist or falangist states. The Vargas and Perón administrations in Brazil and Argentina were of the same cloth. Even the occupational organization of Mexico's official party is in this tradition.

The negative purpose of modern falangism is to prevent the emergence of a secular institution, the state, as the ultimate arbiter of social conflict. Its philosophical function is to continue the identification of social choice with rigid criteria of universal good. The results of such ideas and organization are many: social mobility is rigidly contained and often reduced; the recruitment of able members of the population is inhibited; compromise solutions are made difficult and are often considered cowardly and immoral; class conflict is intensified in periods of crisis; government remains inherently weak and thus unstable; scientific pursuits and attitudes have barren soil on which to grow; problems remain unsolved for extremely long periods; privilege tends to absolute levels, impeding the growth of internal markets and thus limiting the chances for further economic growth; revolution becomes attractive as the only way in which substantive and fundamental change can be attempted; and so on in this vein.

Not all Latin Americans share these views any longer, of course. Significantly large groups in all but the least developed countries have become modern in outlook, although not as yet supported by an institutional order through which they can confidently and predictably work. The transitional nature of Latin American society can be seen in the co-existence not only of urban and rural sub-cultures and of European and Indian ethnic groups, but also, in the major cities, in the co-existence of those persons with the Mediterranean ethos and those who have—not the classically Liberal—but the more fundamental relativistic and partially secularist views of the modern civic pragmatist. This latter dichotomy is not class-bound. Through the social order there are persons of both persuasions. The party structure clearly reflects this schism.

In Chile, for example, [Ed. note: before the rise and fall of Allende] there [were] parties of the Right, the Liberals and the Conservatives; two parties of the center, the Radicals and somewhat to their left the Christian Democrats; and on the left the division between the Castroite Socialists and the traditional, cautious, opportunistic Communists, as well as other splinter groups. The Argentine and Brazilian cases are even more explicit. Enormous confusion has attended the question of whether Vargas and Perón led leftist or rightist movements. Because of the populism they espoused, they are called leftist. Because of their quasi-fascist views, they are called rightist. In reality, they may be considered to the left of the traditionalist spectrum: falangists seeking to corral the lower classes into a syndicalist attachment to the government in order that a contained industrialization and pseudo-modernization could proceed. Is it to be so soon forgotten that Vargas and his disciple, Goulart, represent classically rightist social segments, including certain landowners? Is it to be so soon forgotten that Perón was an army officer and that his aristocratic support came from the most traditional farming sectors in the far interior of Argentina, or that the first Peronist governor to be elected after the fall of Perón in 1955 was from the Province of Tucumán, a sugar growing area of traditional haciendas?

This construction leads to the conclusion that class position, in itself, is no determinant of political attitudes. The minimum further conceptual complication needed for transitional Latin America is to project class effects through the prism of the conflicting value systems involved. Thus middle groups in themselves offer no automatic reason to hope for stability and progress in Latin America, as the easy American dream world would often have it. Nevertheless the presence of certain middle, upper, and lower groups who combine their class position with a modern attitude toward life does indeed offer grounds for optimism, as well as a guide to policy. In general terms those persons and groups espousing non-absolutistic, relativistic, and nationalistic views should be supported in Latin America if modernization is what we seek. The issue cannot be whether governments are democratic or authoritarian; rather, the question is whether the governing groups are laying the basis for fuller and more participant lives for themselves as well as for the dispossessed, whether the governors use the freedom of action they are endowed with by their power actually to exercise freedom (in its pragmatic and relativistic and rational sense) in their manner of governance. To say that alienated, illiterate populaces cannot be democratic and modern participants in social development is obvious. For them, central government must be necessarily authoritarian. But the same is clearly not true for those groups that are literate, trained, imbued with some degree of social, economic, and political power potential. Do they indeed participate? Is there civil freedom for them? Do they enter the political process to make decisions designed to help them broaden the range of decisions they may make in the future? Or are they so humanly limited that they would rather literally die than change? As Matthew Arnold has put it: "Perfection will never be reached; but to recognize a period of transformation when it comes, and to adapt themselves honestly and rationally to its laws, is perhaps the nearest approach to perfection of which men and nations are capable. No habits or attachments should prevent their trying to do this; nor indeed, in the long run, can they."[2]

Latin American countries are not ruled only by blind oligarchs. Some of their rulers fit that description; but others clearly do not. Middle classes in at least half the countries have substantial political power, and they too sprout imitators of the oligarch as well as persons of much broader generosity. Even the alienated lower classes offer their cadres of persons eager to assume the burdens of responsible participant citizenship. The spectacle is not a totally gloomy one. On the contrary, I should argue that the restiveness of today's Latin America offers at least the promise of fundamental decisions for the sorrows as well as joys of relatively complete modernism. Indeed, I feel it not unwarranted to go further and say that in some countries significantly powerful groups have arrived at consensus concerning the full meaning of development, but that they are hindered by a lack of technique, anachronistic institutions, and competing loyalties too strong to be lightly cast aside.

Sociologists have long distinguished among various kinds of change. In their turn, the economists, too, widely (although rather informally) understand differences among "economic change," "economic growth," "economic development," and, most specifically, "industrialization" and "economic modernization." Political scientists, although members of the last of the three disciplines to enter into the development studies game, have perhaps been most persistent about attempting to define the unique nature of a modern polity, and most remiss in discerning the characteristics of the several categories into which non-modern political systems may be put for their finer analysis. This paper argues that the nation-state in a particular definition is the modern polity (not necessarily the super-modern one—but that would be another discussion), and by inference that an industrial urban lifestyle is the modern economy, and that both must relate to social structure, mobility patterns, and value systems in certain ways if the combination is to permit self-sustaining institutional change. This total set of relations does not come into being by magic, however. As Leonard Reissman has put it:

> [Modernization] . . . is not accident or a historical metaphysics at work. It is not . . . that once a new nation buys part of the Western package— say, technology—that it must also buy with it Western reason and Western political institutions, simply because they are all glued together. They are not so glued together in any metaphysical sense. Rather, the new elites are forced into accepting all the other features of the "package" they buy for the same dynamic reasons that the Western elites had to buy them earlier. It is in this sense, then, that the Western experience of a nationalizing history was a "necessary" development. For the same reasons, too, it is "necessary" for the developing nations as well if they are to achieve successful political and social integration of the nation and continuing development.[3]

We simply do not know how much of the enormous change to be seen in Latin America during the post-war period is truly modernizing change. That a great deal has happened is indubitable: enormous industrial cities have grown; the population in general has increased sharply; there has probably been much acculturation as Indians have become cultural mestizos, and much mobility as individuals have shifted about on the social scale laterally as well as vertically; production has increased enormously in absolute terms (whose significance is often eluded because per capita figures are used); and so on. In a political sense, too, there have been great changes:

1. Falangist experiments have been attempted since the 1930s, and so far all relatively full-blown ones have failed.
2. The old-fashioned *caudillos* have been dwindling in numbers, until now they are almost a rarity.

3. New forms of praetorianism and other styles of military government have been tried, but so far without long-term success in the more developed countries, although a sophisticated "mercantilistic caudillismo," so to speak, is exemplified in the administrations of Trujillo, Batista, the Somoza brothers, and others.
4. Outright Marxist experiments have been launched. Cuba is the most notable case, of course, but the embryonic Marxism of the Arbenz period in Guatemala should be mentioned, as well as the programs of such classically Marxist groupings as Chile's Popular Front and the traditional left parties of Argentina and Uruguay.
5. Christian Democracy, advanced as a Catholic developmental alternative to Marxism, is also beginning to have its day. The September 1964 victory of Eduardo Frei in Chile is but the first campaign in what is designed to be a hemispheric war.
6. Middle-class politics are moving away from the old-style Radical politics to identification with the old elites on the one hand, and toward the opening of true national community in identification with lower elements on the other.
7. Mass movements have appeared, but so far they have not contributed significantly and unequivocally to nation-building. In Brazil and Argentina mass participation was drained off into neo-corporativism, in Mexico it is so far safely held within the single-party and its occupationally based sectors, in Bolivia peasant revolt was satiated with land and transformed into a power to contain the appetites of the miners, and so on.
8. Communications networks have grown enormously, almost certainly reducing the "inertness" of Latin Americans not participant in the national community. In the jargon of the trade, it might be said that most nationally non-participant Latin Americans are now "mobilized" and seeking institutionalized means of "integration" in the national community.
9. The "new nations" and European "Third Forcism," combined with the neutralism of the underdeveloped, added to the tug-and-pull of the Cold War, have all changed Latin America's international position. More attention is being paid to Latin problems, as the Alliance for Progress, renewed European interest, and the growing communications among the developing nations attest.

Obviously, the list could be prolonged, or reviewed and revised from other angles. The only point I wish to make is that in Latin America recent political change has been at least as profound as economic and demographic change. But only a subjective judgment can be made at this point concerning the degree of modernization involved in these changes. It is my impression that ever increasingly the changes are in the direction of the establishment of truly modern polities, and that the "bundles" or "packages" of relationships required for self-sustaining change are being formed. The failure of neo-falangism in such major states as Argentina and Brazil, for example, implies a rejection of a particular style of working economic and social change which conduces inevitably to a dead end. That neo-Liberalism under military tutelage should have supplanted the Vargas-Goulart and Perón regimes is, in my opinion, not the "best" decision from a modernizing standpoint, but it is at least not as counter-productive as falangism. At the other ideological pole, Cuba has become the society closest to being a modern nation-state in the Iberian world. The costs in all senses have been high and the process wasteful; whether enough rationality and impersonalism have been worked into the Cuban structure to permit that state to weather an elementary crisis of succession remains doubtful. Still, to deny the high order of supra-class identification with nation which Cuba has probably attained is to render one unable to explain the survival of the regime.

Another possible evidence of political modernization is that, increasingly, economic affairs are taken to be instrumental and not in themselves both promise and fulfillment. The economists of the United Nations Economic Commission for Latin America, when they advance their "structuralist" views of such problems as inflation and industrialization, are moving away from an ingenuously materialistic view of the development process. In governmental policy an increasing eclecticism toward the establishment of mixed economies—as in Mexico and Venezuela— is a hopeful sign of the discarding of more dogmatic ideologies for more relativistic and pragmatic ones.

The criers of Latin American doom can usually be at least dampened by the simple exclamation of how miraculous it is that one Latin American country in dire crisis after another manages to survive to pass through yet another dire crisis. I am suggesting, however, that the picture is yet brighter. Structural changes conducive to national integration are taking place. Millennial, and thus simplistic, ideologies of easy and miraculous development are being discarded. The quality of intellectual thought—at least in the social sciences—is improving, as the increasing contributions of Latin Americans to international academic conferences demonstrate in such easily available fashion.

These massive political, social, and economic changes lead to the antechamber of the truly modern state. It is probably a useful analytical device to see the asynchronous development of Latin America as so out of phase that there already are groups living in substantially modern styles alongside semi-nomadic villages, isolated settled villagers, serfs with their requisite masters, mercantilistic towns, and pseudo-modern falangist urbanites. If that construction is correct, then some of the change occurring must be reinforcing the modern sectors.

Conversely, of course, some of the change must also be ratifying the position of the urban traditionalist and his class colleagues in the countryside. I do not mean to be naively sanguine but to say that they are there at all seems to be something of a novelty among Latin American specialists who, depending on their ideological prejudices, see everybody on top as bad, everybody in the middle as good, everybody on the bottom as dough; or, everybody on the top as good, everybody in the middle as potentially good, and everybody on the bottom as a pest; or, everybody on the bottom as free of original bourgeois sin, and everybody else as black oppressors or guilt-ridden revolutionaries aching to wash their sins away in the blood of the landed.

Instead of seeing Latin America in such facile terms, the true complication of a transition covering almost the entire spectrum of types of human community must be appreciated. Long years of difficulty lie ahead, of course, as competing *kinds* of human beings wrapped into their overlapping class and kin and colleagueship identifications strive for a coherent world. If this kind of tension is extreme in the more developed countries of Latin America, it is also somewhat descriptive of the United States, the Soviet Union, or any other society.

Notes

1. This paragraph is a paraphrase of a section from the first chapter of a study of education and social development in Latin America which I am preparing with Frank Bonilla, associate professor of Political Science at the Massachusetts Institute of Technology.
2. *Mixed Essays* (1880), p. 74.
3. In K. H. Silvert, ed., *Discussion at Bellagio* (1964), p. 138.

4 / Political Change in Latin America: The Emergence of the Middle Sectors

John J. Johnson

The crucial role of the middle classes in the process of modernization is a theme that runs through much of the modernization literature. This is particularly evident in the selection from historian John J. Johnson's classic work on the emergence of the middle sectors in twentieth-century Latin American society. Johnson argues that between 1880 and 1920 Latin America entered a period of rapid, technologically induced economic growth that reflected its transition from "neo-feudal agriculture to semi-industrial capitalism." The most visible aspect of this transformation, in a sociopolitical sense, was the rapid expansion of what Johnson called the middle sectors.

Bearers of modern, particularly entrepreneurial values, the people of these middle sectors coalesced into new political parties that transformed the nature of Latin American politics. These people also shared, according to Johnson, a number of characteristics:

> They are overwhelmingly urban. They not only have well above average educations themselves but they also believe in universal public education. They are convinced that the future of their countries is inextricably tied to industrialization. They are nationalistic. They believe that the State should actively intrude in the social and economic areas while it carries on the normal functions of government. They recognize that the family has weakened as a political unit in the urban centers, and they have consequently lent their support to the development of organized political parties.

The implications of emergent middle sectors on Latin American development was, for Johnson as well as other modernizationists, salutary. On the one hand, as development-minded new political segments of society, the middle sectors would accelerate the process of modernization. On the other hand, solid, prosperous middle classes, inserted between the historical extremes of rich and poor, were the harbinger of a politically stable and democratic society.

In the late nineteenth century a number of the republics of Latin America began to undergo technological transformations. By 1920 the impact of those transformations was widely felt. One of the most profound developments to come from them was the emergence of the urban middle sectors of society as an aggressive political force. Today these groups hold a prominent position in the social-political amalgams that control Argentina, Brazil, Chile, Mexico, and Uruguay. These five countries contain two-thirds of the land area and two-thirds of the population, and produce more than two-thirds of the gross product, of the twenty Latin American republics.

The behavior of the urban middle sectors as political entities has been determined by the changes they have undergone as a result of the technological transformations and by their bid for popular support outside their own groups—a support that has ordinarily come from the industrial proletariat. The constant search for a balance between values they hold to be basic and those dictated by political expediency has been a primary characteristic of their political conduct in this century.

Before the five republics began the transition from neo-feudal agriculture to semi-industrial capitalism, the composition of the middle sectors was essentially static: they were members of the liberal professions, such as law and medicine; they were writers, publishers, and artists; they were professors in secondary schools and institutions of higher learning; they were bureaucrats; they were members of the secular clergy of the Catholic Church and of the lower and middle echelons of the officer corps. This composition began to change as soon as the technological transformations gained momentum, and it continues to change as the component groups remain fluid and as movement in and around them accelerates. Before 1900, representatives of commerce and industry were notably absent from the composition of these middle sectors; the same technological developments that gave the other components an opportunity to improve their political status also created the conditions

---

Reprinted with permission from *Political Change in Latin America: The Emergence of the Middle Sectors*, by John J. Johnson, pp. 1–14. Stanford University Press. © 1958 by the Board of Trustees of the Leland Stanford Junior University.

for the emergence of the commercial and industrial elements—owners as well as managers, applied scientists, and highly trained technicians.

Numerically, the middle sectors formed, until well into this century, a small minority. Until 1900 they might be described as a thin intermediate layer separating the elite from the inarticulate masses; their growth after 1900 was stimulated by the requirements of technology and by the expansion of education and of the functions of the State. Even so they remained, for the first two decades of this century, a small percentage of the total population in each of the five republics. The sharp upswing in their growth curve coincided with World War I. Since 1919 their numerical expansion has been large both in absolute figures and relative to the other elements of society, except the industrial proletariat. Today the middle sectors probably constitute at least 35 percent of the population in Argentina, 30 percent in Chile and Uruguay, and 15 percent in Brazil and Mexico.

In the course of the middle sectors' rapid expansion since World War I their ranks have been infiltrated by appreciable numbers from other levels of society. As long as the demand for their skills rose gradually, as was the case throughout the colonial period and the nineteenth century, the increments to middle sector positions came almost wholly from the middle elements themselves, although occasionally individuals from the elites would drift down and become permanent members, and isolated individuals belonging to the working groups could and did lift themselves up—usually via the Catholic Church or the military. Generally, though, the sons of middle sector families followed in the footsteps of their fathers or moved horizontally within the middle groups. There was nothing approaching the vertical social mobility, limited as it remains, found in the republics today.

When the members of the middle sectors could no longer satisfy the increased demands for skills associated with their status, individuals from other groups began to bid successfully for recognition. In Argentina, Brazil, Chile, and Uruguay many naturalized citizens or sons of immigrants entered the ranks of the middle sectors as the owners of commercial and industrial establishments. Others came from the old rural families who for various reasons—as, for example, scarcity of land in Chile—had invested in urban industry and commerce. The salaried elements—teachers, bureaucrats, technicians, managers—drew an important share of their accretions from the working groups.

Clearly, the middle sectors are anything but a compact social layer. They do not fulfill the central condition of a class: their members have no common background of experience. On the contrary, among them are representatives of nearly the entire cultural and economic range. Members of old Spanish and Portuguese families co-exist with mestizos, mulattoes, Negroes, and newcomers from Europe. Some are members of the middle sectors because of their intellectual attainments; some, because they have combined education and manual labor in proportions that meet the standards of those middle sector elements that still look askance at men who depend upon their hands for a livelihood; others, more because of their wealth than because of their learning. Property owners are associated with persons who have never possessed property and have little prospect of ever operating their own businesses. Some members are strongly committed to the defense of personal initiative and private property; others may be little concerned with property rights or infringements upon what are often considered the domains of private enterprise. Some take their status for granted: their lives are organized, they know where they are headed and what they want when they get there. Others are undergoing the frustrating and unsettling experiences and tensions inherent in passing from one socioeconomic group to another. Some have only a paternalistic interest in, and a theoretical understanding of, the working elements. Others know the lower levels of society because they have risen from them, and their feeling for those groups is likely to be highly personal.[1] They are all the more aware of the existing social and economic inequities because as new members of the middle sectors they are more often confronted by them than they were as members of the lower levels. Some have inherited an almost congenital abhorrence for the labor movement, while others come from families that have depended upon the labor leader as their sole representative before their employers and public officials.

The differentiations in their social backgrounds and economic interests have prevented the middle sectors from becoming politically monolithic. Individual members have reserved the right to act independently. At times large components find the prevailing middle sector attitudes unacceptable and either refuse to exercise the suffrage or make *ad hoc* arrangements with the elites or the workers, or both, in order to oppose the dominant elements. But the differences have not prevented large and ordinarily major segments of the middle sectors from finding common ground for joint political action.

To the extent that the middle sectors have had political cohesiveness and a continuity of common interests, this cohesiveness and continuity seem to have been due to six characteristics they hold in common. They are overwhelmingly urban. They not only have well above average educations themselves but they also believe in universal public education. They are convinced that the future of their countries is inextricably tied to industrialization. They are nationalistic. They believe that the State should actively intrude in the social and economic areas while it carries on the normal functions of government. They recognize that the family has weakened as a political unit in the urban centers, and they have consequently lent their support to the development of organized political parties.

1. *Urbanization.* Whether they are salaried persons, self-employed professionals, or property owners and *rentiers;* whether they belong to the middle sectors because of their learning or their wealth, the members of the intermediate groups are almost solidly urban. It has been thus historically. The great and rapidly expanding centers—Mexico City, Rio de Janeiro, Buenos Aires, Montevideo, Santiago—where the middle sectors are presently found in large numbers were, from their beginning, the centers of concentration for professionals, educators, bureaucrats, and other components of the early middle sectors. The metropolises were first of all administrative centers with revenues that provided the means for their becoming oases in what was otherwise largely a cultural and intellectual void. As industry developed it too has, in general, concentrated in cities, and thus the new components of the middle sectors have been added to the old. Since the middle sectors are predominantly urban, they favor, as they traditionally have, national policies that promote urban growth and economic development and assign a disproportionately large per capita share of public revenues to the urban centers.

2. *Public education.* Before 1900 all other determinants of middleness paled before the educational requirement. It was assumed that the student who entered school would eventually go on for a higher degree. Consequently primary and secondary schools were viewed not as ends in themselves but as stepping-stones on the way to a university. In the universities logic and dialectics were emphasized. Empiricism and pragmatics were slighted in favor of deductive reasoning. A humanistic education was the trade-mark of nearly every member of the middle sectors. The rigid quantitative and qualitative requirements of education gave ground to the conditions created by the economic transformation and the entrance into the middle sectors of the commercial and industrial elements. Members could no longer be expected to hold a degree from an institution of higher learning. The needs of industry and commerce provided the impetus that made scientific training an acceptable substitute for the traditional humanistic training. Trade schools and high schools began to turn out semiprofessionalized graduates able to use their limited educations along with their other qualifications to achieve middle sector status.

Although middle sector families have themselves shown a strong preference for private schools, their leaders have for a century used the political forum to champion mass public education. In the nineteenth century they associated education with representative government and national progress. As industrial and commercial proprietors began to wield their influence upon political thinking, they added a demand that public schools provide the trained personnel needed to operate their plants more efficiently. Political leaders of the middle sectors have continued their demands for public elementary and secondary schools to ensure a literate electorate and a supply of semiskilled and skilled industrial artisans.

3. *Industrialization.* Industrialization has become an obsession within the middle sectors. The urgent need to industrialize further is accepted as a self-evident truth by all components, although in periods of stress differences may arise as to the degree of urgency. The cries for industrialization have mounted to a crescendo since World War II. Today it would be political suicide for a member of the middle sectors publicly to recommend a national policy founded on the economic doctrine that holds that each geographic area should produce only what it can turn out most efficiently. In each of the republics such a position would be interpreted by the political opposition as advocating that the nation remain a producer of unfinished goods and hence an economic colony of the industrial powers.

The middle sectors reached their present views on industrialization in four stages. In the late nineteenth century those concerned with industrial development were by and large content to promote the extractive and processing industries and to support technological development as requisite to continued industrial expansion. Ordinarily, the major enterprises were foreign financed and managed. In the second stage came the clamor for more processing industries. The breakdown of normal trade channels during World War I showed the inconveniences that nonindustrial countries could expect in periods of international catastrophe. The politicians made capital of proposals to avert any recurrence of widespread shortages resulting from dependence upon outside sources of supply. Meanwhile the economics of industrialization remained largely unaltered, although the nature of the new enterprises, many of which required only limited amounts of capital, opened the way for considerably greater domestic financial and managerial participation.

Industrialization and politics became increasingly entwined in the third stage, which corresponded to the world depression of the 1930s. Domestic ownership of natural resources and industry was the cliché of politicians in Uruguay and Mexico and to a lesser extent in the other republics. Substantial expansion in the production of semidurables requiring raw materials as well as capital goods from abroad increasingly involved the politicians in the economic sphere, particularly when foreign-exchange shortages developed. But the important increment to the industrial environment in this phase was the politicians' discovery of the power and appeal of their solicitude for the protection and welfare of the industrial workers. The new concern for the workingman had many facets. He had won a new status throughout the Western World. An aggressive labor movement in Europe had spread to other nations and had helped to strengthen the bargaining power of working groups in Latin America. The laborer had become more politically articulate. His vote was in large part responsible for the success of the political amalgams that the middle sector leadership headed.

Since World War II, in the fourth stage, two aspects of the political-industrial scene have become particularly pronounced. The demands that industry be expanded to include heavy industry have become incessant. The iron and steel plant has become the symbol of progress. On the other hand, serious doubts have been raised whether the republics can achieve the industrial development they seek without a greater price to labor than it has been asked to pay since the 1930s. Differences of opinion on this question have provided the fuel for political fireworks, particularly in Argentina, Brazil, and Chile.

4. *Nationalism.* Nationalism of an assertive xenophobic nature is for all intents and purposes a twentieth-century phenomenon in Latin America. In the course of their drives to power, the middle groups in the five republics have raised nationalism to the level of a major political ideology. Its effectiveness in arousing the emotions of a broad segment of the electorate gives every indication that it will remain a weapon or a potential weapon in the arsenal of the middle sector politician.

During the relatively brief period that it has enjoyed currency, the concept of nationalism has had several dimensions as it has responded to stimuli originating at home and abroad. It was initially nourished by individuals acting in a private capacity. In that stage its juridic and cultural features were presented in abstract terms by intellectuals. The two aspects were often viewed as independent.[2] Not unusually, the advocates of cultural and juridic nationalism condoned the alienation of natural resources and the granting of long-term concessions of a monopolistic nature to foreigners as the price of technological development. As long as private individuals supplied the driving force and the concept remained abstract, nationalism was largely devoid of political appeal because of the narrow audience reached.

In Uruguay and Mexico between 1910 and 1920 and in Argentina, Brazil, and Chile in the 1930s the State replaced the intellectual as the chief propagandist for nationalism. Under the sponsorship of the State two outstanding current characteristics of nationalism soon manifested themselves. Its economic aspect was given greater stress than its cultural and juridic aspects. No longer confined to the abstractions of a few intellectuals it was brought down to the masses in its dynamic and politically charged form.

5. *State intervention.* Statism and middle sector political leadership have become closely linked. The middle sectors early in their bid for political recognition rejected the laissez-faire doctrines of the nineteenth century. As a substitute they offered planned societies. When their recommendations were popularized, the middle sectors rode to new political heights.

Social welfare and industrialization have been the first concerns of the state interventionists. Under the sponsorship of the middle groups the states by 1940 had taken over many of the responsibilities for the welfare of the distressed elements formerly delegated to private and semipublic institutions. The duties of the State in providing educational facilities, medical care, food, and housing for the working groups were written in minute detail into the laws of several of the republics. Also, "in fulfillment of the State's social functions" the governments of Argentina, Brazil, and Mexico took over the direction of the labor movement. As a result the laborer was encouraged to view any benefits he received as coming from the State and to conclude that his well-being and that of his fellow workers lay in political action rather than in direct negotiations with management. With their welfare written into law, laborers ordinarily have preferred to ally themselves with the groups in power, reasoning that only through support of those who administer the laws could they hope to attain what by law is theirs.

State intervention in the economic sphere has been justified on the basis of three socioeconomic tenets upheld by the middle sectors: (1) Industry cannot survive without protection from outside competition, and only the State can provide this protection. (2) Since the accrual of domestic private capital is slow, the State, with its ability to accumulate capital relatively rapidly through taxation and foreign loans, must intercede in the industrial sphere in order to maintain the highest possible rate of development at the same time that it reduces the share of private foreign capital in the economy. (3) Solicitude for the working groups requires that the State exercise some control over prices of necessaries.

6. *Political parties.* After World War I, important elements within the urban middle sectors began to substitute the organized political party for the family as the focus of political thinking. When this transformation is completed, a whole era—politic, social, and economic— will have passed.

For over three centuries after the initial phase of the conquest ended and the stabilization of the social order began (about 1580), the family— or, more properly speaking, the extended family, kin group, or clan—

was traditionally a social, economic, and political institution. The status of each member within the family and his relationship to every other member were rigidly defined. After winning independence (1810–1825), the patriarchal heads of families often became political bosses wielding control over sprawling domains. Political leadership ordinarily passed from father to eldest son.

But the family as a political entity probably never operated as effectively in the cities as it did in the country. In this century it has been progressively less successful as new social and economic forces have undermined the interdependence of the members. The mobility offered by modern means of transportation has encouraged the younger generation to make associations outside the family. Cinemas, clubs, public parks and beaches, and social activities sponsored by the schools increasingly compete with the family for the leisure time of its members. Women have won new freedoms and have taken on new obligations. In ever growing numbers they leave the home to engage in education, business, and the professions, and return with the information that permits them to reach political decisions independently of the male members of the household.

The appearance of large and impersonal businesses has tended to reduce the role of the head of the family in finding employment for the various members of his immediate and extended family. The large corporate enterprises, which are becoming ever more common and which often offer the greatest opportunities for advancement, are inclined to consider individual qualifications more than family credentials. A similar condition is developing in government, which also has become more impersonal as it has become more complex. In the process, nepotism has gradually given ground to civil service systems and professional bureaucracies. The independence which has come with obtaining and holding positions on the basis of merit has helped to sunder allegiances to the family as a political unit. There has been a strong tendency to transfer allegiances to political parties, which provide a common ground for those who have similar objectives based on educational and occupational interests and on social relationships outside the home.

During the decades that the middle sectors have shared power or controlled political decisions in the five republics, the influence of their several components has fluctuated significantly. The pattern of these shifts of relative influence emerges most clearly when the political trends of the five republics are viewed in the long range. Viewed episodically, the trends dissolve into mere political maneuverings in search of short-range solutions, and the main currents of middle sector thinking lose their distinct outlines.

Until World War I, the members of the liberal professions constituted a numerically large segment of the middle sectors in each of the republics. As a group they were learned, and learning conferred considerable prestige. They held a near-monopoly on the formulation of political theory, and, to the extent that the middle sectors participated in practical politics, they were the most active component as well. In recent decades, the influence of the professions on middle sector thought has declined, partly as a result of their loss of relative numerical importance, partly because of their very success; indeed, as the middle sectors as a whole gained in political stature, the rewards of practical politics increased and groups other than the liberal professions began to compete for them.

The role of the Catholic clergy in politics has also been in a general decline in recent decades. This would seem to be true despite the evident part that the Catholic Church played in the overthrow of Juan Domingo Perón in Argentina in 1955, of Gustavo Rojas Pinilla in Colombia in 1957, and of Marcos Pérez Jiménez in Venezuela in 1958. The decline has been more the result of the changing functions of the clergy than of its composition.

The middle sectors continue as always to provide an important part of the Catholic clergy. But the place of the Church in society has been modified and in the process its activities have been circumscribed. This development has been particularly apparent in the urban centers. The urban elements are less inclined than formerly to look to the Church for leadership in those "extra-spiritual" areas on which it traditionally depended for much of its prestige and influence. The State has taken over many of the welfare functions previously performed by the Church. Public elementary, secondary schools, and institutions of higher learning have reduced its share in the field of education. It has lost its semi-monopoly on learning in the smaller cities and towns as persons educated and professionally trained at secular institutions have filtered outside the centers of heaviest population. Mass communications have also lessened the dependence upon the clergy outside the large cities. To a considerable degree the popular groups have substituted the motion picture, radio and television, public recreation, and the diversions offered by the labor unions for the holy days and feast days that for four centuries were the accepted source of release from the humdrum activities of everyday life.

As the Church's temporal responsibilities have been circumscribed, the ministering to the spiritual needs of the people has taken up a larger share of its activity, and the opportunities have been reduced for the clergyman to be an individual personality dispensing personal ideas and expressing personal convictions on nonspiritual issues. Consequently clergymen normally are not today politically influential in any of the five republics except inasmuch as they reflect the thoughts of the Church hierarchy, whose thinking may or may not conform to that of the politically dominant segments within the middle sectors. When the political policies of the hierarchy are acceptable to the middle sectors, as they appear to be more and more often, they are disseminated more by Catholic lay organizations than by the clergy.

While the influence of the professional groups and the clergy declined, teachers acquired added political prestige with the public recognition of the importance of universal education. Where schools have been used for the propagation of political ideologies among the masses, the teachers have become essential parts of the political machinery. In recent years, as elementary school teachers have become better trained, they have been accorded middle sector standing in growing numbers. Teaching staffs in high schools and institutions of higher learning—groups traditionally included in the middle sectors—have expanded.

The bureaucrats too have proliferated and their influence has grown accordingly. As the responsibilities of government expanded, the bureaucrats carried out new functions and assumed many of those previously performed by private citizens.

Given the great number of imponderables involved, it would perhaps be impossible to establish whether the political influence of the officer corps has increased or decreased since World War I. There is some indication that the proportion of officers engaging in politics has declined in recent decades. In the author's opinion, however, there is no doubt that at least since 1930 the social and economic orientation of the politically active officers has been away from that of the old ruling groups and toward that of the civilian middle sectors. The new position of the officers stems primarily from three circumstances: (1) The various branches of the military have become more professionalized and, consequently, less attractive to the old elite groups. But since they continue to offer security at reasonably high salaries, they open up opportunities to men from the middle sectors. (2) As the civilian middle sectors have improved their political status vis-à-vis the elites, military officers have inclined to retain their social contacts with the middle sectors rather than to associate with the elites, as they did in the past. (3) The economic policies of the middle sectors, emphasizing industrialization, conform to those held by the armed forces. Under the widening impact of nationalism, both the civilian and the military elements have tended increasingly to equate industrial growth with national progress. Officers, thanks to their training in organization, have found employment as directors of State-controlled economic enterprises, and the armed forces look forward to domestic production of war matériel. Thus, despite differences in their approach to politics, the military and the civilian components of the middle sectors tend to agree on their broad social and economic objectives.

The swift rise of the commercial and industrial segments has profoundly affected the composition of the middle groups since the end of World War I. The acceptance of industrialization as national policy in each of the republics made the owners of industrial and commercial enterprises a highly effective force both as a constructive and as a veto group. Commercial and industrial leaders today exercise the most powerful influence on middle sector politics. The scientists, technicians, and managers, benefiting as they do from industrial development, have in general identified themselves politically with their employers. . . .

Notes

1. In Latin America the privileged groups are strongly inclined to look for cultural symbols rather than biologically inherited characteristics. Race, consequently, tends to be subordinated to human and social values. For this reason racial differentiations are dealt with only obliquely in this study. In any event, only in Brazil was the racial composition of the middle sectors notably changed when workers began to find their way into them. There, although most of those entering the middle sectors from the working elements have been European in racial origin, for the first time the mestizos, mulattoes, and Negroes in substantial numbers have been provided opportunities to improve their social status. In Argentina, Uruguay, and Chile the new members of the middle sectors have been almost wholly European or mestizos with a decided preponderance of European blood. In Mexico, the new elements entering the middle sectors from the laboring groups have been basically mestizo, but the mestizo has been entrenched in the middle sectors there at least since the mid-nineteenth century. (The term "mestizo" in Spanish America is used to refer to persons of mixed European-Indian blood. In Brazil those of mixed European-Indian descent are normally referred to as *caboclos*.)

2. Economic nationalism commanded only sporadic attention at that stage.

5 / Responsibility of the Latifundios for Lags in Social Development

Jacques Lambert

Although some modernizationists touted the development potential of the new middle classes, others, such as French social scientist Jacques Lambert, were more structurally oriented in their analysis. In our final selection on modernization, Lambert pins responsibility for lags in Latin American social development squarely on the latifundia (great landed estates) that dominated the rural hinterland. On the one hand, the latifundia monopolized the land tenure system in such a way as to relegate the rural population, both on and off the great estates, to small, inadequate parcels (*minifundios*) that produced only a bare, subsistence standard of living. On the other hand, the isolation of the latifundia as well as the system of paternalistic social relations sapped the peasantry's incentive for self-improvement because it guaranteed, in all but the most abusive cases, a minimal, however substandard, level of welfare.

Furthermore, the pervasive and insidious economic and social influence of the latifundia contributed to the formation of what Lambert and others perceived as a dual society, polarized between an unproductive, feudalized backland and a modernizing, urban sector. The solution was to promote agrarian reform and the "defeudalization" of the countryside through the encouragement of modern, capitalist techniques. Other adherents to the modernizationists' diffusion thesis argued that encouraging foreign investment from the West would also serve to promote the process of development.

In most of Latin America the rural societies are much too far behind the urban societies. Many factors account for this lag, which almost everywhere accompanies rapid change—isolation, transportation difficulties, lack of capital, and especially the resistance of the existing social structure and rural society to any drastic change. In Latin America, however, the action of these factors is intensified and perpetuated by the existence of the latifundios.

Hoarding of Land and Agricultural Underemployment

The Latin American countries, like so many other underdeveloped countries, suffer from agricultural underemployment except in the southernmost developed regions of South America, around the cities, and in a few areas where new lands are being developed. It is typical that the masked underemployment prevailing in two-thirds of Latin America's territory stems not from the shortage of arable land but from its overabundance. Underemployment did not spread as a result of rural overpopulation and an attendant surplus of agricultural manpower. In many cases it is due to the fact that excessively large estates monopolize lands of which they can farm only a small portion, using methods that do not allow for full use of the available manpower.

It is true, if paradoxical, that wherever the latifundios predominate— in Brazil, Venezuela, Colombia, Peru, Chile—it has been established that insufficient agricultural production causes part of the population to suffer from undernourishment or malnutrition; the shortage of agricultural manpower prevents the use of perfectly good farmlands, or badly run estates have a surplus of agricultural manpower but cannot use it for more than a few days a year.

Even when the latifundio owners do not use all the manpower available, they seldom complain of an excess of laborers, since they do not have to pay them. The extra land enables the owner whose capital is short to maintain a cost-free reserve of manpower on subsistence farms on his idle land. Thus, in case of emergency, he is conveniently assured of a massive labor force. One owner who had let about a hundred families settle on his estate without working for him explained they would be very handy to have around in case of a fire on the land during a drought. He added that these families had been there so long

Reprinted with permission from *Latin America,* by Jacques Lambert, pp. 75–88. Berkeley: University of California Press, 1967.

he did not have the heart to evict them. (The case is exceptional, to be sure, but significant nonetheless.)

True, some latifundio masters were tyrants who oppressed their subjects, but an institution should not be judged solely by its shortcomings. Considering the archaic social relationships within the rural Latin American world, the authority of the big landlord has generally been paternalistic rather than tyrannical. Otherwise, the latifundio could not have survived through all of Latin America's revolutions. Land reforms are necessary mainly because the latifundio keeps its subjects outside the mainstream of political and economic life and gives them no incentive to improve their condition, rather than because it is cruel, oppressive, or hated. The antiquated large estate demands personal loyalty rather than work and productivity. It accommodates itself very comfortably to its subjects' semi-idleness. It provides a shelter for those who have neither the desire nor the initiative to seek anything else. Provided the patrón is not a tyrant, his traditional mission toward his perennial dependents includes many social obligations but too few economic demands. If he is conscientious about the functions assigned to him by a paternalistic society, he must protect and help those who depend upon him and must always take their side even against the law and the state. In exchange for blind loyalty he owes them relative security at the poverty level.

Contrary to frequent allegations, the social problem caused by the concentration of land in the latifundios is not that the peasants are landless but rather that by accepting less than full freedom they are granted the use of patches too small to deliver them from squalor but which they are understandably reluctant to give up, since they are their family farms. It is also typical that, if certain reports are to be believed, even the Latin American agricultural laborers who are closest to serfdom, the *huasipungeros* in Ecuador, are not wholeheartedly in favor of agrarian reforms that would free them, for fear their freedom would mean the loss of the small plot the master lets them have. It is also typical that in Brazil many of the poor colonos on the decadent fazendas of Rio de Janeiro or Minas Gerais hesitate to give up the relative security of the latifundio in order to take up work in northern Paraná for wages two or three times higher. Modern coffee plantations, after hiring all available Italian immigrants, had to seek out laborers fleeing from the drought in the remote states of the Northeast. The latifundio is at the root of the social problem in Latin American agriculture, while the minifundio is responsible for its economic problem. The reason is that, in addition to the minifundios recorded in censuses as belonging to peasants, many more minifundios situated on only partly developed large estates are farmed by peasants under precarious tenure.

At the cost of personal subjection, the latifundio gives its subjects relative security as well as the satisfaction of enjoying some freedom in the work itself. It gives freedom not to work beyond what is needed to avoid starvation. Above all, it leaves the peasants free to refuse change and to remain outside a society that is changing too fast. The latifundios are always economically inefficient, but they are cruel only when the masters are bad. This happens all too often today. Some landowners refuse to behave like feudal lords and have given up their social role, leaving their estate in the hands of a manager. Other landowners want money more than power and seek profit from the estates. Their farming methods make this possible only if they oppress the workers. Whether the latifundio owner wishes to be a good master or not, in the second half of the twentieth century his paternalistic role, which tends to perpetuate an irrevocably doomed archaic society, is antisocial. . . .

Rigidity of Social Structure

It is widely recognized that in complete contrast to the developed countries of Europe or North America, whose social structure is complex and flexible, Latin America—like all underdeveloped areas—seems to be dominated by a very rigid, simple form of hierarchical society. Because of the lack of large diversified middle classes, social mobility is almost impossible. It is thought by certain analysts that this situation prevails in Latin America even at levels that are no longer truly underdeveloped. The Latin American aristocratic tradition and lack of social spirit are held responsible.

As an acknowledged generalization, this is not wholly untrue. But as far as Latin American urban societies are concerned, a number of reservations are called for. As a matter of fact, large middle classes have existed in the cities for a long time. Even during the colonial era not all Spaniards and Portuguese were big landowners. Very few of the poor immigrants settled on the land, and Spain and Portugal tried to attract artisans to the cities. Together with the small businessman and the lower civil servants, they formed a large segment of the urban populations and were joined by many mestizos. These middle classes were sufficiently large by the end of the eighteenth century to play a crucial role in the independence movement. . . .

Deepening Rural Isolation

In Latin America the danger of a break between the rural and the urban society is far greater now than in Europe in the nineteenth century because change is more rapid and urbanization is concentrated in the very large cities. In seven countries—Brazil, Mexico, Bolivia, Peru, El Salvador, Panama, and the Dominican Republic—the urban population increased by 53.4 percent in the ten years from 1945 to 1955. In Cuba, Chile, Venezuela, and Uruguay, the average increase was 44.4 percent, and in all of them it was felt mainly in the national capitals and the largest cities. Since 1955, the rate of concentration of population in cities has accelerated. Thus between the censuses of 1950 and 1960, the Latin American urban population increased at an annual rate of 4.5 percent (it might double in 16 years) while the population in cities of over one million inhabitants increased at the rate of 6 percent (it might double in 12 years). Despite a fairly low level of industrialization, by 1970 over half of Latin America's population will be living in the cities.

The possibility of employment in industry has been a negligible factor in this urban population growth in Latin America. In the most industrialized countries, the proportion of the urban population employed in industry did not exceed 8 percent in 1950, and in the least industrialized it was only 3 percent. Between 1950 and 1960 these percentages decreased even further. The country dwellers in flight from the large estates only increase underemployment in the cities.[1]

In all countries except Brazil and Colombia, the population of the capital city is larger than the combined population of all cities of over 100,000 inhabitants. In 1960, half of Uruguay's population lived in Montevideo, one-third of Argentina's in Buenos Aires; in Chile, Cuba, [and] Panama, one-fourth of the inhabitants lived in the capital; and in Peru, Venezuela, Paraguay, and Costa Rica, one-fifth. In extreme cases like Peru there is no real urban society outside the capital. Under such conditions, although Latin America is highly urbanized—excessively so, considering her level of development—urbanization is narrowly circumscribed. The concentration in large cities magnifies the characteristics of urban societies and their adaptability to change, while in the countryside isolation perpetuates the complete alienation of the rural way of life. The large estate has its share of direct responsibility for this, along with the facts that the rural population is too small and scattered and transportation is lacking. Actually it is responsible even for the scattering of the population and the shortage of roads because by wasting land it has vastly increased the distances to be covered.

Nothing has fostered isolation and an archaic way of life more than the manorial aspect of the latifundios. They tend to imprison their subjects within a rigid social structure that fills all needs provided they are the needs of a past age and remain on a primitive level. At the estate center, around the master's large house, stand the heavy agricultural equipment (if there is any), the draft and pack animals, a sugarcane mill, a still, and the truck (if there is a road). Sometimes there is an electric generator, and all those who live nearby have electricity. The artisans receive wages from the landowner; the storekeeper (if there is one) is his dependent. Some owners have built a school on the estate center and have provided living quarters for a teacher, either because it is required by law or because they feel it to be their moral duty. Schooling is of little use because in this society lessons have no practical application and hence are soon forgotten. The lord or his overseer are equipped to give first aid and legal advice. There is a small supply of drugs on the estate, and sometimes the big house takes in a passing priest.

As long as the latifundio discharges its social function and its subjects ask for nothing more, it fulfills so many needs—and these are so primitive—that the village and the small town have never had much opportunity to develop. The large estate usurps their function. At the same time its limits are too narrow, and its activities not diversified enough, to truly replace the village and town. Thus, by assuming a role it cannot effectively fulfill, the estate completely isolates its peasants from urban society instead of being an intermediary between the country and the city.

Social and Political Need for Agrarian Reforms

The form of feudalism that the latifundios established in Latin America was an inferior one since it lacked the hierarchies of true feudal societies; the big landowners were lords, but they had no overlord. It was difficult for national governments later to reunite authority that had been so dispersed. The task has not yet been completed, and it will be a difficult one if thorough agrarian reforms do not take place.

This is why the need for land reforms in Latin America is so urgent, for political and social reasons even more than for economic ones. It is doubtful that distribution of land to peons or colonos used to a subsistence life—without capital, uneducated and ill-prepared to assume any responsibilities after having lived always under a paternalistic system—can in itself improve the economic condition of rural populations and increase the production of foodstuffs, which are in such short supply that a large part of Latin America has become a land of malnutrition.

The risks that must inevitably attend agrarian reforms, no matter how inadequate they may be, are minimal, however, since by definition the latifundios are estates farmed through antiquated methods, and their yield is so low that splitting them up among poor, ignorant peasants cannot substantially decrease their productivity. Besides, the latifundios are operated in such a way that a very large portion of the lands is already in the hands of these poor, ignorant peasants. It is only the ownership of the land that is concentrated, not the farms themselves. Appearances notwithstanding, the fact that half of Latin America is occupied by estates over 2,500 acres does not make it a land of large farms; neither is it a single-crop land. Most of the peasants grow food crops—corn, cassava, sweet potatoes, beans, and sugarcane—on very small patches of land using hand methods almost exclusively. Between the hoe of the latifundio and the tractor of the modern plantation, the plow has seldom found a place.

The latifundio combines the shortcomings of the too large holding with too little exploitation: the farms are too small and the people too backward to make them produce; land tenure is too precarious for full use of its potential.

But inadequate reforms, limited to the splitting up of large estates, could merely deprive the peasant of services maintained by the master's paternalism. These services are social rather than economic. They lost much of their effectiveness long ago, and are further deteriorating as the feudal organization disintegrates. Too often, though, no other services have taken their place. The most elementary community services accompanying a land reform would be better than the present ones. After distribution of land to those who wish to farm it, the peasants should be helped to give up their pre-Columbian or African farming methods, which were satisfactory on the latifundio, for newer ones. They also should be helped to break the isolation brought about by the latifundio.

Notes

1. United Nations, *The Economic Development of Latin America in the Post-war Period* (1964), p. 77.

Selected Bibliography

Almond, Gabriel A., and James S. Coleman (eds.). *The Politics of the Developing Areas.* Princeton, N.J.: Princeton University Press, 1960.

Almond, Gabriel A., and G. B. Powell, Jr. *Comparative Politics: A Developmental Approach.* Boston: Little, Brown, 1965.

Apter, David. *The Politics of Modernization.* Chicago: University of Chicago Press, 1965.

Black, Cyril E. *The Dynamics of Modernization.* New York: Harper & Row, 1966.

Coleman, James S. (ed.). *Education and Political Development.* Princeton, N.J.: Princeton University Press, 1965.

Germani, Gino. *Authoritarianism, National Populism, and Fascism.* New Brunswick, N.J.: Transaction Books, 1977.

Giddens, Anthony (ed.). *Emile Durkheim: Selected Writings.* New York: Cambridge University Press, 1972.

Hagen, Everett. *On the Theory of Social Change.* Homewood, Ill.: Dorsey Press, 1962.

Hirschman, Albert O. *The Strategy of Economic Development.* New Haven, Conn.: Yale University Press, 1958.

Huntington, Samuel P. *Political Order in Changing Societies.* New Haven, Conn.: Yale University Press, 1968.

Johnson, John J. *Political Change in Latin America.* Stanford, Calif.: Stanford University Press, 1958.

Lenzer, Gertrud (ed.). *Auguste Comte and Positivism: The Essential Writings.* New York: Harper & Row, 1975.

Lerner, Daniel. *The Passing of the Traditional Society.* Glencoe, Ill.: The Free Press, 1958.

Lewis, W. A. *The Theory of Economic Growth.* London: Allen & Unwin, 1955.

Lipset, Seymour Martin, and Aldo Solari (eds.). *Elites in Latin America.* New York: Oxford University Press, 1967.

McClelland, David. *The Achieving Society.* Princeton, N.J.: Von Nostrand, 1962.

Parsons, Talcott. *The Social System.* London: Routledge & Kegan Paul, 1971.

Redfield, Robert. *Tepoztlan, a Mexican Village: A Study of Folk Life.* Chicago: University of Chicago Press, 1930.

Rostow, Walt W. *The Stages of Economic Growth.* New York: Cambridge University Press, 1960.

Rustow, Dankwart A. *World of Nations: Problems of Political Modernization.* Washington, D.C.: Brookings Institution, 1967.

Stavenhagen, Rodolfo. "Seven Fallacies About Latin America," in *Latin America: Reform or Revolution?* edited by James Petras and Maurice Zeitlin. Greenwich, Conn.: Fawcett Publications, 1968, pp. 13–31.

Weber, Max. *The Theory of Social and Economic Organization,* edited by Talcott Parsons. New York: Oxford University Press, 1947.

PART 2
DEPENDENCY AND MARXISM

Dependency analysis emerged in the 1960s as a direct challenge to the theories of the modernizationists. Although it was a complex and varied school of thought, it tended to draw on two traditions: (1) the economic analyses of the United Nations Commission on Latin America (ECLA), which found severe weakness in the processes of growth that depended on the export of primary products, and (2) the Marxist concerns with the role of imperialism, economic transformations from feudalism to capitalism, and the opportunities for revolution. In general, dependency analysts found that the modernizationists had missed, or severely underestimated, the determining role of Latin America's links to the economies of Western Europe and the United States, the countries at the "center" of the world economy. These links, rather than assisting in the development of Latin America, actually inhibited growth and reinforced the control of the traditional landed oligarchy. It was not the values of tradition that held Latin America back; ironically, it was the diffusion of modern capitalism that helped to maintain a backward economy and to reinforce the political power of an elite that was not particularly entrepreneurial.

Some dependency analysts, like Andre Gunder Frank, argued that these links to countries at the world's economic center prevented the development of Latin America by draining resources and capital that were used to build the economies of the "center" rather than the "periphery." Other dependency analysts saw the development process as being more complex and less determined. Celso Furtado and Fernando Henrique Cardoso (along with his colleague Enzo Faletto) represented a school within dependency that defined a historical-structural approach through which different nations followed slightly different paths. First dependent on the export of primary products, most Latin American nations began a process of industrialization during the depression. This development meant that newly emerging classes—the bourgeoisie and the increasingly proletarianized lower classes—formed an alliance called populism that wrested political power from the traditional oligarchy.

Like the modernizationists, the dependency analysts saw the importance of the middle sectors, but they were most concerned with the role of the national bourgeoisie. While Frank found this class already too linked to the international economy to be able to promote real development, Cardoso and Faletto saw the possibilities of "associated-dependent" development of capitalism under the tutelage of the bourgeoisie. Nevertheless, the process of growth required changing linkages with international capitalists, and as the 1960s began new alliances were formed in which the bourgeoisie became closely tied to multinational corporations. Thus, the bourgeoisie began a process of integrating their economies into a new international division of labor. This transition often necessitated severe repression of the lower classes.

Despite having origins in Marxist conceptualization, dependency analysis was criticized by some Marxists for its overemphasis on external economic factors and its insufficient attention to the domestic organization of production. These Marxists saw greater importance in the complex and varied modes of production in each nation. They also took issue with the dependency analysts' tendency to focus on the bourgeoisie while regarding the lower classes as an undifferentiated mass. For these Marxists, the specific and crucial role of the proletariat was central to understanding the processes of change.

6 / The Development of Underdevelopment

Andre Gunder Frank

Andre Gunder Frank is the author of the controversial and widely read *Capitalism and Underdevelopment in Latin America*, which introduced dependency theory to North Americans. Frank begins his contribution by refuting the main precepts of the modernizationists: their emphasis on endogenous factors as the main cause for the region's underdevelopment, the "stages of growth" theory, and the dualism thesis. According to Frank, capitalism, by its penetration of Latin America, was the main cause of the region's underdevelopment. Through capitalism, Latin America was incorporated into the world economic system, but also through capitalism a series of asymmetrical, metropolitan-satellite relationships, which exploited the region by draining resources and surplus capital from the periphery and moving it toward the center, were established.

In a controversial assertion, Frank maintains that Latin America had never been feudal but rather had been capitalist since its colonization in the sixteenth century. Rejecting the dualist structure—traditional society, modern society—Frank envisioned a linkage between the two systems, in which capitalism worked from the latter to exploit and expropriate surplus from the former. Since underdevelopment resulted from close ties with the metropolitan West, Frank reasoned that in order for development to occur those ties should logically be severed. As Frank acknowledged, this idea owed much to the work of Paul Baran, a Marxist theoretician whose classic work *The Political Economy of Growth* contained many of the ideas later elaborated by Frank.

We cannot hope to formulate adequate development theory and policy for the majority of the world's population who suffer from underdevelopment without first learning how their past economic and social history gave rise to their present underdevelopment. Yet most historians study only the developed metropolitan countries and pay scant attention to the colonial and underdeveloped lands. For this reason most of our theoretical categories and guides to development policy have been distilled exclusively from the historical experience of the European and North American advanced capitalist nations.

Since the historical experience of the colonial and underdeveloped countries has demonstrably been quite different, available theory therefore fails to reflect the past of the underdeveloped part of the world entirely, and reflects the past of the world as a whole only in part. More important, our ignorance of the underdeveloped countries' history leads us to assume that their past and indeed their present resembles earlier stages of the history of the now developed countries. This ignorance and this assumption lead us into serious misconceptions about contemporary underdevelopment and development. Further, most studies of development and underdevelopment fail to take account of the economic and other relations between the metropolis and its economic colonies throughout the history of the worldwide expansion and development of the mercantilist and capitalist system. Consequently, most of our theory fails to explain the structure and development of the capitalist system as a whole and to account for its simultaneous generation of underdevelopment in some of its parts and of economic development in others.

It is generally held that economic development occurs in a succession of capitalist stages and that today's underdeveloped countries are still in a stage, sometimes depicted as an original stage, of history through which the now developed countries passed long ago. Yet even a modest acquaintance with history shows that underdevelopment is not original or traditional and that neither the past nor the present of the underdeveloped countries resembles in any important respect the past of the now developed countries. The now developed countries were never *under*developed, though they may have been *un*developed. It is also widely believed that the contemporary underdevelopment of a country can be understood as the product or reflection solely of its own economic,

Reprinted by permission of Monthly Review Foundation from *Latin America: Underdevelopment or Revolution: Essays on the Development of Underdevelopment and the Immediate Enemy,* by Andre Gunder Frank, pp. 3–17. New York: Monthly Review Press, 1969. © 1969 by Andre Gunder Frank.

political, social, and cultural characteristics or structure. Yet historical research demonstrates that contemporary underdevelopment is in large part the historical product of past and continuing economic and other relations between the satellite underdeveloped and the now developed metropolitan countries. Furthermore, these relations are an essential part of the structure and development of the capitalist system on a world scale as a whole. A related and also largely erroneous view is that the development of these underdeveloped countries, and within them of their most underdeveloped domestic areas, must and will be generated or stimulated by diffusing capital, institutions, values, etc., to them from the international and national capitalist metropoles. Historical perspective based on the underdeveloped countries' past experience suggests that on the contrary, economic development in the underdeveloped countries can now occur only independently of most of these relations of diffusion.

Evident inequalities of income and differences in culture have led many observers to see "dual" societies and economies in the underdeveloped countries. Each of the two parts is supposed to have a history of its own, a structure, and a contemporary dynamic largely independent of the other. Supposedly only one part of the economy and society has been importantly affected by intimate economic relations with the "outside" capitalist world; and that part, it is held, became modern, capitalist, and relatively developed precisely because of this contact. The other part is widely regarded as variously isolated, subsistence-based, feudal, or pre-capitalist, and therefore more underdeveloped.

I believe on the contrary that the entire "dual" society thesis is false and that the policy recommendations to which it leads will, if acted upon, serve only to intensify and perpetuate the very conditions of underdevelopment they are supposedly designed to remedy.

A mounting body of evidence suggests, and I am confident that future historical research will confirm, that the expansion of the capitalist system over the past centuries effectively and entirely penetrated even the apparently most isolated sectors of the underdeveloped world. Therefore the economic, political, social, and cultural institutions and relations we now observe there are the products of the historical development of the capitalist system no less than are the seemingly more modern or capitalist features of the national metropoles of these underdeveloped countries. Analogous to the relations between development and underdevelopment on the international level, the contemporary and underdeveloped institutions of the so-called backward or feudal domestic areas of an underdeveloped country are no less the product of the single historical process of capitalist development than are the so-called capitalist institutions of the supposedly more progressive areas. I should like to sketch the kinds of evidence which support this thesis and at the same time indicate lines along which further study and research could fruitfully proceed.

The Secretary General of the Latin American Center for Research in the Social Sciences writes in that Center's journal: "The privileged position of the city has its origin in the colonial period. It was founded by the Conqueror to serve the same ends that it still serves today; to incorporate the indigenous population into the economy brought and developed by that Conqueror and his descendants. The regional city was an instrument of conquest and is still today an instrument of domination."[1] The Instituto Nacional Indigenista (National Indian Institute) of Mexico confirms this observation when it notes that "the mestizo population, in fact, always lives in a city, a center of an intercultural region, which acts as the metropolis of a zone of indigenous population and which maintains with the underdeveloped communities an intimate relation which links the center with the satellite communities."[2] The Institute goes on to point out that "between the mestizos who live in the nuclear city of the region and the Indians who live in the peasant hinterland there is in reality a closer economic and social interdependence than might at first glance appear" and that the provincial metropoles "by being centers of intercourse are also centers of exploitation."[3]

Thus these metropolis-satellite relations are not limited to the imperial or international level but penetrate and structure the very economic, political, and social life of the Latin American colonies and countries. Just as the colonial and national capital and its export sector become the satellite of the Iberian (and later of other) metropoles of the world economic system, this satellite immediately becomes a colonial and then a national metropolis with respect to the productive sectors and population of the interior. Furthermore, the provincial capitals, which thus are themselves satellites of the national metropolis—and through the latter of the world metropolis—are in turn provincial centers around which their own local satellites orbit. Thus, a whole chain of constellations of metropoles and satellites relates all parts of the whole system from its metropolitan center in Europe or the United States to the farthest outpost in the Latin American countryside.

When we examine this metropolis-satellite structure, we find that each of the satellites, including now underdeveloped Spain and Portugal, serves as an instrument to suck capital or economic surplus out of its own satellites and to channel part of this surplus to the world metropolis of which all are satellites. Moreover, each national and local metropolis serves to impose and maintain the monopolistic structure and exploitative relationship of this system (as the Instituto Nacional Indigenista of Mexico calls it) as long as it serves the interests of the metropoles which take advantage of this global, national, and local structure to promote their own development and the enrichment of their ruling classes.

These are the principal and still surviving structural characteristics which were implanted in Latin America by the Conquest. Beyond examining the establishment of this colonial structure in its historical context, the proposed approach calls for study of the development—and underdevelopment—of these metropoles and satellites of Latin America throughout the following and still continuing historical process. In this way we can understand why there were and still are tendencies in the Latin American and world capitalist structure which seem to lead to the development of the metropolis and the underdevelopment of the satellite and why, particularly, the satellized national, regional, and local metropoles in Latin America find that their economic development is at best a limited or underdeveloped development.

That present underdevelopment of Latin America is the result of its centuries-long participation in the process of world capitalist development, I believe I have shown in my case studies of the economic and social histories of Chile and Brazil.[4] My study of Chilean history suggests that the Conquest not only incorporated this country fully into the expansion and development of the world mercantile and later industrial capitalist system but that it also introduced the monopolistic metropolis-satellite structure and development of capitalism into the Chilean domestic economy and society itself. This structure then penetrated and permeated all of Chile very quickly. Since that time and in the course of world and Chilean history during the epochs of colonialism, free trade, imperialism, and the present, Chile has become increasingly marked by the economic, social, and political structure of satellite underdevelopment. This development of underdevelopment continues today, both in Chile's still increasing satellization by the world metropolis and through the ever more acute polarization of Chile's domestic economy.

The history of Brazil is perhaps the clearest case of both national and regional development of underdevelopment. The expansion of the world economy since the beginning of the sixteenth century successively converted the Northeast, the Minas Gerais interior, the North, and the Center-South (Rio de Janeiro, São Paulo, and Paraná) into export economies and incorporated them into the structure and development of the world capitalist system. Each of these regions experienced what may have appeared as economic development during the period of its golden age. But it was a satellite development which was neither self-generating nor self-perpetuating. As the market or the productivity of the first three regions declined, foreign and domestic economic interest in them waned and they were left to develop the underdevelopment they live today. In the fourth region, the coffee economy experienced a similar though not yet quite as serious fate (though the development of a synthetic coffee substitute promises to deal it a mortal blow in the not too distant future). All of this historical evidence contradicts the generally accepted theses that Latin America suffers from a dual society or from the survival of feudal institutions and that these are important obstacles to its economic development.

During the First World War, however, and even more during the Great Depression and the Second World War, São Paulo began to build up an industrial establishment which is the largest in Latin America today. The question arises whether this industrial development did or can break Brazil out of the cycle of satellite development and under-development which has characterized its other regions and national history within the capitalist system so far. I believe that the answer is no. Domestically the evidence so far is fairly clear. The development of industry in São Paulo has not brought greater riches to the other regions of Brazil. Instead, it has converted them into internal colonial satellites, de-capitalized them further, and consolidated or even deepened their underdevelopment. There is little evidence to suggest that this process is likely to be reversed in the foreseeable future except insofar as the provincial poor migrate and become the poor of the metropolitan cities. Externally, the evidence is that although the initial development of São Paulo's industry was relatively autonomous it is being increasingly satellized by the world capitalist metropolis and its future development possibilities are increasingly restricted.[5] This development, my studies lead me to believe, also appears destined to limited or underdeveloped development as long as it takes place in the present economic, political, and social framework.

We must conclude, in short, that underdevelopment is not due to the survival of archaic institutions and the existence of capital shortage in regions that have remained isolated from the stream of world history. On the contrary, underdevelopment was and still is generated by the very same historical process which also generated economic development: the development of capitalism itself. This view, I am glad to say, is gaining adherents among students of Latin America and is proving its worth in shedding new light on the problems of the area and in affording a better perspective for the formulation of theory and policy.[6]

The same historical and structural approach can also lead to better development theory and policy by generating a series of hypotheses about development and underdevelopment such as those I am testing in my current research. The hypotheses are derived from the empirical observation and theoretical assumption that within this world-embracing metropolis-satellite structure the metropoles tend to develop and the satellites to underdevelop. The first hypothesis has already been mentioned above: that in contrast to the development of the world metropolis which is no one's satellite, the development of the national and other subordinate metropoles is limited by their satellite status. It is perhaps more difficult to test this hypothesis than the following ones because part of its confirmation depends on the test of the other hypotheses. Nonetheless, this hypothesis appears to be generally confirmed by the non-autonomous and unsatisfactory economic and especially industrial development of Latin America's national metropoles, as documented in the studies already cited. The most important and at the same time most confirmatory examples are the metropolitan regions of Buenos Aires, and São Paulo, whose growth only began in the nineteenth century, was therefore largely untrammeled by any colonial heritage, but was and remains a satellite development largely dependent on the outside metropolis, first of Britain and then of the United States.

A second hypothesis is that the satellites experience their greatest economic development and especially their most classically capitalist industrial development if and when their ties to their metropolis are weakest. This hypothesis is almost diametrically opposed to the generally accepted thesis that development in the underdeveloped countries follows from the greatest degree of contact with and diffusion from the metropolitan developed countries. This hypothesis seems to be confirmed by two kinds of relative isolation that Latin America has experienced in the course of its history. One is the temporary isolation caused by the crises of war or depression in the world metropolis. Apart from minor ones, five periods of such major crises stand out and are seen to confirm the hypothesis. These are the European (and especially Spanish) depression of the seventeenth century, the Napoleonic Wars, the First World War, the Depression of the 1930s, and the Second World War. It is clearly established and generally recognized that the most important recent industrial development—especially of Argentina, Brazil, and Mexico, but also of other countries such as Chile—has taken place precisely during the periods of the two world wars and the intervening Depression. Thanks to the consequent loosening of trade and investment ties during these periods, the satellites initiated marked autonomous industrialization and growth. Historical research demonstrates that the same thing happened in Latin America during Europe's seventeenth-century depression. Manufacturing grew in the Latin American countries, and several, such as Chile, became exporters of manufactured goods. The Napoleonic Wars gave rise to independence movements in Latin

America, and these should perhaps also be interpreted as in part confirming the development hypothesis.

The other kind of isolation which tends to confirm the second hypothesis is the geographic and economic isolation of regions which at one time were relatively weakly tied to and poorly integrated into the mercantilist and capitalist system. My preliminary research suggests that in Latin America it was these regions which initiated and experienced the most promising self-generating economic development of the classical industrial capitalist type. The most important regional cases probably are Tucumán and Asunción, as well as other cities, such as Mendoza and Rosario, in the interior of Argentina and Paraguay during the end of the eighteenth and the beginning of the nineteenth centuries. Seventeenth- and eighteenth-century São Paulo, long before coffee was grown there, is another example. Perhaps Antioquia in Colombia and Puebla and Querétaro in Mexico are other examples. In its own way, Chile was also an example, since before the sea route around the Horn was opened this country was relatively isolated at the end of a long voyage from Europe via Panama. All of these regions became manufacturing centers and even exporters, usually of textiles, during the periods preceding their effective incorporation as satellites into the colonial, national, and world capitalist system.

Internationally, of course, the classic case of industrialization through non-participation as a satellite in the capitalist world system is obviously that of Japan after the Meiji Restoration. Why, one may ask, was resource-poor but unsatellized Japan able to industrialize so quickly at the end of the century while resource-rich Latin American countries and Russia were not able to do so and the latter was easily beaten by Japan in the War of 1904 after the same forty years of development efforts? The second hypothesis suggests that the fundamental reason is that Japan was not satellized either during the Tokugawa or the Meiji period and therefore did not have its development structurally limited as did the countries which were so satellized.

A corollary of the second hypothesis is that when the metropolis recovers from its crisis and re-establishes the trade and investment ties which fully re-incorporate the satellites into the system, or when the metropolis expands to incorporate previously isolated regions into the worldwide system, the previous development and industrialization of these regions is choked off or channeled into directions which are not self-perpetuating and promising. This happened after each of the five crises cited above. The renewed expansion of trade and the spread of economic liberalism in the eighteenth and nineteenth centuries choked off and reversed the manufacturing development which Latin America had experienced during the seventeenth century, and in some places at the beginning of the nineteenth. After the First World War, the new national industry of Brazil suffered serious consequences from American economic invasion. The increase in the growth rate of Gross National Product and particularly of industrialization throughout Latin America was again reversed and industry became increasingly satellized after the Second World War and especially after the post-Korean War recovery and expansion of the metropolis. Far from having become more developed since then, industrial sectors of Brazil and most conspicuously of Argentina have become structurally more and more underdeveloped and less and less able to generate continued industrialization and/or sustain development of the economy. This process, from which India also suffers, is reflected in a whole gamut of balance-of-payments, inflationary, and other economic and political difficulties, and promises to yield to no solution short of far-reaching structural change.

Our hypothesis suggests that fundamentally the same process occurred even more dramatically with the incorporation into the system of previously unsatellized regions. The expansion of Buenos Aires as a satellite of Great Britain and the introduction of free trade in the interest of the ruling groups of both metropoles destroyed the manufacturing and much of the remainder of the economic base of the previously relatively prosperous interior almost entirely. Manufacturing was destroyed by foreign competition, lands were taken and concentrated into latifundia by the rapaciously growing export economy, intra-regional distribution of income became much more unequal, and the previously developing regions became simple satellites of Buenos Aires and through it of London. The provincial centers did not yield to satellization without a struggle. This metropolis-satellite conflict was much of the cause of the long political and armed struggle between the Unitarists in Buenos Aires and the Federalists in the provinces, and it may be said to have been the sole important cause of the War of the Triple Alliance in which Buenos Aires, Montevideo, and Rio de Janeiro, encouraged and helped by London, destroyed not only the autonomously developing economy of Paraguay but killed off nearly all of its population unwilling to give in. Though this is no doubt the most spectacular example which tends to confirm the hypothesis, I believe that historical research on the satellization of previously relatively independent yeoman-farming and incipient manufacturing regions such as the Caribbean islands will confirm it further.[7] These regions did not have a chance against the forces of expanding and developing capitalism, and their own development had to be sacrificed to that of others. The economy and industry of Argentina, Brazil, and other countries which have experienced the effects of metropolitan recovery since the Second World War are today suffering much the same fate, if fortunately still in lesser degree.

A third major hypothesis derived from the metropolis-satellite structure is that the regions which are the most underdeveloped and feudal-seeming today are the ones which had the closest ties to the metropolis in the past. They are the regions which were the greatest exporters of primary products to and the biggest sources of capital for the world metropolis and were abandoned by the metropolis when for one reason or another business fell off. This hypothesis also contradicts the generally held thesis that the source of a region's underdevelopment is its isolation and its pre-capitalist institutions.

This hypothesis seems to be amply confirmed by the former super-satellite development and present ultra-underdevelopment of the once sugar-exporting West Indies, Northeastern Brazil, the ex-mining districts of Minas Gerais in Brazil, highland Peru, and Bolivia, and the central Mexican states of Guanajuato, Zacatecas, and others whose names were made world famous centuries ago by their silver. There surely are no major regions in Latin America which are today more cursed by underdevelopment and poverty; yet all of these regions, like Bengal in India, once provided the life blood of mercantile and industrial capitalist development—in the metropolis. These regions' participation in the development of the world capitalist system gave them, already in their golden age, the typical structure of underdevelopment of a capitalist export economy. When the market for their sugar or the wealth of their mines disappeared and the metropolis abandoned them to their own devices, the already existing economic, political, and social structure of these regions prohibited autonomous generation of economic development and left them no alternative but to turn in upon themselves and to degenerate into the ultra-underdevelopment we find there today.

These considerations suggest two further and related hypotheses. One is that the latifundium, irrespective of whether it appears today as a plantation or a hacienda, was typically born as a commercial enterprise which created for itself the institutions which permitted it to respond to increased demand in the world or national market by expanding the amount of its land, capital, and labor and to increase the supply of its products. The fifth hypothesis is that the latifundia which appear isolated, subsistence-based, and semi-feudal today saw the demand for their products or their productive capacity decline and that they are to be found principally in the above-named former agricultural and mining export regions whose economic activity declined in general. These two hypotheses run counter to the notions of most people, and even to the opinions of some historians and other students of the subject, according to whom the historical roots and socioeconomic causes of Latin American latifundia and agrarian institutions are to be found in the transfer of feudal institutions from Europe and/or in economic depression.

The evidence to test these hypotheses is not open to easy general inspection and requires detailed analyses of many cases. Nonetheless, some important confirming evidence is available. The growth of the latifundium in nineteenth-century Argentina and Cuba is a clear case in support of the fourth hypothesis and can in no way be attributed to the transfer of feudal institutions during colonial times. The same is evidently the case of the post-revolutionary and contemporary resurgence of latifundia, particularly in the north of Mexico, which produce for the American market, and of similar ones on the coast of Peru and the new coffee regions of Brazil. The conversion of previously yeoman-farming Caribbean islands, such as Barbados, into sugar-exporting economies at various times between the seventeenth and twentieth centuries and the resulting rise of the latifundia in these islands would seem to confirm the fourth hypothesis as well. In Chile, the rise of the latifundium and the creation of the institutions of servitude which later came to be called feudal occurred in the eighteenth century and have been conclusively shown to be the result of and response to the opening of a market for Chilean wheat in Lima.[8] Even the growth and consolidation of the latifundium in seventeenth-century Mexico—which most expert students have attributed to a depression of the economy caused by the decline of mining and a shortage of Indian labor and to a consequent turning in upon itself and ruralization of the economy—occurred at a time when urban population and demand were growing, food shortages were acute, food prices skyrocketing, and the profitability of other economic activities such as mining and foreign trade declining.[9] All of these and other factors rendered hacienda agriculture more profitable. Thus, even this case would seem to confirm the hypothesis that the growth of the latifundium and its feudal-seeming conditions of servitude in Latin America has always been and is still the commercial response to increased demand and that it does not represent the transfer or survival of alien institutions that have remained beyond the reach of capitalist development. The emergence of latifundia, which today really are more or less (though not entirely) isolated, might then be attributed to the causes advanced in the fifth hypothesis—i.e., the decline of previously profitable agricultural enterprises whose capital was, and whose currently produced economic surplus still is, transferred elsewhere by owners and merchants who frequently are the same persons or families. Testing this hypothesis requires still more detailed analysis, some of which I have undertaken in a study on Brazilian agriculture.[10]

All of these hypotheses and studies suggest that the global extension and unity of the capitalist system, its monopoly structure and uneven development throughout its history, and the resulting persistence of commercial rather than industrial capitalism in the underdeveloped world (including its most industrially advanced countries) deserve much more attention in the study of economic development and cultural change than they have hitherto received. Though science and truth know no national boundaries, it is probably new generations of scientists from the underdeveloped countries themselves who most need to, and best can, devote the necessary attention to these problems and clarify the process of underdevelopment and development. It is their people who in the last analysis face the task of changing this no longer acceptable process and eliminating this miserable reality.

They will not be able to accomplish these goals by importing sterile stereotypes from the metropolis which do not correspond to their satellite economic reality and do not respond to their liberating political needs. To change their reality they must understand it. For this reason, I hope that better confirmation of these hypotheses and further pursuit of the proposed historical, holistic, and structural approach may help the peoples of the underdeveloped countries to understand the causes and eliminate the reality of their development of underdevelopment and their underdevelopment of development.

Notes

1. *América Latina,* Año 6, No. 4 (October–December 1963), p. 8.

2. Instituto Nacional Indigenista, *Los centros coordinadores indigenistas* (Mexico, 1962), p. 34.

3. Ibid., pp. 33–34, 88.

4. "Capitalist Development of Underdevelopment in Chile" and "Capitalist Development of Underdevelopment in Brazil," in *Capitalism and Underdevelopment in Latin America* (New York & London: Monthly Review Press, 1967 and 1969).

5. Also see "The Growth and Decline of Import Substitution," *Economic Bulletin for Latin America,* 9, No. 1 (March 1964), and Celso Furtado, *Dialectica do Desenvolvimiento* (Rio de Janeiro: Fundo de Cultura, 1964).

6. Others who use a similar approach, though their ideologies do not permit them to derive the logically following conclusions, are Aníbal Pinto, *Chile: Un caso de desarrollo frustrado* (Santiago: Editorial Universitaria, 1957); Celso Furtado, *The Economic Growth of Brazil* (Berkeley: University of California Press, 1963); and Caio Prado Júnior, *Historia Económica do Brasil,* 7th ed. (São Paulo: Editora Brasiliense, 1962).

7. See for instance Ramiro Guerra y Sánchez, *Sugar and Society in the Caribbean* (New Haven: Yale University Press, 1964).

8. Mario Góngora, *Origen de los "inquilinos" de Chile central* (Santiago: Editorial Universitaria, 1960); Jean Borde and Mario Góngora, *Evolución de la propiedad rural en el Valle del Puango* (Santiago: Instituto de Sociología de la Universidad de Chile); and Sergio Sepúlveda, *El trigo chileno en el mercado mundial* (Santiago: Editorial Universitaria, 1959).

9. Woodrow Borah makes depression the centerpiece of his explanation in "New Spain's Century of Depression," *Ibero-Americana,* No. 35 (Berkeley, 1951). François Chevalier speaks of turning in upon itself in the most authoritative study of the subject, "La formación de los grandes latifundios en México," *Problemas Agrícolas e Industriales de México,* 8, No. 1, 1956.

10. "Capitalism and the Myth of Feudalism in Brazilian Agriculture," in *Capitalism and Underdevelopment in Latin America.*

7 / Economic Development of Latin America

Celso Furtado

Celso Furtado, a Brazilian economist and historian, discusses the new international division of labor that emerged in the world economy between 1820 and World War I. During this period, the Latin American periphery specialized in primary production for the industrializing West, particularly England. Furtado constructed a typology of economies that exported raw materials, dividing Latin America into three primary producing zones: countries exporting temperate agricultural commodities (principally Argentina and Uruguay, which relied on extensive land use); countries exporting tropical agricultural commodities, such as sugar, tobacco, and coffee (lowland regions); and countries producing mineral products (Mexico, Chile, Peru, and Bolivia, and later Venezuela, an oil producer). Furtado then describes the impact of the 1929 world economic crisis, which abruptly terminated this long phase of Latin American export expansion. This crisis was followed by the emergence of import-substitution industrialization (ISI), a crucial economic process that had profound political implications for dependency analysis, as we will see in Chapter 8.

The Transformation of International Trade in the Second Half of the Nineteenth Century and Its Impact on Latin America

International Division of Labour

During the first half of the nineteenth century, the Industrial Revolution was essentially an English phenomenon. For this reason the structural evolution of the English economy provides the key to the radical changes which took place during this period in the world economy as a whole. The economists who witnessed the beginnings of these changes, and interpreted them from the English viewpoint, immediately realised that it was in England's interests to become a vast factory, opening its doors to primary products from all over the world. In fact, industrial activity, violating the law of diminishing returns, stimulated qualitative changes without precedent in economic processes.

In economies in which technology had made little or no progress—based essentially on agricultural activity—it was evident that there were limits to the degree to which the relative proportions of the productive factors employed could be altered. Beyond a certain point, the output obtained per unit of agricultural land necessarily tended to decrease, regardless of the amount of labour added, which meant that availability of land governed the use of the other factors. Industrial activity made it possible to break this barrier, since growth itself, by creating the possibility of further specialisation in labour and equipment (greater division of labour additional and more complex machinery), became the source of increased productivity, which meant increasing returns. In such circumstances, even if prices of imported agricultural products remained stable and were the same as those of home-produced goods, it would still be to the advantage of a country like England, where land was scarce, to be able to pay for them with industrial products. On the other hand, once England had established an important industrial nucleus and consolidated its advantage over other countries, it would not be difficult to demonstrate that, in terms of the principle of comparative advantage, considered from the static point of view, it would be in the interests of other countries to buy industrial products from England and pay for them with raw materials. However, despite the enormous advantages it represented for England (since it implied

Reprinted with permission from *Economic Development of Latin America*, by Celso Furtado, pp. 27–42, 82–92. New York: Cambridge University Press, 1970. (Ed. note: Some nonessential passages and footnotes have been deleted.)

nothing less than the concentration in this country of those activities in which rapid technological progress was being made), this pattern of development met with resistance on the part of agricultural interests, and its acceptance was much slower than is generally supposed. Throughout the first half of the nineteenth century, English agriculture continued to enjoy effective protection through an adjustable tariff mechanism which permitted customs barriers to be automatically raised whenever world prices fell below a certain critical point. However, faced with the growing power of the industrial bourgeoisie, resistance gradually broke down and, between 1846 and 1849, England eliminated barriers to external trade without expecting other countries to follow suit.

The complete victory of free trade ideas in some ways marked the end of the first phase of the Industrial Revolution. During this phase a dynamic nucleus was formed and consolidated in England, which was to lead, in the second half of the nineteenth century, to the establishment of a system of international division of labour, based on a world market. Of decisive importance in the transition from the first to the second phase of the Industrial Revolution was the application to the transport sector of technology originally developed in connexion with manufacturing industries. Railroads made possible the rapid integration of the domestic markets in European countries, while the mechanisation of maritime transport brought about radical changes in the conditions of international trade. The propeller was invented around 1840, and in the course of the following decade the introduction of iron hulls, reducing the resistance of water, permitted an increase in the size of vessels. From then on, the total world tonnage of the merchant marine was to increase with extraordinary speed: from 6.7 million tons in 1840 it rose to 12.8 million in 1860, and to 43 million in 1913. The impact on long-distance freight charges was dramatic, and in many cases ocean freight rates were cut by as much as 70–90 percent. The consequent fall in the prices of raw materials, particularly of cotton, reinforced England's competitive position. By pursuing a policy of free trade and substantially reducing her own agricultural activities, England was able to extract the maximum advantage from the fall in raw material prices brought about by the cut in shipping costs. In this way, English manufacturers managed to "internalize" the external economies resulting from the technological revolution in transport. It should be recalled that in the first few decades of the second half of the nineteenth century, two-thirds of the manufactures circulating in the world market were made in England.

The century between the 1820s and the outbreak of the First World War saw the establishment of an international division of labour and the shaping of a world economic system. The economic activities of a growing proportion of the world's population became interdependent elements of an integrated complex. The new pattern of the world economy displayed some notable features. The first was the rise in the economic growth rate of many of the countries that made up this pattern. This applied not only to countries which specialized in activities benefiting from rapid technological progress, but also to those making more rational use of their natural resources. This phenomenon had far-reaching historical consequences. Up to this time, growth rates had been irregular and, even when they showed a long-term upward trend, were too weak to bring about really significant changes in standards of living within the lifetime of a single generation. It seemed natural, therefore, to assume, as did the mercantilists, that the enrichment of one community inevitably meant the impoverishment of another. With the Industrial Revolution, the accelerated output of goods and services made it possible to double a community's purchasing power in the course of a single generation.

The second significant change was the dramatic rise in the rates of population increase brought about by urbanisation, improvements in public services, and the rise in real incomes. Immediately afterwards, the striking advances of medical science greatly improved life-expectancies. Expectation of a longer life and the possibility of seeing it dramatically altered produced a new outlook, based on the awareness that the horizon of possibilities open to mankind could be vastly extended on both individual and social planes. The great collective movements, which in the past had had a religious or military inspiration, became increasingly orientated towards understanding and mastering the physical world and reshaping social structures.

The third noteworthy characteristic is the creation and rapid expansion of a fund of transmittable technical knowledge related to the forms of production.[1] In the pre-industrial epoch, production techniques were the result of the gradual accumulation of empirical knowledge, handed down from generation to generation through apprenticeship in the skilled trades. Productive activity gave rise to further productive activity, just as one generation gives birth to the next. With the growing importance of an equipment industry based on advanced technology, the situation was radically altered. Transmission of techniques took the form of a straightforward commercial transaction, and it became possible to transform an entire productive sector at a hitherto-undreamed-of speed. By creating a transport equipment industry, England set in motion a process that was to transform the means of transport throughout the world. Further, by providing adequate financing for this industry, it created a mechanism for exporting capital which was to be a decisive factor in shaping the world economic system and in creating new forms of hegemony outside the traditional framework of colonial administration.

The result of the interplay of these factors was the growth and integration of the world economy in the nineteenth century and the intensification of international specialisation. World trade expanded rapidly; its growth rate was far higher than that of the domestic products of the nations that took the lead in bringing about the transformation of the world economy. The value of world trade, which was no more than 1.5 billion dollars in the 1820s, rose to 3.5 billion in the 1840s and to 40 billion just before the outbreak of the First World War. This growth was reflected in the growing "internationalisation" of the industrialised economies and more particularly of the British economy. Thus, Great Britain's external trade coefficient,[2] which was 8.5 percent in the period 1805–19, rose to 29.4 percent in the period 1910–13. Generally speaking, the external trade coefficient rose in all the European countries that started industrialising in this period. The same phenomenon occurred in countries exporting primary products—the case of the Latin American countries—in which exports were developed at the expense of subsistence economic activities. This was not the case in countries whose development was essentially an expansion of the European economic frontier, i.e., countries such as the United States,[3] Canada, Australia, and New Zealand, whose development was dependent on an inflow of European labour and capital. In these countries development took the form of incorporating new territories and was an extension of the European economic space, whose basic natural resources, thus enriched, permitted a rise in agricultural productivity. The tendency to diminishing returns in agriculture was avoided by increasing the supply of good agricultural land. Thus, Britain could curtail agricultural production while prices of agricultural products could be reduced thanks to the incorporation of land in the temperate zones of North America and Oceania. The economy that developed in these new areas was specialised from the start, that is, it had a high coefficient of external trade and a high level of productivity and income. These conditions made it possible to attract the European immigrants on whose labour these developing areas depended. The result was that when they entered the world economy they already had effective domestic markets for industrial products and a labour force equipped for industrial activity, a circumstance which accounts for their early industrialisation. Since the newly established industries competed with imported manufactures, the external trade coefficient, which was high to begin with, showed a tendency to decline or level off rather than follow the upward trend noted in the first two cases.

In summary, the following features of the formative process of the world economic system are worth emphasising because of their significance in shaping international relations:

1. the existence of a nucleus which achieved a considerable advance in the process of capital accumulation, concentrating a large proportion of industrial activity, practically all centred on the production of equipment; this nucleus was also the finance centre for world exports of capital goods, controlled the transport infrastructure in international trade, and was the major import market for primary products.
2. the emergence of the system of international division of labour under the hegemony of this growth pole; the inducement to specialise favoured rapid settlement of vast empty spaces in temperate zones and the integration of other areas into the world market through the export of primary products.
3. the creation of a network for transmitting technological progress as a subsidiary of the international division of labour; this network facilitated the export of capital and at the same time linked capital outflows to the system of international specialisation which it tended to consolidate; since production of capital goods was concentrated in the nucleus described above, new production techniques also remained geographically concentrated, benefiting those activities in which the dominant economy already had experience or in which it had more direct interest. Hence the evolution of technology was conditioned by the system of international division of labour that emerged with the Industrial Revolution.

Typology of Economies Exporting Raw Materials

The Latin American countries began to enter the channels of expanding international trade in the 1840s. The primary exporters involved in this process tended to fall into three groups: (1) countries exporting temperate agricultural commodities; (2) countries exporting tropical agricultural commodities; (3) countries exporting mineral products. In each case, foreign trade helped to establish a distinctive economic structure whose characteristic features should be borne in mind when studying its subsequent evolution.

The first group is composed essentially of Argentina and Uruguay. In this case, exportable agricultural production was based on the extensive use of land and was destined to compete with the domestic production of countries undergoing rapid industrialisation. Extensive use of good agricultural land made it possible to achieve high profitability from the start. On the other hand, the very extensiveness of the agriculture practised and the sheer volume of freight involved necessitated the creation of a widespread transportation network which indirectly led to the rapid unification of the domestic market, focusing on the major ports of shipment. This group of countries displays the characteristics of regions referred to earlier as constituting an expanding frontier of the industrialising European economy. This frontier, to which European agricultural technology was transplanted in the early stages, soon became an important centre for developing new agricultural techniques of its own. Both the techniques of farming vast open spaces and of large-scale transportation, storage, and shipment of cereals originated in the United States. In sum, the countries in this group, precisely because they competed with the domestic production of countries at a more advanced stage of development and with regions of recent European settlement enjoying a high standard of living, were from the start integrated into a productive sector of the world economy characterised by constant technological advance. Throughout the phase of expansion in their foreign trade, these countries achieved high rates of growth.

The second group, consisting of countries exporting tropical agricultural products, includes more than half the Latin American population. It includes Brazil, Colombia, Ecuador, Central America, and the Caribbean, as well as certain regions of Mexico and Venezuela. Countries in this group entered international trade in competition with colonial areas and the southern region of the United States. Sugar and tobacco remained typically colonial products until the last years of the nineteenth century. It was the rapid expansion of the world demand for coffee and cacao from the mid-nineteenth century onwards that enabled tropical commodities to play a dynamic role in integrating the Latin American economy into world trade during the period under consideration. In this case, structural changes in the British economy had less direct impact, since the British market continued to be abundantly supplied by colonial regions where labour was plentiful and wages were low. The role of dynamic centre fell to the United States and, to a lesser extent, to the European countries. On the whole, tropical commodities were of little significance as a factor in development, although they did involve the opening up of large areas for settlement. On the one hand, their prices continued to be influenced by the low wages prevailing in colonial regions, which had long been traditional tropical commodity producers. On the other, they did not usually require the creation of a complex infrastructure; on the contrary, in many regions traditional means of transport continued to be used. Finally, since they were produced in areas lacking the capacity to develop new techniques for themselves, tropical products tended to remain within the framework of the traditional economies. Nonetheless, in certain regions tropical export agriculture did manage to play an important role in development. The most notable instance is probably that of the coffee region of São Paulo, in Brazil. Here the physical and chemical qualities of the soil permitted extensive coffee planting over large areas. The relatively high productivity of labour and the vast size of the area planted favoured the creation of an infrastructure and promoted home market expansion. The special nature of this case becomes evident when we recall that at the end of the nineteenth century the São Paulo highlands supplied two-thirds of the total world coffee output.

The third group, consisting of countries exporting mineral products, includes Mexico, Chile, Peru, and Bolivia. Venezuela entered this group in the 1920s as an exporter of petroleum. By creating a rapidly expanding market for industrial metals, the transport revolution of the mid-nineteenth century brought about a radical change in Latin American mining. In the first place, precious metals, notably silver, rapidly lost their importance. Secondly, small-scale mining operations of the artisan or quasi-artisan type were gradually replaced by large-scale production controlled by foreign capital and administered from abroad. The considerable rise in the world demand for non-ferrous metals coincided with major technological progress in production methods which permitted or required the concentration of production in large units. This process of concentration, carried out initially in the major producing country— the United States—soon spread to other areas, where local producers were marginalised by American organisations with heavy financial backing and the technical "know-how" required to handle low-grade ores. Thus, the development of the export mining industry entailed not only denationalisation but the establishment of a productive sector which, given its marked technological advance and high capital intensity, tended to become isolated and to behave as a separate economic system, or rather, as part of the economic system in which the decision centre controlling the production unit belonged. Foreign control of a highly capitalised activity, employing a small labour force, meant that the major share of the flow of income generated by this activity was deflected from the domestic economy. In these circumstances its value as a factor for inducing direct change in the domestic economy was practically nil. Moreover, since the infrastructure created to serve export mining industries is highly specialised, the resultant external economies are minimal or non-existent for the economic system as a whole. Finally, since this type of mining activity called for specialised imports and created a limited flow of wage income, it made no significant contribution to the creation of a domestic market. Its potential as a dynamic factor became evident only when the State intervened, obliging mining companies to acquire part of their inputs locally and collecting, in the form of tax revenue, a significant share of the flow of income traditionally remitted abroad.

• • •

Reorientation of the International Economy in the Present Century

Export Expansion Phase

The three decades preceding the First World War were a period of rapid economic development and intense social change for Latin America as a whole: in Mexico, where the Porfirio Díaz administration created the conditions for a large inflow of foreign capital directed mainly into mineral production; in Chile, whose victory in the War of the Pacific against Bolivia and Peru enabled her to monopolise the sources of nitrate; in Cuba, where, even before independence was attained in 1898, the country's increasing integration into the United States market had brought about a dramatic expansion in sugar production; in Brazil, where the spread of coffee over the São Paulo highlands and the influx of European immigrants hastened the collapse of the slave economy; finally, in Argentina, where economy and society underwent drastic changes under the impact of the great wave of immigration and the penetration of substantial foreign capital.

A closer look at the three largest countries reveals the importance of the changes that occurred during this period. In Mexico, the population increased from 9.4 million in 1877 to 15.2 million in 1910. In the last decade of the Porfirio Díaz administration (1900–10), the annual average growth rate of the real per capita product was 3.1 percent. During this decade the production of minerals and petroleum, the country's basic export sector, grew at an annual rate of 7.2 percent, that is, twice as fast as manufacturing production and nearly three times as fast as agricultural production.[4] In Brazil, the population increased from 10.1 million in 1872 to 17.3 million in 1900. In the last decade of the nineteenth century, the rate of population increase in São Paulo was over 5 percent a year, while for the country as a whole it was under 2 percent. Nearly all the 610,000 immigrants entering Brazil during this decade went to the State of São Paulo. Between 1880 and 1910, the total length of railways increased from 3.4 to 21.3 thousand kilometres. Coffee exports, which amounted to around 4 million 60-kilogram bags in 1880, rose to almost 10 million in 1900 and to over 16 million on the eve of the First World War, a total seldom surpassed in later years. In the same period, exports of cacao rose from 6,000 to 40,000 tons, and rubber exports from 7,000 to 40,000 tons.[5] However, it was in Argentina that the changes brought about in this phase were most marked. Between the periods 1890–1904 and 1910–14, Argentina's population doubled, increasing from 3.6 to 7.2 million; the country's railway network was extended from 12.7 to 31.3 kilometres; cereal exports rose from 1,038,000 to 5,294,000 tons, and exports of frozen meat rose from 27,000 to 376,000 tons.

In short, during the period under consideration, Latin America became an important component of world trade and a key source of raw materials for the industrialised countries. In 1913, the Latin American share in world commodity exports was as follows: cereals—17.9 percent; livestock products—11.5 percent; coffee, cocoa, and tea—62.1 percent; sugar—37.6 percent; fruit and vegetables—14.2 percent; vegetable fibres—6.3 percent; rubber, furs, hides, and leathers—25.1 percent.[6]

New Trends in the International Economy

After the First World War there were important changes in the long-term trends of the international economy. These changes were accentuated by the 1929 crisis. In the first place, there was a reversal of the upward trend in the external trade coefficient of the industrialised countries. In Britain, for instance, it fell from around 30 percent (for the period 1910–13) to 25 percent in 1927–9 and to 17 percent in the 1930s. In the United States, Germany, France, and Japan, the coefficient levelled off in the 1920s and declined in the 1930s.[7] This downward trend shifted again only after the Second World War, this time within a new international economic framework in which the central feature of world trade had become the exchange of manufactured products between industrialised countries.

In the second place, there was a persistent deterioration in world market prices of primary products. This tendency, already discernible in the preceding period, became more pronounced after 1913. To the short-term inelasticity of supply of primary commodities and the structural rigidity of countries specialising in primary production for export, was added the effect of technological progress as a factor responsible for this downward trend in world prices of raw materials. After the First World War, synthetic nitrates progressively displaced Chilean nitrates. Synthetic fibres and synthetic rubber appeared shortly afterwards. Greater efficiency in the industrial use of mineral products was to have a similar effect.

The third tendency worth noting is the steady change in the composition of world trade, a tendency that became apparent only after the Second World War. In the three decades preceding World War I, the quantum of world trade in primary products increased at just about the same rate as the trade in manufactures. In the two decades following, as a result of the sharp rise in petroleum exports and the protectionism prevailing in the industrialised countries, the quantum of exports of

Table 1. World Trade Composition

	1913	1953
	% of total	
foodstuffs	29	23
agricultural raw materials	21	14
minerals	13	20
manufactures	37	43

primary products increased more than that of exports of manufactures. However, the most significant shifts in trend have occurred only since the 1950s. As Table 1 indicates, the situation in 1953 was already quite different from that of 1913 with regard to the share of foodstuffs and manufactures in the composition of world trade.[8]

The relative decline in natural fibres and the rise in petroleum are the main changes that took place in the period indicated. It was from the 1950s onwards that the new trends, which were to radically alter the composition of world trade in the course of a decade, became apparent. Between 1953 and 1967, the annual rate of growth of world exports of foodstuffs was 3.5 percent, that of other primary products (excluding fuel) was also 3.5 percent, of fuel 7 percent, of chemical products 15 percent, and of other manufactures 8.5 percent. As a result of these trends, exchanges between industrialised countries have become of growing significance in world trade. Thus, in 1966, the total exports of developed countries with a market economy amounted to 139 billion dollars, of which 106 billion were accounted for by their exports to each other.[9]

If we compare the overall pattern of development of the world economy in the half-century following the end of World War I with the half-century preceding it, significant differences become immediately apparent, particularly from the point of view of the underdeveloped countries. The earlier period was marked by the emergence of a system of international division of labour under the hegemony of the group of countries which had begun to industrialise during the first half of the nineteenth century. This system permitted the concentration in certain areas of production activities which benefited most from technological progress, as well as the fuller and more rational utilisation of abundant resources (labour and land) in other areas. The increased overall activity of an expanding world economy was accompanied by the establishment or accentuation of interdependence between its various parts. If we look more closely at this process, it becomes immediately apparent that it involved two forms of development. On the one hand, we have the development of industrial centres based on technological progress and a rapid accumulation of capital. This type of development entailed increasingly complicated production processes, which required both a change in the relative quantities of productive factors, with more capital per unit of labour, and a change in their quality, more particularly a progressive improvement in the human factor. On the other hand, we have the development of the so-called periphery, or outpost areas, induced by changes in overall demand and effected through the external sector. This second type of development was nearly always extensive in character; that is, it made it possible to increase the economic productivity of available factors without requiring significant changes in the forms of production. Thus, the substitution of a subsistence crop such as maize by an export crop such as coffee brought about an increase in overall output while requiring no major changes in production techniques. In other instances—the case of mining production—this peripheral development took the form of assimilating modern techniques and increasing the input of capital in a production sector strictly geared to exports and lacking the capacity to transmit its growth to the economy as a whole. In either case, peripheral development had little capacity to transform traditional techniques of production. Nevertheless, by requiring the modernisation of infrastructures and of part of the State apparatus, it set in motion an historical process which opened up important new possibilities.

The 1929 Crisis and Its Impact on Latin America

In the period which began with the First World War and assumed marked characteristics with the 1929 crisis, the traditional system of international division of labour played a progressively less important role. International demand for primary products lost its dynamism as a reflexion of the structural evolution that had taken place in the industrialised countries. Full realisation of the nature and magnitude of the problem and of its repercussions on the international economy was delayed by the Great Depression. The extent and severity of the depression obscured all other causal factors. It was not easy to perceive that the very magnitude of the crisis already reflected the important changes that were taking place in the world economy. The quantum of world exports fell by 25 percent between 1929 and 1933, and the general level of export prices by 30 percent, entailing a fall of over 50 percent in the total value of world trade. Moreover, the change in flow of international capital movements greatly aggravated the situation of countries exporting primary products. Britain, the United States, and France, who had exported an annual average of 3,300 million dollars in the form of short- and long-term capital in the period 1928–30,

Table 2. Latin America: Evolution of External Trade

	quantum of exports	terms of trade	capacity to import
1930–4	− 8·8	− 24·3	− 31·3
1935–9	− 2·4	− 10·8	− 12·9

SOURCE: ECLA, *Economic Survey of Latin America, 1949*.

became net importers of 1,600 million dollars, on yearly average, in the period 1931–2. Britain, who in the period 1925–9 had paid for 22 percent of her imports out of the income earned on British capital abroad, raised this proportion to 37 percent in the period 1930–4. In Latin America, the crisis assumed catastrophic proportions, precisely because it was one of the underdeveloped regions which had been most closely integrated with the international system of division of labour. The entire modern sector of the Latin American economy was geared to external trade. In Mexico nearly 30 percent of the country's reproducible capital was controlled by foreign groups, and in Argentina more than 40 percent. The situation in the other countries was much the same. The external debt and its servicing conditioned not only the behaviour of the balance of payments but also that of public finance and the monetary system. Throughout the decade following the crisis, the capacity to import was severely curtailed, not so much as a result of the decline of the quantum of exports but mainly as a reflexion of the adverse trend in the terms of trade, as Table 2 clearly indicates.

Taking into account the population increase, the capacity to import declined by 37 percent in the period 1930–4 relatively to the pre-crisis period, and by 27 percent in the five-year period following. The impact of the crisis was felt most violently in the public sector because of its dependence on revenue from foreign trade and also as a reflexion of the financial significance of the external public debt. With the exception of Argentina, all the Latin American countries suspended debt-service payments for more or less lengthy periods, which made it even more difficult to obtain foreign capital to pay for badly needed imports of equipment.

Although the whole region was hard hit, the consequences of the 1929 crisis varied in accordance with the degree of the country's integration into the system of international division of labour and the nature of this integration. Countries such as Argentina, exporting temperate-zone food products, were *relatively* less severely affected, in the first place because demand for these products has a low income elasticity, particularly in countries with high living levels and, secondly, because

Table 3. *External Trade Indicators for Selected Latin American Countries (% variation from annual average for 1925-9)*

	quantum of exports	terms of trade	capacity to import	quantum of imports
Argentina				
1930–4	− 8	− 20	− 27	− 32
1935–9	− 11	0	− 11	− 23
Brazil				
1930–4	+ 10	− 40	− 35	− 48
1935–9	+ 52	− 55	− 32	− 27
Chile				
1930–4	− 33	− 38	− 58	− 60
1935–9	− 2	− 41	− 42	− 50
Mexico				
1930–4	− 25	− 43	− 55	− 45
1935–9	− 11	− 36	− 39	− 26

SOURCE: ECLA, *Economic Survey of Latin America, 1949.*

the supply of these commodities, nearly all annual crops, is relatively elastic, since it is possible to reduce the crop areas from one year to the next. Finally, since these products compete with surpluses produced in developed countries, markets are relatively better organised.

In the case of tropical products, demand is also relatively inelastic in terms of income. But, given the inelasticity of supply in the case of perennial crops, any decline in demand provokes catastrophic falls in prices, which tend to become even more accentuated in the absence of any possibility of financing surpluses and withdrawing them from the market. In the case of mineral products, we have a different picture: the curtailment of industrial production in the importing countries led to the liquidation of stocks and the collapse of production in the exporting countries. The fall in the volume of exports tended to be considerable. The external trade statistics of Argentina, Brazil, Chile, and Mexico for the decade following the crisis illustrate the different forms of reaction in underdeveloped structures. Given the extreme inelasticity of coffee production and other tropical commodities, Brazil attempted to offset the fall in commodity prices by increasing her quantum of exports, which rose by 10 percent in the 1930–4 period, relatively to the period 1925–9. Argentina reduced hers by 8 percent, Chile by 33 percent, and Mexico by 25 percent. The deterioration in Brazil's terms of trade was twice as severe as in Argentina's, but not very different from that in Chile and Mexico. The hardest-hit countries were the mineral exporters, affected both by the fall in prices and the reduction in the quantum of exports. The countries in the least vulnerable position were those exporting commodities with annual crop cycles, whose production structure was more flexible. In the following five-year period (1935–9) Brazil continued to force the external markets, making a concerted effort to dispose of her enormous output of coffee, since the accumulation of stocks was proving a heavy financial burden. This effort was completely defeated by the deterioration of trade. In Argentina, the reduction in the quantum of exports was accompanied by a significant improvement in the terms of trade. The Chilean economy, more closely integrated with the system of international division of labour than any of the other three economies mentioned, was easily the most severely affected. Its behaviour during this decade revealed the extreme vulnerability of primary-exporter economies within the framework of the international division of labour established in the nineteenth century.

• • •

The Industrialisation Process: Import Substitution

Intrinsic Limitations of the First Phase of Industrialisation

The industrialisation process that had started in some Latin American countries was profoundly affected by the 1929 crisis. This does not mean that the crisis represents a watershed between a period of prosperity and a period of depression. Indeed, some countries had already shown symptoms of a decline in the export sector in the period immediately preceding the crisis. In Brazil, for instance, there had been recurrent crises of overproduction in coffee since before the First World War, and rubber had lost its privileged position in world trade in the decade following the war. In Chile, the nitrate crisis sparked off by competition from the synthetic product had been a burden on the country's economy for more than a decade. Nonetheless, with the exception of Brazil, in all the region's most economically significant countries the quantum of exports was 50 to 100 percent higher in the 1925–9 period than in the first decade of the century. It was in connexion with the industrialisation process that the 1929 crisis constituted a landmark. Until then, the development of the industrial sector had been a reflexion of export expansion; from then on, industrialisation was induced largely through the structural tensions provoked by the decline or inadequate growth of the export sector. The exception to this rule is represented by countries that were to experience a phase of vigorous export growth in a later period: Venezuela, Peru, and the Central American countries.

In the countries in process of industrialisation, the industrial sector's contribution to the product in 1929 was:[10]

	industrial sector as % of GDP
Argentina	22·8
Mexico	14·2
Brazil	11·7
Chile	7·9
Colombia	6·2

Before considering the features of the new phase in industrialization, the following question must be tackled: what possibilities were there for industrialisation in Latin America within the framework that prevailed before 1929? In other words, to what extent did the sudden disruption of world trade frustrate an industrialisation process already making rapid headway?

A careful scrutiny of the data available for Argentina, Brazil, and Mexico shows that the industrialisation process stimulated by the expansion of exports was already showing clear symptoms of exhaustion before the 1929 crisis. Thus, structural changes in the Argentine economy had been of little significance since 1910. In that year, industrial output contributed 20 percent to the gross domestic product, a proportion that remained virtually unchanged until 1920. In 1920 it rose to 23.6 percent, but declined to 22.8 percent in 1929. This structural immutability coincided with the vigorous growth of the Argentine economy. In the course of the two decades mentioned, the volume of industrial output increased by 120 percent and the quantum of exports by 140 percent. In Mexico, the coefficient of industrialisation (share of industrial output in gross domestic product) began to decline in the first decade of the twentieth century, before the revolutionary period. In the period 1900–10, the average yearly rate of growth of the gross domestic product was 4.2 percent, whereas that of industrial output was only 3.6 percent. In Brazil, where the industrialisation process lagged behind that of the other two countries, the index of industrial output rose by 150 percent between 1914 and 1922, but between the latter year and 1929 it remained practically stationary.

To grasp the intrinsic limitations of this initial phase of industrialisation in the Latin American countries, some of its basic features should be borne in mind. It consisted essentially of the establishment of a nucleus of industries producing non-durable consumer goods—textiles, leather goods, processed foodstuffs, clothing—which had become a feasible proposition as a result of the increased income made available for consumption with the expansion of exports. Moreover, the urbanisation process that was taking place at the same time created new demands in the building sector, opening up prospects for manufacturing building materials, which largely replaced the traditional materials produced by local craftsmen. But these industries—non-durable consumer goods and building materials—had little power to generate sustained growth. In the case of consumer goods of a non-durable nature, the vigorously upward shifting trend of the growth curve in the early stages was due simply to the fact that they were replacing goods hitherto imported. Thus, the output of textiles in Brazil increased from 22 million metres in 1882 to 242 million in 1905 and 470 million in 1915.[11] After 1915, however, the growth of the textile industry was extremely weak since import substitution had exhausted its possibilities and the growth of the export sector had slowed down or levelled off.

Given an elastic supply of labour—even when largely recruited abroad, as in the case of Argentina—the growth of the industrial sector will proceed under conditions of steady wage rates as will the expansion of the export sector in an economy with a sizeable subsistence sector. Increased industrial output is due largely to the addition of new units of production similar to those already in existence, and is dependent on imported equipment. There is no question of creating a system of industrial production by steadily diversifying production. What is involved is simply the addition of similar units in certain sectors of industrial activity. The labour force absorbed, benefiting from a wage rate above the national average, provides reinforcement for the domestic market in the same way that growth of the export sector, by absorbing part of the surplus manpower, contributes to the expansion of the home market. Thus there was no essential difference between industrial expansion in this initial phase and the growth of export agriculture. The main difference was that the latter, dependent on overseas demand, acted as an exogenous variable, whereas investment in the industrial sector was dependent on the growth of a market created by the expansion of exports. In fact, the export sector acted as a multiplier of employment in the industrial sector. The industrial sector could overcome this dependence only if it became sufficiently diversified to generate its own demand. In other words, it required the establishment of machine-making and other industries whose output could be absorbed by the industrial sector itself and by other productive activities. But the facilities available abroad for financing investments in infrastructure and even industrial investments were tied to the acquisition of equipment and technology in foreign centres. Financial dependence made it necessary to buy equipment from foreign suppliers, with the result that industrial activity was limited to the processing of local raw materials or to the finishing of imported semi-manufactured consumer goods, the equipment used being invariably purchased abroad. With an industrial complex

Table 4. *Evolution of Import Coefficient in Selected Countries*
(imports as % of GDP)

	Argentina	Mexico	Brazil	Chile	Colombia
1929	17·8	14·2	11·3	31·2	18·0
1937	13·0	8·5	6·9	13·8	12·9
1947	11·7	10·6	8·7	12·6	13·8
1957	5·9	8·2	6·1	10·1	8·9

geared to the processing of consumer goods, there was little need to assimilate modern technology. The only technical assistance given to existing industries was the replacement of worn-out equipment, which could be handled by agents acting for the import houses. This apparent initial advantage turned out to be negative in the next phase, since industries could be established without the emergence of a genuine industrial outlook, which presupposes not only the encouragement of managerial skills but the training of skilled personnel equipped with a thorough knowledge of technical processes.

Structural Changes Induced by the Crisis of the Export Sector

The sudden collapse of the capacity to import, the contraction of the export sector and the ensuing fall in export profits, the blocking of international channels of finance, all provoked by the 1929 crisis, profoundly altered the course of development of the Latin American economies, particularly of those that had already begun to industrialise. The contraction of the export sector led to two types of reaction, depending on the degree of diversification attained by the economy concerned: (1) factors of production were shifted back into the pre-capitalist sector—subsistence agriculture and craft manufactures—as the money economy shrank; (2) the industrial sector geared to the home market was expanded in an effort to replace, wholly or in part, goods previously purchased abroad. The second case constitutes what has been called the import-substitution process. . . .

The evolution of the import coefficient from 1929 onwards in the Latin American countries with the longest-established industries is indicated in Table 4. Estimates are based on GDP and imports series, both at constant prices, taking 1960 as the base year.

In the decade following the crisis, there was a substantial decline in the import coefficient in all the countries mentioned and in the case of Chile it fell dramatically. Of the countries included in the table, Chile is the only one in which the domestic product had not recovered its

Table 5. *Evolution of Industrialisation Coefficient in Selected Countries
(industrial output as % of GDP)*

	Argentina	Mexico	Brazil	Chile	Colombia
1929	22·8	14·2	11·7	7·9	6·2
1937	25·6	16·7	13·1	11·3	7·5
1947	31·1	19·8	17·3	17·3	11·5
1957	32·4	21·7	23·1	19·7	16·2

Table 6. *Intensity of Industrialisation Process in Selected Countries*

	1929–37	1937–47	1947–57	1929–57
Argentina	23	73	50	220
Mexico	46	86	98	407
Brazil	42	82	123	475
Chile	16	9	58	100
Colombia	90	110	130	830

1929 level in absolute terms by 1937. The extremely high degree of its integration into the pattern of world trade—for a country exporting raw materials—and its dependence on imports of food products which would be difficult to replace (tropical commodities and sugar, for instance) made Chile not only the country most violently affected by the crisis but also the one in which the import-substitution process faced the greatest obstacles. The reduction in the import coefficient was made possible by the more than proportional growth of the industrial sector, i.e., the increase in the industrialisation coefficient. Table 5 shows the evolution of the industrialisation coefficient based on the GDP and industrial output series, calculated in 1960 prices.

Chile shows the most significant rise in the industrialisation coefficient in the course of the 1930s. Even so, the rise in industrial output would not be sufficient to account for the considerable decline observed in this country's import coefficient, which also reflects substitution for imports in the agricultural sector, a substantial reduction of investments, and their reorientation with a view to cutting down on their import content. . . .

Table 6 indicates the percentage increases in industrial output in the periods under consideration.

We have already referred to the special features of the Chilean case. Being a mineral-exporting country, Chile's industrial activity was partly integrated with the export sector whether through the processing of ores or the development of by-products. As a result of the sharp decline in these activities during the 1930s, the overall index does not reflect the substitution process that really took place in the manufacturing sector. For example, between 1929 and 1937 the output of cotton textiles was more than quadrupled, that of clothing more than doubled, and that of paper more than tripled. However, the impossibility of curtailing food imports and the need to increase imports of fuels and raw materials, such as cotton, in a phase when the import capacity had been reduced by one-half, account for the slow rate of Chilean industrialisation in the 1930s. It was no doubt partly as a result of these difficulties that the country became aware of the urgent need for State action, designed to introduce changes into the economic structure and to foster the development of the industrialisation process. The creation of the Corporación de Fomento de la Producción (CORFO) in 1939, a government agency that was to provide a model for other Latin American countries ten years later, was the point of departure for the second phase of Chile's industrial development. CORFO was responsible for devising and carrying out an electrification plan, for creating the basis for petroleum production and refining, for establishing a modern steelworks at Huachipato, for developing sugar beet production and fostering the paper industry, and for several other initiatives in the industrial field. Chile is thus less a case of industrialisation based on spontaneous import substitution than of industrialisation fostered by State action designed to surmount the obstacles to the country's economic development created by the disruption of the foreign trade sector.

In the case of Colombia, the fact that industrial development was still at an early stage in 1929 permitted the two phases of the industrialisation process in some ways to overlap. The nature of the export sector, dominated by coffee grown mostly on family holdings, fostered the growth of the home market, leading to the establishment of non-durable consumer goods industries as early as the 1920s. The crisis, acting as an additional protection mechanism, speeded up this process. An elastic domestic supply of foodstuffs, agricultural raw materials, and fuel was another favourable factor. Nonetheless, Colombia's industrialisation coefficient in 1947 still lagged behind the coefficient registered in Argentina, Mexico, and Brazil in 1929. It was in the three latter countries that the import-substitution process revealed its full potential as a factor for stimulating industrialisation.

The 1929 crisis, by initially taking the form of a contraction in the capacity to import, provoked exchange depreciations in these countries. . . . Both these factors (exchange depreciation and inflation) had the effect of raising the profitability of the industrial nucleus geared to the domestic market. The process can be clearly observed in the case of the Brazilian textile industry. This industry, which had undergone remarkable expansion before the First World War, continued to increase its productive capacity in the 1920s. Between 1915 and 1929, the number of spindles in operation increased from 1.5 to 2.7 million and the number of looms from 51,000 to 80,000, an increase reflected in the creation of a relatively large margin of idle capacity.[12] . . . Once [the] first phase of import substitution had run its course, the expansion of this sector became dependent on the growth of overall demand which, in the period that came to an end with the crisis, was closely bound up with the behaviour of the export sector. The existence of unused capacity in the Brazilian textile industry, and the fact that the industry was only very marginally dependent on imported raw materials, enabled it to expand its output rapidly in the period that followed. Thus, between 1929 and 1932 output increased by one-third, and between 1929 and 1939 by two-thirds. This vigorous growth is accounted for by the fact that certain sectors of the market, formerly supplied by imports— particularly of better-quality articles—were now supplied by domestically produced goods. A second factor was the enlargement of the existing market brought about by industrial expansion itself, which raised the level of overall demand. We see here the twin aspects of the substitution process. On the one hand, domestic production improves its competitive position and supplies a wider section of the market; this becomes possible because the level of money demand remains constant while relative prices of imports rise, and because domestic supply has a certain degree of elasticity—otherwise marginal costs would rise, offsetting the fa- vourable effect for the domestic product of the price increase in imports. On the other hand, the development of industrial production creates an additional flow of income which enlarges the domestic market.

Substitution Process and State Action

Import substitution took place only in countries that had already completed the initial stage of industrialisation, i.e., countries that already possessed a significant nucleus of non-durable consumer goods industries. By and large, these industries could make more intensive use of equipment and plant by introducing one or more extra shifts. This made it possible to increase output without further fixed capital investment, that is, without importing additional equipment. In conjunction with this elas- ticity of supply, the other essential condition for embarking on import substitution is the expansion of money income, which should be sufficient to offset the depressive effects of the contraction in export activities on the level of employment. This additional condition was more easily met in countries with a perennial cash crop, such as Brazil, where the government began to buy up coffee stocks, financing this operation with credits provided by the monetary authorities. Where these conditions were met, industrial production expanded rapidly and its profitability increased even faster. Bearing in mind the acute depression of the export sector, it is easy to understand why not only available financial resources but entrepreneurial capacity should have been attracted by industrial activities.

The increase in the output of manufactured non-durable consumer goods that took place at the beginning of the import-substitution process was matched by a rising demand for intermediate products and equipment in general. Given the limited import capacity, costs of industrial inputs tended to rise, opening up new sectors to investment. In countries with considerable metallurgical experience, such as Mexico, or in those where the government's action in promoting basic industries had proved most effective, the import-substitution process was able to continue and extend its range. Comparison of the Argentine, Brazilian, and Mexican experiences illustrates this point. In Argentina, a considerable effort was made, during the 1930s, to maintain the country's credit-worthiness abroad. This required a policy of domestic restraint. Production of import substitutes in the agricultural sector—cotton and other agricultural raw materials—was encouraged, and industrialisation was orientated towards the manufacture of non-durable consumer goods. The concern to defend the level of domestic activity during phases of cyclical depression involved favouring industries with a less elastic demand, i.e., the non-durable consumer goods industries. It was assumed that the demand for consumer durables and equipment could be more easily curtailed as a means of coping with the sharp decline in the country's capacity to import. In other words, Argentina's chief concern was to adapt itself to the unstable conditions prevailing in the world market for raw materials. Mexico's position differed in certain fundamental aspects. In contrast with Argentina, the export sector was controlled by foreigners in the 1920s, which tended to clarify the demarcation line between the interests of the Mexican State and those of the export groups. In the 1920s and early 1930s, the Mexican State was already preparing the ground for far-reaching action in the economic sector, with the creation of the central bank, a government development bank (*Nacional Financiera*), and the Federal Electricity Commission. The expropriation of the petroleum industry in the late 1930s marks the culmination of the crisis between the Mexican State and the powerful foreign groups controlling the country's export activities. Brazil's position was somewhere between that of Argentina and Mexico. In contrast with Argentina, where the exporting interests managed to strengthen their position in the State through the military coup of 1930, in Brazil the position of exporting interests was weakened.[13] However, there was nothing like the dichotomy noted in the Mexican case. The Vargas government, in spite of the defeat of the counter-revolution backed by traditionalist groups in 1932, pursued a policy of compromise with the coffee growers, buying up surplus coffee stocks even when these mostly had to be destroyed. Nonetheless, the acuteness of the crisis in Brazil made it extremely difficult to foster any illusion that the export sector could be restored to its former role. Thus, during the 1930s, the Brazilian government tried to unify the home market by eliminating the surviving trade barriers between states; it created the National Steel Company, which was responsible for building the steel plant at Volta Redonda, and it promoted the training of industrial workers on a nationwide scale.

In the post-war period, the industrialisation process in the three countries under consideration came to depend far more on State action designed to concentrate investment in the basic sectors, on the temporary recovery of the export sector, and on the introduction of foreign capital and technology than on import substitution. However, it was still regarded as import substitution since industrial production was strictly geared to domestic demand and took over markets formerly supplied, albeit on a small scale, by imports. Strictly speaking, new markets were created by the expansion of overall demand that accompanies industrialisation. Since these economies reproduced forms of consumption that already existed in other countries, the supply of a particular commodity was bolstered by imports in the initial stage although this stage tended to become increasingly brief.

In the four countries under consideration—Argentina, Mexico, Brazil, and Chile—industrialisation induced by import substitution is, strictly speaking, a phenomenon of the 1930s and the war period, that is, the period when the decline in the capacity to import permitted the intensive use of an industrial nucleus formed in an earlier period. The fact that industrialisation in these countries was intensified during the depression of the external sector is a clear indication that the process could have started sooner if these countries had had the benefit of appropriate policies. In other words, advance beyond the first stage of industrialisation required economic measures designed to change the structure of the industrial nucleus, and in default of such measures the industrial sectors found themselves in a relatively depressed situation. By creating the conditions for an intensive use of existing capacity and by broadening the demand for intermediate products and equipment, the crisis made it clear that the industrialisation process could only move one stage further if it extended its range. State action, leading to the creation of basic industries, was to open up a third stage in the process of industrialisation in Latin America.

Notes

1. Simon Kuznets, *Modern Economic Growth,* Yale University Press, 1966, p. 286.

2. The coefficient of external trade is defined as the ratio between the average value of imports and exports and the domestic product. For historical data see C. P. Kindleberger, *Foreign Trade and the National Economy,* Yale University Press, 1962, p. 180.

3. The reference to the United States is restricted to the expansion of its agricultural frontier, particularly in the cereal-growing region. By the time the American provinces gained their Independence, they already had a nucleus of manufacturing activities, including iron and steel works and shipbuilding. During the Napoleonic Wars, the United States benefited considerably from her position as a neutral country and became the possessor of the world's second largest merchant fleet, consisting entirely of vessels built in her own shipyards. Modern textile industries were established at the beginning of the nineteenth century and by the 1820s a textile machinery industry had already been set up. On the other hand, the marked increase in cotton exports produced on the basis of slave labour made it possible to maintain a high level of imports, benefiting regions of the country which were in the process of industrialising. The great expansion of agriculture in the Mid-West was supported by the markets provided by the commercial-industrial Eastern region and the region of specialised agriculture in the South. It was the interconnexion of these three dynamic poles—the industrial-commercial complex of the East, the agricultural exporting South and the food producing Mid-West—that gave the U.S. economic system its extraordinary dynamism. Nonetheless, the expansion of the U.S. agricultural frontier, creating large exportable surpluses, had the same stimulating effect on the European economy as the settlement of other empty spaces in the temperate latitudes outside Europe.

4. For basic data see Daniel Cosio Villegas, *História Moderna de México,* VII, *El Porfiriato: Vida Económica,* Mexico, 1965. See also Leopoldo M. Sólis, "Hacia un Análisis General a Largo Plazo del Desarrollo Económico de México" in El Colégio de México, *Demografia y Economía,* I, no. I, Mexico, 1967.

5. Cf. Instituto Brasileiro de Geografia e Estatística, *Anuário Estatístico do Brasil, Quadros Retrospectivos, 1935–40.*

6. Basic data from P. L. Yates, *Forty Years of Foreign Trade,* London, 1959.

7. Cf. C. P. Kindleberger, *Foreign Trade and the National Economy.*

8. Cf. P. L. Yates, *Forty Years of Foreign Trade.*

9. For the basic data, see UN *Yearbook of International Trade Statistics, 1964,* and *Monthly Bulletin of Statistics, Dec. 1967* and *July 1968.*

10. The basic data on industrial production trends and the share of the industrial sector and imports in GDP are taken from ECLA, *El Proceso de Industrialización en América Latina, Anexo Estadístico.*

11. For data on the evolution of the Brazilian cotton textile industry see Stanley J. Stein, *The Brazilian Cotton Manufacture: Textile Enterprise in an Underdeveloped Area, 1850–1950,* Harvard Univ. Press, 1957.

12. In the latter half of the twenties, Brazilian textile manufacturers conducted a vigorous campaign aimed at persuading the government to prohibit imports of equipment. This clearly indicates the impasse reached at the end of the stage in which the growth of the industrial sector failed to effect any significant structural changes in the economy.

13. The 1929 crisis had far-reaching political repercussions in most Latin American countries, in many instances triggering off military takeovers and popular uprisings. However, these political disturbances did not always mean the same thing. In Argentina, for instance, the Unión Cívica Radical, a party essentially representing the middle classes and particularly the urban middle class, had been in power since the 1916 election; the 1929 crisis, by creating the conditions that led to the military *putsch* of 1930, smoothed the path for the restoration to power of conservative groups, bringing together interests connected with foreign trade, land speculation, and stock-raising. A different process occurred in Brazil: with the 1930 revolution, more in the nature of a popular uprising than a military takeover, the coffee oligarchy was ousted from power under pressure from peripheral groups in the Northeast and the South (Vargas was Governor of the State of Rio Grande do Sul). Since the urban middle class was less influential than in Argentina, the displacement of the oligarchy led the Vargas government to move less in the direction of a formal democracy—as was the case in Argentina under the Unión Cívica Radical—than toward an enlightened authoritarianism.

8 / Nationalism and Populism: Social and Political Forces of Development in the Phase of Consolidating the Domestic Market

Fernando Henrique Cardoso
Enzo Faletto

Cardoso and Faletto are probably the most important theorists of the dependency school. Their contributions were published at approximately the same time as Frank's and show a sophistication and a complexity of greater enduring quality than that of Frank. Cardoso and Faletto developed analyses of several patterns of historical development (what they called a "historical-structural" approach) in which domestic economic processes emerging from the dependence on international markets had strong implications for class alliances and, in turn, political regimes and policies. Building on the periodization of economic dependency, analysts such as Furtado and Cardoso and Faletto saw important differences between economies that were dominated by foreign-owned "enclaves" and those that had an ownership that was primarily national. They suggested that different historical processes emerged from these two types of economies as they moved from an outward orientation toward import-substitution industrialization (ISI).

In the selection presented here, Cardoso and Faletto develop a series of paths, of which national populism was the most important, that emerged during the ISI period. They describe how the economic changes that came after the depression gave rise to new class forces—in particular, the emerging industrialists and the growing urban proletariat—that changed the character of national politics and the role of the state in the economic life of each nation. National populism was a historical period in which an alliance of the new bourgeoisie, the middle classes, and the lower classes controlled the state, taking it away from the oligarchy that dominated during the export-oriented period. This state then pursued active economic policies designed both to protect national industries from foreign competition and to incorporate the lower classes into the economy and society.

As we will see, this populist period would become a crucial one for later analyses. Indeed, Cardoso and Faletto described the postpopulist period as one in which the "in-ward" oriented economic policies would lead to economic crises that could only be solved by "opening the market to foreign capital or making a radical political move toward socialism." If the former path was chosen, as it was in most countries, the result would be an increasing "internationalization" of the Latin American market and the rise of a "new dependency." In many ways this analysis foreshadowed the subsequent work of O'Donnell, which we present in our final section.

The distinctive feature of the transition period [of industrialization] in Latin America in the relations among social groups and classes was the growing participation of the urban middle classes and of the industrial and commercial bourgeoisie in the system of domination.

The social situation was expressed on an economic level by policies to consolidate the domestic market and to industrialize. In countries where the export economy was controlled by national groups that had succeeded in forming an important industrial sector *before* the foreign trade crisis [of 1929], these policies took on a more liberal cast. That is, they were based on the expansion of private enterprise. In countries where exports were controlled mainly by an enclave, groups not tied directly to the import-export system had tried to create an urban-industrial base through state direction. In some countries the state apparatus had been used as an instrument in the formation of an industrial class, which eventually would share entrepreneurial functions with the state-owned enterprises.

The private sector was not excluded from economies where state participation was preponderant, nor was the public sector absent in the initial stage of industrialization, even in countries of liberal tradition. On the contrary, the import-substitution phase of industrialization was characterized by two converging movements: growth of the private sector of the economy, and the creation of new areas of investment concentrated around basic industry and infrastructure works with heavy state participation.

Both of these new economic bases of development required broad changes in the social division of work. Countries that began to grow in these ways underwent a demographic-ecological transformation as a proletariat emerged and as a non-wage-earning popular sector developed in the cities. The growth rate of the latter sector usually was higher than the rate at which new jobs were generated by industrialization. This brought about the formation in Latin America of what came to be called "mass urban societies" in insufficiently industrialized economies.

The presence of masses, together with the beginnings of industry that produced more than just nondurable consumer goods, characterized the initial period of inward development. This period intensified during World War II and reached its peak in the 1950s. During this period, industrialization was "substitutive": it was made possible mainly by difficulties of importation and subsequently by lack of foreign exchange. It used and expanded the production base of the preceding period to meet domestic demand for consumer and intermediate goods. In the process, the role of the state increased and changed in character. The state had fundamentally expressed the interests of exporters and landholders and had acted as agent for foreign investment. Now it intervened to set up protective tariffs, to transfer income from the export to the domestic sector, and to create the infrastructure needed to support the import-substitution industry. This was the time of national steel foundries, oil refineries, and electrical power stations.

These measures were taken in some countries only because they were the result of power alliances made during the transition period. Consequently, the industrialization achieved in these cases was not, at the beginning, the result of the gradual or revolutionary ascent of a typical industrial bourgeoisie.

More precisely, this industrialization was the result of a policy, agreed upon by the various sectors, that reconciled the development needs of a type of economy that not only created an economic base for the new groups (later to share power in the transition period) but also offered opportunities of socio-economic incorporation to the popular groups which because of their number and presence in the cities might otherwise alter the system of domination. The system of domination comprised the ascendant middle classes, the urban bourgeoisie, and sectors of the old export-import system, even including the owners of low-productivity latifundia.

During "substitutive" industrialization the agro-exporting and financial sectors as well as the urban middle and industrial sectors shared and disputed control of the state. Appearing in some cases as the object of domination and in others as the supporting base were the popular sectors made up of their three typical components: the working class, the urban popular mass, and the peasant mass.

The different agreements reached in the various countries by the social forces meant that each country would have its own set of substitutive industrialization policies even when different countries shared the same economic or socio-political problems. These differences were largely related to the ways in which economies and national societies had been formed. The functions of the state and the characteristics of the entrepreneurial groups varied in the transition period according to whether or not the original situation had been one of the enclave. Later on, when the presence of masses became important in determining the forms of domination, there would also be differentiation in terms of the particularities of the popular sector of each country.

The masses were generally oriented toward participation and social and economic distributivism. The new dominant sectors generally favored continued national economic expansion, now directed to the domestic market. Their trend to nationalism made possible incorporation of the masses into the production system and, to varying degrees, into the political systems. The connection thus established gave meaning to "developmentalist populism." This ideology expressed conflicting interests: expanded consumption versus accelerated investment in heavy industries, state participation in development versus reinforcement of the private urban-industrial sector. An ideology like "developmentalist populism," in which contradictory goals could coexist, was an attempt to achieve a reasonable consensus and to legitimize the new power system based on an industrialization program offering benefits for all.

The creation of a domestic market required (1) availability of capital to be reinvested within the country; (2) availability of foreign exchange to finance industrialization; (3) possibilities of income redistribution, even if limited, to permit some degree of incorporation of the masses; (4) public and private managerial ability to expand the domestic economy; (5) a minimum of efficiency and responsibility in state administration; (6) a political leadership capable of reconciling the conflicting interests of the different groups in the interest of the "nation."

Actually, since availability of capital and foreign exchange was in the hands of the exporting group, the above scheme could only be realized by mobilizing the industrial bourgeoisie, the state bureaucracy, and the worker-popular sectors against the interests of the former. The success of such a mobilization depended, on the one hand, on a favorable outlook for prices in the world market that would permit policies to maintain the value of exports while carrying out some form of exchange control. On the other hand, given the developmentalist alliance between the industrialist sectors and the worker-popular sectors, it also depended on tariff and monetary policies that would keep up the rate of industrial investment and simultaneously ensure at least an absolute increase in the number of individuals incorporated from the popular sectors into the industrial system, even if it failed to increase real wages and affected the agrarian sector and the traditional middle groups adversely. Thus the groups that tried to control the decision-making process to obtain a pattern of more distributivist development clashed with those that influenced public agencies to reorient price and fiscal policies toward capitalization of private and public enterprises.

History determined how these conditioning factors of industrialization combined, and how they then devised models of development. Nevertheless, by taking liberties with hallowed concepts we can speak of models of hierarchies of variables.

The distinctive features of industrialization policies in each country depended on how the roles of the state and of the industrial bourgeoisie were reconciled. The economic functions of the state were important, but so was the way in which the state, as an instrument of domination, expressed the interests of various groups.

The masses, already important in this period, were needed for the process of industrialization, as a labor-force but also as an integral part of the consumer market. They had to be taken into account by the groups in power to the extent that they ensured or rejected the latter's hegemony.

The industrial bourgeoisie, whether in an enclave economy or where production was controlled by national groups, typically appeared in the different countries in one of the following ways:

1. "Liberal" industrialization directed by private entrepreneurial sectors; this required the existence of a vigorous and hegemonic agro-exporting sector that was in some way also linked to the domestic market.

2. "National-populist" industrialization oriented politically by the drive of social forces like the bourgeoisie, the middle sectors, and the popular (trade union) sectors, and linked to the power apparatus. Together

with the agro-exporting sector (even if in conflict with it), these forces shared to some extent the direction of the process of development.

3. Industrialization oriented by a "developmentalist state," a process in which the weakness of a domestic capitalist export-import sector was offset by a state program that through a tax system channeled investment and established the bases for an industrial economy. This case appeared more often in the enclave situation.

In all cases, the problem of industrialization consisted in knowing which groups could take investment and market decisions and channel investment into the domestic market. It was, moreover, extremely difficult to incorporate—popular as well as low middle class—socially by industrialization. This was why nationalism and populism together expressed the attempts by developing societies to harmonize the interests of groups that were opposed to each other but that united among themselves for the purpose of finding a new base for national power.

Countries to be considered in the following pages are preferably those in which the characteristics of industrialization were more striking or showed more clearly the various possible alternatives.

Populism and the Free Enterprise Economy

In Argentina, both the phases of outward development [Ed. note: i.e., export-oriented] and the period of transition expressed the dynamism of a hegemonic entrepreneurial agro-exporting sector. The system of domination embraced groups that were differentiated at the regional level. Therefore, when the effects of the crisis in world markets began to be felt and World War II intensified the conditions favoring industrialization, an industrial bourgeoisie already existed. It was linked to the agro-exporting sector through the financial system. There was also a middle class that was part of the political game and was capable of mobilizing, at least electorally, the urban popular sectors. The unionized-worker sectors tried to obtain their own representation chiefly through their unions and in some cases in association with parties such as the socialist one, especially in large urban centers like Buenos Aires and Rosario.

The dynamism and success of the exporting sector permitted the creation of an industrial sector dependent on it, and also a strong financial importing sector. These were the groups that undertook to develop the economy by taking advantage of the favorable prospects for the domestic market derived from economic prospects after the depression and especially during World War II. Politically their problem was to keep control of the expanding economy and, at the same time, to contain the worker-union pressure represented by the guild associations dating from the turn of the century. To this was added the pressure of the radical *Irigoyenismo* of the middle classes. During this period in Argentina there were also efforts to form a popular front (1944–1945) similar to those established in Europe and in Chile. Although unsuccessful, such efforts highlighted the class content of the political confrontation between a dominant bourgeoisie and a worker opposition. Nor were they unrelated to a postwar reaction against segments of the Argentine Right that had been overtly sympathetic to the Axis cause.

Nevertheless, the continued class domination—which eventually excluded all opposition—together with the dynamism of the economy, led to a dead end. The new contingents that were constantly being mobilized and incorporated into the labor force required by economic expansion were not being incorporated politically. Nor were they represented in the old trade union structure, where their presence, although broadening the base of worker policy, would have endangered the economic advantages already achieved. This situation was to end in the breakdown of both the exclusive bourgeois domination and the union structure of the old sectors of the working class.

Peronist populism tried to find a solution to such problems and to give continuity to economic growth by respecting the impetus of the private enterprise sector but setting a general course to accelerate incorporation of the masses not only economically but also socially and therefore politically. The state became arbitrator for the class struggle and was used as a mechanism for income distribution both within the entrepreneurial class and downward.

Conflicts among the various sectors—principally between the worker-popular mass and the bourgeoisie—were expressed mainly as a confrontation between popular sectors and oligarchy without any specific political content beyond an abstract anti-foreign sentiment on the international level and pressure for higher wages. Why then did this confrontation appear crucial to the political reorientation of Argentina?

The agro-exporting groups exercised their hegemony in alliance with rural sectors that were basically of two types: the latifundista groups not directly linked to the exporting sector, and the rural sectors allied with but subordinate to the exporting sector. In Argentina the former were residual because of their low level of investment in agriculture, but the second were significant. They included farmers producing for the domestic market, rural bourgeoisie not linked to the agro-exporting sector, those that raised but did not fatten beef cattle, and finally grain farmers not linked to the marketing groups. The hegemonic group itself was made up precisely of the local sectors tied to the import-export scheme, which was basically foreign and increasingly monopolistic.

The hegemonic group of the agro-exporting sector was, through its investments in the domestic market, dynamic and developmentalist; on the other hand, it was the nexus of dependence. The new power coalition represented by *Peronismo* would be effective if it could reconcile the accumulation interests of the economically dominant sector with the participation interests of the expanding masses. Thanks to the foreign exchange accumulated during World War II, it was possible to improve wages and social conditions of the worker-popular sector and of middle-class white-collar workers without doing too much damage to the economically hegemonic sector of the previous stage, although certainly affecting the latter's subordinate sectors, the estancieros and the traditional urban middle class. These sectors, which in political language would be called the "oligarchy," were increasingly to pay the cost of the new power combination as the favorable balance of the export economy was depleted. They also were to bear the brunt of the political criticism of a system of power that was accused of being reactionary and in which they had hardly participated.

Industrialization under *Peronismo* followed two complementary courses: on the one hand, the import-export and financial sectors tried to regulate the impulse of industrialization in a way that could slow down and limit the policy of import substitution, at least in those products that were of interest to the hegemonic sector in its importing phase; on the other hand, the industrial sector not linked to the agro-exporting group tried to strengthen its economic base by expanding the area of substitutive industrialization and creating its own financing mechanisms, traditionally a weak point in this group. The state was a vital institution for both sectors: for the first, because it still controlled the exchange and tariff systems, which were fundamental to a balanced policy of industrial and agro-exporting interests; and for the second, because the state also represented an important instrument of credit and rapid capital formation.

In this development model the various social forces did not exert sufficient pressure to transform the state from an instrument of economic regulation into one directly promoting production. The already existing former economic base permitted private sectors to diversify the domestic economy without the public sector becoming an indispensable part of the production system. To create an industrial economy, private accumulation required only the state to redistribute income into its own investment channels. The resulting growth would generate employment opportunities at the rate adequate to incorporate the urban mass into the economic system.

This development model was possible because the economy was dynamic enough to convert the agricultural worker into a wage earner and to expand rapidly enough to absorb a large part of the rural-urban migration. Migration was accompanied by strong socio-political pressures that, nonetheless, were not directed toward creating a state production base to control economic decisions. Even when pressure for redistribution led to direct economic action by the state, the result was to reinforce the private sector because of the corporative linkage between the bourgeoisie and the new state enterprises.

The presence of masses was felt as a pressure of those who wanted to enter the system as a new partner accepting the already established rules on how industrialization was to be carried out, but who still demanded certain rights. There was strong pressure for higher wages and recognition of the rights of workers. But this did not exclude the possibility of combining the interests of different groups in the new power coalition. The masses were mobilized principally through the unions, and more as an employed mass than as an oppressed class. Their mobilization symbolized the policy of confrontation and of pooled interests through which the popular sectors established their relations with the industrial bourgeoisie. Jointly, these two sectors no longer acted precisely as allies of the monopolistic agro-exporting group, but all three certainly participated in the same power game and together formed a power coalition. So fluid and complex a political connection was made possible by their agreement not to make economic claims for the state; private monopoly was not to be threatened by state monopoly. This arrangement was favored by the prosperity that followed on World War II and by the rapid process of import substitution, which not only expanded mass consumption and raised wages but also capitalized industrial enterprises without lowering the profits of the monopolies.

This development was limited by the progressive exhaustion of the economic process of rapid import substitution of nondurable and durable consumer goods. It was also limited by the contradiction in giving the masses greater participation in the distribution of national revenues while accelerating capital formation and trying to maintain the incomes of other social groups and, especially, of the agro-exporting sectors.

With the end of the easy phase of import substitution and of populist support within the framework of a liberal economy, reciprocal connections were undone. Simple theories began to give way to polemics over statism versus big business. This issue was to be the crossroads of development. The earlier schemes of political support fell apart, and the apparent polarization of oligarchy and popular sectors that had been cloaked by the "developmentalist alliance" was replaced by a new type of confrontation where certain class values served to catalyze popular behavior and, at the same time, to weaken national emphasis on the activities of the entrepreneurial groups. The latter proceeded to reorganize themselves, and tried to reorganize the state, to express not only their political interests as they related to the interests of the popular sectors, but also and more directly their own specific economic interests.

Populism and National Development

The development model in Brazil was different. Here the phase of outward expansion did not consolidate a hegemonic entrepreneurial sector that was strong and modern enough to neutralize the power of the traditional agricultural sectors, still less to unify the popular, rural, and urban sectors as a wage-earning mass. When substitutive industrialization began in the transition period, power was still in the hands of traditional oligarchy—a term used loosely to cover various segments of the exporting sector and of the non-exploiting latifundista groups. It was also shared with the middle groups with access to control of the state, the industrial bourgeoisie, and the urban merchants.

In Brazil, unlike in other countries that followed a liberal pattern of industrialization, the state emerged as an instrument not only to regulate the industrial system but also to directly participate in it through the creation of public enterprises, autarchic and state-controlled. In Brazil, unlike Argentina, a large sector of nonworker urban masses was added to the lesser weight of the worker sector. This difference became even more marked in the presence of a broad sector of rural masses living in a situation totally removed from that of the popular masses.

Populism appeared in Brazil as the link between the new scheme of power and the urban masses, who were either mobilized by industry or driven to the city by the decline of the agrarian sector. It was to change into a policy by which the masses participated politically in a relatively limited way, owing to their weak union structure. This policy affected neither the rural masses nor the whole of the urban popular sector.

Brazil lacked an agro-importing sector (that is, an economic sector limiting agro-export interests with trade import of industrial goods) that would have generated a significant subsidiary industrial economy. Substitutive industrialization was achieved, on the one hand, by direct state action and, on the other, by an industrial bourgeoisie largely unconnected with the agro-exporting sector. Not only did the state promote and even create the traditional branches of basic industry, it also participated in the initial development of industries of consumer durables such as automobiles, as well as industries of intermediate products such as cement or steel. These industrialization policies followed a line of "economic nationalism." How could this type of orientation occur in a power situation where the basic political alliance embraced such diverse sectors—some of them very traditional—as landholding groups, urban popular sector, middle classes, and entrepreneurial groups of industry and commerce?

The answer is partly that the existing *private* groups capable of capitalizing industrial development were in a weaker economic position than in Argentina, for example, and were thus unable to impose a liberal industrialization policy. As industrialization gained momentum the agro-exporting groups lost control of the state apparatus to groups without common interests that could be satisfied through development of a liberal type.

The groups that reached power after 1930 were influenced more by political than by economic considerations in pursuing industrialization. Had they been influenced by economic considerations, they would have been concerned with forming a domestic market that would stimulate development and lead to self-sustained growth. But it was only at a later date—when industrialization was well under way—that they became interested in a policy of this kind. So the state's industrialization policy was not just thrust on it by the force of economic circumstances—it was a political decision.

Government participation in the emergence of an industry can be explained politically by the existence of masses that were mobilized without effective employment having been created to absorb them. This caused a dangerous situation for those who held power. In an urbanizing country with an agrarian economy in decline and a capitalist sector unable to respond rapidly to massive employment requirements, it was imperative that development be made a national undertaking—that is, one in the interest of all the people—and that the state be charged with leading the nation to prosperity.

The alliance that was to carry out the new policy incorporated at the outset the most backward groups of landholders, the farmers who produced for the domestic market, the urban middle class, the already existing industrial sectors, and the urban mass. Not included were the agro-exporting groups (coffee growers) that had controlled the system before the 1930 revolution, or the rural masses. Although the former were to join the "developmentalist alliance" later, the peasants were to be permanently excluded.

Domestic development in Brazil was supported politically by groups with conflicting interests. To create modern economic sectors capable of employing the masses, it was necessary to make a political alliance with the most backward sectors of the Brazilian production structure, the non-exporting latifundistas. On the other hand, the viability of such a policy of domestic development came to depend precisely on a division between the urban mass that benefited from development and the rural mass that was marginal to it. The system of accumulation and economic expansion—given their limited rate of growth—could not withstand the wage pressures that would result from incorporating broad rural sectors into the labor market. Moreover, the political strength of the landholding sectors depended on preventing the rural mass from receiving the benefits of economic, political, and social participation. Since the "developmentalist alliance" encompassed the hacendados, the alliance would be shattered by incorporating the peasants.

It was the excluded sectors that would pay the costs of industrialization. In the early stages, industrialization depended on the power of the state to tax the exporting sector and to exclude the rural and urban masses. Eventually, the export sector became diversified, and certain groups within it began to participate in development by reorienting their capital toward production for the domestic market. Nonetheless, because the rural mass continued to be isolated from the benefits of development, it constituted one of the structural limits to the political possibilities of development. Attempts to expand the "developmentalist alliance" with such groups were counterproductive, and populism could not be used as a base for legitimizing power.

The populism of Vargas was a rather vague movement of people's incorporation into the nation, but without entailing, as in the case of Perón, stronger trade unions and increased pressure for higher wages. It was less an economic definition of workers' rights, which would imply political participation, than a political movement in favor of the "humble." Since the emerging worker class was diluted in the urban mass, the need to accumulate capital did not seem to be much opposed to the pressures for redistribution during the phase of substitutive industrialization. Populist leadership could also be entrepreneurial; hence the state appeared not only as employer but also, from the viewpoint of the masses, even as a good employer. At the economic level, popular protest could be taken care of because it was relatively weak; at the political level, it coincided with the interests of groups that, having reached power without a solid economic base of their own, were in favor of development under state direction.

Even if this alliance favored nationalism and statism, it did not in any way exclude participation of the private sector, which—as the market was consolidated by the state—increasingly invested in the domestic economy. The private sector also needed the state as an instrument of bank-credit allocation and of income redistribution. But once the industrial sector was supported by a broader economic base and could get capital not only from the export sector but also from abroad, pressures rose against the inefficiency of the state as entrepreneur and against populism as a development policy. These pressures could be resisted by the urban middle classes, by the entrepreneurs who feared competition from efficient private monopolies, and by the private sectors organized around the state. But as soon as it became clear that intermediate and capital goods production and heavy industry would be controlled by either the state or big business (private monopolies), it was apparent that the populist scheme was too fragile to frustrate the hegemonic designs of the private groups. As the process of import substitution began to require better technology, higher accumulation, and more efficiency, this became even clearer. Thus, populism and nationalism gave way to other social forces and to another political orientation of development.

It should be mentioned that the state was again briefly able to make populism its political line after the domestic market, now dominated by national and foreign private enterprise, had begun to be developed. The policy of the Goulart government was to try to broaden its base of support by organizing and incorporating peasant sectors as well as by expanding participation and economic benefits for the urban popular sector. Such an effort only demonstrated the impossibility of reconciling interests now clearly contradictory. Not only did it split off the apex of the nationalist-developmentalist alliance, the bourgeois and landholding sectors that were still committed to it, but it also jeopardized accumulation, mainly in the public sector: its social costs were high enough to put a drain on investment. Thus the limits of populism as a form of mobilization of the masses and as a development policy were reached.

The Developmentalist State

In an enclave economy, the domestic market expanded in the process of development. This transition required the state to allow broader political participation of the middle class and to enlist the support of the popular sectors for such a reorganization. In this sense, both the new industrial sectors and the popular sectors were either engaged in or associated with the state. The state promoted industrialization because the industrial sectors needed a mechanism of rapid capital accumulation, but it also did so because these industrial sectors represented an alliance between workers and middle groups, the middle groups being made up principally of the bureaucracy and the beginnings of the new bourgeoisie. This alliance could be maintained only by creating and expanding employment opportunities for the masses.

Such a situation occurred in Mexico and Chile. In Chile, for example, the urban economic sector that had formed in the previous phase continued to be important enough to try to control development or to use the favorable prospects for development for its own advantage. The popular sectors, because they were already established and organized, could try to impose their participation in development policies. In other words, the conflicts or alliances in the Chilean situation always involved class interests. There follows a discussion of how, in both Mexico and Chile, alliances and confrontations helped consolidate a policy of industrialization.

Industrialization in Mexico

The new political power created by the Mexican Revolution (1910–1920) was seriously weakened by economic elements that the Revolution did not change. The basic sectors of the economy, transport,[1] mining, petroleum, and electric power, remained in the hands of foreign companies that were strong enough to restrain the Mexican government. Because of the destruction of the previous agrarian power structure, the peasants, although fervent defenders of the Revolution, were too dispersed to constitute a solid economic base for the revolutionary process. Nor could the workers, with their parallel and fragmented trade unions, bargain successfully with the foreign companies, much less contribute to government stability. The weakness of the system, then, was reflected in its lack of structure for political support from workers and peasants, and in the pressures put on it by an economy that was controlled from abroad.

The only way for the government to reinforce its position against the foreign companies was to organize and unite the worker-peasant movement. Having carried out this policy, Cárdenas (1934–1940) was able to challenge the foreign companies in the petroleum industry, which resulted in its nationalization.

The state, with popular support, began industrialization in Mexico. But its socialistic orientation alarmed not only foreign investors but also vast sectors of the national economy. Although everyone agreed on the need for industrialization, how and by whom was not clear. The relative national unity created by the revolutionary process was in jeopardy. A formula for industrial development was finally arrived at that welcomed foreign investment within limits set by the state. This policy was initiated by Avila Camacho and continued by Alemán. It was hoped that the economic development resulting from industrialization would make it possible to meet popular demands rapidly. Therefore, a large part of the industry established was subsidiary to the United States, which made investments in Mexico that benefited from the guarantees and facilities granted by the state itself. Foreign investment flowed not only into industry but also into the financial and commercial sectors; the state saw to it that the new market was advantageous and, without intending to, helped create conditions for monopolistic operations.

The state continued to develop the basic structure and to ensure the best market conditions. It required only that industrial investors produce within the country. However, not only industrial activity but also agriculture began to attract foreign investment. The agrarian reform, and especially the ejidos, had provided the Revolution with political support. Now it became necessary also to integrate agriculture into an economic policy. The state carried out investments that improved agricultural productivity, but it began to favor the more capitalist sectors among the farmers, owing to the pressure it was under to create an agricultural base quickly. As had occurred in industry, foreign investment was encouraged in agriculture in order to accelerate development. The typical example was the cotton economy, where through market mechanisms the most developed groups began to dominate the noncapitalist producers.

A very close relationship was established between those who controlled the state politically and the new economic sectors. In this way, the fortune of the former came to depend on the growth capacity of the modern economic groups, both private and public. Nonetheless, it should be pointed out that urban popular sectors did not remain marginal. Perhaps the foregoing partly explains the continuance of a complex alliance among the most disparate social sectors.

The Chilean Case

After the 1929 crisis in nitrate, employment could only be maintained by state subsidies. With nitrate being replaced by chemical fertilizer on the world market, the foreign companies began to dismantle their plants. If balance was to be restored, a new economic structure had to be created to sustain it. During this period, the government took measures to expand or in some cases to create the industrial sector. The economic measures devised for this purpose were far from elaborate, but they had important effects. Perhaps the most far-reaching policy was that of exchange control, which forced the old importing sectors to invest their available capital in the national sphere, thereby creating industries that would replace former imports. Therefore, the state began to promote public works and other activities in order to generate employment; there could be no hope of resolving the existing unemployment by limited actions taken by the entrepreneurial sector. The creation of an import-substitution industry, and the direct intervention by the state to guide the economy, were two important consequences of the 1929 crisis.

Perhaps because of the weakness of the power structure, which only looked for new economic bases of support, politics appeared more often as a confrontation than as an alliance. The popular sectors were organized, had political representation, and were crucial elements for any new agreement. The middle sectors, especially those that in some way depended on the state, were also organized, and they aspired to an alliance that would permit them to share in power. The Popular Front (1937) sealed this possible alliance; to the middle and popular sectors were added some stronger economic and social groups that hoped to improve their position within the new order. With political power in its hands, the Popular Front began in 1939 a deliberate planning of the national economy through CORPO (Corporation to Promote Production), in which the state took an active part. One external factor, World War II, favored and to some degree even imposed the new policy by making it necessary to replace imports. Nevertheless, although the intention had been to plan the economy on a large scale, more work was done to create new activities, such as industrial development, electric power, and basic industries, than to modify existing activities.

In agriculture, a policy was proposed to diversify crops for export purposes, but this policy implied no change in the land tenure system and therefore none in the social order it supported. For industry the goal was to help form an industrial bourgeoisie through bank credits. Many industries, even those of foreign origin, could be installed and operated thanks to the facilities and guarantees furnished by the state. With renewed vigor, certain sectors of the existing bourgeoisie began to invest their capital in industry and to reinforce the commercial sector. The middle sectors, which largely managed the state apparatus, found in the revitalized bourgeoisie an ally that permitted them to resist popular and worker pressures. The development program promoted by this alliance was based on the willingness of the state to grant the new group bank credits and favorable conditions to operate in the market.

On the other hand, the external sector, now totally controlled by the United States, recovered. Copper replaced nitrate, and the state could count on revenue from this sector. Nevertheless, this recovery signified a slowdown in industrial development. The rate of growth in this sector declined, and in that sense there was stagnation.

Displacement of the popular sector as an ally produced serious political conflicts resulting in direct repression of the workers and especially the breakdown of their organized expression through the 1948 Ley de Defensa de la Democracia (Law of Democratic Defense). The middle sectors, by their turnabout, also left themselves in an extremely weak position with their recent allies. A new effort was made to reestablish their alliance with the popular sector, but in the absence of the political organizations that had formerly represented the various social sectors, the alliance as adopted took the form of a completely amorphous populism.

This populism—the first phase of the second government of Ibáñez—was of short duration, ending almost before the year was out. Its principal difficulty was to find a way to end Chile's runaway inflation. Orthodox measures to try to stabilize the situation were advised by the Klein-Sacks Mission and also were made a condition for external credit. With this policy the government lost its initial popular support.

The chaos of populism had an unexpected consequence in the restructuring of the political organizations representing the dissident factions. After the disappearance of populism, the new government thus clearly had a new socio-political character; the industrial, financial, and agrarian sectors bent their efforts to gain control of the domestic market. But they no longer did this through the state and even returned state economic activities to private capital. From a socio-political standpoint, the most notable feature of the regime of Jorge Alessandri (1958–1964) was the political polarization between the various social sectors.

Notes

1. Although the Diaz government created a national administration for much of the Mexican railroad system, substantial parts remained under the control of foreign-owned companies.

9 / Feudalism and Capitalism in Latin America

Ernesto Laclau

Although dependency analysis was inspired in part by Marxism and although several of the original thinkers of the school called themselves Marxists, many orthodox Marxists were quite critical of the theory. One of the most influential of these orthodox Marxists is Ernesto Laclau, an Argentine political scientist at the University of Essex in England, whose arguments heralded the "modes of analysis" approach. Laclau takes on the dependency approach through a critique of Frank and therefore does not address the more sophisticated thinkers like Cardoso and Faletto, although some of his criticism could be applied to them as well. His central argument is that Frank has a mistaken definition of capitalism, having overemphasized the importance of trade and commerce while having underestimated the mode of production—the way society is organized to produce goods. Laclau suggests that a more accurate analysis would seek to define the mixture of feudal, slave, and capitalist ways of producing goods, rather than simply lumping all these disparate modes of production under the single rubric of capitalism. The most significant implication of this greater complexity in analysis is that the optimism of Frank and others, who believed that socialism was the next historical stage (since capitalism was already well-established), was unfounded. Laclau implies that the options for the future of Latin America are not to be reduced to such simplistic formulae but rather will emerge from a long and complex process of class struggle in various mixed modes of production. Since Laclau's writing might be especially difficult for readers not accustomed to Marxist terminology, we have added an appendix with a brief overview of pertinent Marxist concepts.

Debate on the left in the last decade over the origins and present nature of Latin American societies has focused on the problem of whether they should be seen as feudal or capitalist in character. A complex and lengthy discussion has taken place whose importance is not diminished by the conceptual confusion which has often accompanied it. Its significance, moreover, has not been confined to theory, since different theories have led to different political conclusions. Those who maintain that the Latin American societies were historically constituted as feudal in character and have remained so ever since, wish to emphasize that they are closed, traditional, resistant to change, and unintegrated into the market economy. If this is the case, then these societies have still not yet reached a capitalist stage and are, indeed, on the eve of a bourgeois-democratic revolution which will stimulate capitalist development and break with feudal stagnation. Socialists should therefore seek an alliance with the national bourgeoisie and form a united front with it against the oligarchy and imperialism. The advocates of the opposite thesis claim that Latin America has been capitalist from its inception, since it was already fully incorporated into the world market in the colonial period. The present backwardness of Latin American societies is precisely the outcome of the *dependent* character of this incorporation and they are in consequence fully capitalist. It is therefore meaningless to postulate a future stage of capitalist development. It is, on the contrary, necessary to fight directly for socialism, in opposition to a bourgeoisie that is completely integrated with imperialism, forming a common front against the masses.

In this article I hope to contribute to a clarification of the basic terms of the polemic.[1] For despite their contradictory appearance, both the positions first cited coincide in one fundamental respect: both designate by "capitalism" or "feudalism" phenomena in the sphere of commodity exchange and not in the sphere of production, thus transforming the presence or absence of a link with the market into the decisive criterion for distinguishing between the two forms of society. Such a conception is clearly alien to Marxist theory, which maintains that feudalism and capitalism are, above all, *modes of production.* Andre Gunder Frank is one of the best-known defenders of the thesis that Latin America is and always has been capitalist.[2] For this reason the present essay will concentrate on his work since it raises the theoretical issues at stake in the debate in their sharpest and clearest form.

Reprinted with permission from the *New Left Review,* Vol. 67 (May-June, 1971), pp. 19–38.

Frank's Theoretical Scheme

Frank's theoretical perspective can be summed up in the following theses:

1. It is false to suppose that economic development occurs through the same succession of stages in each country or that the underdeveloped nations today are at a stage which has been long surpassed by the developed countries. On the contrary, today's developed capitalist countries were never *under*developed in this way, although there was a time when they were *un*developed.

2. It is incorrect to consider contemporary underdevelopment as a simple reflection of the economic, political, cultural, and social structures of the underdeveloped country itself. On the contrary, underdevelopment is in large part the historical product of relations between the underdeveloped satellite and the present developed countries. These relations were, moreover, an essential part of the structure and evolution of the capitalist system on a world scale. Thus Frank declares: "To extract the fruits of their labour through monopoly trade—no less than in the times of Cortez and Pizarro in Mexico and Peru, Clive in India, Rhodes in Africa, the 'Open Door' in China—the metropoli destroyed and/or totally transformed the earlier viable social and economic systems of these societies, incorporated them into the metropolitan dominated world-wide capitalist system, and converted them into sources for its own metropolitan capital accumulation and development. The resulting fate for these conquered, transformed, or newly acquired established societies was and remains their decapitalization, structurally generated unproductiveness, ever increasing misery for the masses—in a word, their underdevelopment."[3]

3. The conventional "dualist" interpretation of Latin American societies must be rejected. The dualist analysis maintains that underdeveloped societies have a dual structure, each one of whose sectors has a dynamic of its own, largely independent of the other. It concludes that the sector which is under the sway of the capitalist world has become modern and relatively developed, while the other sector is confined to an isolated, feudal or pre-capitalist, subsistence economy. According to Frank, this thesis is quite erroneous; the dual structure is wholly illusory, since the expansion of the capitalist system during the last centuries has effectively and completely penetrated even the most apparently isolated sectors of the underdeveloped world.

4. Metropolitan-satellite relations are not limited to the imperial or international level, since they penetrate and structure economic, social, and political life in the dependent Latin American countries, creating sub-metropoles within them to which the interior regions are satellites.

5. From the above propositions, Frank derives the following combination of hypotheses: (1) In contrast to the world metropolitan centres which are not satellites, the development of the subordinate metropoles is limited by their satellite status; (2) the satellites experienced their greatest economic development, including their classical industrial capitalist growth, only when their links with the metropolitan centres were weakened, as was the case during the Spanish Depression of the seventeenth century, the Napoleonic Wars at the beginning of nineteenth century, the Depression of the 1930s, and the two World Wars in the twentieth century; by contrast these impulses to development were extinguished whenever the metropolitan centres recovered economically; (3) those regions presently most underdeveloped were in the past those most tightly linked to the metropolis; (4) the latifundia, whether in the form of plantations or haciendas, were originally typically capitalist commercial enterprises, which themselves created the institutions which enabled them to respond to growing demand in the international and national market by expanding the aggregate of their capital, land, and labour in order to increase their supply of their products; (5) latifundia which today are isolated, engaged in subsistence agriculture, and apparently semi-feudal were not always so, but were sectors that underwent a drop in the demand for their output or their productive capacity.

6. Whenever dualism is introduced into a Marxist analysis the implication is that feudalism comprises a conservative sector at one end of the social structure and capitalism a dynamic sector at the other end of it. The strategic consequences are then clear: "Both in the bourgeois and the supposedly Marxist version of the dual society thesis, one sector of the national economy, which is claimed to have once been feudal, archaic, and underdeveloped as well, took off and became the now relatively developed advanced capitalist sector, while the majority of the population stayed in another sector which supposedly remained as it was in its traditionally archaic, feudal, underdeveloped state. The political strategy usually associated with these factually and theoretically erroneous interpretations of development and underdevelopment is for the bourgeois the desirability of extending modernism to the archaic sector and incorporating it into the world and national market as well, and for the Marxists the desirability of completing the capitalist penetration of the feudal countryside and finishing the bourgeois democratic revolution."[4]

Against this, Frank maintains that Latin America has been capitalist since its very colonization by European powers in the sixteenth century. His proof is to show by numerous examples that even the most apparently remote and isolated regions of Latin America participated in the general process of commodity exchange and that this change was to the advantage of the dominant imperialist powers. It would only be appropriate to speak of feudalism, according to Frank, if it could be proved that the most economically backward regions of Latin America constituted a closed universe in which a natural economy predominated. Given that, on the contrary, they participated in a process whose motor force was the thirst for riches of the dominant classes and powers, it is only possible to conclude that we are in the presence of a capitalist economic structure. Since the colonial conquest, capitalism has been the basis of Latin American society and the source of its underdevelopment; it is therefore absurd to propose as an alternative to it a dynamic capitalist development. The national bourgeoisie, in those cases where it exists, is so inextricably linked to the imperialist system and to the exploitative metropolitan/satellite relationship, that policies based on alliance with it can only prolong and accentuate underdevelopment. The national-bourgeois phase in the underdeveloped countries must in consequence be eliminated, or at least abbreviated, rather than extended in the name of the existence of a dual society.

It can be seen that Frank's theoretical schema involves three types of assertion: (1) Latin America has had a market economy from the beginning; (2) Latin America has been capitalist from the beginning; (3) the dependent nature of its insertion into the capitalist world market is the cause of its underdevelopment. The three assertions claim to refer to a single process identical *in its essential aspects* from the sixteenth to the twentieth century. We will analyse in turn each of these aspects.

The Critique of Dualist Conceptions

Frank's criticism of the dualist thesis and his consequent insistence that Latin American societies have always constituted a complex internally structured by, and fully integrated into, market economy are indisputably convincing and correct. Here Frank has developed the cumulative critique of that dualism which received its most celebrated formulation in the work of W. A. Lewis.[5] According to Lewis, who expressed a standpoint to be found in numerous partial studies by social scientists of the previous decade, it was necessary to distinguish carefully between the "capitalist" sector and the "subsistence" sector of the economy. The latter was presented as completely stagnant and inferior to the former in capital, income, and rate of growth. All relations between the two were reduced to the provision by the backward sector of an unlimited supply of labour to the advanced sector. It has been now repeatedly shown that this model underestimates the degree of commercialization which is possible in rural areas, as well as the degree of accumulation in peasant enterprises. It furthermore greatly over-simplifies and distorts the relations which exist between the two sectors of the economy which it presupposes. A more refined knowledge of the inter-connections between the different sectors of the Latin American econ-omies makes the dualist thesis today no longer tenable in its initial formulation.

Moreover, in the concrete case of Latin America, the evidence accumulated over recent years has completely undermined the idea that a pure, natural economy is to be found in the rural areas of the continent. On the contrary, everything appears to suggest that even the most backward peasant regions are bound by fine threads (which have not yet been adequately studied) to the "dynamic" sector of the national economy and, through it, to the world market. Alejandro Marroquin in an excellent book[6] has made a regional study of this system of relations. Rudolfo Stavenhagen, analyzing the Maya zone of Chiapas and Guatemala Heights, has shown how inter-ethnic relations serve as the basis for class relations based precisely on a widespread incorporation into the market.[7] Moreover, in Latin America during the colonial period— so often referred to as a phase of closed economy—a wide circulation of commodities prevailed, the axis of which were the mining regions, while the marginal zones were organized as sources of consumption products. In the South of the Continent, for example, the central nucleus was the consumption area of Upper Peru near the Potosi mines, while Chile was transformed into a wheat producer and the Argentinian interior provided manufactured goods for this central nucleus. It is hard to conceive such regional specialization as a pure, natural economy.

The idea of a society with dual structures has a long tradition in Latin America. It was initially formulated in the nineteenth century by the liberal elites which integrated their countries into the world market as primary producers, thus accommodating them to an international division of labour dictated by the metropolitan imperialist countries. The formula "civilization or barbarism," coined by Sarmiento, became the watchword of this process. It was necessary to use every means to discredit the reaction of those interior regions whose relatively diversified economies disintegrated under the impact of competition from European commodities. For this purpose liberal spokesmen created a mythology according to which everything colonial was identified with stagnation and all things European with progress: in this Manichean image of the historical dialectic, coexistence between both segments of society became impossible.

This ideological tradition was to prove a heavy impediment to any adequate understanding of the processes which have formed Latin American societies and we cannot say that it has been entirely superseded even today. Much ground has still to be covered by social, economic, and anthropological investigation in order to reconstruct the hidden channels of commercialization by which apparently closed economic zones were linked with world markets, and the economic surplus collected from the direct producers. Frank is therefore on solid ground when he criticizes theories of dualism and affirms the predominance of the market economy in Latin America. But can we accept his second assertion, that these economies are capitalist?

The Theoretical Mistakes in Frank's Conception

It is not so easy to answer this question since, although his two books are dedicated to the analysis of capitalism, at no time does Frank explain exactly what he means by it. The closest we get to a conceptual characterization in his work is in such expressions as the following: "Capitalism's essential internal contradiction between the exploiting and the exploited appears within nations no less than between them."[8] But this does not take us very far, since not only capitalism, but feudalism and indeed every class society has been characterized by the contradiction between exploiters and exploited. The problem is to define in each case the specificity of the exploitative relationship in question. This lack of rigour in determining the object of his analysis is, moreover, only one example of the conceptual imprecision from which all Frank's work suffers; an imprecision that is all the more serious in that Marxists should be well aware of the extensive debates that have occurred over the concept of capitalism,[9] a term which can by no means be taken for granted.

If we nevertheless try to infer what Frank understands by capitalism, I think we can conclude that it is approximately the following: (1) a system of production for the market, in which (2) profit constitutes the motive of production, and (3) this profit is realized for the benefit of someone other than the direct producer, who is thereby dispossessed of it. On the other hand, by feudalism we should understand a closed subsistence economy. The existence of a substantial market therefore constitutes the decisive difference between the two.

The first surprising thing is that Frank totally dispenses with *relations of production* in his definitions of capitalism and feudalism. In the light of this, his earlier characterization of the relationship between exploiters and exploited as the fundamental contradiction of capitalism ceases to be so puzzling. For, in effect, Frank's ideological perspective obliges him deliberately to omit the relations of production from his definition of capitalism; only by abstracting them can he arrive at a sufficiently wide notion of capitalism to include the different exploitative situations suffered by the indigenous Peruvian peasantry, the Chilean *inquilinos,* the Ecuadorian *huasipungueros,* the slaves of the West Indian sugar plantations, or textile workers in Manchester. For all these direct producers assign their produce to the market; they work for the benefit of others, and they are deprived of the economic surplus which they help to create. In all these cases the fundamental economic contradiction is that which opposes the exploiters to the exploited. The only trouble is that the list is too short, for it could also have included the slave on a Roman *latifundium* or the gleb serf of the European Middle Ages, at least in those cases—the overwhelming majority—where the lord assigned part of the economic surplus extracted from the serf for sale. Therefore, we could conclude that from the neolithic revolution onwards there has never been anything but capitalism.

Of course, Frank is at liberty to abstract a mass of historical features and build a model on this basis. He can even, if he wishes, give the resulting entity the name of capitalism, though we cannot see much point in using, to designate such a variety of relations, words which are normally employed in a different sense. But what is wholly unacceptable is the fact that Frank claims that his conception is the Marxist concept of capitalism. *Because for Marx—as is obvious to anyone who has even a superficial acquaintance with his works—capitalism was a mode of production.* The fundamental economic relationship of capitalism is constituted by the free labourer's sale of his labour-power, whose necessary precondition is the loss by the direct producer of ownership of the means of production. In earlier societies the dominant classes exploited the direct producers—that is, expropriated the economic surplus they created—and even commercialized part of this surplus to the extent of permitting the accumulation of large *capitals* by the commercial class. But there was not *capitalism* in the Marxist sense of the term, since no free labour market existed. The following quotation from *Capital* makes this clear:

> . . . otherwise with capital. The historical conditions of its existence are by no means given with the mere circulation of money and commodities. It can spring into life only when the owner of the means of production and subsistence meets in the market with the free labourer selling his labour-power. And this one historical condition comprises a world's history. Capital, therefore, announces from its first appearance a new epoch in the process of social production.[10]

For Marx, the accumulation of commercial capital is perfectly compatible with the most varied modes of production and does not by any means presuppose the existence of a capitalist mode of production:

Hitherto we have considered merchant's capital merely from the standpoint, and within the limits of, the capitalist mode of production. However, not commerce alone, but also merchant's capital, is older than the capitalist mode of production, is, in fact, historically the oldest free state of existence of capital. . . .

. . . The metamorphosis of commodities, their movement, consists: (1) materially, of the exchange of different commodities for one another, and (2) formally, of the conversion of commodities into money by sale, and of money into commodities by purchase. And the function of merchant's capital resolves itself into these very acts of buying and selling commodities; yet this exchange is not conceived at the outset as a bare exchange of commodities between direct producers. Under slavery, feudalism, and vassalage (so far as primitive communities are concerned) it is the slave-owner, the feudal lord, the tribute-collecting state, who are the owners, hence sellers, of the products. The merchant buys and sells for many. Purchases and sales are concentrated in his hands and consequently are no longer bound to the direct requirements of the buyer (as merchant).[11]

Frank's claim that his conception of capitalism is the Marxist one seems to be based on nothing more than his desire for this to be the case. But before leaving this point let us return again to the texts, because, in a polemic that occurred in Mexico and is reflected in his second volume, he was accused *precisely* of ignoring the mode of production in his definition of capitalism. Frank replied with two quotations from Marx which, he claimed, proved his case. The first quotation is taken from the *History of Economic Doctrines* and affirms:

In the second class of colonies—the plantations, which are from the moment of their inceptions, commercial speculation, centres of production for the world market—a regime of capitalist production exists, if only in a formal way, since slavery among the negroes excludes free wage-labour, which is the base on which capitalist production rests. However, those who deal in slave-trading are capitalists. The system of production introduced by them does not originate in slavery, but was introduced into it. In this case the capitalist and the landlord are one person.

According to Frank, this paragraph proves that for Marx it is not the relations of production that define the nature of an economy (at least I deduce as much since it is his answer to Rodolfo Puiggros's question as to what "happened inside colonies such as Brazil and those in the Caribbean, that is, where the mode of slave-holding prevailed?"). In reality, the quotation proves exactly the reverse of what Frank intends, since what Marx says is that in the plantation economies the dominant mode of production is only formally capitalist. It is formally capitalist because its beneficiaries participate in a world market in which the dominant productive sectors are already capitalist. This enables the landowners in the plantation economy to participate in the general movement of the capitalist system without, however, their mode of production being capitalist. But what is the essential condition for such a situation is its exceptional character. I think this will be very clear if we compare the paragraph quoted by Frank with another passage by Marx, from *Pre-Capitalist Formations*:

> However, this error is certainly no greater than that of, e.g., all philologists who speak of the existence of *capital* in classical antiquity, and of Roman or Greek capitalists. This is merely another way of saying that in Rome and Greece labour was *free,* an assertion which these gentlemen would hardly make. If we talk of plantation owners in America as capitalists, if they *are* capitalists, this is due to the fact that they exist as anomalies within a world market based upon free labour.[12]

Did the structural conditions of capitalism exist in sixteenth-century Europe when, according to Frank, the process of capitalist domination started in Latin America? Could we consider free labour to be the rule then? By no means. Feudal dependence and urban handicrafts remained the basic forms of productive activity. The existence of a powerful commercial class which greatly enlarged its stock of capital through overseas trade did not in the least modify the decisive fact that this capital was accumulated by the absorption of an economic surplus produced through labour relationships very different from those of free labour. In a classic article, Eric Hobsbawm has located the seventeenth century as the period of general crisis in the European economy which marked the point of transition towards the capitalist system. As far as the expansion of the fifteenth and sixteenth centuries is concerned, however, he affirms on the contrary that:

> Under certain circumstances such trade could, even under feudal conditions, produce a large enough aggregate of profits to give rise to large-scale production; for instance if it catered for exceptionally large organizations such as kingdoms or the church; if the thinly spread demand of an entire continent were concentrated into the hands of businessmen in a few specialized centres such as the Italian and Flemish textile towns; if a large "lateral extension" of the field of enterprise took place, e.g., by conquest or colonization. . . .
>
> The expansion of the fifteenth and sixteenth centuries was essentially of this sort; and it therefore created its own crisis both within the home market and the overseas market. This crisis the "feudal businessmen"— who were the richest and most powerful just because the best adapted

for making big money in a feudal society—were unable to overcome. Their inadaptability intensified.[13]

Frank, on the contrary, maintains that European expansion was thoroughly capitalist from the sixteenth century onwards. He corroborates his assertion with a second quotation from Marx in which the latter declares: "The modern history of *capitalism* begins with the creation, in the sixteenth century, of world trade and a world market." But this time Frank happens to have transcribed the quotation badly. In the original, Marx, in fact declares, that: "The modern history of *capital* dates from the creation in the sixteenth century of a world-embracing commerce and a world-embracing market."[14]

Given the distinction emphasized above between *capital* and *capitalism*—which permits the coexistence of commercial capital with earlier modes of production—the meaning of this passage is totally different. Marx only says that the enlargement of the world market during the sixteenth century, brought about by overseas expansion, created the conditions and the global framework in which the *modern* expansion of capital could take place. He takes for granted that anterior forms of capital existed—e.g., in the Middle Ages or in antiquity. But he by no means speaks of capitalism.

The errors of Frank's conception can be seen from the fact that he has defined capitalism so loosely that he is unable legitimately to derive any concrete consequences from it about anything. This is, of course, not his own belief; he is confident that he can demonstrate on this ground the irrelevance of the bourgeois-democratic stage in Latin America. Let us consider this demonstration. Frank's basic assertion is that since the task of the bourgeois-democratic revolution is to destroy feudalism, whereas capitalism has always existed in Latin America *ab initio,* the bourgeois democratic revolution disappears from the revolutionary calendar, and is replaced by a direct struggle for socialism.

But Frank has again confused the terms of the problem. For when Marxists speak of a democratic revolution sweeping away the vestiges of feudalism, they understand by feudalism something very different from Frank. For them feudalism does not mean a closed system which market forces have not penetrated, but a general ensemble of extra-economic coercions weighing on the peasantry, absorbing a good part of its economic surplus, and thereby retarding the process of internal differentiation within the rural classes, and therefore the expansion of agrarian capitalism. This is also what the French revolutionaries of 1789 understood by feudalism when they thought they were suppressing it by abolishing the *gabelles* and seigneurial privileges. When Lenin speaks of the growing weight of capitalism in the agrarian structure of

Russia in *The Development of Capitalism in Russia,* his aim is to demonstrate a growing process of class differentiation which was gradually producing a class of rich peasants, on the one hand, and an agricultural proletariat, on the other. It would not have occurred to Lenin to base his demonstration of this process on a progressive expansion of production for the market, for such production had *precisely* formed the source of feudalism in Russia several centuries before, when growing opportunities for commercialized wheat production had led the landowners to increase—indeed to establish—the oppression of serfdom. When the Bolsheviks maintained that the tasks of the Russian Revolution were bourgeois-democratic, they meant that it would eliminate the vestiges of feudalism and open the door to capitalist expansion (in 1905 only Trotsky and Parvus grasped that Russian conditions made possible the inauguration of the direct transition to socialism). Given the inability of the bourgeoisie to carry through its democratic tasks and the numerical weakness of the proletariat, they imagined that the peasantry would have to play a decisive role in the alliance which seized power. For such a strategy, it was crucial that the peasant problem could not be solved by the existing régime, since otherwise Tsarism could have built its own road to capitalism and the revolution would have been postponed *sine die.* Stolypin, the Tsarist Minister who used every device to promote the emergence of a strong class of peasant proprietors to become a bulwark of reaction—somewhat similar to the French peasantry from Napoleon I to de Gaulle—understood this as well as the Bolsheviks. The danger of his policy was clearly perceived by Lenin when he wrote in 1908:

> The Stolypin Constitution and the Stolypin agrarian policy mark a new phase in the breakdown of the old, semi-patriarchal and semi-feudal system of Tsarism, a new movement towards its transformation into a middle-class monarchy. . . . If this should continue for very long periods of time . . . it might force us to renounce any agrarian programme at all. It would be empty and stupid democratic phrase-mongering to say that the success of such a policy in Russian is "impossible." It is possible! If the Stolypin policy is continued . . . then the agrarian structure of Russia will become completely bourgeois, the stronger peasants will acquire almost all the allotments of land, agriculture will become capitalistic, and any "solution" of the agrarian problem—radical or otherwise—will become impossible under capitalism.

This passage limpidly illustrates the conditions in which Lenin considered capitalist development could remove the bourgeois-democratic stage from the agenda of the revolution—exactly the problem with which Frank is grappling. These conditions were the mergence of a strong kulak class at one extreme, and the growth of a rural proletariat on the other. Frank's denial of the possibility of a bourgeois-democratic revolution in Latin America in effect only amounts to this: he takes a political schema based on an analysis of social relationships respectively designated feudalism and capitalism, he modifies the content of these concepts in mid-stream and then concludes that the political schema is false because it does not correspond to reality. There is no need to insist on the validity of this type of reasoning. (Let me add that I am in no way concerned here to assess the possibility or impossibility of a bourgeois-democratic stage in the various countries of Latin America. I have limited myself to pointing out the impossibility of formulating any prognosis on this question on the basis of Frank's analysis.)

Furthermore, if we took Frank's definitions of capitalism and feudalism literally, we would have to derive much more from them than Frank claims. In fact if capitalism had already become general in the metropolitan countries by the sixteenth century—and it is not clear why he stops there when trade and a market economy prevailed from much earlier times—we would have to conclude that Elizabethan England or Renaissance France were ripe for socialism, something I do not think even Frank himself would be prepared to suggest.

If we now confront Frank's affirmation that the socio-economic complexes of Latin America have been capitalist since the Conquest Period (bearing in mind that capitalism and feudalism are modes of production in the Marxist sense of the term) with the currently available empirical evidence, we must conclude that the "capitalist" thesis is indefensible. In regions with dense indigenous populations—Mexico, Peru, Bolivia, or Guatemala—the direct producers were not despoiled of their ownership of the means of production, while extra-economic coercion to maximize various systems of labour service—in which it is impossible not to see the equivalent of the European *corvée*—was progressively intensified. In the plantations of the West Indies, the economy was based on a mode of production constituted by slave labour, while in the mining areas there developed disguised forms of slavery and other types of forced labour which bore not the slightest resemblance to the formation of a capitalist proletariat. Only in the pampas of Argentina and Uruguay, and in other similar small areas where no indigenous population had previously existed—or where it had been very scarce and was rapidly wiped out—did settlement assume capitalist forms from the beginning, which were then accentuated by the massive immigration of the nineteenth century. But these regions were very remote from the dominant pattern in Latin America and were more akin to the new settlements in temperate zones like Australia and New Zealand.

Now this pre-capitalist character of the dominant relations of production in Latin America was not only *not* incompatible with production for the world market, but was actually intensified by the expansion of the latter. The feudal regime of the haciendas tended to increase its servile exactions on the peasantry as the growing demands of the world market stimulated maximization of their surplus. Thus, far from expansion of the external market acting as a disintegrating force on feudalism, its effect was rather to accentuate and consolidate it. Let us take an example from Frank's analysis: the evolution of *inquilinaje* (a form of leasehold) in Chile. During the seventeenth century, the tenant obtained lease of his lands in lieu of a symbolic payment, but this payment began to acquire economic significance and to weigh ever more heavily on the peasant holding as wheat exports to Peru developed following the earthquake of 1688. The nineteenth century witnessed an aggravation of this process, determined yet again by the increased cereal exports; the labour exacted was often equivalent to that of a permanent worker while the traditional rights of the peasant were simultaneously reduced, especially his right to *talaje* or pasturage. The money wage he now obtained was lower than that of a day labourer or a journeyman. It would be a mistake to see in this process the emergence of a rural proletariat. If this had been the case the wage should have become the major part of the *inquilinos'* means of subsistence. But all the signs show that, on the contrary, the wage was merely one subordinate element in a subsistence economy based on land tenancy. That is to say, we are faced with a peasant subjected to servile obligations and not with an agricultural wage-earner who completes his income with customary privileges and a piece of land.[15]

This situation—with some variations—was repeated monotonously throughout the Continent. Thus Latin America was not an exception to the process by which heavily settled marginal regions experienced a strengthening of servile relations to increase production for external markets. This is what Eastern Europe progressively experienced from the sixteenth century onwards, when a substantial growth in the export of primary products to the West became possible. This process was the basis for the re-feudalization of peripheral areas, the "second servitude" of which Engels speaks. No doubt from the end of the nineteenth century these conditions were gradually modified in Latin America with the progressive growth of a rural proletariat. It is difficult to say how far peasant proletarianization has reached in different areas today, since we lack sufficient studies of it, but there is no doubt that the process is very far from being concluded, and semi-feudal conditions are still widely characteristic of the Latin American countryside. There is no need whatever to draw dualist perspectives from this position, because we have already seen that the basis of the modern, expanding sector was provided by increased servile exploitation in the backward sector.

We now reach the point where the fundamental misunderstanding in this polemic rests: *to affirm the feudal character of relations of production in the agrarian sector does not necessarily involve maintaining a dualist thesis.* Dualism implies that no connections exist between the "modern" or "progressive" sector and the "closed" or "traditional" sector. Yet we have argued that, on the contrary, servile exploitation was accentuated and consolidated by the very tendency of entrepreneurs—presumably "modern" in type—to maximize profits; the apparent lack of communication between the two sectors herewith disappears. In such cases we can affirm that the modernity of one sector is a function of the backwardness of the other, and that therefore no policy is revolutionary which poses as the "left-wing" of the "modernizing sector." It is, on the contrary, correct to confront the system as a whole and to show the indissoluble unity that exists between the maintenance of feudal backwardness at one extreme and the apparent progress of a bourgeois dynamism at the other. I believe that in this way we can effectively demonstrate, in agreement with Frank, that development does generate underdevelopment, except that we base our reasoning on relations of production and not only on those of the market. Frank can, nevertheless, argue that the defenders of the "feudal" thesis—notoriously the Latin American Communist Parties—have upheld dualist positions. There is undoubtedly much truth in this. For in their interpretation of the nature of the Latin American economies, the "feudalists" have employed definitions of feudalism and capitalism similar to Frank's own. It would take too long to explain the reasons for this deformation now, but I believe they can be summed up in this fact: historically, the Latin American left emerged as the left wing of liberalism and its ideology was correspondingly determined by the basic categories of the liberal elites of the nineteenth century, which we have already outlined. Dualism was an essential element in this system of categories. From this source there derived a constant tendency to identify feudalism with stagnation and closed economy, and capitalism with dynamism and progress. This typical deformation of Marxism then generated its dialectical complement in the diametrically opposite position that has emerged during the last decade. Since knowledge of historical and present reality made it increasingly evident that the Latin American economies had *always* been market economies, and since the political failure of reformist and allegedly progressive elites in Latin America revealed ever more clearly the intimate interconnections between "modern" and "traditional" sectors, a new school concluded that Latin America had always been capitalist. Frank and those who think like him—and there are many—accept the terms of the dilemma as the Latin American CPS and nineteenth-century liberals have posed them, but they place themselves at the opposite extreme. They thus undoubtedly break with dualism—and their point of view is therefore relatively more correct—*but by trying to situate the fundamental contradiction in the field of circulation rather than production they can go no more than half-way towards an explanation of why development generates underdevelopment.* This becomes very clear once we move on to analyse Frank's third type of assertion, to which we have previously referred: those [hypotheses] according to which the origins of underdevelopment lie in the dependent character of Latin American economic insertion into the world market. But before dealing with this point, it is necessary to introduce a greater degree of precision into the analytic categories we will use by distinguishing in particular between modes of production and economic systems.

Modes of Production and Economic Systems[16]

We understand by "mode of production" an integrated complex of social productive forces and relations linked to a determinate type of ownership of the means of production.[17] From among the ensemble of relations of production, we consider those linked to the ownership of the means of production to be the essential relations, since they determine the forms of canalization of the economic surplus and the effective degree of the division of labour, the basis in turn of the specific capacity of the productive forces for expansion. Their own level and rhythm of growth depends in turn on the destination of the economic surplus. We therefore designate as a mode of production the logical and mutually coordinated articulation of: (1) a determinate type of ownership of the means of production; (2) a determinate form of appropriation of the economic surplus; (3) a determinate degree of development of the division of labour; (4) a determinate level of development of the productive forces. This is not merely a descriptive enumeration of isolated "factors," but a totality defined by its mutual interconnections. Within this totality, property in the means of production constitutes the decisive element.

An "economic system," on the other hand, designates the mutual relations between the different sectors of the economy or between different productive units, whether on a regional, national, or world scale. When, in Volume One of *Capital,* Marx analysed the process of production of surplus value and the accumulation of capital, he described the *capitalist mode of production.* On the other hand, when he analyses the interchange between Department One and Department Two and introduces problems such as rent or the origin of commercial profit, he is describing an "economic system." An economic system can include, as constitutive elements, different modes of production—provided always that we define it as a whole, that is, by proceeding from the element or law of motion that establishes the unity of its different manifestations.

The feudal mode of production is one in which the productive process operates according to the following pattern: (1) the economic surplus is produced by a labour force subject to extra-economic compulsion; (2) the economic surplus is privately appropriated by someone other than the direct producer; (3) property in the means of production remains in the hands of the direct producer. In the capitalist mode of production, the economic surplus is also subject to private appropriation, but as distinct from feudalism, ownership of the means of production is severed from ownership of labour-power; it is what permits the transformation of labour-power into a commodity, and with this the birth of the wage-relation. I believe it is possible within this theoretical framework to situate the problem of dependence at the level of relations of production.

The Stages of Dependence

Frank refers throughout his works to the relation of dependence between satellite and metropolis; indeed this is the axis along which his theoretical schema is organized. Nevertheless, throughout his writings there is no attempt whatever to define the nature of this relationship of dependence—that is, to situate the specific economic contradictions on which the relationship of dependence hinges. Frank describes for us a situation in which the underdeveloped country is totally integrated into the expansive processes of the great metropolitan countries; he then shows us *how* the advanced countries have exploited the peripheral countries; what he at no time explains is *why* certain nations needed the underdevelopment of other nations for their own process of expansion. The most he provides on this point is a vague general reference to Paul Baran's *The Political Economy of Growth.* But as we know, Baran deals with a very specific situation of underdevelopment, which we cannot extrapolate into the past and which is becoming constantly less applicable today to contemporary Latin America. Or does Frank believe that Baran's model is applicable to such countries as Argentina, Brazil, or Mexico—the three most important areas of investment in the continent, after Venezuela, for North American imperialism?

It is not very difficult to find the reasons for this notable gap in Frank's theoretical schema. For his notion of capitalism is so wide that, given the level of abstraction on which he moves, he cannot define any contradictions that are specific to it. If Cortes, Pizarro, Clive, and Cecil

Rhodes are all one and the same, there is no way of tracing the nature and origins of economic dependence in relation to production. If, on the other hand, we cease to regard capitalism as a *Deus ex Machina* whose omnipresence frees us from all explanatory problems, and try instead to trace the origins of dependence in concrete modes to production, the first step we must take is to renounce all talk of a single unique contradiction because relationships of dependence have always existed on the margins of the existence of capitalism.

During the Middle Ages, for example, advances in historiographic studies have made it clear that an unequal exchange existed between Western Europe and the Eastern Mediterranean. Ashtor's works on prices in medieval Syria, in particular, show that the latter were stationary while prices in Western Europe were oscillating with a long-term tendency to rise. This disjuncture provided a channel of absorption of economic surplus for the Western bourgeoisies from their Eastern periphery. Since economic dependence means the constant absorption by one region of the economic surplus of another region, we must categorize medieval trade between East and West as a relation of dependence, because the disparity in price levels—the basis of any commercial activity—was always to the advantage of one against the other. Yet this activity, which greatly stimulated the accumulation of commercial capital in the great European cities, by no means implied the generalisation of wage relationships in the sphere of production. On the contrary, it corresponded to a feudal expansion, in which servile ties were very often reinforced to maximise the surplus. Was not the European expansion of the mercantilist epoch perhaps an extension of this process on a world scale? Through its monopoly positions, metropolitan Europe fixed the price of commodities in its overseas empires—with the aim of securing a permanent disparity in its favour—while, by means of extra-economic coercion, it exploited labour-power in the mines and plantation systems. Romano asks: "Can the problem of disparity of prices, observed between different regions of the Near East, find an explanation, an attempted explanation, in the light of the example of Spanish America? Might not these zones of lower price levels be the fate of sub-colonies, such as are so often found in the Spanish Empire in America: for example, Chile and Peru were both colonies of Spain, yet the first was also the sub-colony of the second?"[18] It is thus possible to see how the development of the dominant economic structure of the metropolitan countries in the mercantilist epoch could generate underdevelopment: reducing the economic surplus of the peripheral countries and fixing their relations of production in an archaic mould of extra-economic coercion, which retarded any process of social differentiation and diminished the size of their internal markets.

This type of dependent relationship is nevertheless very different from that which was to predominate in the specifically capitalist epoch of European expansion. For this is where the central problem arises. Because if we want to show that in this epoch, too, development generates underdevelopment, what we have to prove is that the maintenance of pre-capitalist relations of production in the peripheral areas is an inherent condition of the process of accumulation in the central countries. At this point we enter territory where unfortunately empirical investigation is too inadequate to permit our reaching any definitive conclusion[19]; nevertheless I believe we can legitimately formulate a theoretical model which establishes the variables at play and the form of their articulation to which the available evidence points. This theoretical model can be summarized in the following terms. The process of capital accumulation—which is the fundamental motor force of the ensemble of the capitalist system—depends on the rate of profit. Now the rate of profit is in its turn determined by the rate of surplus-value and the organic composition of capital. A rise in the organic composition of capital is a condition for capitalist expansion, since technological progress is what permits the reconstitution of the reserve army of labour and the maintenance of a low level of wages. But unless a rise in the organic composition of capital is linked to a more than proportional increase in the rate of surplus value, it will necessarily produce a decline in the rate of profit. This tendency is partially compensated by capital movements from industries with a high organic composition to those with a low organic composition: from this there emerges an average rate of profit which is always higher in value terms than the corresponding rate of profit in the technologically more advanced industries. Nevertheless, since a growing augmentation in the organic composition of the total capital is inherent in capitalist expansion, in the long term there can only be a permanent tendency for the rate of profit to decline. These are, of course, the terms of the famous law formulated by Marx.

It will be seen that in this schema—which describes precisely enough the dominant tendencies at work in a free competitive capitalism—what seems to be the key to a sustained process of accumulation is the expansion, in any sector of the system, of productive units in which either low technology or super-exploitation of labour makes it possible to counteract the depressive effect on the rate of profit of the increasing organic composition of capital in the dynamic or advanced industries. Now the enterprises of the peripheral areas are in an ideal position to play this role. Let us take the example of plantations or haciendas. In these the organic composition of capital is low[20]—as is always the case in the production of primary products as against industrial output; the labour force is in general subjected to the forms of extra-economic coercion characteristic of the feudal or slave modes of production; finally, to the extent that free labour exists, it is generally superabundant and therefore cheap.[21] If it could then be proved that investment in these sectors has played an important role in determining the rate of profit, it would follow that the expansion of industrial capitalism in the metropolitan countries necessarily depended on the maintenance of pre-capitalist modes of production in the peripheral areas. However it is at this point that the evidence so far available becomes suggestive, but not conclusive. If this thesis were established it would be possible by starting strictly from relations of production to show that development generates underdevelopment and to refute, from a Marxist perspective, the traditional dualist schema.

Returning, then, to our previous terminology, we can affirm that the world capitalist system—which finds it regulating principle in the average rate of profit produced by the interaction between different enterprises—includes, *at the level of its definition,* various modes of production. For if our previous line of argument is correct, the growth of the system depends on the accumulation of capital, the rhythm of this accumulation depends on the average rate of profit, and the level of this rate depends in its turn on the consolidation and expansion of pre-capitalist relationships in the peripheral areas. The great flaw in pure underconsumptionist theories is that they interpret external expansion as a response to the pressure for markets; they thereby overlook the decisive fact that colonial exploitation, by helping to raise the average rate of profit, ensures the system's capacity for expansion not only at the moment of *realisation* but also at the moment of *investment.*

This is as far as we can go by purely theoretical argument. The above assertions are subject to two series of empirical verifications. It will be necessary to demonstrate: (1) that during the nineteenth century the growth in the organic composition of capital was in fact more rapid than the growth in the productivity of labour; (2) that the capital invested in peripheral countries played an important role in the maintenance of an adequate rate of profit in the metropolitan countries. Only empirical investigation can prove that both these conditions existed in reality.

On the other hand, if these conditions did exist in the past, there is no doubt that they no longer apply today.[22] The enormous increase in the productivity of labour in the present stage of monopoly capitalism—related to technological changes—has tended to make pre-capitalist super-exploitation of labour power anti-economic, and to concentrate investment in the central countries. At the same time—Latin America is a clear example of this—imperialist investment has tended to shift from its traditional patterns into the production of either strategic materials—the typical case is oil—or into industrial output. The nature of the relationship between metropolis and satellite—to use Frank's terminology—is no less one of dependence, but it operates in each case as a very distinct type of dependence. It seems to me more useful to underline these differences and discontinuities than to attempt to show the continuity and identity of the process, from Hernan Cortes to General Motors.

Returning, then, to the debate over "feudalism vs. capitalism," I think it should by now be clear that its protagonists have constantly confused the two concepts of the *capitalist mode of production and participation in a world capitalist economic system*. I consider that the distinction between these concepts is not a purely academic matter since, if the foregoing argument is correct, it enables us to clarify important aspects of the ensemble of relationships between metropolis and satellite. On the other hand, to equate the two can only perpetuate the misunderstanding that haunts Frank's contribution to the debate. The final comment on the traditional form of the polemic can perhaps best be left to Marx himself. In a celebrated reflection on the economists of his day he wrote a passage that has still not lost its relevance:

> The first theoretical treatment of the modern mode of production—the mercantile system—proceeded necessarily from the superficial phenomena of the circulation process as individualised in the movements of merchant capital, and therefore grasped only the appearance of matters. Partly because merchant's capital is the first free state of existence of capital in general. And partly because of the overwhelming influence which it exerted during the first revolutionising period of feudal production—the genesis of modern production. The real science of modern economy only begins when the theoretical analysis passes from the process of circulation to the process of production.[23]

Notes

1. This article develops some ideas which I have earlier explored in "Feudalism and Capitalism as Categories of Historical Analysis" (Internal publication of the Institute Torcuato Di Tella), Buenos Aires, 1968.

2. Andre Gunder Frank, *Capitalism and Underdevelopment in Latin America,* New York, 1967, and *Latin America: Underdevelopment and Revolution,* New York, 1969.

3. *Latin America: Underdevelopment and Revolution,* p. 225.

4. Ibid., p. 225.

5. W. A. Lewis, "Economic Development with Unlimited Supplies of Labour," *Manchester School,* May 1954, pp. 139-191, and idem., *Theory of Economic Growth,* London, 1955. A summary of the criticisms that Lewis's model have aroused can be found in Witold Kula, *Theorie Economique du Systeme Feodal,*

Paris, 1970, pp. 9–12. Cf. also P. T. Bauer, "Lewis's Theory of Economic Growth," *American Economic Review,* XLVI, 1956, 4, pp. 632–641.

6. Alejandro Marroquin, *La Ciudad Mercade* (*Tlaxiaco*), Mexico, 1957.

7. Rudolfo Stavenhagen, "Clases, colonialismo y aculturacíon. Ensayo sobre el sistema de relaciones inter-etnicas en Mesoamerica," *América Latina,* Año 6, No. 4, Octubro–Diciembre 1963, pp. 63–104.

8. *Latin America: Underdevelopment and Revolution,* p. 227.

9. See, for example, Maurice Dobb, *Studies in the Development of Capitalism,* London, 1946, Chapter I, and R. H. Hilton, "Capitalism—What's in a Name?" *Past and Present,* Number I, February 1952, pp. 32–43.

10. Karl Marx, *Capital,* Vol. I, Moscow, 1959, p. 170.

11. Ibid., Vol. III, pp. 319–321.

12. Marx, *Pre-Capitalist Economic Formations,* London, 1964, pp. 118–119.

13. E. J. Hobsbawm, "The Crisis of the 17th Century," *Past and Present,* No. 5, May 1954, p. 41.

14. Marx, *Capital,* Vol. I, ed. cit., p. 146.

15. In an unpublished note that the author has kindly made available to me, Juan Martinez Alier has pointed out that on the haciendas of the Peruvian Sierra, where the formal elements of extra-economic coercion—such as *corvée* in economic and *gamonalismo* in political relations—have not disappeared, they have nevertheless been transformed to the extent that the peasants' land hunger is now an instrumental end and not an end in itself: land hunger now stems in reality from hunger for employment. He adds: "The aim of a classical jacquerie is to throw off the boss: that is to say, to recover full possession of the land, to get rid of the obligation to pay rent, and as a result, to change the political structure of the distribution of power. The aims of a struggle by peasants with a proletarian mentality will be, on the other hand, to obtain higher pay and greater security, and for these goals the acquisition of land or its take-over by the State can seem appropriate means. If we think . . . that, for the non-wage earning peasant of the Sierra who has gone to work in the haciendas, the principal problem is security of employment, then the possibilities of locating an agrarian structure which permits later socialist development are greater than if we think that the possession of the land is an end in itself for the peasants."

Martinez Alier here points out one of the ways in which a process of proletarianisation can effectively start. Nevertheless, the operation of this process presupposes the concurrence of two conditions: (1) that there is a progressive loss of ownership of the means of production; (2) that another optional system of employment, subject to cyclical fluctuations, is permanently available. Otherwise we should have to maintain that where the demand for service labour is lower than the supply, coercion is economic and not extra-economic, and that therefore the serf is a proletarian and not a peasant. But this situation was a frequent occurrence during the European Middle Ages in periods of rising population, which enabled the lords to intensify the services due to them. On the other hand, periods of declining population—such as that which followed the Black Death in the fourteenth century—enabled the peasants to improve their negotiating position vis-à-vis the lord. The situation described by Martinez

Alier only exists when land has become simply one possible field of employment alongside others. In all other cases, we cannot speak of a dissociation in the peasant's consciousness between the land as a source of employment and the land as an end in itself.

16. What follows is a resumé of arguments advanced in my study mentioned above (See footnote 1).

17. Oscar Lange, *Economia Politica*, Roma, 1962.

18. Ruggiero Romano, "Les Prix au Moyen Age: Dans le Proche Orient et dans l'Occident Chretien," *Annales E.S.C.*, Juillet-Aout 1963, pp. 699–702.

19. See, however, the information contained in the essays by Cristian Palloix, "Imperialisme et mode de production capitaliste" in *L'Homme et la Societe*, 12, Avril-Juin 1969, pp. 175–194, and Samir Amin, "Le Commerce International et le Flux Internationaux de Capitaux," ibid., 15, Janvier-Mars 1970, pp. 77–102.

20. Under feudalism the ownership of the means of production by the direct producer is an obstacle to technical progress. Under a slave mode of production the tendency of the slave to destroy the machine creates barriers to investment of constant capital. See Marx, *Capital*, Vol. I, pp. 196–197, where several examples are cited, and Manuel Moreno Fraginals, *El Ingenio*, La Habana, 1964.

21. The importance of this fact was already noted by Marx, who nevertheless did not analyse its relative weight in the formation of average rate of profit: "Another question—really beyond the scope of our analysis because of its special nature—is this: Is the general rate of profit raised by the higher rate of profit produced by capital invested in foreign, and particularly colonial, trade?

"Capital invested in foreign trade can yield a higher rate of profit, because, in the first place, there is competition with commodities produced in other countries with inferior production facilities, so that the more advanced country sells its goods cheaper than the competing countries. In so far as the labour of the more advanced country is here realised as labour of a higher specific weight, the rate of profit rises, because labour which has not been paid as being of a higher quality is sold as such. The same may obtain in relation to the country to which commodities are exported and to that from which commodities are imported: namely, the latter may offer more materialised labour *in kind* than it receives and yet thereby receive commodities cheaper than it could produce them. Just as a manufacturer who employs a new invention before it becomes generally used, undersells his competitors and yet sells his commodity above its individual value, that is, realises the specifically higher productiveness of the labour he employs as surplus labour. He thus secures a surplus profit. As concerns capital invested in colonies, etc., on the other hand, they may yield higher rates of profit for the simple reason that the rate of profit is higher there due to backward development, and likewise the exploitation of labour, because of the use of slaves, coolies, etc." *Capital*, Vol. III, pp. 232–233.

22. See for example, the discussion initiated by Charles Bettelheim in his preface to the French edition of Baran and Sweezy's *Monopoly Capital*, Paris, 1968, and by Pierre Jalée, *L'Imperialisme en 1970*, Paris, 1970.

23. *Capital*, Vol III, p. 331.

Editors' Appendix: Overview of Marxist Concepts

Laclau focuses on a central problem for Marxists: defining and periodizing the transition from one distinct historical stage—in this case feudalism—to another—capitalism. Each stage for Marx was marked by a dominant "mode of production" that described the "forces of production"—the nonhuman resources such as land, raw materials, machinery, and other technologies—and the "relations of production"—the human aspects such as ownership, labor, and payment systems. In feudal systems, the forces of production were mainly large landed estates owned by aristocratic landlords who were not particularly entrepreneurial. The peasants who worked the land were "coerced" (by "extra-economic" means, i.e., physical force or custom) to work, usually through serfdom, for landowners, and they produced very little surplus beyond their own subsistence. In capitalism, new technology, in particular manufacturing, allowed the production of greater "surplus value," which a new class— the capitalists or "bourgeoisie"—accumulated as profit and appropriated for their own individual use as entrepreneurs, rather than sharing with the actual producers—the "proletariat." The proletariat, unlike feudal serfs, were not coerced by extra-economic means; rather they were disciplined by their dependence on selling their labor (in Marxist terms, "labor-power") for a wage, having lost the possibility of subsistence production. Capitalism, much more than the prior modes of production, depended on "commodity exchange" and money, both for the development of a market for manufactured goods, and for the development of a mobile work force that was forced to sell its labor.

During the transition from the feudal to the capitalist mode of production, the emerging new class—the bourgeoisie—would have to take control of the state from the aristocratic feudal class. This process usually involved some form of "bourgeois-democratic" revolution (the French Revolution being a central model) in which the bourgeoisie allied itself with the lower classes to overthrow the monarchy. In the twentieth century, many Marxist debates centered on the inability of the bourgeoisie in countries outside Europe to fulfill this historic mission. Marxists then were forced to decide whether the proletariat or the other lower classes (i.e., peasants, urban poor) should ally with the bourgeoisie or should take a leading and radical role.

Once established, capitalism required growth and consumption in order to remain healthy, and the accumulation of surplus value from labor had to continue. However, Marx predicted that economic crises would occur as the result of changes in the "organic composition of capital," i.e., capital accumulated from the past would grow faster than the surplus value produced by the current work force. This process would lead to a "falling rate of profit"—the first step in the decay of capitalism in which the enlarged proletariat eventually would overthrow the bourgeoisie and establish the egalitarian economic and social system that Marx called socialism and communism.

Selected Bibliography

Amin, Samir. *Unequal Development*. London: Monthly Review Press, 1976.

Bagú, Sergio. *Economia de la sociedad colonial: Ensayo de historia comparada de América*. Buenos Aires: Ateneo, 1949.

Baran, Paul. *The Political Economy of Growth*. New York: Monthly Review Press, 1957.

Bath, C. R., and D. J. James. "Dependency Analysis of Latin America: Some Criticisms, Some Suggestions," *Latin American Research Review* 11:3 (1976), pp. 3–54.

Caporaso, James A. (ed.). *Dependence and Dependency in the Global System*. Special issue of *International Organization* 32:1 (Winter 1978).

Caputo, O., and R. Pizarro. *Imperialismo, dependencia y relaciones internacionales*. Santiago: 1970.

Cardoso, Fernando Henrique. "Associated Dependent Development," in *Authoritarian Brazil*, edited by Alfred Stepan. New Haven, Conn.: Yale University Press, 1973.

Cardoso, Fernando Henrique. "The Consumption of Dependency Theory in the United States," *Latin American Research Review* 12:3 (1977), pp. 7–24.

Cardoso, Fernando Henrique, and Enzo Faletto. *Dependencia y desarrollo en América Latina*. Mexico, D.F.: Siglo Veintiuno Editores, 1969. (English translation, Berkeley: University of California Press, 1979).

Chilcote, Ronald (ed.). *Dependency and Marxism: Toward a Resolution of the Debate*. Boulder, Colo.: Westview Press, 1982.

Chilcote, Ronald, and Joel Edelstein (eds.). *Latin America: The Struggle with Dependency and Beyond*. New York: John Wiley & Sons, 1974.

Cueva, Agustín. *El desarrollo del capitalismo en América Latina*. Mexico, D.F.: Siglo Veintiuno Editores, 1977.

Emmanuel, Arghiri. *Unequal Exchange: A Study of the Imperialism of Trade*. London: New Left Books, 1972.

Evans, Peter. *Dependent Development: The Alliance of Multinational, State, and Local Capital in Brazil*. Princeton, N.J.: Princeton University Press, 1979.

Foster-Carter, A. "From Rostow to Gunder Frank: Conflicting Paradigms in the Analysis of Underdevelopment," *World Development* 4:3 (March 1976), pp. 167–180.

Foster-Carter, A. "The Modes of Production Controversy," *New Left Review* 107 (Jan.-Feb. 1978), pp. 47–78.

Frank, Andre Gunder. *Capitalism and Underdevelopment in Latin America.* New York: Monthly Review Press, 1967.

Frank, Andre Gunder. *Latin America: Underdevelopment or Revolution.* New York: Monthly Review Press, 1969.

Frank, Andre Gunder. *Lumpenbourgeoisie—Lumpendevelopment.* New York: Monthly Review Press, 1972.

Frank, Andre Gunder. *Critique and Anti-Critique: Essays on Dependency and Reformism.* New York: Praeger, 1984.

Furtado, Celso. *Economic Growth of Brazil.* Berkeley: University of California Press, 1963.

Hilton, R., et al. *The Transition from Feudalism to Capitalism.* London: New Left Books, 1976.

Hindess, B., and P. Hirst. *Pre-Capitalist Modes of Production.* London: Routledge & Kegan Paul, 1975.

Hindess, B., and P. Hirst. *Mode of Production and Social Formation.* London: Macmillan, 1977.

Hobson, J. A. *Imperialism: A Study.* New York: J. Pott & Company, 1902.

Ianni, Octavio. *A formaçao do estado populista na América Latina.* Rio de Janeiro: Civilizacao Brasiliera, 1975.

Ionescu, G., and E. Gellner (eds.). *Populism.* London: Weidenfeld & Nicolson, 1969.

Kay, G. *Development and Underdevelopment: A Marxist Analysis.* London: Macmillan, 1975.

Laclau, Ernesto. *Politics and Ideology in Marxist Theory.* London: New Left Books, 1977.

Lall, S. "Is Dependence a Useful Concept in Analysing Underdevelopment?" *World Development* 3:11 (Nov.-Dec. 1975), pp. 799–810.

Lenin, V. I. *Imperialism: The Highest Stage of Capitalism.* Moscow: Progress Publishers, 1968. (First published in Russian in 1917).

Owen, R., and B. Sutcliffe (eds.). *Studies in the Theory of Imperialism.* London: Longman, 1972.

Oxall, I., et al. *Beyond the Sociology of Development.* London: Routledge & Kegan Paul, 1975.

Palma, G. "Dependency: A Formal Theory of Underdevelopment or a Methodology for the Analysis of Concrete Situations of Underdevelopment?" *World Development* 6:7/8 (July-Aug. 1978), pp. 881–924.

Pinto, Aníbal, and Jan Kñakal. *América Latina y el cambio en la economia mundial.* Lima: Instituto de Estudios Peruanos, 1973.

Prado Júnior, Caio. *The Colonial Background of Modern Brazil.* Berkeley: University of California Press, 1969.

Prebisch, Raúl. *The Economic Development of Latin America and Its Principal Problems.* New York: United Nations, 1950.

Santos, Theotonio dos. *Dependencia y cambio social.* Santiago: CESO, Universidad de Chile, 1970.

Santos, Theotonio dos. "The Structure of Dependency," *American Economic Review* 60:2 (May 1970), pp. 231–236.

Smith, Tony. "The Dependency Approach," in *New Directions in Comparative Politics,* edited by Howard J. Wiarda. Boulder, Colo.: Westview Press, 1985, pp. 113–126.

Stein, Stanley J., and Barbara H. *The Colonial Heritage of Latin America: Essays on Economic Development in Perspective.* New York: Oxford University Press, 1970.

Sunkel, Osvaldo. "Transnational Capitalism and National Disintegration in Latin America," *Social and Economic Studies* 22:1 (March 1973), pp. 132–176.

Sunkel, Osvaldo, and Pedro Paz. *El subdesarrollo Latinoamericano y la teoria de la desarrollo.* Mexico, D.F.: Siglo Veintiuno Editores, 1970.

Taylor, J. *From Modernization to Modes of Production: A Critique of Sociologies of Development and Underdevelopment.* London: Macmillan, 1979.

Tucker, Robert C. (ed.). *The Marx-Engels Reader.* 2d ed. New York: Macmillan, 1978.

Wallerstein, Immanuel M. *The Modern World-System. Capitalist Agriculture and the Origins of the European World-Economy in the Sixteenth Century.* New York: Academic Press, 1974.

Wallerstein, Immanuel M. *The Modern World-System II: Mercantilism and the Consolidation of the European World-Economy, 1600–1750.* New York: Academic Press, 1980.

Warren, B. "Imperialism and Capitalist Industrialization," *New Left Review* 81 (Sept.-Oct., 1973), pp. 3–44.

PART 3
CORPORATISM

A third major approach to the problem of development in Latin America is corporatism. This theory, whose origins can be traced back to Aristotle and St. Thomas Aquinas, stands in sharp contrast to both dependency and modernization. Corporatism stresses the enduring character of Latin American society, which it attributes to the persistence of Catholic and Thomistic values, an authoritarian political heritage, and a corporatist economic organization. The underdevelopment of Latin America is a product of its uniquely Catholic, Mediterranean tradition that not only stood apart from but rejected the revolutionary spirit that animated the West in the age of capitalism and modernity after 1500.

Corporatists see society organized into limited numbers of specialized groups that are given autonomy by the state to run their specific social or economic sectors. These "functional groups," such as guilds, the Catholic church, chambers of commerce, and multiclass political parties, are organized hierarchically and cut across class lines, usually through personalistic ties, which are best illustrated by the paternalistic relationship between patrons and peons.

Both anticapitalist and anti-Marxist, corporatists reject what they see as the imposition of foreign—alien—developmental models onto Latin America. Modernity and development, if they are to come to the region, must be filtered through and adapted to what the corporatists see as a uniquely Latin American tradition and ethos. For many this distinctiveness is found in the authority of the state and the central role it has played in shaping the society and the economy. Thus, some corporatists envision a third, noncapitalist/non-Marxist road to modernity and development—a road that is led by a powerful, activist, and interventionist state, but one that remains decidedly within the essentially Catholic cultural and philosophical framework of Latin American tradition.

10 / Social Change, Political Development, and the Latin American Tradition

Howard J. Wiarda

A leading exponent of corporatism in Latin America is political scientist Howard J. Wiarda. He argues here that "there is a distinct Latin American/Southern European counterpart to the great sociological paradigms formulated by Marx, Durkheim, or Weber." In Wiarda's view, Latin America's corporatist tradition is antithetical to democratic and liberal values, having remained largely untouched by the liberal revolutionary currents that transformed the West. As such, Latin America remains "locked in this traditional pattern of values and institutions that has postponed and retarded development."

Instead of examining Latin America in terms of Western development, therefore, the region must be taken on its own terms, without imposing a particular model of change along U.S. or European lines. Wiarda thus questions the convergence thesis that Latin America will automatically pass through the Western stage of development. Rather, he notes that "many traditional societies, and particularly those of the Iberic Latin nations, have proved remarkably permeable and flexible, assimilating at various points more 'modern' and 'rational' elements, but without losing their characteristics."

Appreciating Latin America

Before the dramatic onset of revolution in the Caribbean and Central America, Latin America was generally ignored in the United States and worldwide, in the books people read and the courses they took, because of a widespread sense of the area's unimportance. Latin America was viewed as something of an aberration, an area where democracy failed to work, constant coups and military takeovers occurred, and "underdevelopment" (social, moral, and political, as well as economic) persisted. Our popular image of the nations to our south was (and in some quarters still is) shaped by stereotypes, magazine cartoons, and old movies: peasants with big sombreros either taking siestas or dancing gaily in the streets, and mustachioed, comic-opera men-on-horseback galloping in and out of presidential palaces with frequent regularity.

Scholarship and teaching often reflected both this ignorance and the bias and ethnocentrism of the popular stereotypes. Latin America was thought to have little to contribute materially or from a social-science point of view. It had "no history" according to Hegel, "no political culture" according to many sociologists and political scientists. The few books on Latin America that appeared were preoccupied with lamenting the weakness of legislatures, the strength of various dictators, and the absence of elections and United States style democracy. Reflecting this North American ethnocentrism, the focus of most studies was on explaining why Latin America failed to measure up to United States or Western European standards of the "good" democratic society and polity. On the international front, meanwhile, despite some occasional flare-ups, Latin America remained marginal to the major balances of power, an "American backyard" protected by the Monroe Doctrine and "safe" from communism.

Castro's revolution in Cuba began to change all this. Students, scholars, and government officials were suddenly confronted with a new situation that thrust Latin American affairs to the forefront. A great deal of scare literature was produced on Latin America, books with the titles of *The Eleventh Hour* or *One Minute to Midnight*. Suddenly the Congress was concerned, new "task forces" to study "the problem" were set up, and a host of fellowships materialized to help channel our best young minds into Latin American studies. A new image, that of the guerrilla revolutionary, replaced the older stereotype of the sleepy peasant. New aid

Reprinted with permission from *Politics and Social Change in Latin America: The Distinct Tradition,* 2nd edition, edited by Howard J. Wiarda, pp. 3–25. Amherst: University of Massachusetts Press, 1982.

programs and cooperative endeavors were suddenly announced by the United States government and various private agencies. Stemming initially from the Cuban revolution and then reinforced by upheaval in Nicaragua and El Salvador, the concern was widespread that unless *we* did something, the fire would spread up and down the Andes, and the entire Hemisphere would fall prey to Castro-Communist takeovers.

The potential for revolution spreading throughout the Hemisphere tomorrow is surely greatly exaggerated, but one cannot fall back into the older habits of neglect and indifference either. Indeed, there is a whole body of literature that argues that Latin America is a profoundly "unrevolutionary society," perhaps inherently and permanently so, that genuine social revolution is unlikely to occur in any but two or three spots in the Hemisphere. Neither the peasants, the workers, nor the students in the major countries are really very revolutionary; their guerrilla movements have not achieved widespread popular support or great success; the local communist parties are generally old and tired; revolutionary strategies have not proved successful. Moreover, the area's traditional structures and institutions—the extended family pattern, the assumptions of hierarchy and authority, the Church and the Army, traditional beliefs and culturally conditioned habits—have proved to be remarkably flexible and persistent, bending and adapting to change instead of giving way or necessarily being crushed under the onslaught of modernization. Midnight has not tolled—or if it did, nothing very dramatic happened. The choices of reform or revolution, or of dictatorship versus democracy, have proved to be false, or at least did not take into account all the varied Latin American possibilities. In Washington this perception of the essentially conservative nature of Latin America, particularly during those periods when no "threatening" Castro-like revolutions loomed, was reflected in a renewal period of official neglect and indifference.

Neither of these scenarios or models, the revolutionary or the conservative, necessarily describes or delineates accurately and completely the nature of the Latin American development process. The apocalyptic "eleventh-hour" theme is probably useful for prying aid funds from a reluctant United States Congress, for getting students interested and involved in the area, and for raising the level of public consciousness about Latin America. But the idea that all Latin America is about to explode in violent upheaval has proved to be a myth, a phantom notion that has greatly obscured our understanding of how the Latin American systems do, in fact, change and modernize. The social and economic transformations occurring in Latin America are considerable, but these have not always or uniformly produced fundamental alterations in the class structure or political behavior. Nor have they given rise, except in a handful of countries and for some quite special circumstances, to a noticeable strengthening of revolutionary sentiment and movements. The fundamental assumptions on which the scare literature and the dramatic, hyped-up television specials were based have proved to be inaccurate or at best only half-truths, a reflection once again of the inappropriateness of trying to interpret Latin America through the lenses of United States political understandings. Not only have we persisted in viewing Latin America through our own rose-colored glasses and our own preferred political perceptions but—through our aid, our Peace Corps, our human rights policy and other initiatives—we have often sought to impose United States or Western European solutions and political formulae on societies where they simply do not fit.

The scare tactics and verbal overkill employed in much of the literature have not only produced wrong and misleading interpretations but they have also produced the inevitable reactions in the form of renewed public and official indifference and in the production of a new body of literature that, in seeking to correct past misconceptions, overcompensates by focusing solely on Latin America's conservative aspects. But the image of Latin America as a wholly static and reactionary area is not very accurate either. In fact, the changes occurring throughout the area have been many and profound—class changes, social and economic changes, and political transformations as well. But these changes have not often been in the direction or the precise form envisioned in most of the "development" literature written by North Americans or Northwest Europeans. For example, the Latin American middle class does not behave as this literature leads us to expect, political parties seldom play the same role as in the United States, the military continues to intervene, and so on. Our biases and ethnocentrism have helped both to perpetrate some fundamental misunderstandings of Latin America, as well as to render a positive disservice to a more accurate comprehension of how the Latin American systems do in fact function, change, and modernize.

These criticisms of some of the conventional "wisdom" regarding Latin America—a wisdom derived from divergent poles on the political spectrum and from different assumptions about development, but none of it very useful for comprehending Latin America—serve as the point of departure for the main theme of [our discussion], namely, that there are some distinctive aspects to the process of social and political change in Latin America that do not correspond to the development models usually employed. Latin America has its own social and political institutions and its own ways of achieving change, and it is both presumptuous of us and detrimental to a proper understanding of the area to look at it exclusively through the prism of the United States or the Western European developmental experience. If we wish to appreciate and come to grips realistically with Latin America and its change processes, we must do so on Latin America's own terms and in its historical context, not through some model of society derived from outside the Hemisphere and rooted in circumstances having little to do with the present conditions of Latin America itself. We cannot seek to impose some narrow, preconceived general theory on a set of societies to which it does not correspond, nor seek to understand Latin America's often times unique developmental pattern exclusively in the light of the Northwest European–North American experiences. Instead we must look at Latin America through its own eyes and institutions and seek to come to grips with the processes of change there using a framework for analysis and understanding that grows out of Latin America's own history, tradition, and special circumstances. That is precisely what the [our discussion] seeks to provide: an understanding of the historical and cultural conditions and determinants of Latin American social and political behavior that shows also the implications of these factors for understanding concrete contemporary issues of political change and social and economic development.

Let us be more specific in our criticisms of the Western model of development and why it has but limited relevance to Latin America. *First,* the timing and context are entirely different. The United States and Western Europe began their drive to accelerated development in the nineteenth century, and it seems obvious that for countries like those of Latin America that began a full century later, the conditions and circumstances are quite dissimilar. *Second,* the sequences of development are distinct. In the European context economic development and the rise of capitalism served as the motor force of modernization, stimulating social change that in turn triggered political reform. But in Latin America the social, economic, and political transformations are occurring all at once, and a good case could be made for its being political requirements that stimulated economic growth rather than the other way around. *Third,* the international settings are wholly changed. Countries like the United States, Britain, and Japan were able to develop relatively autonomously and on their own; Latin America, in contrast, cannot do so and is caught up in a web of international dependency and interdependency over which it has no control. One need only look at market and trade patterns, the dependence on foreign, OPEC-produced oil, the Cold War and the alliance systems and rivalries to which it gave rise, and the important role of the international lending agencies (the World Bank and others) to see how different the conditions are for Latin America.

Fourth and most important for our purposes here, we have learned that "traditional institutions," in Latin America and elsewhere, have remarkable persistence and staying power. Whether it is African tribalism, Indian caste associations, Islamic theocracy, or Latin American personalism, Catholicism, and familism, we now know that these institutions are not fated inevitably to disappear or be submerged as modernization advances. Rather, traditional institutions have proved to be adaptable and accommodative, absorbing some elements of Western modernization, transforming others to fit local circumstances, and often rejecting the rest. There has been no one-way, automatic, or unilinear process by which traditional institutions have been *replaced* by modern ones. Rather, the process has been much more complex, involving blends and fusions of traditional and modern. Instead of being replaced by modern (read Western) institutions, traditional institutions have overlapped with them. Traditional institutions have also served as filters and brokers of the modernization process, absorbing that which was useful from the outside world and keeping out the rest. In this way the historic institutions of Latin America have not only survived but thrived. Moreover, as nationalism has intensified throughout Latin America and as the institutions imported from the West have proved unworkable and dysfunctional, a new pride has developed in indigenous institutions. An effort has been made to adapt them to modern circumstances, to fashion an indigenous model of development instead of seeking to preserve the rather pale and artificial institutions imported earlier from the outside.

The Latin American systems have their roots in the ancient Greek notion of organic solidarity; in the Roman system of a hierarchy of laws and institutions; in historic Catholic concepts of the corporate, sectoral, and compartmentalized organization of society based on each person's acceptance of his or her station in life; in the similarly corporate organization (Army, Church, towns, nobility) of Iberian society during the late medieval era; in the warrior mentality and the walled enclave cities of the period of the Reconquest of the Iberian Peninsula from the Moors; in the centralized bureaucratic systems of the early modern Spanish and Portuguese states; and in the absolutist, scholastic, Catholic, political culture and institutions of Spain of the Inquisition and the Counter Reformation. Of course, in the vast empty and "uncivilized" Western Hemisphere, which was under the constant threat that the thin veneer of Spanish and Portuguese culture and institutions would be submerged, and which had huge Indian (ten times larger in Latin America than in North America) and later African populations, the institutions transplanted from Iberia underwent various changes and permutations. The amazing thing is their capacity to survive, persist, and adapt even into the contemporary period.

Latin America is essentially Western, but it represents a particular tradition in the West and one with which we are not very familiar.

Latin America is a fragment of Europe circa 1492–1570 (the era of the Conquest), and a fragment of a quite special part of Europe, the Iberian Peninsula. As a fragment of Catholic, corporate, Roman, semifeudal Europe at that time, and as a reflection of the main institutions of Spain and Portugal and not of France, Germany, Great Britain, or other of the Northwest European countries, Latin America has some special characteristics. Its economy was mercantilist and state-directed rather than capitalist and individually directed; its social structure was two-class rather than multi-class and pluralist; its political institutions were hierarchical and authoritarian rather than democratic; its culture and religion were orthodox, absolutist, and infused with Catholic precepts as contrasted with the religious nonconformity and Protestant precepts of the North American colonies. Latin America was condemned eventually to lag behind the United States in terms of its economic growth, but that should not lead us to assume its political, moral, or social institutions were also "retarded" or "underdeveloped." If nothing else, [our discussion] conveys the idea that Latin America socially, politically, and culturally represents an *alternative* to the Northwest Europe and United States model, not an "undeveloped" version of it.

Latin American development, therefore, was bound to take on some special features that reflected the area's historic past. Moreover, as the change process began to accelerate in the late nineteenth and early twentieth centuries, Latin American development acquired some special dynamics and went forward in ways that were consonant with its own traditions and institutions but that often bore only superficial resemblance (its constitutions and formal structures) to the North American or Northwest European examples. . . .

The change process throughout Latin America has gained increased momentum in recent decades and some far-reaching socio-political transformations have occurred. The middle class has grown greatly in size and influence, peasants and workers are being mobilized and organized, new ideological currents are being felt, the level of popular demands is rising, and new institutional paraphernalia and policy programs have appeared. Despite these changes, however, the traditionalist, elitist, clientelistic, authoritarian, corporatist, and paternalistic structures of Latin America have proved amazingly adaptive and durable. Some sweeping changes are under way throughout Latin America (thus demonstrating that its institutions are not nearly so rigid, unyielding, and reactionary as we had thought), and yet this has seldom resulted in very many fundamental alterations in Latin America's basic structures (thus confounding the classic theories of revolution). Latin America has modernized and developed, but it has done so in its own way and without sacrificing those elements considered valuable from its past. In

Latin America, to use the old saw, the more things change, the more they remain the same. . . .

The Latin American nations have proved remarkably adept at accommodating their traditional institutions to modernity and at reorienting their modernizing forces in traditional or system-conforming directions. In the process they have evolved quite a distinctive way of assimilating and absorbing the newer social forces and of managing the entire development process without destroying or sweeping away the traditional institutions themselves. One must guard against romanticizing this process, however, for the inequities and injustices existing in Latin America are great and plain for all to see. Nor can one have great sympathy for those Latin American systems where the legitimate demands of the people have been consistently smothered, or for those Latin American leaders who, in the name of "tradition," have exercised brutal and repressive power. And yet, our attention must be commanded by the ability of many of the Latin American nations to manage the change process in a relatively peaceful and orderly fashion, to provide for economic growth and considerable social justice even in contexts of dependency and limited natural resources, and to preserve, albeit unevenly, those institutions and societal norms considered valuable from the past (the extended family, personalism and humanism, a sense of community, individual dignity and worth, social solidarity and mutual interdependence, moral and ethical values) even in the face of the immense pressures toward impersonality, mass society, and alienation imposed by the impact of modern, twentieth-century life. Surely as confidence wanes in the capacity of the United States and other "advanced" industrial societies to cope with their social ills, as we lament the passing of our own sense of community, family, individual worth, and mutual respect and tolerance, it is worth examining closely a society and cultural tradition seeking—with some success—to preserve the heritage deemed valuable from its history while at the same time adapting it to the currents of modernization.

No claim is here made that this is the one and exclusive explanation of Latin America. Other major explanations—class analysis, international economic dependency relations—must also be employed. Nor should it be thought that the explanation offered here applies to all the Latin American countries uniformly. It applies to some more than others and in varying degrees within the several countries. But although not a complete explanation, the interpretation offered here is an essential one and one that is often ignored in the literature; furthermore, it represents a model or "ideal type" that should be tested comparatively in the different national contexts. But with these qualifications, the main point should not be lost: because of their distinct backgrounds and the pattern of their socio-cultural evolution, the Latin American nations merit separate treatment and interpretation. Their development patterns are unique and poorly understood. Because of the biases within the social sciences that focus on the Northwest European and United States experiences, the Latin American system and model seldom find expression in our studies of political theory, sociology, or political development. Indeed in Latin America it is likely we are looking at a "Fourth World of Development," one that corresponds neither to the "First World" of liberal-capitalist countries, nor to the "Second World" of Soviet-type socialism, nor to the "Third World" either, which is such a big category and spans so many diverse continents as to be almost worthless as a descriptive or analytical term. Latin America has evolved its own ways of seeking to manage the major challenges of modern times, one that borrows from the models of the first and second worlds but is not identical to either, one which increasingly builds on indigenous, *Latin American* institutions. That model, which is quite distinct from the United States and the dominant Northwest European systems, has not received the attention it deserves, nor have its implications been adequately explored. . . .

The Place of Latin America in the Literature on Development

In recent years the fields of economic development studies and social and political modernization and development have mushroomed. This corresponds both with the sudden entrance of a host of new nations in Africa, Asia, and the Middle East onto the world stage, and with a dawning realization in the West that such developing or emerging nations can no longer be safely ignored. The study of development has itself become a growth industry, and there can be no doubt that the analysis and understanding of how societies change, modernize, and reorient their institutional life correspondingly are and will remain among the most exciting, challenging, and important subject areas with which we and the world, both those in the so-called developed world and those in the developing one (even the phrases used illustrated the paternalism and ethnocentrism involved in much of the literature), must be concerned.

Unfortunately, in the rush to study such development, two major problems have emerged. The first has to do with the pervasive ethnocentrism with which we view Latin America. Almost everything said and written about the developing nations has been from a Western, white, Northern European and United States perspective. The assumption is widespread that to be developed is to be "just like us"—presumably that means liberal, democratic, moderate in our policies, pluralist, middle class, and so on. The second problem is that in all the new, grand, and universal theories of development, Latin America is largely left out of consideration. This is a curious omission because with their common cultural background, histories, colonial past and parallel development experiences, the Latin American nations provide a particularly fertile area—almost a living laboratory of sociological and political development—for comparative analysis and the testing of distinct theoretical models of the change-modernization process. The trouble is that Latin America doesn't fit very well into the great designs that sociologists, economists, and political scientists have erected. But rather than revising the theory to deal with these distinct realities, social scientists have often preferred to ignore the entire area. Obviously that is unacceptable from any point of view that presumes to social-science accuracy.

The ethnocentrism of our familiar approaches to studying development has already been noted, but a further point needs to be made here. Most of us are students of what we call the liberal arts, but it must be remembered that liberal-arts education is concerned almost entirely with the Western tradition. Sociology, political science, and economics all have their roots in the Western experience of Europe and North America, and that is where their major concepts and understandings derive from. That is not bad, of course, so long as we recognize the narrowness and particularism of that approach and its limited relevance in the rest of the globe. The trouble is that in our models of development we have generalized from the Western experience to the entire world, and the same categories do not fit very well. We have made the mistake of assuming that development necessarily means Westernization. That is not only wrong and inappropriate, contributing to a perpetuation of our lack of comprehension regarding other culture areas, but it represents some of the worse forms of what we might call cultural imperialism. Liberal-arts education, by which we mean the Western European tradition, is really the first area study; but it is erroneous and presumptuous to assume that the concepts and categories derived from that area have universal validity.

As to why Latin America is not included in the major general books on development, several reasons may be offered. First, there exists a series of prejudices about Latin America. The area is based upon hierarchical, elitist, Catholic, corporatist, and authoritarian assumptions, and the fact is that social scientists, like most Americans, do not like societies based on such assumptions. A second reason is that those most prominent in the field of development studies—Gabriel A. Almond, W. W. Rostow, S. M. Lipset, Lucian Pye, Bert Hoselitz, David Apter, Karl Deutsch—have all been European, African, or Asian experts and therefore have concentrated in their writings on erecting models based on the areas they know best. Third, the knowledge (and appreciation) of Latin America in the general social-science disciplines remains limited, and in the general studies of development written by social scientists, Latin America is usually ignored or glossed over quickly. The comments about Latin America in the general development literature are often limited to a few unenlightening (and often dead wrong) paragraphs or, in some cases, a meager footnote. This omission has resulted in a large body of literature propounding a supposedly universal model of development that, in fact, ignores a major area of the globe, one that has much to tell us concerning the processes of development particularly of nations in the intermediary and transitional stages. If one remembers, moreover, that a number of these leading development theorists were also among the new mandarins (those foreign policy advisers helping design the often misconceived, misapplied, and ruinous United States programs directed toward Latin America in the 1960s and 1970s), then this indictment becomes even stronger.

But the problem is not simply ethnocentrism, a lack of empathy, and a lack of knowledge concerning Latin America. The difficulty also lies in the fact that Latin America does not fit very well the models and metaphors that scholars and government officials (for the most part, from the United States) have concocted. With more than a century and a half of independent life behind them, the Latin American countries could hardly be called "new nations." With its Catholic, Iberian, and Southern European heritage, Latin America is certainly not "non-Western"—though, as we shall emphasize, it represents a quite distinct set of threads and socio-political currents within that Western tradition which is quite at variance with the better known (and usually more admired) northern example. Nor has Latin America followed the sequential "stages of growth" that these same Northwestern European nations and the United States went through. And the classical Marxian categories—in a continent where capitalism in its laissez-faire form hardly exists, where the workers and peasants are not always revolutionary, and where class and economic variables may be part of the superstructure and largely determined by socio-political factors instead of the other way around—provide only a partial and often incomplete explanation. In short, Latin American development resembles only in limited ways the African, Asian, or Middle Eastern patterns, fits uncomfortably in any pancontinental or Third World category, and corresponds only partially to the major theories and frameworks of "modernization" growing out of the Northwest European and United States experiences. Any effort toward grand theory construction on a global basis that seeks to stuff Latin America into some narrow and ill-fitting intellectual straitjacket is bound to be misleading and inaccurate.

The community of Latin America scholars, however, must also shoulder part of the blame. Long apart and isolated from the most recent theoretical thinking in their respective disciplines, they have tended to reject out of hand the newer analytical tools and models or to use them only half-heartedly. Rather than update their own thinking and research, the older school of Latin Americanists has often sought refuge in arguments for the discreteness of all historical events and the noncomparability of times and nations. In contrast, the younger generation of Latin Americanists have often accepted the universalist models learned in graduate school uncritically and indiscriminantly, applying them to an area where they may not fit or may fit only partially. Little effort has been made to sort out, with empathy and rigor, in what precise areas Latin America is in fact unique and where it conforms to more universal—i.e., Western— modes of development.

That is what [our discussion] is all about. Clearly Latin America can and must be included within the broader, global context of change, development, and modernization. To ignore the Latin American experience because it does not exactly fit our preconceived, generally Western and hence ethnocentric notions of how the development process unfolds is both bad scholarship and disastrous for our understanding of the area. It is clear also that the Latin America area specialist must have a firm grasp of the general development and theoretical literature and must be able to conceptualize the area's change processes within this larger historical and comparative perspective. At the same time he must be sensitive to the area's distinctiveness and recognize that the major development models fashioned for Northwest Europe and the United States must be modified, reshaped, supplemented, and sometimes rejected and reformulated altogether in order to have relevance for Latin America. Only by bridging our broad and theoretical understanding of the overall development process (adjusting, amending, and recasting that understanding to account for major national and cultural area-specific variations) with a thorough mastery of the functioning of particular institutions, processes, and countries in Latin America—only then can significant and useful advances occur in our learning of how development generally proceeds and of the alternative forms development may take. . . .

The Pattern of Latin American Development:
An Overview

Latin America's roots lie deep in the past.[1] History hangs heavily over the area. Its historical traditions are both strong and persistent.

The major historical influences on the Iberian mother countries of Spain and Portugal were the Roman system of law and governance,

Christianity and the Thomistic tradition, the centuries long Reconquest of the peninsula from the Moors, and the special character of Iberian feudalism, the guild system, and corporatism. Roman law helped provide Spain and Portugal with both unity and a hierarchical, structured, integral, and imperial political foundation; Christianity provided not only a religious and moral base but also a strong scholastic and natural law tradition and a pervasive Catholic political culture that still undergirds behavior and institutions. The Reconquest of Iberia from the Moorish "infidels" helped give religion a more militant, crusading, and intolerant attitude and also shaped the Iberian pattern of walled enclave cities, military order and special privileges, and the class *and* caste stratification system that persists even today. Spanish feudalism and the guild system also emerged from the Reconquest period and thus became especially rigid and hardened in place. At the same time, the early forms of Iberian corporatism were forged in the relations between such institutions as the Church, the towns, the military orders, the universities, and the privileged castes with each other and with an emerging central state. These traditions and institutions came together and were becoming firmly established in Iberia at precisely the time Spain and Portugal launched their great overseas ventures.

Latin America may thus be viewed as a fragment of Southern European and Iberian culture and civilization of approximately 1500. The time period and the Iberian heritage were especially important in shaping Latin America's future. In terms of the history of Western civilization, Latin America was founded on a basis that was precapitalistic, preenlightenment, pre-Protestant Reformation, prescientific revolution, and prerepresentative government. These features not only helped retard Latin America's later development but also gave it some of its most distinctive characteristics. An understanding of this also enables us to see why Latin American development should be both slower and quite different from the pattern in the North American colonies. . . .

It goes a long way toward understanding Latin America if we comprehend the time frame in which the area was settled, colonized, and its major institutions established, *and* the special character of these institutions as offshoots not of Elizabethan and Stuart England but of the Spain of Ferdinand and Isabella, Charles I, and Philip II. The major institutions transferred to the New World were "feudal," not "modern." In the Spain and Portugal of that time, and now in their colonies, the dominant institutions were a feudal-patrimonial system of land ownership and of lord-peasant relations; an authoritarian, absolutist, hierarchical, and organic structure of political authority; a similarly authoritarian and absolutist Church that buttressed and reinforced the state concept and provided little room for pluralism; a social order divided vertically in terms of segmented corporate units (Church, Army, bureaucracy, university) and horizontally according to a rigid system of classes, estates, rank orders, castes, and purportedly God-given inequalities; an exploitive, centralized, monopolistic, statist, and mercantilist economic system; and an educational system and intellectual tradition based on scholastic learning, rote memorization, absolute truth, and deductive reasoning. Forged and crystallized during and in the aftermath of the centuries long crusade against the Moors, these traditions and institutions had been firmly established in Spain and Portugal by the end of the fifteenth century. Beginning in 1492 they were transferred to the Americas where they not only were strongly institutionalized but also received a new lease on life—either as established forms or as goals and aspirations for Latin American society to achieve. The theme does not get much attention in [our discussion], but it should be noted that one reason for the durability of the institutions carried over from Iberia is that they closely paralleled and reinforced the similarly authoritarian, absolutist, and theocratic institutions of the indigenous, pre-Columbian Indian civilizations in the Americas. . . .

The isolation of Latin America from the outside world during the next three centuries of colonial rule, buttressed both by Iberian colonial policy and by immense distances and premodern communications, combined with the fact that it was largely unaffected by the powerful modernizing forces stirring elsewhere in the West—the rise of capitalism and accelerated social change, religious nonconformity and pluralism, the scientific revolution and the Enlightenment, the thrusts toward representative government and participation—served to lock Latin America into the fifteenth- and early sixteenth-century pattern and to prevent its evolution along other lines. In contrast to the North American colonies, settled more than a century later when the hold of feudal institutions had been considerably weakened in England, the Latin American colonies remained essentially authoritarian, absolutist, feudal (in the peculiarly Iberian sense), patrimonialist, elitist, and organic-corporatist.

Right from the start, therefore, the Latin American colonies were destined both to lag behind their North American counterparts and to evolve in some quite distinct directions. If we recall, for instance, that in our usual history texts the modern era is thought to commence in roughly 1500, then we may begin to comprehend the fundamental differences between the colonies in the two parts of the Americas. Latin America was settled and colonized on the basis of a set of essentially feudal and medieval institutions still reigning at that fundamental breakpoint, and it took on a special character because of its bases in the Iberian tradition; North America, on the other hand, was colonized a full century later when the thrusts of capitalism, religious and political pluralism, modern science, concepts of limited and representative government, and a new enterprising middle class had all begun to have a powerful impact.

Given the time period and the Iberian background it should not be surprising that Latin America was established on this authoritarian, feudal, Catholic, scholastic, mercantilist, patrimonialist, and corporatist basis. What is remarkable is that these institutions proved so long lasting. They survived not only three centuries of colonial rule but also, with some modifications and restructuring, the transition of the colonies to independent nations early in the nineteenth century and even the immense pressures that began to be thrust upon them in the twentieth century by the newer forces of modernization. It is in this sense of having been cut off from and only marginally affected by the great transformations that molded the modern world, while keeping its traditional institutions largely intact, that Latin America may be referred to as a profoundly, historically conservative and nonrevolutionary area. . . .

This of course is not to say there were no significant changes at all or that Latin America remained wholly static. New laws and changes were continually promulgated by the Crown, considerable reorganization of the institutional mechanisms took place, foreign interlopers seeking to break the Spanish monopoly system had to be dealt with, Spanish power waxed and waned, there were depressions and population shifts, a new merchant class eventually began to grow up, some Enlightenment ideas filtered in, the Spanish Bourbon kings of the eighteenth century sought to streamline and modernize colonial rule, and the revolutions in North America and France eventually had an impact. Nevertheless, the basic structures and pillars of the system remained intact. The social and political institutions developed by Spain and Portugal proved flexible enough to accommodate themselves to the changes while also persisting without any revolutionary challenges and with only minor modifications in the fundamental character of the system.

It is not our intention here to review the chronology of events and battles that led to independence. Suffice it to say that by the end of the eighteenth century independence sentiment had grown and that between 1807 and 1824 all Latin America (except Cuba and Puerto Rico) became independent—in some areas as the result of vigorous fighting and in others peacefully, as the result of administrative fiat or the withdrawal of the Spanish military forces and the Crown's authority. It does need emphasizing, however, that these were wars of separation rather than genuine social revolutions and, hence, that the essential structure of top-down authority and society continued, for the most part, as it had been. In many respects the independence movements in

Latin America should be seen as conservative movements rather than liberalizing ones, designed to secure and enhance the status of traditional institutions and of the native-born oligarchies. The local elites wanted not to destroy the ancient system but to make it their own, unfettered by the inconveniences of Spanish decrees and officialdom.

Royal authority, the apex of the Spanish-Portuguese pyramidal system, had been lopped off by independence, but the role and power of the Church, the system of patrimonialism and of lord-serf relations, the hierarchical and rigidly stratified system of power and society, and the norms and values of traditional Catholic political culture all continued. Some of the ancient guilds were abolished and there was a reordering of Church-state relations, but these were more in the nature of adjustments within the system than they were fundamental alterations to it, and soon new corporate units were created as replacements for those abolished. Into the power vacuum created by the Crown's withdrawal stepped the indigenous oligarchies and the armies created during the independence struggles and their *caudillo,* men-on-horseback leaders, seeking to take over the mantle of authority previously centered in the king and to reestablish the time-honored system of authority and power, but now with themselves in charge.

In keeping with the preferences then current, the constitutions adopted in Latin America for these "new nations" provided for civil, republican, representative rule. But the Iberic-Latin social structures underneath were hardly conducive to or supportive of liberal or democratic government. Latin America adopted the forms of democracy but not its substance. Indeed when one examines these constitutions closely . . . one sees that the principles of democratic government were largely concessions to a foreign (United States and European) fad and had little basis in Latin American reality. Rather than instituting democratic rule, the founding fathers of Latin America were chiefly concerned with preserving existing hierarchies and the authoritarian and nondemocratic institutions of the past (which they would of course dominate), while paying only lip service (and occasionally somewhat more than that) to democratic principles. The elitist, absolutist, authoritarian, and patrimonialist structure of Latin America thus demonstrated remarkable staying power, both before independence and after it.

The legitimacy vacuum ushered in by the Crown's withdrawal, however, coupled with the lack of nationally organized institutions and the typical discontinuities attendant upon new nationhood, resulted in a period of considerable instability in the immediate postindependence period. Neither the creole oligarchies nor the new armies were able to fill the void entirely. In a number of countries periods of anarchy alternated with periods of dictatorship. Rival *caudillos* and their retinues vied for control of the presidential palace, which in the absence of the Crown was now the center from which power, patronage, and spoils flowed. From the 1820s to the 1950s the efforts to create viable nation-states out of the fragmented elements that made up society resulted in discord and instability. Only Brazil, which solved its legitimacy problem by continuing as an independent monarchy, and Chile, which quickly reestablished conservative oligarchic rule, were able to avoid the disruptions experienced by the other nations.

From roughly the 1850s, varying somewhat from nation to nation, the situation began to stabilize. The first postindependence generation of men-on-horseback had passed from the scene. The Church-state issues were largely settled. Agriculture and commerce began to expand and a new merchant and artisan class began to grow up in the cities. The first national banks and industries were established. The romantic political notions of the French Revolution—liberty, equality, and fraternity— gave way to more realistic assessments of the area's realities and possibilities. The early rejection of Spain and what it had stood for was now replaced by an effort to come to grips practically with Latin America's own past and historic traditions.

By the last quarter of the nineteenth century, in virtually all the Latin American nations, a considerable degree of order had been achieved. This was a period of national consolidation; of the growth, enlargement, and increasing centralization of national armies and bureaucracies; of immigration and population increase; of rising nationalism; of increased foreign investment and national infrastructure building (railroads, highways, port facilities); of gradually rising affluence and economic expansion. In some countries (Argentina, Brazil, Chile) power was firmly consolidated in the hands of landed oligarchies; in others (Mexico, Venezuela, the Dominican Republic) a new breed of stable, nation-building "order and progress" *caudillos* arose to replace the unstable men-on-horseback of the past. A third pattern occurring a decade or two later in a number of the Caribbean and Central American countries involved direct United States military occupation, which, in alliance with the indigenous oligarchies, helped produce some of the same consolidating and infrastructure-building trends.

Although this was a period of increasing change and development in Latin America, it implied few fundamental breaks with the past. The growing stability and progress of the late nineteenth century came not through any revolutionary transformations but essentially through a reconsolidation of the old colonial system of hierarchy and elites— albeit now without the Crown and often dressed up in republican garb— with some new elements added to the prevailing systems. Whether *caudillo* or oligarchic dominated (or even under United States hegemony) the Latin American nations sought to achieve growth within the structural framework of the past, which thus included authoritarianism, monopoly, hierarchy, elitism, and patrimonialism. Considerable development occurred in terms of economic growth and greater institutionalization, but very little democraticization resulted. For instance, a new commercial, import-export merchant class rose up but it was quickly absorbed within the elitist and oligarchic structure (now expanded somewhat) and came to share the values and assumptions of the older elites. In many instances the older elites either intermarried with the children of the rising entrepreneurial class or themselves went into business, thus both diversifying and modernizing their economic activities while also maintaining an elite-dominated monopoly on wealth and power. Concurrently, a new and fledging middle class emerged, but it lacked coherence and consciousness as a class. Its members, once they had "made it" economically and politically, also aped upper-class ways and the traditional elitist disdain both for manual labor and for the lower classes. Elections even in the "liberal" regimes remained controlled so as to perpetuate rule by a small minority. The beginning of the economic "take-off" in Latin America thus produced some new social and political forces but implied no fundamental realignment of the socio-political order, nor did it give rise to the political pluralism and greater egalitarianism that these transformations sparked elsewhere in the West. . . .

The period from roughly 1890 to 1930 was the heyday of oligarchic rule in Latin America. The terms of trade were advantageous and, by exporting their mineral wealth and agricultural products, many nations of the area prospered. A new era of order, stability, and progress ensued; it was hardly democratic but represented chiefly the reinstitutionalization and further elaboration of the older pattern of autocracy and special privilege. In some countries "revolutions" continued, but these were not social upheavals and implied usually the changing of only the names and faces of those in the presidential palace, a rotation of the ruling elites rather than any fundamental restructuring. Seldom in any of these revolts were there many people killed or much property destroyed for that was costly and not in accord with the accepted rules of the game.

In this way the Latin American nations began to adjust and accommodate themselves to modernization, but it did not result in any genuinely revolutionary changes in the structure of elite and oligarchic rule or even in much alteration in the prevailing political culture. Authoritarianism, patrimonialism, hierarchy, elitism, monism as distinct from pluralism . . . , these remained the dominant institutional norms. Development in Latin America thus went forward within the framework, which was still only slightly altered, of an older historic pattern that stretched back to colonial and precolonial eras; it was a framework that was more conservative and "feudal" than liberal. Only in Mexico from 1910 to 1920 did a full-fledged social revolution occur, and even that was a limited and essentially middle-class revolution not out of harmony with the historic Latin American pattern and eventually evolving a similar authoritarian and corporatist structure. Argentina in 1916 and Chile in 1920 also experienced middle-class takeovers that served to incorporate these rising elements into the system but did not change the system very much itself.

A major break came in 1930. The world-market crash of 1929-30 and the ensuing Depression eroded the demand abroad for Latin America's primary products and helped undermine the older system of oligarchic rule. In 1930 and the years following, a rash of revolts occurred throughout the area, reflecting the dissatisfaction of the rising middle classes with the traditional elitist system and their demand for a restructuring of it—chiefly to include themselves. Hence, even the accelerated changes and search for new solutions in the post-1930 period have generally had as their goals the remodeling of the traditional system of authority and privilege, now updated to include some of the newer social groups and political "power contenders," . . . but not repudiating the older historic system. In some countries there ensued a period of alternation between traditional and more forward-looking regimes; in others what we think of as right-wing dictators (Trujillo in the Dominican Republic, the elder Somoza in Nicaragua) reestablished order—often with a vengeance—but also brought the new middle classes into power and accomplished a variety of changes necessary for adaptation to the new circumstances of greater (albeit still severely limited) pluralism; in still others, civilian and military populist leaders (Vargas in Brazil or Perón in Argentina), backed usually by middle sector and often some emerging labor elements, redirected and restructured the prevailing systems. Nineteen thirty marked a significant turning point in Latin America, but in the classic fashion the changes did not often produce a very sharp or revolutionary break. It signified the grafting on of a number of new social elements to a system that had been absorbing such new elites in this manner for centuries. Some new pillars were added but Latin America's historic pyramidal structure was maintained. . . .

As the development process began in Latin America in the nineteenth century, the new merchant and entrepreneurial elements had been quickly absorbed within the dominant elitist system. The continued growth of the middle classes throughout Latin America has implied since the 1930s the increased participation (and, now, often dominance) of these elements in politics, government, the Church, and the armed forces officer corps. Significantly, however, though the class composition of these institutions has been altered, there have been few changes in the cultural norms and elitist-authoritarian behavioral patterns that predominate in them. The middle sectors have absorbed the elitist ways and often have been stronger defenders of the traditional order than even the traditional elites themselves. There are a number of new elites but the patterns of elite rule and circulation in power persist. Since the 1930s also, as Latin America has increasingly industrialized, the urban (and sometimes rural) trade-union movement has also emerged as an influential force in all the Latin America nations. But as with other groups, organized labor led by middle-class spokesmen has generally also been assimilated into the prevailing system through the creation of government-sponsored and controlled labor movements, paternalistically directed from above rather than reflecting much mass or grassroots challenge from below. A manifestly *corporatist* system of controls on trade-union activity and incorporation of cooperative labor elements into the prevailing system represents the historic elites' response to the rise of this new social force. . . .

More recently, as a result of the transistor radio and the extension of other communications and transportation grids that have brought new demands and expectations to the previously isolated countryside, it has become the peasants' turn to be assimilated in a partial fashion. The laws governing the "rights" (in Latin America still more a feudal than a modern concept, implying group obligations and privileges rather than individual rights) of organized labor have now been extended to rural workers; similarly "agrarian reform" became more an instrument to structure and control peasant participation in the national life than to liberate or bring revolutionary transformation to the countryside. These same laws in many of the countries of the area have also been extended recently to women workers and domestics. In a few countries (Cuba, Nicaragua, El Salvador) such changes came too slowly or were perverted under brutal dictatorship and revolutionary upheavals resulted. But in the majority of countries the pattern has been one of continued "civilization" of new social groups into the prevailing political culture and the incorporation of such groups into the system under elite tutelage and direction, rather than one of revolutionary overthrow.

All this has given the development process in Latin America a distinctive flavor and structure that help distinguish it from the Western European and United States pattern. Not only are the times and circumstances obviously different in Latin America today from what they were for the Western nations in the nineteenth century; but the process by which modern institutions are filtered in and out, the timing and sequences of development, and the social and political concomitants of economic growth are quite different as well. In Latin America the traditional structures have, for the most part, proved remarkably malleable and adjustable. With some exceptions, they have accommodated the forces of change instead of being overthrown by them. In contrast to our more familiar models of development, which picture traditional institutions as hardened shells that must either crack and disintegrate under the onslaught of modernization or else be overthrown, the Latin American systems have proved both remarkably tenacious and surprisingly adjustable, absorbing what is useful in modernity, rejecting most of the rest, and in the process largely retaining their historic tradition, essence, and distinctiveness. In these ways Latin America has sought to adapt to the main currents of the modern industrial world while also maintaining what it considers valuable and characteristic of its own civilization.

Latin America should thus be looked on as having opted for and chosen because of historical circumstances a developmental path that is *alternative* to the United States model, not some pale, retarded, "unsuccessful" version of it. Moreover, as the United States cracks and creaks; as we realize this nation had no monopoly on virtue or efficient political institutions; as hierarchy, corporatism, and centralized state-directed control and direction grow in the United States and other advanced industrial nations; *and* as we long for the sense of community, moral values, and unity that we seem somehow to have lost, the Latin American experience may offer some valuable instruction from which we can learn. The question cannot be finally answered in [our discussion] but it is too important to be ignored: Can it be, heretical though it seems in the United States, that the Latin American nations with their organic, unitary, and patrimonialist conception of the proper ordering of state and society will in the long run prove to have coped better with the wrenching crises of modernization than the United States with its secular, divisive, fragmented interest group pluralism? That is a question that transcends the study of Latin America, but it is one whose implications we must begin to consider.

The focus in [our discussion] is on the historic and prevailing political culture of Latin America, the institutional and socio-political context in which development takes place and which shapes it in various ways. That is an important, often neglected, and necessary explanation, but no claim is put forward that it is the only explanation. We must also, as indicated in the preceding discussion, examine the great motor forces of economic development and class change, and also the patterns of Latin American dependency. But religion, culture, values, language, law, and history are also crucially important in understanding the institutional framework through which development is fashioned and filtered, and even in shaping the processes of economic development and class change themselves. Although the particular form that development has taken in Latin America has both multiple causes and has produced multiple effects, anyone with even a nodding acquaintance with the area cannot help but be impressed by the continuing importance of the historical, sociological, and political-cultural variables stressed here as fundamental in molding and determining development's direction.

Latin America, we shall see, remains hierarchical, authoritarian, paternalistic, Catholic (in the broad political-cultural sense as used here), elitist, corporatist, and patrimonialist to its core. These ingredients have been *and remain* at the heart of its development tradition and are what help make it distinctive. At present, however, new ideologies and movements have begun increasingly (and in several countries successfully) to challenge the traditional ones, the bases of order and legitimacy of the old system are being progressively undermined, the outside world has had more and more of an impact, and a new framework of class and issue-oriented politics has appeared. The clash between traditional and modern has intensified throughout the Hemisphere, raising strong doubts as to whether Latin America's traditional structures are any longer capable of managing and controlling the rising tide of popular demands, and whether its historic patterns and institutions can survive. Yet even in the face of these newer and in some cases revolutionary pressures for change, the traditional Latin American ways of adapting and accommodating to the pressures of modernization are often dominant—and they may well remain so. Thus the model and explanation of Latin American development presented here may not only help us understand the more traditional regimes in Latin America but also the revolutionary ones, where hierarchy, top-down authority, and institutionalized corporatism also prevail. As Claudio Véliz reminds us, Cuba is highly centralized and authoritarian not just because it is socialist but also because it is Latin America. . . .

Notes

1. No attempt in these few pages is made to present a complete picture and history of Latin American development. This discussion is purposely brief and interpretive, designed to provide only a skeletal outline and overview of the Latin American development pattern as a way of introducing the area.

11 / Natural Corporatism and the Passing of Populism in Spanish America

Ronald C. Newton

Ronald Newton, a historian at Simon Fraser University, Vancouver, B.C., opens his chapter by suggesting that a revival of corporatism occurred in Chile following the overthrow in 1973 of the Marxist regime of Salvadore Allende Gossens by General Augusto Pinochet. Newton describes corporatism in terms of the "limited pluralism" of "functional groups" with "cross-cutting solidarities" that break down class distinctions. These groups are given a monopoly by the state to aggregate and articulate their political demands. In the case of Chile, he argues that the Pinochet regime was merely the first overt manifestation of a "'natural corporatism' that has been evolving obscurely behind the epiphenomena of *movimientos* and insurrections, electoral campaigns and *golpes,* since the depression of the 1930s and, more markedly, since the late 1940s." In particular, Newton links the idea of natural corporatism and the phenomenon of populism, which emerged in Latin America during the 1930s as a political response to the generalized societal crisis precipitated by the worldwide depression. He proposes that "the two are not only roughly coeval, but that in natural corporatism are found the typical structures and processes of populism." Finally, Newton considers natural corporatism to form an integral part of the "new authoritarianism" that characterized the rise of military rule in Latin America after 1964.

In the aftermath of the military revolt that overthrew the Popular Unity government of Dr. Salvador Allende in September 1973, reports began to seep out of Chile that the junta was supervising revision of the constitution in a "corporativist" sense. . . . These are early days yet to attempt an analysis. . . . What is reasonably apparent, however, is that the Chilean right has resurrected a variant of the corporate state.

Most observers must find themselves bemused at this, for in the experience of the Atlantic world the corporate state is an anachronism, and a faintly tawdry one at that. I propose to argue, however, that in the larger Latin American context the Chilean episode is merely the first *overt* manifestation of a "natural corporativism"[1] that has been evolving obscurely behind the epiphenomena of *movimientos* and insurrections, electoral campaigns and *golpes,* since the depression of the 1930s and, more markedly, since the late 1940s. This essay will define the concept of natural corporatism, and mark the limits of its usefulness. Beyond that, in an attempt to discover leads to answers to questions that the concept raises but of its nature cannot cope with satisfactorily, I will consider some historical and situational factors that suggest reasons why natural corporatism should have arisen at a particular place and time. This in turn necessitates examination of the relation between natural corporatism and the political mood of "populism"; I shall propose that the two are not only roughly coeval, but that in natural corporatism are found the typical structures and processes of populism. Finally, it seems appropriate to touch briefly upon the function of natural corporatism in the contemporary transition in the more advanced states of Spanish America to more comprehensive forms of autocratic rule—the "new militarism" that has become a major preoccupation of Latin Americanist scholars since the Brazilian coup of 1964.[2]

The corporate state, idea and praxis, has not fared well at the hands of historians and political sociologists, certainly not those of the erstwhile Allied nations of World War II. The modern idea of corporatism has been around for a long time. Its origins go back to the conservative reaction against the Enlightenment and the French Revolution, to the "organic" sense of society in Burke, de Bonald, in some aspects de Maistre, and a major line of German theorists from Herder through Hegel and Savigny to Gierke. But toward the latter part of the nineteenth century, the accelerating processes of industrialization and urbanization,

Reprinted with permission from *The New Corporatism: Social-Political Structures in the Iberian World,* edited by Fredrick B. Pike and Thomas Stritch, pp. 34–51. (Notre Dame, Ind.: University of Notre Dame Press, 1974), copyright © 1974 by University of Notre Dame. (Ed. note: Some nonessential passages and footnotes have been deleted.)

with their attendant phenomena of disruption of traditional class and status relationships, dissolution of long-standing social solidarities (which in extreme form would become "alienation" and/or "anomie"), proletarianization and gathering class conflict—all these made more urgent, by reaction, the quest for organic concepts of society, or organic "solutions." These were compelling modes of thought for writers who, with diverse rationales, rejected both the postulates of liberal bourgeois capitalism and the liberal state (with its mechanistic social relationships determined by the marketplace), and the Marxian dialect (whose implacable unfolding also implied change of unknown magnitude). The "organic-mechanistic" antithesis was assimilated to formal sociology by, among others, Ferdinand Tönnies, who reformulated it as *Gemeinschaft-Gesellschaft,* an organizing concept whose ramifications would preoccupy sociologists for generations. The like concern of many writers with "primary" groups and solidarities led them to a reexamination of family, clan, commune, and occupational group, and generated in turn a revival of scholarship into the guilds and corporations of medieval Europe. Neo-medievalism was clear in the Catholic social thought of such ideologues as La Tour du Pin and Pope Leo XIII, but is equally evident in the somewhat later work of the secular humanitarians of the English circle of Guild Socialists. And derivations from the same loose idea system are clear enough in the evolving doctrines of revolutionary syndicalism that found their most fertile ground in pre-1914 Latin Europe.

Thus in the first decades of the twentieth century there was no single coherent corporatist doctrine, nor any dominant corporatist doctrinaire. Corporatism was, rather, an untidy intellectual kitchen midden comprised of brilliant social insights as well as the effluvia from some badly cracked pots, strategies of working-class resistance to the capitalist order and proposals for the reconstitution of a harmonious and hierarchical Christian society, limited projects for political and administrative reform through functional representation and the garbled verbalizations of the insecurities of individuals—artisans, intellectuals, aristocrats—threatened by marginalization in the onrushing change of industrializing Europe. But at the end of World War I the very incoherence of corporatism facilitated its assimilation, or fragments thereof, to the ideological reaction, first, to the immediate threat of the spread of the Bolshevik Revolution, and secondly, to the protracted crisis of liberal democracy and liberal capitalism that had been exposed by the war and deepened by postwar economic depressions. In a limited pragmatic response to the collapse of 1929-30, the devices of corporatism, in the form of industrial self-government through preexisting cartels, trade associations, and chambers, were applied briefly by nonfascist capitalist systems, including the United States of the New Deal era (the NRA) and Nazi Germany.[3] But elsewhere, most particularly in Latin and Catholic Europe, corporatism was heralded forth as a multipurpose nostrum in the context of authoritarianism and (often largely rhetorical) nationalism. In industrial relations, the creation, with the participation of state functionaries, of functional corporations grouping together owners, managers, and workers, and the public arbitration of disputes, offered surcease from conflict between capital and organized labor (and among capitalists); but unlike the Bolshevik solution corporatism promised to leave property rights, religion, the family, and hierarchical social status virtually untouched. Its political corollary, functional representation through corporate chambers, offered a seemingly rational alternative to the disarray and ineffectuality of parliamentary systems, or to the class bias and latent (if somewhat tarnished) internationalism of the socialist movement, or to the despotism of a Leninist vanguard. Indeed, it offered a means to the depoliticization of society, hence to a renewal of ordered performance of functions in the body politic, hence also to the enlightened rule of technical and administrative expertise. The nation-state thus came to be the reason for being of corporatist structures. In view of the libertarianism and emphasis upon the autonomy of social solidarities that had formed important though not dominant strands of pre-1914 corporatist thought, there is abundant irony in this.

Although the Italian Corporate State was not legislated into existence until 1934, and led at best a shadowy half-life thereafter, the international notoriety that the fascist regime had enjoyed for more than a decade caused Italy to serve as the best-known paradigm of corporatism. There, before the end of the 1930s, the disparities between rhetoric and praxis suggested to many that the Corporate State (and its predecessor, the Syndicalist State) had served mainly as a façade behind which the regime had destroyed the autonomy of the Italian trade union movement and reduced the living levels of Italian workingmen.[4] Marxists asserted at the time that "social peace" was but a code word for the obliteration of socialism within the working class, and "economic coordination" but a sanction for the monopolies, oligopolies, and cartels demanded by a faltering capitalist order; and subsequent historians have described the Italian Corporate State in such uncommonly blunt terms as "wind" and "a confidence trick."[5] But in the deepening international crisis of the late 1930s and the descent again into war, corporatism was much more generally discredited in the Western democracies by its frequent appearance in the ideologies, action programs, and (less commonly) institutional structures of the movements and regimes in alliance or sympathy with the Rome-Berlin Axis. The states in which it achieved some semblance of implementation—pre-*Anschluss* Austria, Vichy France,

Mussolini's Italy—were in their turn absorbed by Nazi Germany and perished with it. Save for vestiges in the Iberian dictatorships that survived at the margin, corporatism as a formal doctrine has lain buried amidst much other trumpery paraphernalia of the European catastrophe for more than a quarter of a century.

In interwar Europe, corporatism was an explicit if not altogether coherent doctrine advocated by political movements seeking power, and an organizational principle imposed by regimes *in* power, often in the wake of substantial socio-political turbulence or violence. Until the very recent events in Chile, this has nowhere been the case in postwar Latin America. On the contrary, *natural* corporatism, as the adjective implies, has evolved slowly, unacknowledged, within or parallel to the conventional and more or less constitutional processes of electoral politics, civic paralysis, *golpes,* caretaker administrations, *pactos, convenios, acuerdos,* and more electoral politics. Where European-derived corporatism has figured at all in the doctrinal writings and programs of political activists, it has been the property of isolated sects and sectarians of the extreme right with few prospects of immediate access to power.[6] What is under discussion here, rather, is an *organizing hypothesis,* a mental construct developed by scholars with which to examine and explain socio-political phenomena which have not, generally, proved responsive to explication in terms of the postulates and categories of conventional liberal-developmental scholarship on Latin America.[7] Although one may feel—with no elation whatever—that the recent turn of events in Chile confirms some of the insights of this line of scholarship, the concept itself . . . needs much further work. The starting point, I suspect, has been the commonsense assumption that, despite the notorious frailty of Latin American party systems and legislatures and the frequent and apparently ruinous breaks in executive continuity, the essential business of politics— the transmutation of claims, demands, and grievances into legislation and dispensation, *input* into *output*—continues, after a fashion, to get done. . . .

Let me attempt to outline the historical emergence of natural corporatism and summarize its salient characteristics.[8] It is first of all a function of the increase in complexity of social and economic organization attributable to urbanization and industrialization. Its beginnings in Latin America, therefore, are located in the limited import-substitution industrialization of the 1930s, and its further evolution in the patterns of rural-urban migration, expansion of urban white-collar and working-class aggregates, and spasmodic industrialization, since the World War II period. The phenomenon is consequently identified with Latin American states at "advanced" levels of socio-economic evolution; it is not found in the small peripheral states that have not experienced significant development of both urbanization and industrialization.[9] Apace with this evolution, there has emerged a new congeries of urban secondary groups based upon occupation or function; these complement, though, rarely supersede, the older primary solidarities of kinship, ethnicity, locality, and work place, and the intricate obligations of friendship and *relaciones*. These secondary groups have rapidly achieved formal organization and, in virtually all cases, legal recognition. They span a great range in terms of their attributes of social solidarity: from purely mechanical or contrived solidarities (trade associations, public bureaucracies staffed by place hunters), through professional organizations or paternalistic small and medium enterprises (in which the web of personal interaction grows denser), to those rooted in a shared way of life not yet seriously disrupted by change (landowning cliques, older skilled-trade unions, the military, the Church, until lately the university). Many toward the latter end of the scale have been effective in providing creature satisfactions, material and psychological; in doing so they have become partially closed social environments affording individuals a single source of authority and a single focus of allegiance: the group's leadership or functional elite or *patrón*. These are, to a degree, "inclusive" social solidarities, and correspondingly isolated from other such solidarities—the characteristics of a more traditional, preindustrial order of secondary-group structure.[10] Or to put it another way, in comparison with the unlimited pluralism of, for example, industrializing Great Britain or the United States, the number of secondary groups in contemporary urban Latin America is small (by virtue of lesser and later industrialization, and the hostility of the authoritarian state to the creation of voluntary groups, noted below), and the multiple affiliations or cross-cutting solidarities possible to or demanded of individuals are few. "The habit of voluntary association," in de Tocqueville's phrase, is not strong.

This pattern is reinforced by the controlling concepts and institutions of a traditional politico-legal culture, the Hispano-Roman, which is throughout antagonistic to the autonomous existence of secondary groups, but which conduces to the institutionalization—including, by legal or quasi-legal means, the bestowal of economic or social monopoly—of dependent, *non*autonomous secondary groups. In the classic situation of natural corporatism, however, the latter are not completely subordinated and articulated to the structure of government. Rather, in the mode of what Juan Linz describes as the "limited pluralism" of Hispanic authoritarianism,[11] they possess the ability to mobilize men and influence, legal legitimacy and *fueros,* and, as *intereses creados,* the sanction of tradition to support their claims of respect for customary privilege. Indeed, this equilibrium between the state's authority to grant life to intermediary bodies, and the extensive defenses of the latter behind which to perpetuate their existence unmolested, is, it seems to me, a key to any understanding of the long-term immobility of the forms of Hispanic statecraft.[12]

Such a relationship implies continuing one-to-one interaction between functional elites and political elites, which means, where little or no permanent bureaucracy exists, the executive and his ministers and advisors. The vertical nature of these relationships provides channels of political flow that circumvent those of the constitutionally envisioned electoral and legislative processes. As the former prove ever more effective for the articulation of political demands—whether behind closed doors or through street *manifestaciones* or strikes, or some combination thereof—and for their satisfaction, the conventional structures can only decline further in prestige and legitimacy. The constant febrile effort, in an atmosphere of struggle necessary to keep the system in some sort of balance conduces to in-group solidarity, exacerbates the differences among groups, and strengthens the configuration of multiple lines of vertical interaction converging within the apparatus of government.

Nevertheless, in its earlier stages the system—which is rather too elegant a term—of natural corporatism was tolerably effective. It has ceased to be so because socio-economic change has altered the preconditions that once made it viable. One of these is, obviously, that the number of *intereses* to be satisfied be relatively small. This was true in the beginnings of urbanization and industrialization; it is true no longer. Similarly, increasing socio-economic complexity and shifts in the locus of power have undermined the ability of elites to manipulate the informal arrangements of corporatist politics and make them work. Traditional elites, not far removed from the classic complementary nineteenth-century triad of landowners, ecclesiastics, and soldiers, were— even when they were fighting among themselves—relatively homogeneous; shared status and values bound functional and political leadership together (indeed, at times they were indistinguishable), informal channels of communication linked them together. Their social distance from the commonality, the relatively low levels of participation, the buffer provided by the melodrama of party politics, all contributed to the atmosphere of tranquility in which competing demands could be balanced off more or less rationally, crises managed more or less imperturbably. But older agrarian and extractive interests have had to cede place to newer and ever more ramified commercial and industrial interests. This has not, of course, spelled the wholesale eclipse and demise of older elite families. But the diversification of elite structures and the co-optation of the newly successful *have* meant a degree of fragmentation, more tenuous communications, and in turn far greater difficulties in the management of politics. This has been compounded, further, by the greater accessibility and visibility of elites. It may be that the economic gap separating functional elites from their constituencies has not appreciably lessened in the past two generations, but social distance certainly has. Status is less fully ascriptive; performance is more susceptible to scrutiny by an occasionally obstreperous press and a rather more exigent public.

The consequences can be schematized in structural-functional terms. Organized secondary groups are clearly serviceable vehicles of interest *articulation*. But as the sheer number of groups availing themselves of these procedures grows, in function both of economic diversity and the increasing intrusion of urban (and occasionally, rural) underclass aggregates into the circle of organized interests permitted to participate, the problem of interest *aggregation*—the compromises, operationalization and translation into legislation, adjustment of political demands to majority or national priorities—becomes ever more acute. It is hypothesized that in the earlier stages of this process the aggregating function was performed primarily through the informal horizontal solidarities of elite structures, and secondarily through the formal horizontal solidarities of parties and legislatures, or some combination thereof. But the formal processes have fallen into an advanced state of decrepitude through the success of the informal ones; the latter in turn, for very different reasons, have more lately also lost their capacity to aggregate effectively. Thus for a conventional regime forced to maneuver in the exquisitely narrow space between the "populistic" priorities of distribution and the "developmental" demands of production, a sequence of unprocessed and uncompromising demands is in all likelihood catastrophic, whether all the demands be satisfied or not; and the military authoritarian solution has proven all too obvious. It should be added that in the Mexican and Cuban systems the crucial slippage between formal polity and secondary groups, and their respective elites, has been diminished or eliminated through the interpenetration of elites and the subordination of functional leadership to men—party members and/or permanent bureaucrats—who are bearers of a more or less homogeneous national ideology and program; this process is best described by the Hitlerian term *Gleichschaltung*. In the more recent "modern" military regimes, those in which liberal rules and procedures have been definitively abandoned and "development" accepted as an overriding goal, military officers, especially those trained in managerial techniques beyond the requirements of narrow military expertise, and their civilian technocratic associates constitute an analogous horizontal solidarity, with the same aggregating capacity.

Although many subtleties remain to be introduced and ramifications traced out, the concept of natural corporatism *per se* cannot carry us much beyond the present point. If its potential uses are obvious, so also are its limitations. As a method of *static* analysis, it directs a searching light upon a fairly narrow range of phenomena—secondary (or "functional" or "intermediary") groups, and their relation to formal and informal government. To a degree it illuminates closely related areas, but leaves much of *total* socio-political systems in darkness. In structural-functional terms—and the derivation of the concept from structural-functional theory is evident enough—natural corporatism relies heavily upon analysis of *input* functions—interest articulation and interest aggregation—but can tell us little about *output,* except to make clear that the functions under the latter head must be performed with the minimum either of continuity or of rationality. Natural corporatism is not of much help in approaching the classic question, *who gets what?*, although it certainly suggests a means of finding out *how.*

As a means of discovering and analyzing the *dynamics* of socio-political change over time, the concept offers a schematic model, which is again useful though limited. As sketched above, the phenomenon of natural corporatism is restricted to a particular time period, roughly the four decades from 1930 to 1970. This is the phase of Latin American socio-political history that is coming to be called "populist." The descriptive label "populism," it seems to me, lumps together causes, informing assumptions, and processes: the incorporation of ever-greater sectors of populations into political society, attempts to create cross-class coalitions (either under the aegis of quasi-revolutionary *movimientos* such as the Bolivian MNR [Movimiento Nacionalista Revolucionario] or Peronism in its first and second incarnations, or through electoral arrangements such as those associated with Peru's APRA [Alianza Popular Revolucionaria Americana] and its daughter parties), emphasis on (and bitter competition over) *distribution* of the social product, and a peculiar style which one associates with enhanced and strident mobilization, the mass *manifestaciones* of assorted *sindicatos, ligas, gremios, comisiones, federaciones,* and so on. Natural corporatism, it has been argued, arose as a function of urbanization and industrialization, the consequent emergence, growth, and proliferation of organized secondary groups, and the incapacity of traditional liberal constitutional procedures (which have not, however, been explicitly repudiated) to articulate their wants, much less to satisfy them. The two concepts, in other words, are congruent; the latter is, one hopes, a fairly precise model of the mechanics of the former. But it goes further: though effective at first, natural corporatism's inherent inability to afford *orderly* methods in a *national* context for the containment of the competing demands of production and distribution has caused it to break down. Under pressure, natural corporatism, itself the offspring of the traditional Hispanic mode of authoritarianism, has developed easily into regimes more modern and thoroughgoing in their use of command and coercion. But it is clear that although the dynamic schema can lead to a more accurate understanding of *what* has happened, the underlying reasons *why* these particular kinds of change have occurred in this particular place and time remain elusive.[13]

The fact that the concept of natural corporatism is restricted by place and time in its applicability is significant. After all, the industrialization process everywhere has been accompanied by growing social complexity, the proliferation of secondary groups, changes in elite structure and composition, and expansion in the ambit of political participation. In the Atlantic world, many societies, including the United States, have been plagued by the conflict between the sanctioned procedures of electoral politics and the more covert workings of interest group politics. Yet except for affinities to the interwar experiences of the states of Latin Europe, most markedly those that eventuated in the status quo corporatist dictatorships of Salazar and Franco, the natural corporatism of Spanish America appears to be unique in its configuration and in its historical trajectory of rise, dysfunctionality, and transformation into more comprehensive forms of authoritarianism. Thus the obvious next step is some consideration—exploratory at best, in the present state of scholarship—of historical and situational factors.

I have proposed elsewhere[14] that in the sixteenth and early seventeenth centuries the structure of Spanish political society congealed into a stasis from which it has yet fully to extricate itself: an equilibrium between an autocratic central state, which could not tolerate the legal or constitutional autonomy of intermediary bodies, and those intermediary bodies, which succeeded in clothing themselves in legal charters, *fueros,* and customary privilege, and which achieved, especially under weak monarchies, a near-parity of de facto power with the Crown. The first element was created by the centralizing efforts of Ferdinand and Isabella and their successors of the House of Austria through Phillip II (and their bureaucracies), who suppressed in turn the autonomy of the towns, the Church and military orders, great noble houses, and functional corporations such as the *Mesta.* In the process, however, the internal authority and customary privileges of these latter were altered only in small degree; they were, rather, yoked to the fortunes of the Crown as coordinate arms of administration. The second element of the stasis was a function of the psychologically ruinous and financially catastrophic failure of Spain's imperial mission in the seventeenth century, demographic decline, and the concurrent contraction and impoverishment of the nation's internal economy. The Crown's expedients for revenue in a failing cause increased its dependence upon and concessions to intermediary bodies; disillusionment and gross economic recession stimulated in the latter, one might argue, an overriding concern to consolidate past gains. In this stasis, the decay into almost total irrelevancy of the several *cortes* halted the formation of horizontal political solidarities and strengthened the pattern of multiple vertical flows of political interaction.

The weight of historical tradition is also a historian's customary escape hatch, and I do not wish to labor it here. Other states of early modern Europe experienced, and in time evolved away from, centralized autocracy and corporatist socio-legal structures; they have also long since fashioned, often from unpromising beginnings, systems of political representation. The *economic* factor, however, appears to be more suggestive for our purposes—the factor, to be more precise, of the reality or perception or fear of economic collapse and long-term stagnation, which must be taken in conjunction with its implications—legal, administrative, customary, intellectual—for the evolution of secondary-group solidarities. One does not, after all, find enduring corporatist structures in societies, or sectors of societies, characterized by headlong economic growth and its attendant social flux and optimistic view of the future—a point apparent enough to the liberal assailants of corporate privilege of the late eighteenth and nineteenth centuries.

This factor, I suggest, has had ample opportunity to recur, in differing contexts, in the Hispanic lands. Karl Marx's observations at a much later date, for example, echo what has been proposed above:

> We have not here to state the circumstances, political or economical, which destroyed Spanish commerce, industry, navigation, and agriculture. For the present purpose it is sufficient to simply recall the fact. As the commercial and industrial life of the towns declined, internal exchanges became rare, the mingling of the inhabitants of different provinces less frequent, the means of communication neglected, and the great roads gradually deserted. Thus the local life of Spain, the independence of its provinces and communes, the diversified state of society originally based on the physical configuration of the country, and historically developed by the detached manner in which the several provinces emancipated themselves from the Moors, and formed little independent commonwealths—was now finally strengthened and confirmed by the economical revolution which dried up the sources of national activity. And while the absolute monarchy found in Spain material in its very nature repulsive to centralization, it did all in its power to prevent the growth of common interests arising out of a national division of labor and the multiplicity of internal exchanges—the very basis on which alone a uniform system of administration and the rule of general laws can be created.[15]

Spain was not, in the mid-nineteenth century—nor in the seventeenth, for that matter—a "primitive" society flirting with the beginnings of "development." The point of Marx's observation is, rather, the corrosive effect of prolonged economic depression, exacerbated at the time by loss of much of the income from a colonial empire, upon an elaborately developed social system with centuries of complex evolution behind it—one in which, however, the dynamic of capitalist economic development had gone sluggish at an early stage.

In twentieth-century Spanish America, it is not difficult to place this factor in relation to the asymmetries or socio-political evolution that have often been commented upon. The starting point is the growing urbanization since the turn of the century—necessarily, since urbanism is the context and *sine qua non* of the social differentiation and secondary-group development under discussion. Included in this process were the restoration of the city (the primate city, normally) to preponderance in national economic, political, and administrative life, the expansion of urban white-collar population groups, and, in some regions, the beginnings of trade unionism. All were functions, of course, not of indigenous industrialization (except for primary processing) but of the more effective articulation of the Latin American primary-product economies, in subordinate situations, to the European- and North American-dominated world trading system. This meant, among other things, that ever-larger (and more vocal) population segments were exposed more nakedly to the vagaries of world business cycles culminating in the depression of the 1930s. It would be an exaggeration, it seems to me, to regard the depression era as the "crisis of liberalism," except insofar as "liberalism" was equated narrowly with the uninhibited flow of commodities and capital. Otherwise, however, one must be skeptical of the extent to which the postulates either of liberal democracy or free-enterprise capitalism had been absorbed in the first place. By the same token, the corporatist projects of a José Uriburu in Argentina or a Getulio Vargas in Brazil are perfectly comprehensible, if premature, in terms both of their challenge to majority political rhetoric and to important export-oriented sectors; nor was social mobilization sufficiently advanced.

By now it is generally accepted, however, that the limited import-substitution industrialization of the 1930s and 1940s set events in train that would culminate in the crisis of the bourgeoisie. For much of the latter had established itself in the occupations of the preindustrial city—bureaucracy, the professions, commerce, "service"—and participated but little in the industrialization process, such as it was, in competition with immigrant entrepreneurs, foreign branch plants, and state and foreign sources of capital. Industrialization, in any event, proved an inconstant lure, both during World War II when the profitability of primary products diverted capital again into traditional extractive production, and in the late 1940s when the industrial nations were once more able to flood Latin America with consumer goods. The urban middle classes, whose apparent emergence to political self-consciousness was signalized by the wave of democratic reformist regimes of the immediate postwar period, had in fact entered upon modernization very belatedly, and were thus condemned in the main to white-collar functions not directly related to technologically and organizationally advanced manufacturing processes. Moreover, hard on their heels emerged not only a more demanding and politically potent organized working class, but also a rapidly increasing underclass of rural origins, whose potential for turbulence was perceived at the time as incalculably menacing. In the more advanced societies, the nether millstone was set firmly in place by the early 1950s.

The politics of populism and the unacknowledged evolution of what has been described earlier in these pages as natural corporatism expanded from this period onward, in repeated cycles of standpat military regimes, overthrow, reformist projects, multiclass coalitions, stalemate, and military restoration of the situation. The raw increase in population save in a few areas, the even greater demand for social services it provoked, the growing capability of organized interests representing ever-larger population aggregates to articulate their demands, resulted in increasingly bitter competition for the proportion of the social product that could be distributed, and a concern to protect what had been so gotten. For even with foreign borrowings for current expenses, the social product did not keep pace. The provenance of this upper millstone has been a matter of dispute for a decade and more. The shortcomings of Latin American capitalism have been attributed by respectable scholarly opinion, especially in the United States, to the hopelessly preindustrial "attitudes" and "values" of what should be the bourgeois cutting edge of industrialism; given the asymmetries noted above one must concede some substance to this view, despite its all too comfortable congruence with the intellectual needs of United States policymakers. But of course there is here a nice question of an interrelated chain of causes and effects over an extended period of time. It makes more sense to examine, in the first instance, the pressures of industrial trading partners to expand and rationalize production at the expense of indigenous industrialization, the long-term decline in the world prices of those commodities as against the rise in the cost of manufactures, the gradual transfer of foreign investment from the primary to the secondary and tertiary sectors and the expansion of foreign-controlled branch-plant enclaves, and the drainage of capital in the form of remitted profits and payments in service of debt. In any case, the functional and political elites of the

populist phase—the "national bourgeoisie" in current Marxist terminology—have proven unequal to either the developmental or the aggregate
tasks; the "new military," who are among other things counter-elites,
are now proposing to make good these failures.

In summary: it may be that in the hands of the Chilean right and
possibly elsewhere corporatism will be revived as a working ideology—
or, properly speaking, an element of an ideology. The Chilean case could
prove instructive, for it is not certain that the military have been trained
to assume manifold administrative and technical positions as their
brother officers in Brazil and Peru have been; nor indeed is it certain
that they are prepared to make the decisive break with their upper-
status civilian compeers that would enable them to pursue roughshod
the lure of development. In such a situation, the uses of corporatist
structures as means to depoliticization and social demobilization are
apparent; and we may in fact see a true Corporate State, a regime with
strong affinities to the past—post-Civil-War Spain, for example—as well
as to the present of the "new military."

I must emphasize again, however, that for the time being natural
corporatism is an analytical construct, a scholar's tool, and nothing
else. Even for those in the tricky business of operationalizing scholarship
into policy or rationalizations for policy, it must be obvious that the
concept of natural corporatism is not the stuff of which policy recommendations are made.

Notes

1. Adapted from Philippe C. Schmitter, *Interest Conflict and Political Change
in Brazil* (Stanford, 1971), 383 passim. I have earlier objected to the use of
"corporativism" to describe these phenomena; the objection is withdrawn. See
Ronald C. Newton, "On 'Functional Groups,' 'Fragmentation,' and 'Pluralism'
in Spanish American Political Society," *The Hispanic American Historical
Review*, L (1970), 1–29.

2. Brazil will be alluded to in passing, but the main concern of this essay
is with the states of Spanish America and with a specifically Hispanic politico-
legal tradition. For detailed treatment of Brazil see Schmitter, *Interest Conflict
and Political Change in Brazil.*

3. As pointed out recently by John A. Garraty in "The New Deal, National
Socialism, and the Great Depression," *American Historical Review*, LXXVIII
(1973), 914–915.

4. S. Lombardini, "Italian Fascism and the Economy," in S. J. Woolf, ed.,
The Nature of Fascism (New York, 1968), 156–162.

5. H. Stuart Hughes, *The United States and Italy* (Cambridge, 1953), 88, cited by N. Kogan in Woolf, *The Nature of Fascism,* p. 17; anonymous reviewer in the *Times* (London) *Literary Supplement,* March 2, 1973, pp. 225–227.

6. The most significant of these, perhaps, was the old Chilean *Falange Nacional,* which became the Christian Democratic Party in the late 1950s. With the transition the emphasis on corporatism was much diminished.

7. To my knowledge, none of the writers associated with the "New Left" have utilized the corporatist approach. The *concept,* however, is not inherently anti-Marxist, nor an "alternative to Marxism," as the *ideology* has of course been.

8. For a fuller treatment see my 1970 essay cited in note 1.

9. In my earlier essay, I suggested that natural corporatism was also limited by a second set of factors: the existence of durable and viable structures of interest aggregation, the party system and legislature. As examples, I offered in 1970 Uruguay and Chile. In 1973 this no longer applies. Of the major states, only Venezuela and Colombia retain any vestiges of conventional systems. [Ed. note: The factors Newton considers have changed again as many countries that experienced military governments in the 1960s and 1970s have returned to formal democracies. This phenomenon is fairly recent, and it is unclear how the return to party systems and legislatures exemplifies natural corporatism.]

10. The failure to see that in industrialized society *most* secondary structures are of necessity "mechanical" and bureaucratized, are not and cannot be social solidarities, is, it seems to me, a chief weakness of the conservative theorists who sought to recreate harmonious, "integral" societies on what they took to be the preindustrial model.

11. "An Authoritarian Regime: Spain," in E. Allardt and Y. Littunen, eds., *Cleavages, Ideologies, and Party Systems* (Helsinki, 1964), 291–341.

12. See Newton, *The Hispanic American Historical Review, op. cit.,* esp. 22–28.

13. Only time, of course, will prove or disprove the assumption that populism and natural corporatism are drawing to a close. One may be fairly certain, however, that national systems now growing sufficiently "advanced" to experience these phenomena will not in fact do so to any great extent. We are a long way from the crudities of a "stages" thesis, *à la* Rostow, which would demand that each system recapitulate, with perhaps a bit of telescoping, the entire trajectory of more "developed" systems. Within Latin America, the demonstration effect is close enough at hand to obviate this. I suspect also that, on the South American continent, at least, mingled admiration for and fear of the Brazilian model will accelerate present trends toward military authoritarianism.

14. See note 12.

15. Karl Marx and Friedrich Engels, *Revolution in Spain* (New York, 1939), 25–26. Originally published in the New York *Daily Tribune,* 1854.

Selected Bibliography

Chalmers, Douglas A. "Corporatism and Comparative Politics," in *New Directions in Comparative Politics,* edited by Howard J. Wiarda. Boulder, Colo.: Westview Press, 1985, pp. 56–79.

Collier, David, and Ruth Berins Collier. "Inducements Versus Constraints: Disaggregating Corporatism," *The American Political Science Review* 73:4 (Dec. 1979), pp. 967–986.

Erickson, Kenneth Paul. *The Brazilian Corporative State and Working Class Politics.* Berkeley: University of California Press, 1977.

Hammergren, Linn A. "Corporatism in Latin American Politics: A Reexamination of the 'Unique' Tradition," *Comparative Politics* 9:4 (July 1977), pp. 443–446.

Linz, Juan J., and Alfred Stepan (eds.). *The Breakdown of Democratic Regimes: Latin America.* Baltimore: Johns Hopkins University Press, 1978.

Malloy, James M. (ed.). *Authoritarianism and Corporatism in Latin America.* Pittsburgh, Penn.: University of Pittsburgh Press, 1977.

Morse, Richard M. "The Heritage of Latin America," in *The Founding of New Societies,* edited by Louis Hartz. New York: Harcourt, Brace & World, 1964.

Schmitter, Philippe. "Paths to Political Development in Latin America," *Changing Latin America: New Interpretations of Its Politics and Society,* edited by Douglas A. Chalmers. New York: Academy of Political Science, 1972.

Schmitter, Philippe, and Gerhard Lehmbruch (eds.). *Trends Toward Corporatist Intermediation,* Beverly Hills, Calif.: Sage Publications, 1979.

Stepan, Alfred. *The State and Society: Peru in Corporative Perspective.* Princeton, N.J.: Princeton University Press, 1978.

Pike, Fredrick B., and Thomas Stritch (eds.). *The New Corporatism: Social-Political Structures in the Iberian World.* Notre Dame, Ind.: University of Notre Dame Press, 1974.

Reyna, José Luís, and Richard S. Weinart (eds.). *Authoritarianism in Mexico.* Philadelphia: Institute for the Study of Human Issues, 1977.

Veliz, Claudio. *The Centralist Tradition of Latin America.* Princeton, N.J.: Princeton University Press, 1979.

Wiarda, Howard J. (ed.). *Politics and Social Change: The Distinct Tradition.* Amherst: University of Massachusetts Press, 1974, 2d ed., 1982.

Wiarda, Howard J. "Toward a Framework for the Study of Political Change in the Iberic-Latin Tradition: The Corporative Model," *World Politics* 25 (Jan. 1973), 206–235.

Wiarda, Howard J. "Corporatism and Development in the Iberic-Latin World: Persistent Strains and New Variations," *Review of Politics* 36 (1974), pp. 3–33.

Wiarda, Howard J. "The Corporative Origins of the Iberian and Latin American Labor Relations Systems," *Studies in Comparative International Development* 13 (1976), pp. 3–37.

Wiarda, Howard J. *Corporatism and Development: The Portuguese Experience.* Amherst: University of Massachusetts Press, 1977.

Wiarda, Howard J. *Corporatism and National Development in Latin America.* Boulder, Colo.: Westview Press, 1981.

PART 4
BUREAUCRATIC
AUTHORITARIANISM

For Argentine political scientist Guillermo O'Donnell, bureaucratic authoritarianism (BA) emerged as a response to the "crisis" of populism that dominated the politics of Argentina under Juan Perón (1946–1955) and of Brazil during the rule of Getúlio Vargas (1930–1945 and 1950–1954). Once the so-called easy stage of import-substitution industrialization (ISI) was exhausted, having reached the limits of the domestic market, populism, as can be seen in our first selection, confronted serious problems. Rising inflation and balance-of-payment difficulties undermined the economic gains made by the urban middle and working classes and hence eroded the viability of the populist coalitions on which these regimes were based. According to O'Donnell, technocratic elements of the coalition (prominent in the military, state, and private sector), whose numbers had swelled through recent modernization, then sought to attain a dominant position within the coalition. Attributing the crisis to the threat of political activization within the popular groups (which continued to press for improvements in their living standards), technocrats in both Argentina and Brazil encouraged and supported military coups. The new regimes, rather than attempting to reincorporate the popular sectors, moved to exclude and deactivate them by instituting a repressive brand of authoritarianism and to reorient the political economy according to technocratic conceptions of economic growth. These conceptions included a deepening of industrialization through the domestic manufacture of consumer durables and intermediate and capital goods, which required larger, more efficient, and highly capitalized enterprises—often the affiliates of multinational corporations.

237

In the second selection, O'Donnell focuses on the internal dynamics of BA, defining the state in light of recent Marxist conceptions as both a form of maintaining class domination and "the organizational focus of consensus within society." Using this basic vision of the state as both coercive and cooptive, O'Donnell sees particular weakness in making legitimate a nation state that relies on securing transnational capital and on excluding popular sectors from political participation. He notes that it is the fear of the "threat" of lower-class mobilization during populism that forges an alliance between the upper bourgeoisie, the technocrats, the suppliers of transnational capital, and the military. However, O'Donnell envisions this alliance as basically unstable and suggests a variety of possible alternatives, such as Mexico's single-party corporatism or other forms of limited democracy.

12 / Toward an Alternative Conceptualization of South American Politics

Guillermo O'Donnell

The relationships between the political and socio-economic dimensions are a time-bound interplay, and only a longitudinal perspective can reveal their interactions. . . . For this purpose, the accumulation of work in the field (particularly country studies) provides a rich background of information, but unfortunately there are many problems involved in the utilization of these data for comparative purposes. Thus, being careful about the status of the conclusions to be drawn, I will use the term "proposition" for those statements that are reasonably well supported by available data, while reserving the term "hypothesis" for those that, even though they appear plausible in the light of the information at hand, must await more stringent testing.

In this chapter I will make use of a distinction . . . whether or not governmental action is geared to exclude the *already activated* urban popular sector (working class and segments of the lower middle class) from the national political arena. Such exclusion means consistent governmental refusal to meet the political demands made by the leaders of this sector. It also means denying to this sector and its leaders access to positions of political power from [which] they can have direct influence on national policy decisions. This political exclusion can be achieved by direct coercion and/or by closing the electoral channels of political

Reprinted with permission from *Modernization and Bureaucratic-Authoritarianism: Studies in South American Politics* by Guillermo A. O'Donnell, pp. 51–111. Institute of International Studies, University of California, Berkeley, 1973. Abridged by the author. Original version substantially footnoted.

access. (It is important to note that the concept of "exclusion," as I am proposing to use it, assumes previous "presence" in the national political arena: an excluded sector is a politically activated sector. Politically "inert" sectors are not part of the set of political actors . . . ; they remain outside the national political arena.) The exclusion of political actors involves an intentional decision to reduce the number of persons who have a significant voice in determining what goes on at the national political level. Of course, attempts at exclusion have varying degrees of success. At one extreme, the political deactivation of an excluded sector may be achieved: it becomes politically inert through destruction of its resources (especially its organizational bases) and can no longer make . . . political demands. At the other extreme, the attempted exclusion of a sector may not achieve its political deactivation, in which case it will retain the capacity to continue pressing its political demands, and the set of political actors will tend to reconstitute into the number that existed before the exclusion was attempted. A system that attempts the exclusion of the already activated urban popular sector will be called an "excluding political system."

The opposite—an "incorporating political system"—is defined as a political system that purposely seeks to activate the popular sector and to allow it some voice in national politics—or that, without deliberate efforts at either exclusion or incorporation, adapts itself to the existing levels of political activation and the given set of political actors. The "incorporating" categorization allows for a good deal of variation, but it is sufficient for the purposes of our analysis, which will focus on the exclusion systems and the processes that have led to them.

In the sense defined, the only two contemporary (1972) South American systems that are "excluding" are Argentina and Brazil. These are the countries that . . . have advanced furthest in modernization. Here we shall study the processes that in both countries led, first, to incorporation and, later, to exclusion. We shall then briefly examine other contemporary South American political systems. Finally, a sketch of the "political game" in highly modernized contemporary South American political systems will be proposed [as will be] a new classification of political systems with respect to modernization. . . .

Argentina and Brazil:
From Incorporation to Exclusion

The Period of Populism and Horizontal Industrialization

Until the 1930s, in both Argentina and Brazil, the economically more dynamic and politically more powerful sectors were in the nationally owned agrarian areas producing exportable goods, and in the largely foreign-owned network of financial and export intermediaries. In both countries the world crisis of the 1930s greatly accelerated the emergence of domestic industry and an urban working class. The increased urbanization and industrialization changed the distribution of political power and provided the basis for a broad "populist" coalition. It was formed by relatively new sectors.[1] What the coalition was *against* was quite obvious: the oligarchies, the highly visible foreign-owned firms mediating between the international and the domestic market, and the policies of free trade with which the old rulers had traditionally been associated. In terms of what it was *for,* the new coalition agreed on two basic points: (1) industrialization and (2) the expansion of the domestic market. Though it originated in the drastic drop in export earnings due to the world crisis, the growth of industry soon took on a dynamic of its own. For its advocates, industrialization was the way to insulate the country from international crises, as well as the means for eliminating the economic and political dependence that was beginning to be widely resented. These hopes, added to the close ties between foreign-owned firms and the traditional rulers, made industrialization (combined with nationalism) the "ideological glue" of the new coalition.

Argentina and Brazil established import and exchange restrictions for the purpose of saving international currency; this left a wide range of unsatisfied consumer demand, which offered a ready-made market for the expansion of domestic industry. Populist leaders (Perón in Argentina and Vargas in Brazil) made the need to save international currency an argument for a policy of domestic expansion and nationalism, and the high tariff protection that they established preserved the national market for domestic producers after the more severe years of international trade had passed.

As noted, the populist coalition was built around this dynamic core of rapidly expanding domestic industry. The broadening of the functions of the state, entailed by the abandonment of free trade and laissez-faire policies, provided employment for many middle class *empleados* and *técnicos;* the nationalism *cum* industrialization argument had direct appeal for the military; the expansion of industry and government, together with the growth of the economy, benefitted urban workers, created more jobs, fostered migration to the urban-industrial centers, extended the market economy, raised consumption levels, and increased unionization; in the agrarian sector, the producers of non-exportable goods benefitted from the expansion of the domestic market.

The great "but . . . " was that the "enemy"—the export-oriented sector—was the provider of international currency. The populist response was to reduce this sector's real income and redistribute it for the benefit of domestic industrial expansion and consumption. But even though the export sector had lost its traditional hegemony, and the government had succeeded in extracting a significant portion of its income, the exporters' situation as sole international currency earners allowed them to retain a degree of political influence disproportionate to their decreasing share of the Argentine and Brazilian GNP. The nationalistic populist policies never went much further than deprecation of the "oligarchy" and expropriation of the more visible symbols of foreign presence. Under cover of these largely symbolic actions, Vargas' and Perón's governments developed a complex pattern of accommodations and ambiguous relations with the export sector, which in its role as foreign currency earner was crucially important for the carrying out of populist domestic-expansion policies.

An aspect of the drive toward industrialization which would have enduring consequences was that since the 1930s the expansion of industry was "horizontal" or "extensive"—i.e., aimed at satisfying the demand for finished consumer goods (mostly light and nondurable). It is a moot question whether, given the technological, financial, and managerial resources available, it would have been possible to proceed otherwise, but this horizontal expansion of industry meant that few inroads were made into the production of intermediate and capital goods. The results were fractionalization into many consumer-goods producers and very high costs. Another consequence was a heavy dependence on imports of intermediate and capital goods, as well as of technology, without which the industrial establishment could not continue operating.

The entry of vast segments of the popular sector as consumers in the urban economies was fostered by (and a requisite of) the expansion of domestic industry. Their entrance into an expanding governmental and labor market was, of course, part of the same phenomenon. As long as the export sector could provide the necessary international currency and the industrial domestic firms could continue to expand horizontally, no incompatibility seemed to exist among the interests of the members of the populist coalitions. Vargas and Perón encouraged workers' unionization, in part because it provided allegiance for them and in part because it facilitated governmental control over the newly incorporated segments of the popular sector. Both leaders used their control of governmental resources for gaining power over existing labor unions and for creating new ones. This policy deprived the popular sector of the opportunity to develop more autonomous organizations and ideologies, and it gave Perón and Vargas increased capacity for manipulating labor. But it also had the effect of giving urban workers an organizational basis that, with all of its weaknesses considered, was incomparably stronger than anything they had before. Unions would by and large support Perón and Vargas and, during their governments, union leaders would be dependent on their approval for keeping their positions. But even in this subordinate position, the urban popular sector was given its first chances to have some effective weight in national politics, and its leaders were able to participate in bargaining within the populist coalition. When the populist period lost its dynamism and the populist governments had been ousted, in both Argentina and Brazil there remained an urban popular sector with a high degree of organization, political allegiances hostile to the established sectors, and ideological tendencies amenable to more radical formulations than anything proposed by Perón or Vargas during their years in power.

Another aspect of populist policy deserves emphasis here. The period of horizontal economic growth began with a domestic industrial sector having few links with foreign-owned firms, most of which (as noted above) were up to then devoted to export-oriented activities. The expansion benefitted all industry. It seemed merely a matter of maintaining high tariff protection and of obtaining more resources from the state, and industry would be able to meet existing consumer demand and the broadening of demand by the entry of new segments of the popular sector into the market. Public policies reflected the cohesiveness of industrialists' interests and were, in this sense, quite simple and straightforward. The displaced rulers could complain, of course, but to the members of the populist coalition, indiscriminate industrial expansion and tariff protection seemed the obvious policies.

Perhaps above all, the periods of the politically incorporating and economically expanding Argentine and Brazilian populist systems were times of quite generalized exultation. The broad "developmentalist alliance" had found the way for "takeoff into sustained growth," the old rulers had been replaced and the ties of external dependence severed, all participants in the populist coalition were receiving payoffs roughly proportionate to their expectations, and no source of fundamental conflict among them was apparent.

But this situation contained elements that would lead in a short time to its collapse. In the following section we will trace the main features of the crisis of populist policies and the creation of new alignments that would later preside over the "excluding" phase of the Argentine and Brazilian political systems.

The End of Argentine and Brazilian Expansion

What happened in the Argentine and Brazilian economies came to be known as the "exhaustion" of the "easy" stages of industrialization— i.e., the end of the period of extensive, horizontal industrial growth based on substitution for imports of finished consumer goods. Import

Table 1. Compensatory International Financing Plus Decrease in
Net Monetary Reserves Used by South American Countries
to Cover International Balance of Payments Deficits: 1946–1961

(in U$S millions)

Argentina	1,129.0
Brazil	1,471.6
Chile	232.7
Colombia	339.0
Peru	-49.1
Uruguay	207.1
Venezuela	-161.4
Bolivia	37.6
Ecuador	17.7
Paraguay	4.4

Source: Computed from UN-ECLA, The External Financing of Latin America
(New York, 1965).

substitution proved to be an import-intensive activity. During the horizontal industrialization period international prices for exports were erratic, contributing to a declining economic situation further aggravated by the poor productivity of the export sectors, which were "paying the bill" of populist policies. Combined with the increasing need for imports of intermediate and capital goods to support the existing domestic industry, these factors led to severe foreign exchange shortages. As Table 1 shows, increases in import substitution by Argentina and Brazil did not alleviate the problem at all.

The foreign exchange shortage has been at the core of many of the countries' economic problems. It became a question of importing either raw and intermediate materials (thus maintaining existing levels of industrial activity, but hindering growth) or capital goods (thus favoring growth, but creating serious socio-political crises as a consequence of drastic short-term drops in output). More important, it became evident that the existing domestic industrial structure could not effect "intensive" industrialization—i.e., the vertical integration of domestic industry for the production of a wide range of raw, intermediate, and capital goods. The period of "horizontal" industrialization left a schedule of supply which included a disproportionate (in amount and variety) share of consumption and luxury items, as well as myriad small producers coexisting with a few big firms, all under the umbrella of minimum competition and maximum state protection. This composition of the industrial sector has contributed to costs that are well above international standards, has multiplied inefficient allocations, and has exerted an increasingly negative effect on income distribution. When (circa 1960) the economies of Argentina and Brazil had evidently exhausted the possibilities of "easy" horizontal industrial growth, the problems that this generated made clear to many sectors that important and quite painful policy innovations were required—though they were far from agreeing on what those policies should be.

The type of industrial undertaking needed for vertical integration (both for the development of "basic" and capital goods industries, as well as for the huge infrastructure investments required) is very different from the small shop that frequently was sufficient for entrance into industry during the horizontal expansion stage. The size of the new investments, their period of maturation, and their technological requirements in most cases exceed the capabilities of Argentine and Brazilian firms, and greatly strain available public resources. The populist hopes concerning the reduction of foreign dependence have become an unwitting irony. The assimilation of masses into urban life has consolidated consumption expectations modeled after the highly developed economies, "vertical" industrial projects have depended more and more on capital and technology transfers from abroad, and the increasing penetration of technocratic roles has consolidated linkages of dependence with the "originating" societies from which such roles have been "transplanted." Even more important, foreign firms have been encouraged to "jump over" the tariff barriers. The larger the domestic market, the greater the incentives for the "Argentine" General Motors and the "Brazilian" ITT to enter directly into these markets. Table 2 shows how, circa 1960, the pattern of U.S. direct investments varied with the size of each domestic market (and consequently with the differences in degree of modernization of each South American country).

In the more modernized South American countries, foreign-owned industrial firms producing for the domestic market are no longer isolated, highly visible, export-oriented firms characteristic of lower levels of modernization. These firms have created a wide network of satellite, nationally owned production and marketing firms, and pay higher than average wages in the great urban areas.[2] The towering, isolated symbols of foreign presence in former periods have now spread into the largest South American markets, establishing multiple connections with domestic entrepreneurs and with workers who depend on these foreign-owned firms for maintaining their relatively privileged positions. In Argentina and Brazil this new situation reflects profound socio-economic transformations which (as I will argue in more detail below) have had a profound impact on their political problems and have changed their constellations of political actors and policy concerns.

Table 2. *U.S. Private Investment in South American Countries, Direct and Direct Industrial: 1960*

(U$S millions)

Country	Total, Direct Private Investment (1)	Subtotal, Direct Private Industrial Investment (2)	(2) ÷ (1) = Percent
Argentina	828	454	55%
Brazil	1,128	663	59
Chile	768	27	4
Colombia	465	120	26
Peru	448	60	14
Uruguay	51	20	39
Venezuela	2,807	202	7
Bolivia, Ecuador, and Paraguay	635	29	5

Source: U.S. Department of Commerce, *Survey of Current Business*, August 1964.

The foreign exchange shortage, combined with consumption demands from all sectors which became more and more difficult to satisfy, have been at the heart of the inflation that has plagued these nations. The countries that have suffered the most inflation are those which began their drive toward industrialization earliest (Argentina, Chile, and Uruguay) *and* those that, because of their larger domestic markets, have advanced furthest in their industrialization (Argentina and Brazil), as can be seen in Table 3.

With Argentina and Brazil, Chile and Uruguay share a history of "stabilization plans" based on the diagnosis that the containment of excess demand, a restrained monetary policy, and the elimination of "marginal" (i.e., inefficient) producers are prerequisites for stopping inflation and that, in turn, stopping inflation is a prerequisite for further growth. These policies have been the subjects of heated debate. Whatever their merits, they were rendered politically impracticable by the enormous social tensions they created. Inflation and growth followed a wild pattern, alternating between the recessionary effects of the "stabilization plans" and the return to more relaxed policies. Among other important effects, it did not take long for many Argentine and Brazilian sectors to reach the conclusion that stabilization programs (as well as other economic policies to be discussed below) required, as a political precondition, postponement of popular consumption and power participation demands.

Table 3. *Yearly Average Rates of Inflation: 1960–1965*
(Percentages)

Argentina	23.2%
Brazil	60.0
Chile	27.0
Colombia	12.4
Peru	9.4
Uruguay	29.7
Venezuela	0.0
Ecuador	3.8
Bolivia	5.1
Paraguay	5.3

Source: UN-ECLA, *Estudio economico de America Latina, 1969* (New York, 1970).

As a consequence of these policies, inflation was on the average very high in Argentina and Brazil, but with substantial yearly fluctuations. The alternation of recessionary and inflationary public policies created a volatile situation to which many public and private decision-makers found it difficult to adjust.[3] Another important indication of the exhaustion of horizontal industrial expansion is given by data on aggregate economic growth, almost nil in Argentina and declining sharply in Brazil during the years immediately preceding the 1964 military coup. . . .

The crucial point here is that horizontal industrial growth advanced much further in Argentina and Brazil than in the other South American countries. But this growth was severely limited and of short duration. When it was over it left a heritage that included the breakdown of the populist coalition, new policy issues, a profoundly modified social structure, and many shattered illusions. In a fundamental sense, after reaching in this way the high point of modernization of their "centers," Argentina and Brazil have had to deal with "problematic spaces"[4] that have crucial aspects that are significantly different from those of their preexpansion period *and* from the present problematic spaces of other, less modernized South American countries. This is a point that will be stressed and elaborated in the rest of this chapter—i.e., different levels of modernization, in all the dimensions that this concept entails, generate different constellations of issues that define each country's problematic space. In turn, the set of political actors and their political responses (actors' goals and coalitions, public policies, and political system types) are molded by these different constellations and by the different structures in which these constellations have emerged. These are, I believe, useful

Table 4. *Percentages of Total Non-Rural Employment in Industrial (Factory) Employment in South American Countries: 1945–1960*[a]

	1945	1950	1955	1960
Argentina	*20.6%*	18.5%	16.9%	15.3%
Brazil	16.9	*17.3*	15.8	15.0
Chile	12.7	13.1	*13.3*	12.4
Colombia	9.1	*9.8*	9.1	9.6
Peru	8.5	11.0	11.9	*13.0*
Uruguay	N.A.	N.A.	N.A.	N.A.
Venezuela	9.2	8.1	9.7	*10.8*
Other (includes Middle American countries)	11.6	10.7	11.1	*11.4*

Source: UN-ECLA, *The Process of Industrialization in Latin America* (New York, 1966), Statistical Index [mimeo].

[a]Underlined figures are the maximum percentages for each country during the 15-year period.

analytical tools for the comparative exploration of socio-economic and political interactions in contemporary South America.

In Argentina and Brazil, the homogeneity of interests that once existed within the industrial sector has evidently disappeared. More and more "experts" since the late 1950s agree that, if growth is to begin again, the market must be cleared of "marginal" producers by eliminating all restrictions on those firms that are technologically more advanced, more capital-intensive, and financially more powerful. Of course, this issue cuts deep across the industrial sector. In addition to its obvious economic importance, it becomes a major political problem because most of the more advanced firms are foreign (mostly U.S.) owned. In addition to being domestically owned, the more marginal industrial firms tend to employ more labor-intensive production techniques, which means that their elimination would aggravate the unemployment crisis. Thus, what would seem to be "economically rational" (leaving aside for the moment the less than optimal effects of oligopolic concentration) raises prospects of more dependence and more unemployment. . . . Nationalism and preservation of the social peace can be used as effective arguments by those domestic industrialists whose elimination is threatened by expert advice, by "stabilization" plans, and by the interests of the more powerful producers. As will be seen below, this issue also has profound significance for the military and the tecnicos placed in strategic points for national economic planning and decision-making.

The end of horizontal industrial growth had other closely related effects. No longer were there isolated, highly visible "enemies" or the hope of devising policies that would provide satisfactory payoffs for all the participants in the old populist coalition. What remained for some time was the pattern of erratic policies that resulted in more inflation and less growth. In that situation, the nature of salient social problems in Argentina and Brazil profoundly changed: new issues were discussed by a different set of political actors, both of which reflected the changes in social structure and the new cleavages that the high modernization of their "centers" had brought about in these countries. There is little doubt that in all South American countries further growth requires, among other things, quite drastic changes in their economic structures. But in Argentina and Brazil of the 1960s and today, conflict and debate no longer center on solutions to be achieved by expropriating extractive or export-oriented, foreign-owned firms. Before their horizontal industrial growth these were central issues, as they are now central issues in the contemporary scene of most other, less modernized South American countries.

Political Actors in Argentina and Brazil After Populism

Given the strained economic situation that resulted from the "exhaustion" of horizontal industrial growth, the consumption and power demands of the popular sector seemed to other sectors to be very difficult to satisfy. But now those demands were formulated from the more solid and broader organizational bases achieved during populism and were addressed to civilian governments very vulnerable to civilian strife. Furthermore, the populist period generated a large urban electorate to whom political leaders could appeal—mostly with promises of distributionist, populist-type economic policies. Before the 1964 (Brazil) and 1966 (Argentina) military coups, all political actors operated more and more on the basis of pressure and threats. The main assets of the popular sector were its electoral weight and its capacity to strike, demonstrate, and disrupt. As a consequence, the scope and intensity of its political activation grew markedly in both countries in the years that preceded the coups. The active presence of the popular sector in the great urban centers was perceived as profoundly threatening by most other social sectors. After economic expansion had ended, the workers' demands were assessed by their former coalition partners as leading to a reshaping of society far more radical than anything they were willing to accept. In spite of "complications" that originated the new inter-industry cleavage, most propertied Argentine and Brazilian sectors agreed that the popular sector's demands were excessive (both in terms of consumption and of power participation), and that capital accumulation would be impossible if those demands were not tightly controlled.

We have been careful not to equate high modernization with any implication of socio-economic "development." The concept of modernization has been used for studying changes taking place within a national context of manifold social rigidities, a highly skewed distribution of resources, and external dependence. Within such a context, the possibilities of economic expansion were quite limited, as the populist experience showed. But high modernization generated increasing rates of popular political activation. This led most of the propertied sectors to perceive popular political demands as serious threats to the survival of the existing social arrangements—particularly the class structure, the power distribution, and the international alignments of the countries. The resulting polarization made the strong class component of the situation even more visible, facilitating the collaboration of most of the propertied sectors in accepting a political "solution" that supposedly would eliminate such threats by the political exclusion of the popular sector. For reasons that will be discussed below the collaboration did not extend much further than this, and the major role in the determination of the content of the new policies was played by a very small segment of the propertied sectors. This segment was constituted of the individuals that, because of the level of modernization in Argentina and Brazil, controlled the more complex organizations and the more advanced technologies, and had the closest links abroad. But the limited collaboration sufficed for ensuring the united support of the propertied sectors for the coups, and for the initial decisions taken by the new "excluding" political systems of Argentina and Brazil. (We will return to this point below.)

The Cuban revolution frightened many sectors and seemed to confirm their assessment of the implications of popular political activation. The specter of a socialist revolution was raised, and was greatly enhanced by the manifold activities that U.S. policymakers undertook to prevent and repress "subversion" in [Latin] America. The impact of the Cuban revolution and increasing social unrest were at the core of an expanded definition of the role of the military. The United States undertook to provide training in anti-subversive warfare, French and U.S. "anti-subversive" and "civic action" doctrines were taught, and the military's capabilities for political leadership were stressed as parts of the evolution of the military. "National security" was redefined to include the achievement of "socio-economic development" and the suppression of "internal enemies"—the "agents of extremist subversion." Social crises, government inefficiency, and social unrest were perceived to constitute the "internal subversion" whose elimination had fallen within the range of specific military duties.

The income situation of the large salaried middle class deteriorated in both Argentina and Brazil during the years that preceded the 1964 and 1966 coups. This sector showed unequivocal signs of disaffection with the situation, in which deprivation, political disorder, and a formally democratic system appeared linked. Reacting in a characteristic way, they responded to a "law and order" appeal. . . . [Furthermore,] most agrarian exporters reasserted their dislike for mass politics and their conviction that they could not achieve much permanent gain under elected governments subject to the pressure of the urban popular sector.

The result of these developments was the political isolation of the popular sector. Lacking their previous populist allies and direct political access, and suffering from unfavorable income redistribution, they required increasing political activation to obtain decreasing returns on their demands. In the other sectors, growing fears of subversion coupled with shrinking payoffs had the effect of further eroding the weak support they had given to the pre-coup Argentine and Brazilian political systems.

The deteriorating performance of government was reflected in net decreases in the resources available to the governments during the periods that preceded the 1964 and 1966 coups. Lower tax revenues and smaller shares of governmental income in the GNP, decreased real salaries of civil servants, overstaffing at the lower ranks and an exodus at the higher levels, recurrent cabinet crises—all indicated marked decay in governmental problem-solving capabilities in both countries.

Various currents in political development literature have emphasized the importance of some correspondence between the performance of the political system and political demands. As the Argentine and the Brazilian populisms show, periods of socio-economic expansion tend to increase the activation of more political actors. But the many developmental bottlenecks lead to situations in which, while overall social performance is improving slowly, further political demands are being formulated, supported by further political activation. The "gap" between performance and demands generates political action to reduce it. What action will be taken by which political actors? This seems to depend on the patterns of social differentiation resulting from changes in the socio-economic structure.

. . . [We have] suggested [elsewhere] that the size of South American domestic markets and the productive structure of their modern areas—particularly their type of industrialization—are the major factors in determining the pattern of social differentiation of each modern area. (These are the more general aspects of the concept of modernization being used here.) Furthermore, the increased differentiation of the social structure means greater social complexity—i.e., more social units (sectors, classes, institutions, and roles) interrelated in more complex ways. Political pluralization is the political expression of social differentiation: it means greater complexity of political interaction—i.e., more political actors interrelated in more complex ways. In all these dimensions the overarching concept of modernization has guided the analysis and the choice of indicators. More important, in all these dimensions the available information suggests that there are significant differences among the three groups of South American countries. These differences, and the different problematic spaces they entail, are seen here as major determinants of the different patterns of political phenomena (in particular, of the different types of political systems) that distinguish the countries in each group from those in the other groups.

Social differentiation proceeds in a "contrapuntal interplay"[5] with problems of social integration. "Social integration" is almost impossible to define and measure with precision. It is a concept used frequently in social theories that postulate equilibrium assumptions that are not shared here. But in spite of its limitations, it points to an aspect of social reality that cannot be ignored. The emergence of new social units (classes, sectors, institutions, roles) often conflicts with patterns consolidated during previous stages of society—in particular when, instead of emerging from more or less spontaneous processes of conflict and adjustment of internal forces, highly influential social units (in particular, institutions and roles) result from "transplantations" from more advanced and more industrialized societies. Modernization entails social differentiation, and the latter generates competing interests, conflicting normative claims, and divergent behavioral expectations. Insofar as some "fit" is not achieved among these aspects and across social units, social integration lags behind social differentiation. The incorporation of newly differentiated social units exponentially increases the possible permutations and combinations among them, at the same time that structural sources of conflict increase and the commonalities of behavioral expectations decline. A frequent result is a low level of social cohesion and generalized uncertainty. Political actors begin to focus more and more on short-terms gains, the boundaries of socially and politically permissible behavior are blurred, and the capacities of political systems to incorporate sectoral goals into broader perspectives are diminished.

In Argentina and Brazil, the "differentiation-integration gap" contributed to the previously mentioned "demands-performance gap." Both were consequences of the high levels of modernization reached in the national "centers," and led to a political situation that Samuel Huntington has aptly described as "mass praetorianism."[6] The "political game" became, on the one hand, broader, in that more demands, brought forth by more political actors, were focused on governmental decisions. On the other hand, the "game" became more unconstrained, in that formally prescribed political behavior was less and less important vis-à-vis naked power strategies, both among political actors and against the governments. Political institutions in both countries (parties, parliament), which had never been particularly strong, were even further weakened, and the executive became the primary focus of a glut of political demands. In this situation, the pre-coup Argentine and Brazilian governments were victimized by, and collaborated in, praetorianism. Some authors have depicted the situation as a "stalemate," with high levels of unrestrained conflict, sharp differences in demands, and weakness of governments preventing the implementation of *any* policy.[7] This governmental incapacity aggravated the social situation, breeding more praetorianism. Inside the government, with few possibilities for effective decision-making, concern for survival in office became paramount. This led to the adoption of sequences of policies designed to placate the more threatening political actors, with little concern for general problem-solving.

These processes threatened the survival of the existing political system. Salient social problems remained unsolved, competition was increasingly zero-sum, gains were precarious, and praetorianism undermined the problem-solving capabilities of existing institutions. The threshold for a definitive crisis in the political system was reached when most of the political actors focused on changing the rules of the "political game" altogether, instead of trying to obtain gains within the existing rules. Coalitions were formed with the preeminent goal of ending the "stalemate" by implanting a new political system that would allow effective decision-making in line with the preferences of the coalition members. As Huntington's analysis suggests, after a praetorian period the tendency is to define the situation as one requiring the placement of severe constraints on the political activities of those who are outside the winning coalition. The tendency, thus, was toward a highly authoritarian political system, but the specific characteristics of such authoritarianism, as well as the major goals of the winning coalition, were deeply influenced by the degree of [high] modernization and the type of [mass] praetorianism. . . .

Technocratic Roles

Until now we have worked at two levels of analysis. At both levels, important changes have taken place as modernization has proceeded in Argentina and Brazil. The first has been the level of the agenda of salient social problems and developmental bottlenecks; the second, the level of social structure, the productive-industrial base, and the differentiation, emergence, and political activation of new social sectors and political actors. Structural analysis can be carried on at a lower level of generality, focusing on roles—smaller units at the intersection of social structure and the behavioral tendencies of their incumbents. The concept of modernization being used here requires the analysis of roles (particularly of what I have called "technocratic roles") as a crucial component of the overall modernizing situation. In the framework I am proposing, the political variables can readily be seen as interacting with social factors at these three levels of analysis.

Advances in modernization are evidenced by further social differentiation at one level of analysis, and by further penetration of technocratic roles at a lower level. . . . The complexity of social structure produced by high modernization (and its key component, industrialization) creates public and private management needs in which technology plays an ever-increasing part. This seems to be true irrespective of the type of political system. Larger organizations engaged in more complex production, the effects of industrialization upon communications, marketing, publicity, and information-processing services, as well as the need for coordination of more diversified social units and activities— all require increasing "inputs" of persons who have gone through prolonged training in techniques of production, planning, and control. As modernization proceeds, more technocratic roles are to be found in more and more social activities. These roles are always a small proportion of the total population, but both their scope and density of penetration increase markedly with modernization.

Are there stages at which the incumbents of technocratic roles feel capable of dealing with broad social problems in "their own ways"? What are their prevailing biases for perceiving, assessing, and acting upon social problems? These are among the questions to be explored in this section.

A lot of attention has been paid to the "revolution of rising expectations" at the mass level, but very little scholarly effort has been devoted to a closely related and perhaps more important phenomenon: the transplantation of expectations produced by incumbency in technocratic roles in modernizing societies. Executives attending business schools molded after prestigious U.S. models, military officers studying abroad and in military academies that adopt curricula and approaches proposed by foreign advisory missions, and técnicos getting their degrees abroad— all learn role-specific techniques, but above all they learn role-models. How role-incumbents in the "originating" societies perform, what support they have and what rewards they can expect, what the criteria for achievement are—all are transmitted together with the more specific technical expertise of each profession.

This is a crucial point. What is transmitted from the "originating" societies is a complex constellation, of which the technical expertise is only one element. In addition to the latter (rather, encompassing it), the individual learns a role-model; and his conception of his role, which derives from that learning, must interact with a social context that in a modernizing situation differs greatly from that of the society in which his role (and his conception of his role) originated. Given the unavoidable effects of a different social context, a key question is what dimensions of the role-model will be adjusted (and in what directions) in the modernizing situation.

Even the specific technical expertise is more dependent on the social context than is usually recognized. Techniques are "adequate" only in certain contexts. If, as frequently happens, the role-incumbent's social context differs substantially from the one presupposed by the techniques he learned, his specific technical knowledge may be of little use. As would be expected from what has been said here, . . . acquaintance with incumbents of technocratic roles in modernizing contexts reveals severe frustration stemming from a "failure" of the context to meet their expectations. This situation can threaten the achievement of the rewards they feel are "normally due" according to their role-models.

Their frustration can easily be channeled into a drive to reshape the social context in forms that, it is hoped, will be more congenial to the learned expertise and the reward aspirations of these individuals—a course which can easily be rationalized. Their consciousness of their expertise convinces incumbents of technocratic roles that, by molding the social context to serve their own aspirations, they would at the same time improve the social situation. At this point the interaction of roles with the other structural levels is crucial: I hypothesize that the extent to which frustration by incumbents of technocratic roles may be channeled into political action aimed at reshaping the social context is a . . . function of the degree of penetration (density and scope) of these roles in a modernizing situation.

High modernization (including one of its components, the high industrialization of modern national centers) involves the emergence of more technocratic roles in more social sectors and activities. . . . It can quite confidently be asserted that, at the level of productive-industrial processes and their closely related activities, high levels of South American modernization entail a high degree of penetration of technocratic roles in the modern centers. The point to be stressed here is that the possibilities of linkages among incumbents of those roles across the sectors in which they are operating increase as a . . . function of the overall penetration of these roles. Before the 1964 and 1966 coups in Brazil and Argentina, business and military academies became common meeting places for incumbents at the "top" of large business organizations and the military. Several equivalents of *Time* and *Fortune* magazines appeared, providing further intercommunication among these role incumbents and lending them social prestige vis-à-vis other social sectors. Numerous publicists diffused the outlook of what came to be called the "modern" or "technocratic right."

The effects of the penetration of technocratic roles are multiplicative: greater scope and density leads to the emergence of a wide network of institutions and channels of communication across the social sectors in which the roles most deeply penetrate—the military, large and technologically complex business organizations, and governmental areas of economic decision-making and planning.[8] At lower levels of modernization the lesser penetration of technocratic roles hinders the formation of these important linkages, even though individual incumbents have the same training as those operating in more modernized contexts.

Linkages promote mutual recognition. Whatever the social sector in which they operate, the incumbents of technocratic roles share many important characteristics. Their role-models, and through them their basic expectations about the "proper" state of the social context, originate in the same societies. Their training stresses a "technical" problem-solving approach. Emotional issues are nonsense; the ambiguities of bargaining and politics are hindrances to "rational" solutions; and conflict is by definition "dysfunctional." Their underlying "maps" of social reality are similar. That which is "efficient" is good, and efficient outcomes are those that can be straightforwardly measured; the rest is noise that a "rational" decision-maker should strive to eliminate from his decision premises. The texture of social reality is radically (in some cases, one is tempted to say, brutally) simplified. . . . The resistance of so many problems to solution through efficiency considerations alone tends to be interpreted as an indication of how much "progress" in formal rationality remains to be achieved. . . .

Mutual recognition is promoted by the development of a common "language." The old scorn of unlearned military, ignorant businessmen, and humanistic intellectuals for one another has undergone substantial modifications. Many individuals in each of these categories have gained a common technocratic background and have discovered that they share a common technical language (or "jargon"). This facilitates communication across specialties, but makes communication more difficult with other social sectors lacking this background. . . . Mutual recognition and a common "language" promote a heightened assessment of their combined capabilities by incumbents of technocratic roles. The more they penetrate social sectors, the more likely they are to believe that their combined expertise can ensure effective problem-solving throughout a broad range of social problems. In less modernized contexts, the necessarily more isolated incumbents of technocratic roles may withdraw from political involvement or, since a coalition centered around these roles would be too weak to be effective, may search for alliances with other groups for channeling their political action. But in situations of high modernization that have resulted in mass praetorianism, a coup coalition[9] is likely to be formed with the predominant participation of incumbents of technocratic roles. These individuals have already achieved dense penetration (and consequently a high degree of control) of crucial social sectors. Because of this, they are more likely than in less modernized contexts to be confident of their capabilities for governing effectively. The basic goal of these role-incumbents will be a quite drastic reshaping of the social context, aimed at the creation of conditions that will permit much more extensive application of their expertise, and the expansion of influence of the social sectors they have most densely penetrated.[10]

Operating in a different social context, technocratic role-incumbents in situations of high modernization are likely to act in contrast to their usually politically liberal role-models and to constitute the core of the coalition that will attempt the establishment of an authoritarian, "excluding" political system. The usual verbal allegiance to political democracy is apparently the weakest component in their role-models. It is easily abandoned to promote an authoritarian political system that will (it is believed) facilitate more effective performance by the role-incumbents. . . .[11]

There is evidence of the numerous linkages established among incumbents of technocratic roles during the periods of Brazilian and Argentine praetorianism, as well as of their crucial influence in the 1964 and 1966 coups. Their coup coalitions could count on the acquiescence of many sectors for the first round of decisions, which included the exclusion of the popular sector, the postponement of popular demands, and the closing of the electoral channels of political participation. Once in power, the coalitions made a second round of decisions, and the policy implications of the coups were spelled out. Then, many of the original supporters of (or acquiescers to) the coups discovered that the choice of a new political system over continued mass praetorianism was not a very happy one. The first round of decisions is related to the inauguration of the post-1964 and -1966 Brazilian and Argentine political systems, while the second round is related to their performance and subsequent evolution. Strictly speaking, it is the first phase only that falls within the scope of this book; it will be the subject-matter of the section immediately following. . . .

Bureaucratic-Authoritarian Political Systems
in Contemporary South America

The exclusion of an activated popular sector can sometimes be achieved with psychological or economic payoffs; otherwise, the exclusion requires the application of strong and systematic coercive measures. This has been the experience of the authoritarian political systems emerging in highly modernized contexts which have attempted to exclude, and eventually to deactivate, the popular sector.

Robert Dahl has proposed a heuristically useful model of the emergence of "polyarchy" ("political democracy," as used here) as a function of decreasing costs of tolerance and increasing costs of suppression ("exclusion," as used here).[12] As social differentiation proceeds, more and more autonomous groups appear, and it becomes harder for the government to suppress them—or for them to suppress each other. At this stage a political system which accepts the legitimacy of diverging interests and actors, and regulates them peacefully, is likely to emerge. Dahl's model ends at this point, but for the sake of my argument I have extended it further (see Figure 1).

In the right hand third of the model depicted in Figure 1, social differentiation has increased with further modernization, and with its increase the costs of suppression (i.e., exclusion) have risen steadily. But social integration has lagged, and praetorianism has resulted, such that the costs of toleration have risen even more rapidly. In this situation, it is likely that suppression will be attempted again, but now at a much higher cost than at any previous stage. . . .

With reference to the "demands-performance gap" discussed earlier, in principle governmental action could be taken to meet any unfulfilled demands. But since on the basis of even the most optimistic assessment, only slow improvements in performance could be expected, immediate political action would be taken to block demands that are perceived as excessive, given the state of the social context. First, political parties and elections would be eliminated, and with them the political personnel who were sensitive to the demands of the popular sector. Second, the "domestication" of the labor unions, the most important organizational channel for the formulation of popular demands, would be attempted by co-optation of the leaders and by coercion. Third, an attempt would be made to bureaucratically "encapsulate" most social sectors, in order to maximize control over them. This would be accomplished by ensuring that the sectors were politically represented by organizations whose legal existence was dependent upon government authorization. Bargaining and interest representation would be limited to leaders at the top of these organizations, and spontaneous modes of demand-formulation, as

Figure 1

An Adaptation of Dahl's Model for the Emergence of Political Systems

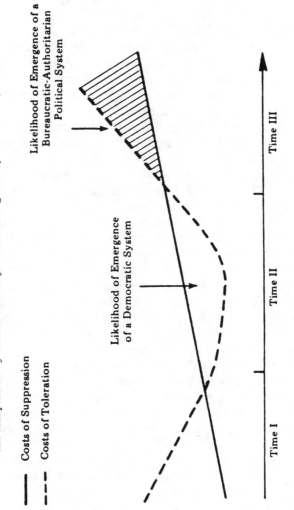

—— Costs of Suppression

- - - Costs of Toleration

Likelihood of Emergence of a
Bureaucratic-Authoritarian
Political System

Likelihood of Emergence
of a Democratic System

Time I   Time II   Time III

well as dissent, would have no legitimate place under the new political conditions.

The proponents of these policies assume that the exclusion of the popular sector and its demands would make possible a reconversion of the socio-economic structure that would stimulate economic growth by a general increase in efficiency and by allowing political hegemony and capital accumulation in the more "dynamic" sectors. Political democracy and wider distribution of wealth and power would *then* be possible. Of course, the main beneficiaries of the earlier accumulation of political power and socio-economic resources would be the sectors most densely penetrated by the coup coalition of incumbents of technocratic roles— the more "efficient" producers (i.e., larger, more modern firms, the armed forces, and, to a lesser extent, the government). As will be seen below, some of these aims were not achieved, but along with the high degree of coercion required if the authoritarian efforts were to succeed, they played an important part in determining the characteristics of the post-1964 Brazilian and the post-1966 Argentine political systems.

These political systems have a theoretical import extending beyond the specific Brazilian and Argentine cases. In his broad-ranging study in historical sociology, Barrington Moore finds, in addition to bourgeois and Communist revolutions, a third historical path toward industrialization.[13] This path involves a coalition of the public bureaucracy and the propertied sectors (including a subordinate industrial bourgeoisie) against the peasantry and an emerging urban proletariat. It is a conservative reaction to "the strains of advancing industrialization," to "a weak push toward parliamentary democracy," and to the entry of the "masses" into the political scene. This "third path" is not unlike what has occurred in Argentina and Brazil.

Moore deals with countries that have come to play an important role in international affairs, but . . . Andrew Janos studies weaker, more dependent countries that bear illuminating similarities to the South American cases analyzed here.[14] Janos deals with the Eastern European countries of the 1930s, many of which became what he calls "bureaucratic regimes." Like contemporary Argentina and Brazil, these countries had advanced well beyond stereotypical "traditional" societies, they had relatively large modern centers, there was high political activation of the urban popular sector, developmental bottlenecks had appeared, social-structural rigidities had persisted longer than in the earlier modernizing countries, and social integration had lagged far behind social differentiation. Eastern European "bureaucratic regimes" were based on a coalition of military, high-level civil servants, big businessmen, and sectors of the traditional landowning strata, with the initial support of a large dependent urban middle class. This coalition attempted to consolidate traditional forms of domination in the rural areas and to deactivate the urban popular sector. In this way the "bureaucratic regimes" tried to accelerate industrialization and to minimize the chances of social revolution.

Janos points out that these regimes were distinguished from those of Italy and Germany during the same period in that they lacked the mobilizational force and ideological appeal of the latter. He attributes this difference to the fact that the elites of the "bureaucratic regimes" (as is true in the Argentine and Brazilian cases under study here) belonged to already well-established sectors of their societies.

There is little doubt that the present political system of Spain can be categorized as a "bureaucratic regime," even though the events that preceded its inauguration differed in several important respects from events in the Eastern European countries. The present-day system of Greece is strikingly similar to such a regime in all the aspects discussed here. The Brazilian and Argentine political systems inaugurated in 1964 and 1966, respectively, also belong in this category. All these political systems are authoritarian systems emerging from conditions of high modernization. It is impossible to say, without systematic comparative research, but it is a disquieting possibility that such authoritarianisms might be a more likely outcome than political democracy as other countries achieve or approach high modernization.

Two authors—David Apter and Juan Linz—have made important contributions to the study of this type of political system. Though Apter's analysis is at a relatively high level of abstraction while Linz's analysis is derived mainly from his examination of the specific case of Spain, a comparison of Apter's "bureaucratic system"[15] and Linz's "authoritarian regime"[16] reveals that they are referring to the same empirical phenomenon. Apter's bureaucratic system emphasizes control and vertical authority arrangements, operating by means of predominantly instrumental norms (i.e., without consummatory, mobilizational ideologies). Linz's authoritarian regime is characterized by limited pluralism and low ideological content, as well as by attempts at political deactivation and the development of relative autonomy of government vis-à-vis social groups. Linz points out that these regimes come to power "after periods of considerable *organized* political strife, lack of consensus under democratic governments, and aborted revolutions."[17]

If these systems obviously are not political democracies, they also have characteristics that clearly distinguish them from totalitarianism. They lack solid legitimation and a comprehensive ideology; they do little to indoctrinate the population; they prefer political apathy and accept "limited pluralism." . . . As Linz says:

We prefer for purposes of analysis to reject the idea of a continuum from democracy to totalitarianism, and to stress the distinctive nature of authoritarian regimes. Unless we examine the distinctive nature of authoritarian regimes, the conditions under which they emerge, the conception of power held by those who shape them, regimes which are not clearly democratic or totalitarian will be treated merely as deviations from those ideal types and will not be studied systematically and comparatively.[18]

I will call the political system that was implanted in Brazil in 1964 and in Argentina in 1966 "bureaucratic-authoritarian." This awkward term is in part used to indicate its derivation from Apter's and Linz's contributions, but also because it facilitates the use of the term "authoritarian" as a *genus* that includes other types of non-democratic South American political systems associated with lower levels of modernization.[19] The term "bureaucratic" suggests the crucial features that are specific to authoritarian systems of high modernization: the growth of organizational strength of many social sectors, the governmental attempts at control by "encapsulation," the career patterns and power-bases of most incumbents of technocratic roles, and the pivotal role played by large (public and private) bureaucracies. . . .[20]

Until now the focus of my analysis has been on the factors that in Argentina and Brazil led to the military coups that attempted (and, at least in the short term, achieved) the implantation of bureaucratic-authoritarian political systems. For such a focus it has seemed sufficient to use a set of concepts and variables at a fairly high level of generality which reflected important similarities in the Argentine and Brazilian centers. A different problem (or, to use the jargon, a different "dependent variable") is to explain the differences in the performances and degrees of consolidation of these two political systems. This task cannot be undertaken here, but I cannot resist the temptation to speculate briefly about the main reasons for these differences. In terms of strategy of analysis, what is required for such an explanation is the examination of factors more specific than those used for establishing the typological similarity of Argentina and Brazil. More specific analyses would enable us to make distinctions among units within the same general type. The preliminary typological task undertaken here is useful for such purposes in a double sense—first, for drawing . . . distinctions across types (e.g., Argentina and Brazil vis-à-vis the other two groups of South American countries); second, for underscoring . . . specific differences among countries of the same type, which facilitates comparative analysis within the same type.

In this matter it is necessary to stress again the crucial importance of governmental coercion for bureaucratic-authoritarian "success" in excluding and deactivating the popular sector, as well as for enforcing decisions tending to facilitate economic concentration in the more "dynamic" or "efficient" sectors, and for repressing the opposition of intellectuals and university students. . . . The use of coercion (especially that geared to effectively exclude and deactivate the popular sector) is required for achieving the extreme concentration of wealth and power epitomized in the socio-economic policies of Ministers Campos of Brazil and Krieger Vasena of Argentina. The Brazilian bureaucratic-authoritarian system was able (and willing) to apply the degree of coercion required to achieve the complete political exclusion *and* deactivation of its popular sector. On the other hand, the Argentine bureaucratic-authoritarian system implemented its policies in a context in which the popular sector retained a high level of political activation, even though the sector's main channels of political access were suppressed.

To determine what may have led to this difference, it is necessary to recall a factor that was alluded to when discussing the fact that both Argentina and Brazil belong to the "South American high-modernization" type—i.e., the different degrees of intra-country heterogeneity. The big "peripheral" area of Brazil has always provided a huge labor supply that has had very debilitating effects on its labor unions. On the other hand, the Argentine economy has functioned for long periods with full employment. Thus, even though both countries have a similar concentration of unionized and industrial workers in the big urban centers, a careful examination shows that in their pre-coup periods there were already important differences in the strength and autonomy of the political activation of their popular sectors. As a consequence, it could be assumed that to achieve similar results in the political deactivation of the popular sector, the Argentine bureaucratic-authoritarian system would have to apply a significantly higher degree of coercion than the high degree applied in the Brazilian case.

Another factor seems to have contributed to the initially different degrees of coercion applied by the Argentine and Brazilian bureaucratic-authoritarian systems. The political activation of the Brazilian urban popular sector increased at a very rapid rate during the years preceding the 1964 coup. In the Argentine case, though the rate of increase of urban political activation was not as rapid as in Brazil in the period immediately preceding the 1966 coup, the *level* of such activation was higher. Both countries shared the high-modernization characteristic of the presence in the big cities of a large number of politically activated individuals composing the urban popular sector. But it seems that in Argentina it was the *level*, while in Brazil it was the *rate of increase*, of urban political activation that contributed most to the defensive political reactions that led to their coups. This seems to be a reflection of the different sources of the main Argentine and Brazilian pre-coup popular political activation. In Brazil the inducement of popular political activation "from above" (especially by the Goulart government) played an important part. In Argentina the impulse came mainly "from below" (unions and Peronismo), with the governing Radicales definitely not encouraging it. In this respect, the nature of the political system change in Brazil must have exerted a more marked deactivating effect on the popular sector than in the Argentine case.

Finally, the Peronista allegiance of most of the Argentine popular sector was perceived as relatively less threatening by the more established sectors than the suggestion of socialist tendencies among some of the Brazilian governing personnel prior to the 1964 coup. In the latter case the perception of a more immediate threat to the existing social system may have fostered an initially tighter degree of cohesion in the ruling coalition, as well as increased the influence of its more "anti-subversive" and "efficientist" members. Another possible factor in determining the different degrees of coercion initially applied in the two coups is that while by and large the Brazilian urban popular sector supported Goulart, the unions and Peronistas were strongly opposed to the pre-coup Radicales Argentine government. The unions and Peronistas welcomed the 1966 coup for the short period of time that it took for the policy implications of the new political system to be spelled out; this delayed and lessened the degree of coercion applied. In contrast to the Brazilian case, the Argentine bureaucratic-authoritarianism did not begin with the more influential leadership of the popular sector in a markedly antagonistic position.

Obviously, these are only hypotheses about what seem to be important factors for explaining the differences in the degrees of coercion initially applied in the Argentine and Brazilian cases. These hypotheses cannot be tested here; the point to be stressed is that the different degrees of coercion that were applied (and the different degrees of coercion that each case apparently "required") seem to have been influential factors in the deactivation of the popular sector achieved in the Brazilian case and the retention of the relatively high level of political activation by the Argentine popular sector. When the socio-economic implications of the "bureaucratic-authoritarian" systems became fully apparent, they triggered "social explosions" in the Argentine modern areas, while they aroused no significant opposition in Brazil. This may be a basic reason for the different degrees of present-day (July 1971) consolidation of the two systems.

I have hypothesized that the "maps" of social reality of incumbents of technocratic roles tend to emphasize those aspects that secondary socialization has best taught them to measure and deal with. Reality may be confounded with that which is indicated by easily available, "hard" data. In such cases, performance (including a political system's performance) will tend to be measured by these types of indicators and what they reveal, to the neglect of hard-to-decode information coming from the "noisier" channels for the expression of popular preferences. Thus, growth in GNP, diminished inflation, and fewer strikes may be achieved at a huge cost in terms of repression, income redistribution, elimination of national entrepreneurship, liquidation of political institutions, increased poverty of the urban and rural popular sectors, and alienation of intellectuals and students. But it is the former set of indicators that the technocratic outlook is inclined to emphasize. If this set of indicators shows "satisfactory" performance, political rule based on a technocratic outlook will be easily rationalized, the technocratic roles' coalition will be consolidated, and the technocrats' assessment of their capabilities for "solving" social problems will be reinforced.

I suspect that this is the single most important factor for understanding why, in the Argentine case, influential members of the original ruling coalition seem willing to attempt a "return to democracy," whereas the Brazilian system has hardened, and its rulers intend to continue in power for a long time. In Argentina the "failure" of the political system has been blatant, even using the set of indicators that I have hypothesized would be preferentially monitored. This situation has weakened the cohesion of the original ruling coalition and its confidence in its capabilities—as is evidenced by the coups that deposed General Onganía and, more recently, General Levingston.

As a consequence, there is less probability of long-term consolidation of a bureaucratic-authoritarian system in Argentina than in Brazil. But if democratization is seriously attempted in Argentina, the high level of public disaffection will present serious problems. In particular, it will make it especially difficult to create a government built around "friendly" political parties that can successfully compete in the electoral arena. Rather, candidates are likely to win on the basis of appeals to the grievances that have accumulated against the disintegrating bureaucratic system among many sectors of the population. Among the military, the attempt to promote a "return to democracy" has a strong element of self-interest. As events in Argentina have clearly shown, direct rule and "unsatisfactory" governmental performance fractionalize the armed forces and make them the direct target of popular hostility. But the probability of a victorious "anti-system" government could be an even more serious menace to corporate interest (not only of the military). Today (July 1971) it is far from clear what the outcome will be. If the "return to democracy" succeeds, one possibility is the tightly controlled elections in which, as a price for their authorization, political parties will agree to present candidates "suggested" by the military and to accept, when in power, severe constraints on their socio-economic policies. But once the "electoral" option has prevailed, the military's bargaining position vis-à-vis political parties (especially the major ones) would seem to be too weak for extracting such a price. But more important, this would create a . . . huge "vacant" electorate willing to vote for independent candidates and support new socio-economic policies. Such an electorate would constitute such a strong temptation for political parties to appeal to its preferences that the effectiveness of any agreement would seem to be very unlikely. If, on the other hand, the *continuista* option prevails, there is little doubt that there would be an attempt to "deepen the revolution" along the Brazilian model. The problem in that case would be that a bureaucratic-authoritarian attempt to deactivate the popular sector would require an even greater degree of coercion than in 1966, when such an attempt "failed." If we consider that in Argentina in 1966 the degree of coercion "required" was significantly higher than that applied in Brazil in 1964, it is obvious that a new attempt to politically deactivate the Argentine popular sector would entail frightful social costs, with very little chance of success.

This prospect, combined with the disintegration and loss of confidence in their capabilities of the 1966 coalition, may act as a deterrent to the manifold tendencies operating in a continuista direction. The option seems to be between *continuismo* and truly open elections, given the unlikely possibility of controlled elections. The great risk in the continuista option is the huge social costs it would entail, but it is the open elections option that raises the most serious concerns, and most deeply divides the sectors now in power.

The Argentine case highlights the enormous difficulties to be faced in democratizing a bureaucratic-authoritarian system. Unable to solve the salient social problems and developmental bottlenecks, and to institutionalize itself, the Argentine political system must try to find its way through the vacuum left by the destruction of its deteriorated political institutions. After a 1966–1969 "truce," mass praetorianism has re-emerged in Argentina. If the many obstacles to political democratization that remain can be overcome, the new political system will still be instituted under very unfavorable circumstances. The renewal of mass praetorianism can only hinder its problem-solving capabilities and induce many established sectors to consider new authoritarian experiments. The great question would be to what extent the social learning provided by the bureaucratic-authoritarian period had promoted changes in the attitudes of the crucial political actors and persuaded them to forego praetorianism and seek better ways to deal with the still unsolved "problematic space" within a democratic framework.

So far I have analyzed the socio-economic correlates of South American political systems on three levels: (1) social structure, focusing on the productive-industrial base of "modern" areas and on social differentiation, with its correlates of political pluralization and activation; (2) the agenda of salient social problems and developmental bottlenecks that define the problematic space within each country; (3) the penetration of technocratic roles. These are all dimensions of the overarching concept of modernization, and at each level of modernization significant differences can be seen in them.

A fourth important dimension has been mentioned only in passing— i.e., the present position of South American countries in the international context. All the South American countries have very limited influence in international affairs; at most they can hope only to attenuate the internal effects of international events and the decisions of the great powers. They all lack market power in international trade; they are all subject to the virtually undisputed military, political, and economic hegemony of the United States; they are all dependent on scarce foreign capital; and they are all dependent on technologies that have originated in countries that are capital-rich and labor-scarce, and from which many of their role-models, consumption expectations, and ideological influences have been derived.

The particular ways in which these factors impinge on each South American country depend on their different levels of modernization. The problem of economic dependence, for example, is common to all, but it is expressed in Argentina and Brazil in interindustry cleavages, while in most of the other South American countries it is still centered around the expropriation of extractive enclaves and/or export-oriented foreign-owned firms. These similarities and differences must be taken into account in studying the problematic space within each country and in examining the ways different political coalitions deal with that space.

Argentina and Brazil are the most highly modernized South American countries. Combined with the factors deriving from their position in the international context, this modernization has created the problematic space with which their pre-coup and bureaucratic-authoritarian political systems have had to deal. Can we conclude that, as modernization proceeds in other South American countries, there will be similar "pulls" in a bureaucratic-authoritarian direction?

It is basic to the argument [here] that this is a significant question to raise. . . . But in the absence of systematic research, there are too many indeterminate factors to answer that question with any degree of assurance. First, although the general context is common, an assumption of the equivalence of causal processes (here, those of Argentina and Brazil vis-à-vis those of the other South American countries) may be fallacious. Second, even if the tendency were toward bureaucratic-authoritarianism, purposive political action might be able to bring about a change in directions—particularly with the experiences of Argentina and Brazil to alert leaders to the possibilities and generate effective efforts to avoid them. Third, other factors might invalidate any simple attempts at extrapolation—e.g., the existence of solid political institutions in Chile, particularly well-organized, non-personalistic political parties, a working parliament, and effective democratic socialization; "system pride" of many Chilean and (apparently) still some Uruguayan political actors, heightened by the "political primitiveness" of their larger neighbors; a tradition of military non-intervention in Chile and Uruguay [Ed. note: written before the coups in 1970 in Chile and Uruguay]; Venezuela's hard currency income from oil extraction, exceptional by South American standards; the end of the "National Front" in Colombia, with its serious danger of a breakdown leading toward authoritarianism, but also with the opportunities it raises for achieving and instituting open political competition; the exhaustion of "horizontal" industrialization at a lower level than in Argentina and Brazil, and greater difficulties to be faced in attempting vertical integration, which may induce institutional innovations in other South American countries that were absent in Argentina and Brazil.

All these factors are potentially very important, but it should be remembered that they have to operate in a severely strained context. Low levels of performance and growing demands, increased political activation and penetration of technocratic roles, many salient social problems—these can only be seen as pushing societies away from political democracy and toward authoritarian breakdowns that, as modernization proceeds, are quite likely to be of the "bureaucratic" type analyzed in this chapter.

Lacking sufficient evidence for weighing all these factors, one must suspend judgment. But this being the case, suspension of judgment applies both to my speculations and to the more sanguine expectations derived from the basic paradigm. . . . It can be asserted here that clarification of the main historical tendencies in operation can hardly be obtained under the assumptions of linear democratization.

The Vargas and Perón periods have already been referred to as populist authoritarianisms; another case that belongs in this category is the contemporary Peruvian political system. It is ruled by the same type of coalition; it has the same "enemies"; its policies are the same combination of expansion of the domestic market based on a still homogeneous industrial sector, weakening of the traditional ruling sectors, and expropriation of the most visible symbols of foreign presence. It has the same mixture of radical policies that irreversibly change society, leaders with conservative ideologies, and regressive policies in some important areas. Furthermore, as in the Argentine and Brazilian populist experiences, the Peruvian system is attempting the political activation and incorporation of segments of the popular sector "from above"— i.e., from the government—while trying to maintain tight controls over the process. In terms of my analysis, its lower levels of social differentiation, political activation, and penetration of technocratic roles prevented the emergence in Peru of a bureaucratic-authoritarian system and its supporting coalition. These circumstances, together with the concomitant possibilities of further "horizontal" industrial expansion and the prevalence of foreign-owned firms in the export-oriented sectors, permitted the grand coalition typical of populism. There are important differences between the Peruvian *populist* authoritarianism and the *bureaucratic* authoritarianisms inaugurated in Brazil in 1964 and in Argentina in 1966. The fact that in all three cases the military appear to hold governmental power is typologically inconsequential. What matters most are the policies of each system and the social problems to which it responds, the coalition on which it is based, and whether or not it attempts to exclude and deactivate the popular sector. Perhaps the most significant difference between the Peruvian and the older populisms is that the former emerged during a period in which U.S. policies had induced substantial changes in military organization, but it remains to be seen if this will finally result in a better record.

Bolivia and Ecuador also have been going through a period of authoritarian expansion of their political systems. These populisms, however, are following very erratic paths. Constraints derived from the extremely small size of their domestic markets have kept their "horizontal" industrial expansion at a lower level than Peru's. Thus the driving force of the populist policies has been weak, and a crucial element of the coalition (domestic market-producing industrialists) has had to play a lesser role than in countries that have started from a more favorable base.

Finally, in Paraguay is the only survival of traditional authoritarianism in South America. A small and quite homogeneous elite rules over a largely politically inert and scarcely differentiated population. The foreign export-oriented sector is dominant, and there have been no serious attempts to subordinate it to domestic industrial and market expansion.

The Proposed Classification

. . . In Table 5 South American countries, clustered by levels of modernization, are paired with political system types according to the criteria and the definitions set forth in this and the preceding chapter.

Table 5. *A Classification of Contemporary South American Political Systems by Levels of Modernization*

Level of Modernization	Political Democracy?	Excluding System?	Resulting Political Type
High			
Argentina	No	Yes	Bureaucratic-Authoritarian
Brazil	No	Yes	(*Modal type*)
Medium			
Chile	Yes	No	Political
Colombia	Yes	No	Democracy
Uruguay	Yes	No	(*Modal type*)
Venezuela	Yes	No	
Peru	No	No	Populist-Authoritarian
Low			
Bolivia	No	No	Populist-Authoritarian
Ecuador	No	No	(*Modal type*)
Paraguay	No	No	Traditional-Authoritarian

[Ed. note: Data are from 1971, before the coups in Chile, Uruguay, Bolivia, and Ecuador.]

The differences between the classification proposed here and the studies analyzed in Chapter I need not be repeated; but it might be useful to note what this proposed classification and those studies have in common. [Ed. note: O'Donnell's Chapter I does not appear in this collection.] All involve ordering cases along two dimensions (*socio-economic* and *political,* albeit differently defined) and then asking the question "What goes with what?" All stress unidirectional effects—those produced by socio-economic factors on the political "side." All are preliminary operations before the really important theoretical task of specifying the relationships that determine the interactions between these dimensions. If these relationships could be specified, a powerful explanatory theory could be formulated, and more reliable predictions about future trends would be possible.

All this serves to underline the shortcomings of . . . the present study. But strongly influenced by the view that explanation can only be approximated by consideration of dynamic, time-bound processes,

I have taken more steps than are customary in a study of this type. The first step . . . consisted in establishing a pairing—in this case between levels of modernization and political system types. The second step focused on Argentina and Brazil, attempting to bring forth elements to provide a genetic explanation of the implantation of contemporary South American bureaucratic-authoritarian systems. There we examined the main characteristics of the Argentine and Brazilian political systems and tried to place them in comparative perspective vis-à-vis European bureaucratic-authoritarian systems and other South American authoritarianisms. A brief third step, highly speculative, consisted of attempting to assess some trends.

On the basis of this analysis, several points can be made with some confidence. First, the higher levels of contemporary South American modernization are not associated with political democracies. Second, the Argentine and Brazilian bureaucratic-authoritarian systems can hardly be conceived as having increased the probabilities of establishment and consolidation of political democracies in these countries. Third, until much more solid and better focused evidence is brought forth, there are no reasons to believe that the chances of the survival of the existing South American political democracies are significantly higher than those of their breakdown in an authoritarian direction. Fourth, as modernization proceeds there is an indeterminate but considerable probability that such authoritarian breakdowns will fall within the "bureaucratic" category analyzed here. Fifth, the basic paradigm and its underlying assumption of equivalence of causal processes are not supported by the South American cases. . . .

Notes

1. "Relatively" new because some members of the old oligarchy shifted part of their activities toward domestic market-oriented industrial production. In this sense they participated in, and benefitted from, the new economic policies, but a substantial proportion of them, including their associations, maintained their former activities and openly opposed the new policies.

2. This situation contrasts with the still largely prevailing pattern in other South American countries, where the largest proportion of foreign investment is concentrated in export-oriented firms (mainly mining-extractive enclaves, plantations of highly specialized exportable agrarian products, and financial-commercial intermediaries with foreign trade). The links that most of those firms establish with the domestic market and with domestic entrepreneurs are far less numerous than in those cases where marketing and consumption also take place within the same domestic market. Furthermore, even though enclaves and plantations tend to pay higher wages than the national averages, in most cases they are located at great distances from the large urban centers of these

countries. See Celso Furtado, *Teoría y Política del Desarrollo* (Siglo XXI, 1968) and F. Cardoso and E. Faleto, *Dependencia y Desarrollo en América Latina* (Siglo XXI, 1969), p. 48ff.

3. A UN-ECLA study, "Industrial Development," advances the interesting suggestion that these difficulties are greater the more industrially advanced the country is. According to this study, the greater technological requirements for further vertical integration, as well as the greater size of investments and their longer terms of maturation, require a more stabilized context over which public and private decisions can span. In contrast, industrial establishments in which less capital- and technology-intensive firms and projects still predominate are better able to adjust to sudden contextual variations. This suggests the hypothesis (to be explored further below) that the *perceived* need of achieving a high degree of stabilization and predictability in the social context will increase with the degree of modernization achieved in each country. I emphasize that this seems to be a *perceived* need, because the UN-ECLA study presents it as an objective need imposed by a situation of more advanced industrialization.

4. I will use this term to combine two partially overlapping concepts: "salient social problems" (social problems that are high on the agenda of concerns of political actors) and "developmental bottlenecks" (problems that from the point of view of the observer seriously hamper the probabilities of future socio-economic growth).

5. The expression is from Neil Smelser, *The Sociology of Economic Life* (Englewood Cliffs: Prentice-Hall, 1960), p. 110.

6. *Political Order in Changing Societies* (New Haven: Yale University Press, 1968). According to Huntington, "praetorianism" emerges when the levels of political participation and mobilization markedly exceed the level of political institutionalization in a society (p. 80). "*Mass* praetorianism" exists when the institutionalization lag occurs in highly modern and mobilized societies, where large-scale social movements and complex organizations play a decisive role (p. 88ff.). Huntington discusses the main aspects and consequences of "[mass] praetorianism" in several passages; see, e.g., p. 196: "In all societies specialized social groups engage in politics. What makes such groups seem more 'politicized' in a praetorian society is the absence of effective political institutions capable of mediating, refining, and moderating group political action. In a praetorian system social forces confront each other nakedly: no political institutions, no corps of professional political leaders are recognized or accepted as the legitimate intermediaries to moderate group conflict. Equally important, no agreement exists among the groups as to the legitimate and authoritative methods for resolving conflicts. . . . In a praetorian society, however, not only are the actors varied, but so also are the methods used to decide upon office and policy. Each group employs means which reflect its peculiar nature and capabilities: the wealthy bribe; students riot; workers strike; and the military coup."

7. For the initial statement of this concept, see Torcuato di Tella, *El sistema político argentino y la clase obrera* (Eudeba, 1964). Other authors have explored its implications; see, for example, E. Kenworthy, "Coalitions in the Political Development of Latin America," in S. Groennings et al., eds., *The Study of*

Coalition Behavior (New York: Holt, Rinehart and Winston, 1970) and Irving L. Horowitz, "La norma de ilegitimidad: Hacia una teoría general del desarrollo político latinoamericano," *Revista Mexicana de Sociología,* XXX, No. 2 (1968).

8. The concept of "technocratic roles" applies to those individuals who, as an important part of their daily business, *apply* modern technology. This requires fairly prolonged training and continuing attention to developments in the field of technical expertise, but should not be confused with what might be called "scientific roles," which are primarily concerned with expanding knowledge in particular fields—not with the application of what is more or less received wisdom in a specialty.

9. As used here, the term "coup coalition" refers to the military officers and civilian personnel who directly participate in creating the political conditions conducive to a military coup, as well as organizing, setting the main goals, and executing them.

10. There is little doubt that one consequence of the modernization processes in Argentina and Brazil has been a significant increase in the political and economic weight of the social sectors (the armed forces, large modern firms, and the national government) that technocratic roles have most densely penetrated. This is an important link between the social structure and the role levels. It is tempting to interpret this link by postulating that factors at the role level merely "express" the objective interests of social sectors (particularly classes) and organizations. This is a fairly common basis for interpretation, especially in some varieties of Marxism, but it is my impression that the causal processes are far more complicated, with both sets of factors (at the role level and the social-structural level) making independent and important contributions.

11. Of course, this shift produces profound psychological dissonance. Dissonance is evidenced in the repeated Argentine and Brazilian assurances since their coups that the resulting political systems were the only ways to achieve "authentic democracy" in the future.

12. Robert Dahl, *Polyarchy, Participation and Opposition* (New Haven: Yale University Press, 1971), pp. 15–16.

13. *Social Origins of Dictatorship and Democracy* (Boston: Beacon Press, 1966). For another important study that suggests many points similar to Moore's and to the considerations proposed here, see Alexander Gerschenkron, *Economic Backwardness in Historical Perspective* (Cambridge: Harvard University Press, 1962). See also A. Organski, *The Stages of Political Development* (New York: Knopf, 1965). The first detailed analysis of a historical situation marked by defensive political reactions of the propertied sectors was by Marx; see *El 18 Brumario de Luis Bonaparte* (Barcelona: Ediciones Ariel, 1968), which is still a source of valuable insights.

14. Andrew Janos, "The One-Party State and Social Mobilization: East Europe Between the Wars," in S. Huntington and C. Moore, eds., *Authoritarian Politics in Modern Societies: The Dynamics of Established One-Party Systems* (New York: Basic Books, 1970).

15. David Apter, *The Politics of Modernization* (Chicago: University of Chicago Press, 1965), *Conceptual Approaches to the Study of Modernization*

(Englewood Cliffs, N.J.: Prentice Hall, 1969), and *Choice and the Politics of Allocation* (New Haven: Yale University Press, 1971).

16. Juan Linz, "An Authoritarian Regime: Spain," in S. Rokkan, ed., *Mass Politics* (New York: The Free Press, 1970).

17. Ibid.; emphasis added.

18. Ibid.

19. The other South American authoritarianisms, which will be briefly discussed below, will be categorized as "populist" and "traditional."

20. The decision to exclude the Middle American countries from the focus of this study has meant excluding Mexico, a country that clearly belongs in the same group of high modernization as Argentina and Brazil (with a degree of intracountry heterogeneity similar to the latter). In my view the Mexican case highlights the importance of a phenomenon not present in Argentina and Brazil: the entrance into high modernization with a high degree of legitimacy of the political system and generalized allegiance of the population at large (for survey data on this point see G. Almond and S. Verba, *The Civic Culture* [Princeton: Princeton University Press, 1963], and the excellent discussion by Robert Scott, "Mexico: The Established Revolution," in L. Pye and S. Verba, eds., *Political Culture and Political Development* [Princeton: Princeton University Press, 1965]).

Such legitimacy and allegiance—stemming from a revolutionary process that had not occurred in Argentina and Brazil—allowed a high level of institutionalization of the Partido Revolucionario Institucional (PRI), through which it has been possible to achieve a high degree of "encapsulation" of the Mexican popular sector. (The degree to which such encapsulation has been achieved with other social sectors is disputed among specialists, but it seems clear that it holds for the popular sector; see R. Scott, *Mexican Government in Transition* [Urbana: University of Illinois Press, 1959], and the survey of the state of this question in M. Croan, "Is Mexico the Future of East Europe? Institutional Adaptability and Political Change in Comparative Perspective," in S. Huntington and C. Moore, eds.)

These same factors have contributed in the Mexican case to the stability of governments and tenure in public office, which is to be contrasted with the extreme instability of the high-modernization periods in Argentina and Brazil, and which can be interpreted as greatly facilitating more effective public decision-making and a longer-range horizon of decisions for public policy. In terms of my analysis, the Mexican revolutionary heritage made possible the entry into high modernization with a low level of popular political activation and demands, most of them channeled through established and largely "encapsulating" political institutions. By the same token, the demands-performance and differentiation-integration "gaps" have been far less pronounced than in Argentina and Brazil, and have not led to mass praetorianism.

But it should be noted that the consequence of these factors has not been markedly different in terms of political system type and public policies. Rather, the legitimacy of the political system and the low level of popular political activation in Mexico has made it possible for the policies of authoritarianism at high modernization to be pursued at relatively (in comparison to Argentina and Brazil) low cost and high efficiency. Several comments should be made to clarify this statement.

First, only by "conceptual stretching" can the Mexican system be classified as a political democracy. In spite of the broad allegiance that makes electoral defeat unlikely, there are abundant indications that there is no chance for genuine political opposition.

Second, it is clear that "encapsulation" has advanced much further in the Mexican case than under the Argentine and Brazilian bureaucratic-authoritarian systems. An important consequence has been the almost complete "domestication" of Mexican labor unions—an important requisite for the "success" of authoritarian policies and for achieving (maintaining, in the Mexican case) a low level of political activation of the popular sector.

Third, in terms of allocation of resources, Mexico is not more equalitarian than Brazil and certainly much less so than Argentina. Furthermore, the trend since the 1950s has been (as in the other Latin American situations of high modernization) toward income redistribution against the interests of the popular sector and in favor of the more "dynamic" entrepreneurial sectors (see, among others, UN-ECLA, *The Process of Industrial Development in Latin America* (New York, 1966), "Income Distribution in Latin America," *Economic Bulletin for Latin America,* Vol. XII, No. 2 (1968), and *Estudio Economico de America Latina,* 1969 (New York, 1970); M. Singer, *Growth Equality and the Mexican Experience* [Austin: University of Texas Press, 1969]; and P. Gonzalez Casanova, *La Democracía en México* [Mexico DF, 1965]).

13 / Tensions in the Bureaucratic-Authoritarian State and the Question of Democracy

Guillermo O'Donnell

Concerning the State

The state is fundamentally a social relationship of domination or, more precisely, one aspect—as such, comprehensible only analytically—of the social relations of domination.[1] The state supports and organizes these relations of domination through institutions that usually enjoy a monopoly of the means of coercion within a defined territory and that generally are viewed as having a legitimate right to guarantee the system of social domination. As such, the state should be understood from and within civil society, though in its objective, institutional form it appears to be, and proclaims itself to stand, above society.

What interests us here is a type of capitalist state. As such, it maintains and structures class domination, in the sense that this domination is rooted principally in a class structure that in turn has its foundation in the operation and reproduction of capitalist relations of production. These relations of production are the "heart of civil society," within which we view the state as the strictly political aspect of the social relations of domination. From this perspective the state is, first and foremost, a relation of domination that articulates in unequal fashion the components of civil society, supporting and organizing the existing system of social domination. What makes this support effective are certain objective manifestations of the state—its institutions and the

Reprinted with permission from *The New Authoritarianism in Latin America,* edited by David Collier, pp. 285–318. Princeton University Press, 1979. Copyright © 1979 Princeton University Press.

law. Yet the true meaning and consequences of these can be understood only in terms of their being the objective manifestations of certain aspects of the system of domination in society.

I wish to stress two interrelated themes regarding the state—first, its analytic reality as the political aspect of certain social relations of domination, and, second, its concrete objectification as a set of institutions and legal norms. By keeping in mind the interrelation between these two faces of the state—analytic and concrete—one can see the falsity of the claim by the state's institutions to embody a rationality that is distinct from and superior to that of civil society, as well as the corresponding falsity of denying the state's fundamental role in articulating civil society in an unequal (or, more precisely, contradictory) fashion.

Further, the apparent separation of the institutions of the state from civil society fosters the emergence of diverse linkages or "mediations" between the opacity and fractionalization of that which is "private"— i.e., civil society—on the one hand, and the "public" and universalistic role (for the population within its borders) in which the state institutions usually present themselves to ordinary consciousness. I do not have space to develop here the reasoning that underlies this conclusion, but the state is usually also the organizational focus of consensus within society, from which it derives the basis for its own legitimation. In order to achieve consensus, these institutions must appear as *the* state, as agents of a general interest of a community—the nation—that transcends the reproduction of daily life in civil society. The reification of the state in its institutional objectifications obscures its underlying role as guarantor of domination within society; yet—inasmuch as it implies that state and society appear to be separate—it tends to generate various mediations between them through which consensus tends to be created. The state ultimately is based on coercion, but it usually is also based on consensus, which both encompasses and conceals coercion.

The principal mediation alluded to above is the nation. I mean by nation the collective identities that define a "we" that consists, on the one hand, of a network of solidarities superimposed upon the diversity and antagonisms of civil society and, on the other hand, of the recognition of a collectivity distinct from the "they" that constitutes other nations. The nation is expressed through a dense symbolism epitomized by the flag and national anthem, as well as by an official history that mythologizes a shared, cohesive past and extols a collective "we" which should prevail over the cleavages (not only those between social classes) of civil society.

There are two other fundamental political mediations. One is citizenship, in the double sense of (1) abstract equality which—basically by means of universal suffrage and the corresponding regime of political democracy—is the foundation of the claim that the power exercised through the institutions of the state by the occupants of governmental roles is based on the consent of the citizens; and (2) the right to have recourse to juridically regulated protection against arbitrary acts on the part of state institutions. The second mediation is the *pueblo* or *lo popular*.[2] This mediation is based on a "we" that derives neither from the idea of shared citizenship, which involves abstractly equal rights, nor from the idea of nation, which involves concrete rights which apply equally to all those who belong to the nation without respect to their position within society. *Pueblo* and *lo popular* involve a "we" that is a carrier of demands for substantive justice which form the basis for the obligations of the state toward the less favored segments of the population.

Normally, in a capitalist state the subject of the state is the citizen, who has the right, which is not systematically denied, to lodge claims of substantive justice before the appropriate state institutions. Of course, this right is actually limited by the systematic inequalities that arise from the underlying class structure of society and from other forms of social inequality. Nonetheless, this right is partially real, and the belief in its existence is normally an important element of consensus, which entails challenging neither the domination which is exercised in society nor the role of the state as the agent or representative of the general interest of the nation.

The efficacy of this idea of the nation, along with that of citizenship and *lo popular,* allows the state institutions to appear as agents which achieve and protect a general interest—that is, the general interest of a "we" that stands above the factionalism and antagonisms of civil society. Moreover, the effective functioning—as an institutional reality and in terms of subjective acceptance on the part of a large portion of relevant social actors—of the ideas of citizenship and *lo popular* usually provides a consensual basis for the exercise of power, and ultimately of coercion, by the state institutions. They do this because the basis of state power must appear to reside outside the state itself. The state can only be legitimated by appearing to reside in external referents whose general interest the state institutions are supposed to serve. These external referents are normally the nation, jointly with citizenship and *pueblo,* which represent the intersection of an abstractly equal "we" (i.e., citizenship) and a "we" which is concretely unequal (involving the tutelage of the less favored portion of society, i.e., the *pueblo*). From these referents there usually emerge collective identities that stand above the class cleavages that can potentially arise from civil society. Because the state appears separated from society and objectified in its institutions, these institutions cannot by themselves legitimate the power they exercise except by means of the collective referents whose general interests they claim to serve. Each of those collective referents mediates the relation between the state and society, transforming its underlying reality; hence their role in achieving consensus and, correspondingly, in legitimating the power exercised by the state institutions.

On the other hand, these mediations are the means through which the social subject, as a member of society, rises above his private life. Identifying himself in the symbols of the nation, exercising the rights of citizenship, and eventually making demands for substantive justice as part of the *pueblo,* the social subject transcends his daily life and recognizes himself as part of a "we" which is, from another perspective, the referent evoked by the state institutions. Hence, these institutions do not usually appear as the organizers and guarantors of social domination, but rather as agents of the general interests expressed through those mediations. This fact tends to result in a consensus which expresses the belief that what the state institutions do and do not do—even though systematically biased by the underlying system of social domination— is the consequence of the rights derived from being a citizen, as well as a member of the nation and *lo popular.* This tension between the underlying reality of the state as guarantor and organizer of social domination, on the one hand, and as agent of a general interest which, though partialized and limited, is not fictitious, on the other, is characteristic of any state. This tension is the key to the theoretical analysis of the state. We cannot attempt such an analysis here. Yet by examining certain characteristics of the BA state we will be able to see, in a context in which the above-mentioned mediations are largely missing, their crucial importance in facilitating what is fundamental for any system of social and political domination: to mask the reality of domination and to appear to be the expression of a general, encompassing interest.

Before turning to the main topic of this chapter, I must present other observations indispensable for understanding both the situation prior to the installation of BA and its subsequent impact once installed.

1. In Latin America the formation of the nation was accomplished much more through the mediation of *lo popular* than through that of citizenship. Whether or not it occurred through so-called populisms, the political activation of the previously marginal popular sectors occurred through political relationships in which they were treated much more as a *pueblo,* as a carrier of demands for substantive justice, than as citizens.

2. This same process of constituting the nation involved the postulation of a "we" that defined itself as an adversary of an "antinational" social order whose most conspicuous components involved the role of transnational capital in the exportation of primary products

and the dominant national classes that were more intimately tied to transnational capital.

3. This process contributed to the downfall of the system of oligarchic domination and its replacement by a system of bourgeois domination supported by the expansion of the institutional system of the state which opened the way for the supremacy of transnational capital in the urban productive structure.

4. In the periods preceding the installation of BA, the great advance in the transnationalization of the productive structure led to a fundamental alteration in the nature of civil society in relation to the territorial scope of the authority exercised by the state. That is, many of the principal centers of economic decision-making in society, the final destination and criteria for the distribution of the capital generated in the local market, and many aspects of the social relations (not only economic ones) extended beyond the state's capacity for control within the scope of its territorial authority. This "denationalization" was added onto that which had occurred earlier in connection with the exportation of primary products, and now came to affect the most dynamic components of the urban productive and class structure.[3] Other factors that came into play prior to the implantation of the BA state, such as the different levels of "threat," the interaction between the pattern of economic growth that followed the transnationalization of the urban productive structure and the growing popular political activation, and the severity of the crisis that preceded it, have already been treated elsewhere.[4]

We can now delineate the most important features of the BA state as a starting point for analyzing the contradictory dynamic that is set in motion by its implantation.

The Bureaucratic-Authoritarian State

BA is a type of authoritarian state whose principal characteristics are:

1. It is, first and foremost, guarantor and organizer of the domination exercised through a class structure subordinated to the upper fractions of a highly oligopolized and transnationalized bourgeoisie. In other words, the principal social base of the BA state is this upper bourgeoisie.

2. In institutional terms, it is [composed] of organizations in which specialists in coercion have decisive weight, as well as those whose aim it is to achieve "normalization" of the economy.[5] The special role played by these two groups represents the institutional expression of the identification, by its own actors, of the two great tasks that the BA state is committed to accomplish: the restoration of "order" in society by

means of the political deactivation of the popular sector, on the one hand, and the normalization of the economy, on the other.

3. It is a system of political exclusion of a previously activated popular sector which is subjected to strict controls in an effort to eliminate its earlier active role in the national political arena. This political exclusion is achieved by destroying or capturing the resources (especially those embodied in class organizations and political movements) which supported this activation. In addition, this exclusion is guided by a determination to impose a particular type of "order" on society and guarantee its future viability. This order is seen as a necessary condition for the consolidation of the social domination that BA guarantees and, after achieving the normalization of the economy, for reinitiating a highly transnationalized pattern of economic growth characterized by a skewed distribution of resources.

4. This exclusion involves the suppression of citizenship, in the twofold sense defined above. In particular, this suppression includes the liquidation of the institutions of political democracy. It also involves a denial of *lo popular:* it prohibits (enforcing the prohibition with coercion) any appeals to the population as *pueblo* and, of course, as class. The suppression of the institutional roles and channels of access to the government characteristic of political democracy is in large measure oriented toward eliminating roles and organizations (political parties among them) that have served as a channel for appeals for substantive justice that are considered incompatible with the restoration of order and with the normalization of the economy. In addition, BA appears as if placed before a sick nation—as expressed in the rhetoric that derived from the severity of the crisis that preceded its implantation—whose general interest must be invoked; yet, because of the depth of the crisis, BA cannot claim to be the representative of that sick nation, which is seen as contaminated by innumerable internal enemies. Thus, BA is based on the suppression of two fundamental mediations—citizenship and *lo popular.* In an ambiguous way it may evoke the other mediation—the nation—but only as a "project" (and not as an actual reality) which it proposes to carry out through drastic surgical measures.

5. BA is also a system of economic exclusion of the popular sector, inasmuch as it promotes a pattern of capital accumulation which is highly skewed toward benefiting the large oligopolistic units of private capital and some state institutions. The preexisting inequities in the distribution of societal resources are thus sharply increased.

6. It corresponds to, and promotes, an increasing transnationalization of the productive structure, resulting in a further denationalization of society in terms of the degree to which it is in fact contained within the scope of the territorial authority which the state claims to exercise.

7. Through its institutions it endeavors to "depoliticize" social issues by dealing with them in terms of the supposedly neutral and objective criteria of technical rationality. This depoliticization complements the prohibition against invoking issues of substantive justice as they relate to *lo popular* (and, of course, class), which allegedly introduces "irrationalities" and "premature" demands that interfere with the restoration of order and the normalization of the economy.

8. In the first stage that we are considering here, the political regime of the BA state—which, while not formalized, is clearly identifiable—involves closing the democratic channels of access to the government. More generally, it involves closing the channels of access for the representation of popular and class interests. Such access is limited to those who stand at the apex of large organizations (both public and private), especially the armed forces and large oligopolistic enterprises. . . .

Ambiguities in the System of Domination

Fundamentally, BA is a type of state which encompasses sharply contradictory tendencies. On the one hand, BA involves the further denationalization of civil society noted above that occurs first as a consequence of the urgent search for the transnational capital which is a requisite for the normalization of the economy, and later due to the necessity of maintaining a "favorable investment climate" in order to sustain the inflow of such capital. At the same time, BA entails a drastic contraction of the nation, the suppression of citizenship, and the prohibition of appeals to the *pueblo* and to social class as a basis for making demands for substantive justice. This contraction derives from the defeat of the popular sector and its allies; from the reaction triggered by the threat that the political activation of this sector seemed to pose for the survival of the basic parameters of capitalist society; and, once BA is implanted, from the aim of imposing a particular social "order" based on the political and economic exclusion of the popular sector. . . .

On the other hand, like all states, BA claims to be a national state. Lacking the referent of the nation as a universally comprehensive idea that encompasses the entire population, the rhetoric of the institutions of BA must "statize" the meaning of the nation—at the same time that, in relation to the normalization of the economy, the same rhetoric defends an intense privatization. Such statizing of the idea of the nation implies that its general interest be identified with the success of the state institutions in their quest to establish a particular order in society and to normalize the economy. As a result, the state institutions no longer appear to play the role through which they usually legitimate themselves, that of serving an interest superior and external to themselves—i.e., the interests of the nation as a community that encompasses the totality of, or at least most of, the population. On the contrary, when the state institutions attempt to redefine the nation in terms of exclusion and of national infirmity, the power they exercise no longer has an external basis of legitimation and cannot but appear as its own foundation. In other words, domination becomes naked and dilutes its consensual mediations; it manifests itself in the form of overt physical and economic coercion. In addition, the suppression of citizenship, together with the prohibition against invoking *lo popular,* not merely dilutes but radically eliminates other legitimating mediations between the state and society. . . .

The institutions of the BA state attempt to fill the void thus created through an intensive use of the martial and patriotic symbols of the nation. But these symbols must be anchored in some of the aforementioned referents if they are not to be merely grandiloquent rhetoric. The BA leaders attempt to recreate mediations with society by inviting "participation"; but the state's denial of its own role as representative of the nation and the elimination of the ideas of *pueblo* and citizenship mean that such participation can only involve a passively approving observation of the tasks that the state institutions undertake.

Under these conditions, the best that can be hoped for is a "tacit consensus," i.e., depoliticization, apathy, and a retreat into a completely privatized daily existence. And fear. Fear on the part of the losers and the opponents of BA, which results from BA's conspicuous capacity for coercion. And fear on the part of the winners, who face the specter of a return to the situation that preceded the implantation of BA. There is also the fear, on the part of those who carry out the physical coercion, of any "political solution" that could possibly lead to such a return; this last fear at times appears to drive them down a path of coercion that knows no limits.

Tacit consensus is a foundation too tenuous to sustain the state. Fear, together with the upper bourgeoisie and the "modern" sectors of the middle class more closely tied to it, [is] the major social support of the BA state. But fear hardly serves as an adequate mediation between the state and society. Moreover, the fear on the part of the winners tends to diminish with the passage of time (in spite of efforts to refresh their memory) and with an awareness of the costs imposed on many of them by the continuation of BA.

In reality, the surgery that the higher institutions of the BA state attempt to perform upon the nation inflicts heavy costs on many of those who supported the implantation of BA. The imposition of "order" of course severely punishes the political and class organizations that served as channels for the political activation of the popular sector. The economic exclusion of this sector and the prohibition against raising issues of substantive justice around the symbols of *pueblo* and class make it clear that whatever the BA state may proclaim the nation to be, it does not include the popular sector. Those who were until recently an active political presence are ostracized from their own nation through their political and economic exclusion. On the other hand, the attempts to normalize the economy through a close alliance with the upper bourgeoisie (in the first stage of BA, above all with transnational and domestic finance capital) inflict serious hardships on a good portion of the middle sectors and the weakest (and more indisputably national) fractions of the bourgeoisie. As a result, a rapid contraction of the alliance that supported its implantation takes place in the initial period of BA. The supporters who withdraw from the alliance enter into the "tacit consensus" and engage in a disillusioned defense of their specific interests in the interstices of state institutions. Depending on the lesser or greater degree of previous threat, those who withdraw their support because of the policies of economic normalization may or may not, respectively, combine with the excluded sectors and participate, as in Argentina in 1969, in a decisive challenge to the BA state.[6] In cases of a high level of previous threat in which they do not withdraw, these sectors reinforce the silence and opacity of civil society.

The withdrawal of these initial supporters underscores the fact that the principal (and at that moment virtually the only) base of social support of BA is the upper bourgeoisie—i.e., the upper fractions of the local bourgeoisie and of transnational capitalism. But this is—ostensibly—the principal economic beneficiary of the new situation and the most transnationalized and, therefore, the least national component of society. In light of the economic and political exclusion of the popular sector, the economic hardships suffered by an important portion of the original alliance, the contraction of the nation, and the suppression of the mediations of citizenship and *pueblo,* the BA state remains—and overtly appears to be—sustained basically by the oligopolistic and transnationalized fractions of the bourgeoisie, along with—in its own institutional system—the armed forces and the technocrats who attempt the normalization of the economy. These oligopolistic and transnationalized fractions of the bourgeoisie serve poorly as a legitimating referent for the state because they are the antithesis of *lo popular* and of the symbolism of the nation defined as a "we" that stands in contrast to the "they" of other nations. On the other hand, the local bourgeoisie hardly provides an adequate legitimating referent for the state either. Though the BA economic policies have variegated impacts on different economic activities, they further weaken the already weak local bourgeoisie, placing part of it among those who are part of the "tacit consensus" and hardly leaving this class in an appropriate position to fill the role of a dominant class whose interests can plausibly be argued by the state institutions to be coequal with the general interests of the nation. . . .

In the face of these dilemmas, one escape might lie in the possibility that the state can convert itself, not only in its discourse but in the reality of its activities, into the institutional center of a national development project which could be invoked as representing the paramount general interest. That is to say, the state institutions themselves would become the economic and social center of such a project, emerging as the leaders of "development" and taking the place of the absent bourgeois leadership. This approach would lead toward state capitalism. Yet this alternative conflicts with the high degree of transnationalization of the productive structure and with the crucial role that private capital, especially the upper bourgeoisie, must play if BA is to endure. It generates ambiguities and tensions, both within BA and with its principal social base, which we will consider below.

On another level, the institutional system of BA reflects the priorities that its own actors set for themselves. The institutions specialized in the use of coercion occupy the apex of this system by virtue of having themselves ended the crisis that preceded BA and because they remain in charge of imposing order and, no less important, of guaranteeing the future effectiveness of this order. At the same time, the task of normalizing the economy is assigned to civilian technocrats closely identified with the upper bourgeoisie and with transnational financial institutions. The technocrats believe in the rationality of economic orthodoxy, know how to apply it, and are trusted by the local and transnational elements of the upper bourgeoisie. The policies and institutions of the first phase of BA are organized around these two concerns. The two great tasks of imposing order (with its organizational agent, the armed forces) and of normalizing the economy (with its social base in the upper bourgeoisie, and its agents in the technocrats who direct it) are institutionally inserted into the BA state. As a result, BA cannot but appear as the transparent conjunction of coercion and economic domination.

These priorities reflect something fundamental which has already been mentioned, but which I hope we may now understand better. The implantation of BA is an attempt to salvage a society whose continuity as a capitalist system was perceived as threatened. This goal can only be achieved, given the magnitude of this threat, by, on the one hand, severely imposing "order," and, on the other, by carefully obeying the rules of orthodoxy upon which the support of transnational capital and of the most dynamic and economically powerful fractions of these societies is contingent. These measures, together with the suppression of mediations and the resulting exposure of the underlying system of domination, are the immense homage which is rendered to the reproduction of society *qua* capitalist. In the face of the alternative posed by the depth of the crisis that preceded BA and the accompanying threat, the state is first and foremost a capitalist state, rather than a national, a popular, or a citizens' state. Yet the implementation of these measures entails the immense risk of implanting a state that is incapable of converting itself into the foundation of its own legitimacy. The state must rely instead on tacit consensus, coercion, fear, and the support of the least national fractions of its society.

There cannot be consensus unless the connection between coercion and economic domination is veiled. Yet the opposite occurs in BA. Moreover, in BA the proximity of coercion and economic domination juxtaposes two social actors—the armed forces and the upper bourgeoisie—who usually are separated, on a political level, by the mediations mentioned above and, on the institutional level of the state, by other institutions of civilian bureaucracy and democratic representation. That is to say, the social basis of BA in the upper bourgeoisie, their ostensible support for BA, and their "bridgehead" in the institutional system of the state in the form of the economic technocrats intersect directly and visibly with the armed forces. The upper bourgeoisie and the technocrats have a strongly transnational orientation, both in their beliefs and in their economic behavior. For them, the political boundaries of the nation are basically a useless constraint on the movement of the factors of production, on the free circulation of capital, and on considerations of efficiency at the transnational level. They also interfere with the efforts to reintegrate these economies into the world market in the aftermath of the pre-BA crisis. All of these aims clash with what is perceived by these actors as the narrowness of the nation and of "nationalism." On the other hand, these actors are the most fully and dynamically capitalistic members of these societies. Hence, they are unabashedly motivated by profit, the driving force behind an accumulation of capital which is sanctioned by an ideology which claims that the maximization of profit will, in the long run, contribute to the general welfare.

But a great problem within BA is that the other central actor in its institutional system—the armed forces—tends to be the most nationalistic and least capitalistic of the state institutions. With their sense of mission, the martial values with which they socialize their members, and their doctrines of national security which presuppose the existence of a nation characterized by a high degree of homogeneity in the orientations and actions of all civilians, the armed forces are the state institution most predisposed to define the nation as that which is *not* foreign, and to define appropriate behavior as that which is inspired by an introverted and exclusivist vision of the nation. In addition, the profit motive appears to them to be of secondary importance, at most, and sordid in comparison with the larger concerns and ideals that derive from their own orientations. Profit may be necessary, but in any case it should not become "excessive" or work against the mission of homogenizing the totality of the nation.

How is it possible that social actors with such different orientations and values can join together as the principal actors within the institutions of BA? The answer is that with the legitimating mediations suppressed— and, of course, pending always the problem of maintaining the deactivation of the popular sector and the prohibition against evoking *pueblo* and class—economic domination and coercion tend to become transparently close and mutually supportive. Particularly after many of the original supporters of BA withdraw to "tacit consensus" (in addition to the initial exclusion of the popular sector), the upper bourgeoisie needs coercion as a guarantee of present and future social "order," without which it could neither reinitiate accumulation for its own principal benefit nor place its confidence in the future of the economy.[7] On the other hand, without this support and the resulting confidence, a BA state whose alliances have narrowed to such an extent could not even attempt economic normalization and would soon crumble.

In the BA state, economic domination and coercion, along with their social carriers, are mutually indispensable. But this mutual indispensability does not prevent the alliance forged in this way from being marked, on both sides, by numerous tensions. Nor does it prevent the emergence of a desire to reconstitute a system of domination which would again separate these two components by interposing the lacking mediations. This point, fundamental for understanding the dynamic of BA, will receive our attention in the following sections.

Tensions in the Alliance

The mutual indispensability of the upper bourgeoisie and the armed forces is the key to discovering the dissonances and tensions that arise between them. The goal of constructing a more homogeneous nation is inconsistent both with the denationalization of civil society promoted by the most transnationalized actors within society and with their orientation toward a pattern of capital accumulation which cannot remain confined within the local market, either in terms of its principal criteria for decision-making or in terms of the main beneficiaries of that accumulation. The overt alliance of the pinnacle of the state apparatus with the least national elements in the nation occurs in conjunction with the exclusion of the popular sector and with the withdrawal of support by important—and unequivocally national—portions of the middle sectors and the bourgeoisie that actively supported the implantation of BA.

How can the tensions be resolved that arise among the armed forces' conception of the nation, the transnational orientation of their principal allies in the BA state, and the national character not only of the popular sector but also of the original allies who have subsequently suffered from the impact of the normalization policies? One possibility would be the enlargement of the state apparatus that might greatly expand its direct economic role, including its role in economic production. Supposedly, this state role would provide a counterweight to the expansion of large-scale private capital (especially transnational capital) and would permit the state apparatus to ally itself with the local bourgeoisie—admittedly weak, but which could, presumably, recover its dynamism under the tutelage of the state apparatus. This approach would involve a nationally oriented pattern of development in which the principal economic actor would be a productive state apparatus serving as a vanguard for the local bourgeoisie. Yet, at least in the initial stage of the BA state, this approach is most unlikely to meet with success. In the period of normalization, economic orthodoxy must be observed carefully, above all when the pre-BA crisis has been particularly acute. One of the practices that is prohibited in this context is the continuation of "state interventionism," especially in productive or commercial activities. One of the tenets of orthodoxy, on the contrary, is to reduce the fiscal deficit drastically, to return potentially profitable activities to the private sector, and to eliminate subsidies to consumers and inefficient producers (including state enterprises). These policies are explicitly referred to in the agreements on the basis of which transnational financing is acquired, involving not only the International Monetary Fund but other lenders as well. Moreover, they are proclaimed as a central article in the professions of orthodox faith on the part of the BA technocrats. Deviating from these and related criteria would undermine the internal and international confidence without which normalization would be impossible. Hence, a shift toward state capitalism is blocked in the initial period of BA.[8]

The fact that this alternative is precluded is a source of acute concern within the core of the armed forces, many of whose members express their dislike of the emphasis on transnationalizing the economy that the alliance with the upper bourgeoisie entails. To other members of the armed forces—above all those who hold high positions within the government—it is clear that, "for the moment," the viability of BA and the hopes for restoring national cohesion depend on economic orthodoxy and a close alliance with the upper bourgeoisie. Yet the ambivalence that underlies the acceptance of this formula is a sword of Damocles which hangs over the consolidation of bourgeois domination.

The period from 1967 to 1970 in Argentina is an instance of normalization policy under BA in which these tensions manifested themselves most strongly, introducing a major element of uncertainty in a context in which these policies had, in fact, met with an important degree of success. Already by the end of 1967, as an alternative to the policies then being pursued, other proposals were being considered in which the state would take a more active role, encourage the development of certain fractions of the local bourgeoisie, impose significant restrictions on transnational capital, and reincorporate previously domesticated and "de-Peronized" labor unions into the political arena. This alternative had important support in the armed forces, and this support generated within the upper bourgeoisie a grave concern that the armed forces might adopt this path. The bourgeoisie saw in this alternative precisely the consequences which later ensued: the end of all attempts to normalize the economy, a rapid flight of capital, and a renewal of the crisis that the implantation of BA had tried to end. Two factors appear particularly important in determining the speed with which this nationalist and statist path—along with the accompanying reorientation of political alliances, including the search for some support from the popular sector— emerges as an alternative. One of them involves the different levels of threat that precede each BA.[9] The second involves the issue of how quickly and decisively the initial economic policies of the BA state meet with success. The greater the degree to which this occurs, the sooner the nationalist and statist alternative is likely to be posed and the stronger its impact on the armed forces.[10] In Argentina, the level of economic crisis and threat was lower than in other cases of BA, and the stabilization program which began in March 1967 had already achieved some significant success by 1968–1969.[11] It was therefore tempting to discontinue orthodox policies and return to the earlier policies involving state support for weaker, national fractions of the bourgeoisie and a moderate redistribution of income for the benefit of the popular sector. These options only appeared reasonable if one ignored the true parameters of the situation, yet this fact did not prevent a realignment of political forces in a direction that inevitably shook the recently renewed confidence of the upper bourgeoisie. This group, in turn, in addition to warning ominously against this unexpected revival of statist and nationalist tendencies under BA, tried to encourage the replacement of the leaders of the government, including President Onganía, by military groups more attuned to their orientations and interests. Thus, the political concerns of the upper bourgeoisie further eroded the internal cohesion of BA and, along with the great social explosions of 1969–1970, hastened its demise.[12]

In contrast, post-1973 Chile and post-1976 Argentina show that if the pre-BA crisis is significantly more intense and the level of threat—as well as the corresponding fear of winners and losers—is higher, it makes reducing the rate of inflation to minimally acceptable levels more difficult, permits the speculative activities typical of the previous period to continue, diminishes the capacity of the state to invest, and likewise prolongs and deepens the recession provoked by the normalization policies. As a result, orthodox economic policies must be followed closely, in spite of the fact that in significant measure it is these policies that bring on such consequences. This necessity, in turn, means that in spite of innumerable expressions of disagreement, the nationalist and statist alternative delineated above does not really appear possible. As a result, more time is available for the application of orthodox policies and for continuing, in an overt and almost exclusive form, the alliance with the upper bourgeoisie.

Stated briefly, the lower the level of prior crisis and threat, the greater the probability of rapidly achieving normalization and restoring economic growth. But, on the other hand, success in restoring growth will increase the temptation, even within the armed forces, to abandon orthodox economic measures at a point which is "premature" from the perspective of the upper bourgeoisie and of the technocrats who control the economic apparatus of BA. Thus, with a lower level of prior crisis and threat, the confidence of the bourgeoisie is more rapidly and easily achieved, but at the same time this confidence remains subject to a greater degree of uncertainty. Inversely, the higher the level of prior crisis and threat, the less the probability of achieving success (even from the point of view of the leaders of BA and their allies) in the normalization of the economy, but, for this very reason, the greater is the certainty on the part of the upper bourgeoisie that orthodox economic policies will be maintained.

The perpetuation (alleviated in some respects but aggravated in others) of the economic crisis that precedes BA is the best guarantee that its ties with the upper bourgeoisie will be maintained in spite of the tensions discussed above. But this ongoing crisis means, among other things, that high rates of inflation will continue and that, owing to the absence of economic growth and to the drastic reduction in popular consumption prescribed by economic orthodoxy, there exists substantial unused installed capacity for production. As a result, the upper bourgeoisie accumulates capital much more through financial speculation, in which it has numerous advantages over other sectors, than through the production and investment which are supposed to provide the basis for renewed economic growth. This speculation in turn serves to further accentuate the economic crisis. In the cases of Chile and Uruguay, this situation has been prolonged in a pathetic fashion for a number of years after BA was implanted, and no serious challenge to the continuation of orthodox economic policies has occurred. This outcome, perverse even for the leaders and supporters of BA, can be understood from the perspective presented in this chapter. The case of contemporary Argentina, after more than two years of a BA implanted in reaction to a crisis and threat much more profound than those of 1966, has so far exhibited these same characteristics.[13]

The case of Brazil is the only one that, after four years of orthodoxy, experienced, starting in 1968, an important resurgence of economic growth that included a vigorous expansion of the state role in economic production and a return to assisting some of the fractions of the local bourgeoisie, yet without undermining the original alliance with the upper bourgeoisie.[14] This shift coincided with the period of greatest repression. It served to demonstrate what the Argentine BA, and particularly the "Cordobazo" of 1969, could not: that the state continued to be, despite the tensions internal to the alliance and to the armed forces, a power capable of applying the necessary coercion to crush the reemergence of movements that attempted to invoke the excluded sectors as *pueblo* or as class. This renewal of BA's coercive guarantee confirmed the confidence of the upper bourgeoisie and was accompanied by changes in economic policy and by the great wave of investments of transnational capital that launched the "Brazilian miracle." At this point it became possible to pursue simultaneously two goals in a way that had been impossible at the onset of BA: the combination of rapid advances in the transnationalization of the productive structure through the increasingly important role played by transnational financial and industrial capital, on the one hand, and the expansion of the productive activities of the state, on the other. Yet each of these processes imposes limits on the other. The movement toward transnationalization is limited by an expansion of state activities that in the last few years has generated an outcry against the "statization" of the Brazilian economy. On the other hand, such statization could not go further than partial incursions into the areas of capital accumulation that the upper bourgeoisie—transnational and domestic—claims as its own, without undermining the hard-earned climate of "business confidence" and precipitating a crisis whose potential severity frightens all parties involved. Both sides see the precipice that defines the limit of their sometimes noisy debates. As a result, in the midst of such debates, the upper bourgeoisie takes care to reiterate its support of a state whose expansion it wishes to limit, but not to prevent. At the same time, the Brazilian authorities are careful to reiterate that they accept and understand the rules of a game based on maintaining the confidence of the upper bourgeoisie. Meanwhile, the celebration of the Brazilian "miracle," with its evocation of "national grandeur" and of the triumphal fulfillment by the BA state of its goals, has unquestionably facilitated the perpetuation of this system of domination. Yet, as the elections of recent years, among other things, have shown, not even this combination of economic success and political propaganda was sufficient to achieve a more or less solid consensus. Likewise, the evocation of this "miracle" as a legitimation of the state and of the increasingly notorious social costs that it imposes is further undermined because it is impossible to sustain the "miracle" year after year. The risk faced by the allies of the Brazilian BA is not only that of intolerable transgressions of the rules of the game that is the basis for the alliance with the upper bourgeoisie; the risk also involves the very real possibility of an active reemergence of genuine opposition.

Brazilian BA is unique in relation to the others because it has lasted so long and because of the greater degree to which it has been successful in its own terms. Yet, as noted above, it has not been able to escape the dilemmas and fears shared by the other BAs: being a type of political domination which is not veiled by a network of mediations and which is, therefore, permanently haunted by the specter of an explosive negation.[15] . . .

Yet how can the mediations be created that would resolve "the difficulties that derive from the solitude of power"?[16] One solution would be, of course, to reinvent the Mexican political system with its dominant party, the PRI, which provides these mediations and at the same time efficiently helps to prevent popular challenges. However, the PRI can be only a nostalgic aspiration because its origin is precisely the opposite from what occurred in cases with which we are concerned here: a popular revolution, rather than the reaction of the terrified bourgeoisie which implanted the BA states. Another possibility would be that of a corporative structuring of society. But for corporatism to truly take the place of the missing mediations, it would have to incorporate in a subordinate fashion the entire society rather than simply restricting itself to being a form of state control of workers. Yet this outcome is precisely what the upper bourgeoisie cannot accept. With good reason, they have no objection to the reimposition of harsh controls over the popular sector, but why should the upper bourgeoisie, an indispensable supporter of BA, have to be incorporated into a state that subordinates it? For this reason corporatist ideology, in spite of its important influence on many of the actors in BA, represents a Utopia that is as archaic as it is unachievable. Corporatism can serve—in the form of tight control over unions—to consolidate a class victory, but not as a means of replacing the mediations between state and society that BA has suppressed.[17]

If some version of the PRI is not possible, if corporatism cannot replace the mediations which are lacking, and if the state's resonant exhortations for "participation" bounce off of the silence of society, then the only thing that remains is the aspiration for the very thing that BA has radically denied: democracy. The use of this term on the part of those at the apex of state institutions and on the part of the upper bourgeoisie would be inexplicable if we did not recognize that such use reflects the fundamental problem of a state without mediations and, hence, of a system of naked domination. If political democracy were to be restored, at the very least the mediation of citizenship would reappear. As a result, there would once again be a possibility that many members of the society could be treated as, and would also see themselves as, participants in a form of abstract, but not insignificant equality—in addition to the implication of the restoration of some basic legal guarantees to the individual. In this way, the basis of state power could be attributed to this source exterior to the state—a condition which is not sufficient, but yet is necessary, for its legitimation. The restoration of political democracy would also permit the resolution of another problem that arises from the lack of mediations and from the militarization of the state: that of presidential succession. From the perspective of the upper bourgeoisie, solving this problem would have the advantage of reducing the institutional weight of the armed forces, of allowing it to cushion its ties with the armed forces through civilian groups which would have policy-making capabilities regarding non-economic issues, of giving greater access to government to civilians whose orientations are more consonant with those of the upper bourgeoisie, and—ultimately—of reducing the visibility of the coercion through which the state supports its economic domination.[18]

But what kind of democracy? It would have to be one that achieves the miracle of being all of this and that at the same time maintains the exclusion of the popular sector. In particular, it would have to be one that sustains the suppression of invocations in terms of *pueblo* and class. Such suppression presupposes that strict controls of the organizations and political movements of the popular sector are maintained, as well as controls over the forms of permissible discourse and rhetoric on the part of those who occupy the institutional positions which democracy would reopen. The search for this philosopher's stone is expressed in the various qualifying adjectives that customarily accompany the term "democracy." . . .

But, how to democratize? It seems clear to the rulers that any move in this direction can open a Pandora's box of popular political reactivation, along with invocations in terms of *pueblo* and eventually of class, which could lead to a renewal of the crisis that preceded BA. And for the dominant alliance this outcome would be much worse than the continuance of a form of domination without mediations and legitimacy, in spite of the tensions and frailties discussed above. Moreover, if BA originally emerged in response to threatening political activation, and if the silence that is imposed on society does not hide the heavy costs of the economic normalization and the imposition of order, is it not reasonable to fear that this threat would reappear in an even more severe form as soon as the dike of exclusion that has been constructed is even partially opened? Because of this fear, the aspiration to restore at least some of the mediations of citizenship and democracy is simultaneously the hope and the dread of this system of domination.

The philosopher's stone would be a form of democracy which is carefully limited, in the sense that invocations in terms of *pueblo* or class are prohibited, but which at the same time is not such a farce that it cannot provide the mediations and, ultimately, a legitimacy that could transform itself into hegemony. The question of how this form of democracy will be achieved poses an enigma that severely tests the ingenuity of the "social engineers" who offer their expertise to accomplish a task which amounts to squaring the circle. Yet the goal which the most enlightened actors in this system of domination seek to achieve is clearly this type of democracy. In cases of a high level of prior threat and crisis, as in Chile, a democratic alternative was not proposed from within the state apparatus and was introduced instead by members of the initial BA alliance who subsequently withdrew their support: the church and the Christian Democrats. In the case of a low degree of prior threat, as in Argentina in 1966, the issue of democracy was posed almost at the beginning as a goal toward which BA should progress as an alternative to the corporatist leanings of the governing military group. In Argentina in 1976, as a result both of the "lesson" derived from this earlier experience and of the underlying tensions that are the concern of this chapter, the goal of restoring democracy has been mentioned from the start, although the obstacles that must be overcome in order to achieve this goal appear today to be far more difficult than they did in 1966. In Uruguay, the topic continues to be raised, accompanied by the curious contortions intended to preserve an image of civilian government in the form of a figurehead president completely subordinated to the armed forces. In Brazil, there was an attempt during the Castelo Branco period to retain some of the institutions of political democracy. The authoritarian dynamic of the situation took things in a different direction than that foreseen in this initial period, but some elements nonetheless remained: the parliament, the two official parties, and periodic elections for non-executive positions. However, the experience with elections has made quite evident the potentially disruptive dynamic that is set into motion when the alternative of democracy is raised, regardless of how surrealistic this alternative may appear to be when it is done by, and during the period of, a BA state.

The nakedness of BA domination and of the alliance that supports it, as well as the highly visible character of its negative social consequences, generate the great issues raised by those who oppose BA: human rights, economic nationalism, and demands for substantive justice. The great dread of a system of domination which is simultaneously so imposing and so insecure is the fear that the opponents—who, despite their silence, quite clearly exist—will galvanize themselves around these issues into one great explosion that will destroy not only BA but also the system of social domination that it has helped to impose. The "Cordobazo" and the events that followed it are the symbol of this possibility, and not just in Argentina. The unsuccessful attempts to reestablish a cohesive and harmoniously integrated nation, the prolongation of the ominous silence of civil society, and the notoriety of the domination which BA supports, are the basis of the insecurity of this system of domination—which tends to make it more dangerous and more coercive. This coercion further biases the institutional system of BA toward a larger role for the armed forces, and further deepens the silence of society, which is exactly the opposite of what should happen if some legitimacy is to be achieved. Nevertheless, democracy continues to be mentioned, at times being eclipsed, but then reemerging in the official rhetoric or as the proposal of one or another of the groups that struggle for power in the BA state.

The issue of democracy is important not only because it contains the Achilles heel of this system of domination, but also because it contains a dynamic that can be the unifying element in the long-term effort to establish a society that is more nearly in accord with certain fundamental values. The issue of democracy is not equivalent to the other—already mentioned—great issues which BA raises as a result of its policies and their impacts. The proposal for a limited form of democracy, without *pueblo* and ultimately without nation, is not the gracious concession of a triumphant power, but the expression of its intrinsic weakness. The ambivalence with which democracy is mentioned both from the institutional apex of the BA state and by its principal allies, and the evident fear of transgressing limits beyond which it would be too risky to go in a process of democratization, does not generate its own contrasting negation as do the other unequivocal policies and impacts of BA. The antithesis of the distorted and limited democracy proposed by the BA's institutions does not have to be the political and social authoritarianism which is, precisely, the true and evident reality of this state. As a result, the issue of democracy, even the mere mention of the term, remains suspended in political discourse, and thus liable to be expropriated by giving the term meanings that supersede the limitations and qualifications with which the only public voices to be heard in the initial period of BA try to control it.

The possibility of democracy may simply represent an invitation to opportunism for those who wish to use it just to enter into a predetermined game. This possibility may also invite the imbecility of rejecting democracy out of hand because it is initiated from above and because there is such a careful effort to impose limits upon it. But what it can also be, if indeed the powers-that-be are not the only ones who have learned something from the tragedy of the Southern Cone, is the discovery of a purpose and style of politics that would not be limited to a careful calculation of the limits up to which it can be expanded at each point in time. It would be, more fundamentally, a struggle for the appropriation and redefinition of the meaning of democracy, oriented toward impregnating itself with the meanings carried by those who are excluded by the BA state and constituting, together with them, the basis for an alternative system of domination.

There are circumstances in which the discussion of certain topics can seem to be useless nostalgia. But the fact that certain words, such as democracy, are employed at all cannot simply be attributed to idiosyncracies, to tactics of accommodation with the international situation, or to false consciousness. The evident contradiction between the mere mention of democracy and the reality of daily life is much more than this. This contradiction is a key to understanding the weaknesses and profound tensions of the present system of domination. It is also an indication of the immense importance of what remains implicit behind the superficial appearance of these societies—the importance of those who are excluded and forced into silence, who, on the one hand, are the focus of any hopes for achieving legitimacy and yet, on the other hand, are a Pandora's box that must not be tampered with. This implicit presence of those who are excluded and silent is the source of the dynamic and tensions of BA to no less a degree than that which occurs in the grand scenarios of this type of state.

Later on, after the first period of BA—that of the implantation—on which this chapter has focused, the dikes of exclusion begin to crack, the effects of fear begin to be diluted, and some of the voices which had been silenced are heard once again. More or less obliquely, but with a meaning that no one can fail to understand, they begin to resound, not only throughout the society, but also within the state apparatus itself. These changes do not just involve the end of the silence imposed on those who were defeated, nor the thousand ways of demonstrating that the "tacit consensus" in fact represents a suppressed opposition. Nor is it merely a vain search for mediations on the part of those at the apex of the institutions of BA who know, on the one hand, that without them they cannot continue to be dominant and, on the other, that by attempting to restore the mediations they may also revive the old ghosts which, with the implantation of BA, they attempted at such high risk and such a high cost to destroy. At such a point, the fissures which from the very moment of implantation of BA are opened by the absence of mediations pose a great opportunity. The response to this opportunity—in terms of the scope of the potential democratization that it involves—in large measure will depend on those who in the phase of the implantation of BA were so radically excluded. But for a whole series of reasons, this still unmapped future lies beyond the scope of the present analysis.

Notes

This article is dedicated to the memory of Kalman Silvert, whom I admired.

1. This discussion represents a revision of the conception of the state which was implicit in my essay "Reflections." I now view this earlier conception as excessively focused on the institutional features of the state. Unfortunately, I can only briefly introduce here the most indispensable elements of this revised conceptualization. For a more complete discussion, see my "Apuntes para una Teoría del Estado" (Documento CEDES/G.E. CLACSO/No. 9, Centro de Estudios de Estado y Sociedad, Buenos Aires, 1977).

2. Translator's note: These two terms are not translated because the most nearly equivalent terms in English, "people" and "popular," have different meanings. The meaning intended by O'Donnell is indicated in the text above.

3. The most enlightening contribution on this and related topics continues to be that of Fernando Henrique Cardoso and Enzo Faletto in *Dependencia y Desarrollo en América Latina* (Mexico City: Siglo Veintiuno Editores, 1969).

4. Here again, see "Reflections" and the references cited in that article.

5. I use this phrase to refer to the tasks undertaken by the civilian technocrats in charge of the economic apparatus of BA, whose aim is to stabilize certain crucial variables (such as the rate of inflation and the balance of payments) in a manner that will gain the confidence of major capitalist interests—above all, in the first stage of BA, of transnational finance capital.

6. This and other arguments to which I will refer in the following pages have been presented in greater detail in "Reflections."

7. These points, including that regarding the importance of the guarantee that both order and the rationality of the management of the economy (from the perspective of the upper bourgeoisie) will be maintained in the future, are dealt with in my "Reflections."

8. Nonetheless, the relative importance of the state apparatus continues to be substantially greater than the orthodox technocrats would like, and the state's capacity for control increases greatly. The increasing state role in part involves the hypertrophic growth of the institutions most directly linked to coercion and of the rest of the institutional mechanisms designed to guarantee the exclusion of the popular sector. It also involves a major expansion of the state institutions responsible for the normalization policies. These expanded institutions are generally superimposed on the more traditional state agencies. At the same time, the attempts to make the enterprises which remain in the state's control more efficient have an interesting medium-run consequence: the "administrative rationalization" which is carried out in these enterprises, the elimination of subsidies from the central treasury, and the major increase in their relative prices (which typically had been held down as a means of appealing to the popular sector during the period which precedes BA) help these enterprises to become important centers of capital accumulation. This tendency converts them into a seed of state capitalism (which did not exist in the previous period and is a paradoxical result of the orthodox approach which sought to reduce their role), and later allows a major "statization" to be sustained. The clearest example of this is Brazil, but the results of the economic policy in Argentina between 1967–1970 were similar. In Chile, in spite of the orgy of "privatizations," this same phenomenon may be occurring in an important sector of state enterprises.

9. I have dealt with this topic in "Reflections," which, in the interest of brevity, I shall again only cite.

10. For a similar argument from a more general point of view, see Alfred Stepan, *The State and Society: Peru in Comparative Perspective* (Princeton: Princeton University Press, 1978).

11. In particular, the rate of inflation was low, the fiscal deficit had been reduced substantially, the balance-of-payments deficit had been alleviated, and the economy had achieved a respectable rate of growth.

12. A detailed analysis of these processes will be provided in my forthcoming book about the bureaucratic-authoritarian experience of Argentina from 1966 to 1973.

13. This consideration would have to be incorporated in the concept of "deepening" that I presented in "Reflections," along with the arguments regarding this concept that have been made by other authors. . . . As long as a situation such as that described above persists, deepening is clearly impossible, primarily because of the continuation of this speculative behavior on the part of the principal economic actors and because of the existence of an important degree of unused installed capacity. But to the extent that these conditions persist, the orientation of economic policies (which principally focus on the primary sector, and to the extent that they deal with industry are opposed to any effort to carry out the type of import substitution implied by deepening) is much more the result of a crisis which leaves little latitude for divergence from economic orthodoxy. But this pattern will not necessarily be followed in the long run, at least in the cases where economic growth is not excessively limited by a small internal market.

14. This last point represents a crucial contrast with the Argentine case, where a more state oriented and nationalistic pattern of economic policy was adopted toward the end of 1970, at a point when BA was falling apart and the upper bourgeoisie had lost all confidence in the future prospects for stability.

15. No discussion of this theme is complete that does not mention the fundamental contributions of Fernando Henrique Cardoso. See especially his *Autoritarismo e Democratização* (Rio de Janeiro: Paz e Terra, 1975).

16. Phrase used by the president of Argentina, Lt. General Videla, as quoted in *Cronista Comercial* April 27, 1977, p. 1.

17. I have dealt with this topic in my article "Sobre el 'Corporativismo' y la Cuestión del Estado" (Documento CEDES/G.E. CLACSO No. 2, Centro de Estudios de Estado y Sociedad, Buenos Aires, 1976). This was also published in English in James M. Malloy, ed., *Authoritarianism and Corporatism in Latin America* (Pittsburgh: University of Pittsburgh Press, 1977).

18. The concern with these goals is another of the reasons why the Mexican political system and the PRI represent such an attractive (if unattainable) model—since they provide all of these advantages without even raising, in connection with presidential succession, the uncertainties of a genuinely competitive election.

Selected Bibliography

Collier, David, ed. *The New Authoritarianism in Latin America.* Princeton, N.J.: Princeton University Press, 1979.

Hirschman, Albert O. "The Political Economy of Import-Substituting Industrialization in Latin America," *The Quarterly Journal of Economics* 82 (1968), pp. 2–32.

O'Donnell, Guillermo. "Corporatism and the Question of the State," in *Authoritarianism and Corporatism in Latin America,* edited by James M. Malloy. Pittsburgh, Penn.: University of Pittsburgh Press, 1977.

O'Donnell, Guillermo. "Reflections on the Patterns of Change in the Bureaucratic-Authoritarian State," *Latin American Research Review* 12:1 (Winter 1978), pp. 3–38.

O'Donnell, Guillermo O. "Reply to Remmer and Merkx," *Latin American Research Review* 17:2 (1982), pp. 41–50.

Remmer, Karen L., and Gilbert W. Merkx. "Bureaucratic-Authoritarianism Revisited," *Latin American Research Review* 17:2 (1982), pp. 3–40.

Stepan, Alfred. *The State and Society: Peru in Comparative Perspective.* Princeton, N.J.: Princeton University Press, 1978.

CONCLUSION

14 / The Promise of Theory

Thomas J. Bossert

Where has this long journey through the thickets of competing Latin American development theories led us? Our presentation suggests that although the different approaches have competed with one another as major means of describing and explaining the development processes, they also build on one another. Dependency theorists, although rejecting many aspects of modernization theory, built on some of that theory's observations about domestic economies and social structures by placing them in an international context. Modes of production analysts corrected for dependency's overemphasis on external factors by focusing attention on domestic productive forces and lower-class dynamics, without denying the dependent economic context for those processes. Corporatists restored interest in the values and structures that modernizationists defined as "traditional," but saw them in a more positive light and demonstrated their enduring quality. In formulating the theory of bureaucratic authoritarianism (BA), O'Donnell drew eclectically on the previous approaches, borrowing, for example, the value concerns of modernizationists in his discussion of "technocratic roles," emphasizing import-substitution industrialization (ISI) and populism from dependency theory, developing the production concerns of the modes of production school, and exploring the functional corporatist aspects of authoritarianism.

Development theories have usually challenged prior assumptions and explanations, but they have not really followed the process of "scientific revolutions" explored by MIT historian of science Thomas Kuhn (1962).[1] Kuhn argued that science advances by a series of leaps in which established paradigms of explanation fail to account for developing empirical knowledge and are replaced by revolutionary ways of posing the questions for analysis, new central means of finding explanations, and new sets of hypotheses to be explored. The processes we described for development theory have often been debated as if they were paradigm shifts—for instance, the debate between proponents of modernization and of dependency is often argued as such.[2] However, it might be more accurate to see the rhetorical conflicts as part of a remarkably incremental process of winnowing in which the obvious errors of the established approaches are stripped away, leaving a valuable core of understanding on which subsequent theory is built.

If we are right to emphasize the incremental process of theory building, it might be supposed that by placing O'Donnell's BA model last we mean to suggest that BA is the culmination of theories on Latin American development. Had this book been published a decade ago, this argument might have been correct. However, in the last few years the BA model has come under serious criticism, resulting in questions about its utility as an explanatory framework for analysis of Latin America. We will discuss some of these criticisms later, the most serious of which questions the validity of some of the concepts that are central to the model, such as the need for a "deepening" of industrialization and the populist "threat" to the elite. These criticisms suggest the need to develop new theoretical approaches.

If O'Donnell's theory has been shown to be inadequate, why have we not selected another author or series of authors to conclude this reader? It is because, despite its flaws, BA has not been replaced by a significant new approach, another "contending" theory. Critics point out failings without offering new modes of analysis. It might be that we are just in a hiatus in theory building, and an unheralded creative approach will soon revolutionize the debates on Latin America. However, it seems more likely that just as most of the theories examined here were built on the thoughts of prior generations of thinkers, the foundations for new theoretical developments probably already exist.

We chose to give considerable space to O'Donnell in part because we believe he provides a useful methodology for future theoretical endeavors. His model is a clear attempt to be synthetic—to select salient aspects from several theoretical approaches and to integrate them in an imaginative explanation of central events in recent Latin American history. In this chapter, we first discuss the most serious criticisms of BA, illuminating the need for a new theoretical approach. We then review the criticisms of each of the other theories presented in this reader in order to define those areas of each approach that might still prove valuable in future theory-building and to discuss how O'Donnell's synthetic method provides the most likely basis for these future theoretical advances. In addition, because theories of Latin American development have always occurred in relation to thoughts about development in other parts of the world, we briefly review some wider social science trends that we see as converging toward a general consensus on development issues. Finally, we outline a tentative direction that might be fruitful for the advancement of Latin American development theories and apply that approach to the two central events of the 1980s: the debt crisis and the return to formal democracy by most countries.

Critiques of O'Donnell

After O'Donnell's BA theory gained broad scholarly interest in the early 1970s, a group of scholars held a symposium to discuss his theory and published the results in a widely read collection.[3] Several of these scholars—in particular, Albert Hirschman, a pioneering economist of development at the Institute of Advanced Studies at Princeton University; José Serra, an economist at the Centro Brasileiro de Análise e Planejamento in São Paulo; and Robert Kaufman, a political scientist at Rutgers University—were particularly critical of the BA model. Their critiques questioned the applicability of the model to the cases for which it was designed: the military regimes in Brazil, Argentina, Uruguay, and Chile. First, the authors found little evidence for O'Donnell's argument for the exhaustion of ISI and the need for "deepening" of industrialization in the countries he discussed. Indeed, the move from the "easy stage" of ISI toward vertical industrialization (when consumer durables and intermediate goods replace food processing and textile manufacturing as the dynamic industrial sectors) was already occurring, in Brazil at least, in the 1930s, and some evidence suggested that this deepening might have been progressing at a faster rate before the Brazilian coup in 1964 than it did afterward.[4] In a review of the policies adopted by military regimes there was little evidence that the leaders even articulated deepening as a conscious policy, preferring rather to pursue orthodox austerity programs and outward-looking export promotion.

This criticism of O'Donnell's work was profound because it attacked the central basis for the ISI exhaustion thesis, which formed one of main pillars of the BA model. It was obvious that the economies of the countries that suffered military coups were under tremendous stress prior to the coups. However, if deepening was already occurring in the BA countries before the coups, O'Donnell's explanation of the cause of the economic crisis is flawed. Furthermore, if democratic regimes had produced deepening then it is not clear why BA regimes would be necessary to carry out this structural change in the economy. The general argument can be made then that cyclical economic crises threaten the stability of any regime and that major crises in democracies will probably result in those democracies being replaced by some sort of authoritarian regime. Such an argument undermines the persuasiveness of O'Donnell's elaborate explanation for the emergence of BA regimes.

The second criticism addressed the other central pillar of the BA model: the "threat" to the elites that came from the demands of the populist sectors, which were increasingly perceived to be out of control. In a critique of BA and dependency, several authors reviewed the classic populist governments of Vargas, Cárdenas, and Perón and found the concept of populism difficult to define and to apply.[5] Their analysis of the great variety of populist experiences raised questions about the use of the populist concept as a descriptive and explanatory category. If there is no clear and consistent way to define populism, then its contribution to the emergence of BA is also unclear.

In his later work, O'Donnell attempted to redefine the concept of a populist threat and to explain the link between empirical referents of this threat and the future policies of the BA regime. This effort, however, was only partially successful. Karen Remmer and Gilbert Merkx (1982), political scientists from the University of New Mexico, found the concept of threat still difficult to utilize and not particularly successful in predicting variations in economic policies and the exclusion of the lower classes.[6]

Ian Roxborough (1979), a sociologist at the London School of Economics, took Remmer and Merkx's criticism further, reiterating some of the modes of production critiques of the dependency approach and arguing that the concept of populism does not give enough separate weight to the dynamics of working class mobilization, organization, and alliance-building.[7] Roxborough found that the term populism places the working class in an undifferentiated populist mass without taking into account the distinct interests and political power of its members. Roxborough's analysis suggests that if O'Donnell had considered specific working class activities he would have found a clearer explanation for the formation of the BA regimes and their policies.

If these critics are right, and O'Donnell does dispute some of their conclusions, then O'Donnell's concept of populism is undermined, leaving the model without its clearly persuasive empirical basis and suggesting that new approaches must be sought.[8] These criticisms have raised serious doubts about the specific dynamics of the BA model and, for some analysts, questions about the whole enterprise of trying to find consistent relationships between political characteristics and economic conditions. Remmer and Merkx argue that a situational approach is called for—one that examines the entire context of each regime without trying to establish ideal types of "syndromes," such as BA, that specify trends of relationships for more than one case at a time. This argument suggests that there are few generalized patterns that groups of nations might follow and focuses attention on close empirical analysis of separate national histories.[9]

Other analysts, such as Hirschman, Serra, Kaufman, and Roxborough, have tried to retain the general direction of O'Donnell's approach by seeking different areas of commonality and different types of hypotheses to correct the theory by adjusting it to the new data. It is in the search for "multiple paths"—as Roxborough calls them—of historical processes that we find the most fruitful direction for future theory.

We think that O'Donnell's analysis has not been seriously compromised by its failure to account for all empirical challenges to its propositions. Although some concepts, such as deepening and threat, might need to be reformulated or abandoned, O'Donnell's model provides an effective methodology that can be the basis for a general approach to development problems. The model is an attempt to place national processes into distinct patterns that borrow eclectically from all the other approaches discussed here: modernization, dependency, modes of production, and corporatism.

In the following sections we reexamine each of the approaches presented in this book, discussing the major criticisms that have led scholars to seek other theories. We also explore O'Donnell's use of these theories and suggest what elements might be added to O'Donnell's model to form a basis for future theoretical developments.

Modernization Revisited

Modernization theory, it will be recalled, focused attention on internal processes of development within each nation, assuming that less de- veloped nations would follow a unilinear progression from tradition to modernity. Theorists of modernization argued that value changes would lead this process of economic development, and optimistically suggested that democracy would be the result of this value change and economic growth.

Modernization theory was criticized by the dependency analysts for not giving sufficient attention to the external economic constraints that shaped the Latin American economies and class structures. Dependency analysts overemphasized this aspect of development, but it is clear that this omission by modernizationists had to be corrected. External economic conditions have a considerable effect on the internal domestic political and economic processes in countries with important trading and financial links to the developed world. Development simply cannot be the result of national efforts alone.

The second criticism of modernization was its optimistic assumption that countries progressed in a unilinear progressive fashion from tra- ditional to modern. Even analysts within the modernization perspective began to recognize that this assumption might not be valid; indeed, it was not valid for the development of Western Europe. As Samuel Huntington (1968), a Harvard University political scientist, pointed out, the process of modernization was more difficult than the initial postwar optimism would have predicted.[10] He argued that development produced a tendency toward the breakdown of regimes and the emergence of "praetorian politics" in which the military, and not democratic political parties, could play the central role in providing the stable conditions necessary for sustained economic growth. Robert Packenham (1973), a Stanford University political scientist, took the critique further by showing that the liberal assumption that, as he put it, "all good things go together" was unfounded, not only for political processes but also for economic, social, and cultural changes.[11] It was clear that if modernization theory was to be useful, its assumption of unilinear progress would have to be modified.

Nevertheless, the trend in the 1980s toward formal democracies in Latin America suggests that the assumption that Latin America is headed toward a political future similar in many respects to that of Europe and the United States may be less unrealistic than it seemed to be in the 1960s and 1970s. If the process toward democracy is not unilinear, it still might be a secular trend, although it is too soon to tell whether the current wave of democratization will endure.

Modernization was also criticized for its idealist orientation. Deriving considerable inspiration from Weber, modernizationists—especially Lipset—tended to overemphasize the importance of values and value change in their development model. As a result, they paid little attention to the structural constraints of class and to the economic realities that often made holding "unmodern" values quite rational for both peasants—who were caught in corporatist patron-client relations—and entrepreneurs—who could earn more through the state bureaucracy or foreign enterprises than they could through their own Protestant-ethic entrepreneurialism.

Although this criticism of the centrality of values may be valid, the enduring significance of values to development should probably not be overlooked. As we have seen, O'Donnell used the concept of technocratic values when defining particular groups that would join in an alliance with the military in order to create a rationalized state and halt the threat from popular sectors. The values of different participants in development are important and can be examined as part of a larger analysis that places these values in a structural context. As we will discuss later, other aspects of values—their role in creating class consciousness and in legitimizing a state—are also essential to development.

A third criticism of modernization focused on the role of the middle sectors. As these sectors grew in the period of postwar economic growth, they did not provide the democratizing buffer that the modernizationists predicted. Indeed, the middle sectors at first joined with the upper classes to welcome the authoritarian regimes that excluded the popular classes and ended democracy. Nevertheless, the alliances made by the middle classes are contingent on the character of the conflict between the lower classes and the dominant classes and vary from country to country. Although the central role of the middle classes as a stabilizing factor might be highly questionable, their importance in the dynamics of change by larger processes is not. O'Donnell clearly places the middle sectors in a major role as holders of the technocratic values and as allies of the upper classes and the military—indeed, the military is a member of the middle sectors by Johnson's definition. Further, in the modes of production analysis, the middle sectors are considered allies who can, under some conditions, join with the lower classes but also, and in recent history more often, with those who repress the lower classes. Although these new formulations mean that we must develop greater clarity in defining the middle sectors and that their role is not likely to be viewed with the centrality given them by modernizationists, the middle sectors do play a part in the process of development, and their role must continue to examined.

Finally, the predictions of modernizationists that there would be a transition from feudal latifundia to modern forms of capitalist land tenure has withstood the test of time better than their other arguments. Although the links between the latifundia and the capitalist economy are such that they undermine the simplistic assumptions of isolated "dual societies," it is clear that a diffusion of capitalism is occurring. As we show in the next section, dependency analysts, such as Cardoso, and modes of production analysts describe a long-run transition from the feudal traditional economy that was so important in Latin America in the past to a more integrated and dominant capitalist mode of production.[12] While this process might include periods in which capitalism reinforces or recreates feudal relations of production, as the modes of production analysts argue, it nevertheless is part of the secular transition toward worldwide capitalism. The old latifundia are dying out, replaced either by land reform efforts of the 1960s or by agro-industrial enterprises that are run by capitalist managers using resources according to capitalist principles. In addition, in much of Latin America the once-resistant landed oligarchy has increasingly adapted to the intrusion of capitalist forms of production and has begun to join with other owning classes—the industrial, commercial, and financial bourgeoisie. Indeed, it is often through family networks that the old land-holding oligarchy is intermeshed with these classes.[13] The identification of the dominant classes with distinct sectoral economic interests becomes harder to maintain as these classes change their economic activities in each sector, i.e., as agriculture becomes more capitalistic and as networks are formed across sectors.

Because he is examining the already advanced economies of Latin America, O'Donnell assumes this process of expanding capitalism has already been achieved. Indeed, his starting point is the question, Why have these most developed countries not achieved the kind of political system that the early modernizationists had assumed they would? Although O'Donnell refers to the landed economic class as the oligarchy, he tends to see the process of modernization as having forced this class to join with an emerging national bourgeoisie in favor of the development, first of an internal market through ISI, and later through deepening and export expansion.

Several factors from the modernization approach can thus be incorporated in future development theory. First, the unwarranted assumption that economic modernization would be accompanied by a unilinear process of political modernization—the move toward democracy—must be replaced by a contingent understanding of the potential for democracy that is in tune with the Western European experience. As many of the authoritarian regimes return to formal democracies, it is hard to resist the temptation to suggest that authoritarianism was a temporary—though long—period that has been overcome and that Latin America is once again on the road to both economic and political development. Indeed, the secular trend might be toward democratic forms of government, even if the current fragile democracies do not weather the continuing economic crises they all face. If the modernization process is no longer assumed to be unilinear, it may yet be seen as a secular trend. Second, although values are not the driving force in modernization, they nevertheless have to be taken into account in shaping the choices to be made by the various classes. Third, the middle sectors, although not playing the central role in development and the creation of democracy that was assumed in the modernization model, are nevertheless crucial participants in the alliances that will determine the future processes of development. Finally, capitalism will continue to deepen itself in both rural and urban economies, changing the composition of the dominant and subordinate classes in ways that are likely, in the long run, to produce a class structure quite similar to that of the advanced capitalist countries. The feudal characteristics that modernizationists saw holding back development were, as the modes of production analysts argued, important for certain periods in reinforcing the success of capitalism, but over time these advantages shrank, and the dominant oligarchies evolved to participate more and more in the change to the dominant mode of production—capitalism—in both rural and urban areas.

Dependency and Marxism Revisited

The extravagant claims of some dependency analysts, such as Frank, have come under considerable criticism, even by other dependency analysts. The most vulnerable assertion was the claim that the economic links between the center and the periphery prevented growth and development in the periphery. The original argument by the United Nations Economic Commission for Latin America (ECLA) that the terms of trade were detrimental to those who produce primary products has been questioned by the authors of a variety of studies. In a significant analysis of the external economic relationships and the role of foreign investment in both the center and the periphery, Oxford University economist Sanjaya Lall (1975) found that some of the developed nations, such as Canada and Belgium, were more dependent on foreign capital than were some underdeveloped nations, such as India and Pakistan.[14] Other cross-national, quantitative studies provided evidence suggesting that foreign investment in the economies of less developed nations could bring benefits as well as liabilities.[15]

Since World War II, many countries in Latin America have experienced sustained periods of considerable growth—at rates often exceeding those of the developed countries—and this growth has often been accompanied by expanded foreign investment. In recognition of this process, the more sophisticated dependency analysts argued that foreign participation in some Latin American economies was likely to promote growth, or what Cardoso called associated-dependent development. Cardoso suggested that the

> "new international division of labor" put a dynamic element into operation in the internal market. Thus, *to some extent,* the interests of the foreign corporations become compatible with the internal prosperity of the dependent countries. In this sense, they help promote development.[16]

Although these arguments did not completely deny that external links could be exploitative and prevent development, they suggested that Frank's assertion of a universal process that "created underdevelopment" had to be modified. Cardoso's historical-structural approach presented dependency as a complex process in which a variety of factors in both the international and domestic economies shape different and complex patterns of growth or decline. This perspective allowed analysts to account for growth in the new industrializing countries—such as Korea, Singapore, Taiwan, Brazil, and Mexico—as well as the decline in some center countries such as Britain and France.

Another criticism of dependency analysis was that it failed to propose alternative paths to growth that did not depend on trade and foreign investment. While many dependency analysts suggested that socialism and broad-based participation in both economic benefits and political power were the desirable and necessary alternatives to dependent capitalist development, it was not clear how socialism would remove the importance of external linkages and funding. It was difficult to argue that Cuba and Eastern Europe provided evidence of economic autonomy.[17] Dependency analysts did suggest that dependent countries can attempt to shape their external linkages in such a way as to modify or reverse the dependent relationship by enhancing their bargaining power with multinational corporations (MNCs) and financial institutions, as well as by diversifying their markets so as not to be dependent on any one nation. However, few analysts suggested that a real alternative to dependency exists.[18]

The enduring core of dependency analysis appears to be the tremendous importance of the external economy for sustaining growth within Latin American nations. External constraints and the penetration of the national economies by international economic players help define the potentials for growth and development. These constraints are not universal but rather depend on changes in the international economy and the role that each nation is able to play within that economy—a role that is be determined by the interaction of domestic and international factors. Major changes in the international economy—such as depression, war, aggressive expansion of MNCs, credit surpluses or squeezes, and shifting consumption patterns in major markets—force all nations to respond to the new conditions producing the broad historic periodization that Furtado, Cardoso, and Faletto explained in the selections included in this reader. But the patterns of growth for each nation are not simply determined by external constraints and opportunities, they are also the result of internal conditions and choices.

As we noted in our opening chapter, some dependency analysts focused attention on the United States as an imperialist power.[19] This argument was criticized for its tendency to view the U.S. government as simply acting on behalf of U.S. multinational companies, without distinguishing the separate interests of the state, U.S. businesses with interests in Latin America, and the larger business community in the United States. Dependency analysis also tended to disregard the distinction between national security interests and U.S. economic interests. Finally, as Latin American nations began to diversify their trading and financial ties, it became clear that U.S. economic domination of Latin America was on the wane, raising questions about how enduring U.S. hegemony in the Western Hemisphere would be.

However, even if U.S. hegemony in the region is declining, the United States is still the most important of the center countries and is likely to continue to play the major role in Latin American countries for the forseeable future. Although the dependency analysts might overemphasize U.S. power, they are correct to focus attention on the unique role of the United States. The assumption that U.S. government interests are dictated by U.S. businesses is harder to sustain. In Nicaragua under Somoza, for instance, U.S. businesses were considerably constrained, and yet the U.S. government firmly backed the dictator as a vehement anti-Communist. The simplistic conclusions of some dependency analysts must be rejected and replaced with a view of the U.S. role that accounts for both economic and strategic interests and that examines the domestic political processes within the United States as they impinge on U.S. policy in the region.[20]

A fourth criticism of dependency analysis focuses on the class and political implications of the links to external economic forces. The modes of production analysts take dependency analysts to task for not defining classes with sufficient clarity and not focusing enough on the dynamic forces of the lower classes—especially the working class. This criticism has been echoed by non-Marxist critics who focus on the need to find empirical referents for the class categories as well as the need to develop institutional analyses of the state and interest groups.[21] However, some analysts recently have begun refining the analysis of class dynamics and the state within the dependency perspective. Peter Evans (1979), a sociologist from Brown University, focused on the interaction among the "trio" of the MNCs, the national bourgeoisie, and the state in Brazil,[22] and Nora Hamilton (1982), a political scientist from University of Southern California, examined these relationships as they existed during the crucial Cárdenas period (1934–1940) in Mexico.[23] Douglas Bennett and Kenneth Sharpe (1986), political scientists from Temple University and Swarthmore College, respectively, also analyzed relations among the state, class, and MNCs specifically for the case of the Mexican automobile industry.[24] These works represent new efforts to clarify and define class relationships and the state, and in some way respond to the criticisms of the dependency analysts. Nevertheless, additional empirical work involving a clearer conceptualization of the state and of classes must be done.

As Roxborough points out, the central dynamic contributed by the sophisticated dependency analysts is their focus on the interaction between the external economy and the capacity of the dominant classes to incorporate or exclude new challenges from emerging classes, in particular the bourgeoisie and the middle classes.[25] Most important is the analysts' suggestion that for each historical period—outward expansion, ISI, new international division of labor—there are multiple development paths that depend on this interaction. Cardoso and Faletto, for instance, placed considerable importance in their theories on whether the middle classes were incorporated into power in the early twentieth century. In Mexico, the rigid oligarchic regime of Porfírio Díaz (1876–1910) failed to provide opportunities for the inclusion of the emerging middle classes, which enlisted the support of the peasantry in the Mexican Revolution and ended oligarchic dominance. In other regimes, such as that of Peru, the oligarchy was able to form alliances with the foreign enclave and was strong enough to repress the middle- and lower-class challenge. In Chile, the oligarchy and the foreign enclave were not sufficiently powerful to resist the middle-class challenge, but the oligarchy was able to incorporate this class without being overthrown. Although Cardoso and Faletto have been criticized for not clearly defining central concepts such as "oligarchy," "middle classes," and "bourgeoisie" and have been challenged empirically for their characterizations of the class dynamics in specific countries, their theory of multiple development paths that specifies several key structural variables is likely to form part of the basis for future analysis.

The modes of production analysts criticized the dependency theorists for not clearly defining the mode of production. Although their criticism of Frank's definition of capitalism as commodity exchange did not extend to the more sophisticated dependency analysts, the modes of production perspective again raised the problem of clarifying the relationship between capitalist and precapitalist economies. However, the modes of production analysts have themselves been criticized for proliferating the ways of defining the modes of production—suggesting, for example, that the colonial period was a unique mode of production. Although it is generally agreed that the capitalist mode of production is dominant in the industrialized Latin American nations, it is not clear when capitalism became dominant or how much it was based on prior modes of production. Furthermore, as yet there is little agreement on how to define the mixture of production modes that persists today.[26] Nevertheless, there is little reason to suggest that modes of production analysis is incompatible with the more sophisticated dependency theory. These dependency analysts focused on productive issues, as well as commerce and ownership, that would be strengthened by the inclusion of an orientation that specified the type of production and the definition of the different modes of production.

Modes of production analysts also criticized the dependency analysts for not giving sufficient attention to the lower classes. In most dependency analysis, the lower classes are viewed as an undifferentiated mass, with little distinction made between the role of the proletariat, the peasants, and the marginal classes. This problem is clearly apparent in the weak definition of populism as an alliance between the lower and middle classes and the national bourgeoisie. While the dependency analysts tended to focus attention on the upper classes and their relationship with MNCs, their analysis does not completely exclude the role of differentiated lower-class dynamics. It is likely that as modes of production analysts begin to develop their analysis of working class dynamics, this perspective will complement rather than replace the sophisticated dependency approach.[27]

A final debate raised by dependency analysts centered on the implications of their various interpretations for political strategy. As noted in our introduction, Marxist debates over the Russian Revolution and its consequences were replicated in part in the dependency analysis. Frank's analysis was used to justify a more audacious revolutionary strategy, mobilizing the lower classes but rejecting compromises with the national bourgeoisie, which was seen as inextricably linked to international capitalism. More orthodox Marxists took Frank to task for his "voluntarism," suggesting that conditions for lower-class revolution were not present in most countries in Latin America, and therefore alliances with some sectors of the bourgeoisie were necessary.[28] Although debates over revolutionary strategy continue, their links with dependency theory have become less clear. After the failures of the 1960's "voluntaristic" guerrilla movements in Bolivia, Uruguay, Brazil, and Argentina, most analysts have come to reject assumptions that revolutionary conditions are uniform throughout the continent. At the same time, it was apparent that dependency analysis, especially the sophisticated forms, could be used to justify a variety of political strategies and that the debates over revolutionary strategy most likely would have to be developed in terms of specific country conditions.

O'Donnell borrows explicitly from dependency analysis (and the further elaborations of the historical-structural approach of Cardoso and Faletto) in his concern with the external contraints on the economies of the advanced industrializing Latin American nations. He uses dependency analysis to define the periodization of ISI and populism and suggests that the external economic constraints dictating the need for deepening and the importance of foreign investment and foreign technology are part of the broader process that leads to the creation of the authoritarian regimes that would exclude the popular sectors. O'Donnell adds that the international orientation of the new regimes created a nationalistic backlash that undermined their legitimacy in the long run.

From this review of the central criticisms of dependency and modes of production we can identify several possible contributions of these theories to future development theory. Dependency analysts, building on a historical model that assumes dialectical conflict rather than unilinearity, emphasize the importance for development of changes in the international economic structure and the international economic actors who play roles in domestic economies. These analysts underscore the need to examine the effects of economic ties between international actors (MNCs, the International Monetary Fund [IMF], foreign banks) and the dominant classes in each country.

Furthermore, the dependency analysts draw attention to the interaction among classes within each nation, suggesting that this interaction responds to both international and domestic conditions. The dynamics of class analysis then are not likely ever again to be viewed as simply the product of domestic class conflict. By the same token, however, analysts, rejecting Frank's assertions, will not examine class conflict as a mere reflection of external economic contexts. Perhaps the most enduring aspect of the sophisticated dependency approach is the suggestion that different economic, class, and state relations in each historical period allow for multiple paths of development. Modes of production analysis adds to these concerns by suggesting that the different means of organizing production in some areas of national economies might account for different class formations and for different dynamics of alliance and conflict that need to be examined in greater detail than has been the case until now.

Corporatism Revisited

Some critics have considered corporatism to be an apology for conservative or fascist political systems. According to these critics, the "third way" toward development—neither Western democracies nor Eastern communism—that corporatists such as Wiarda argued would be followed by Latin America was, at best, simply a celebration of traditional forms of social and political organization and, at worst, a justification for maintaining strong authoritarian governments similar to those in some fascists states in Europe. Neither of these criticisms is particularly accurate. Wiarda argued that traditional values and structures endure longer than modernizationists had hoped and that they are likely to continue shaping the process of development. However, the third way would not only differ from liberal capitalist and communist models but would also move beyond the traditional societies. Furthermore, although some corporatist arguments might have been used in fascist doctrine, the new corporatism in Latin America lacked the total mobilization of the population that was crucial to nazism and Italian fascism.

While apologists for military regimes may have seen positive value in hierarchical, paternalistic, authoritarian organizations and a preference for functional groups over the chaos of liberal pluralism or the rigidity of totalitarianism, few analysts who used the theory actually praised the model; rather they saw corporatism simply as part of the Latin American reality.

Other critics found the cultural and value emphasis of some corporatists to be simply a variation of the traditional-modern polarity of the modernizationists.[29] However, corporatist analysts such as Newton and Schmitter, who focus on structural rather than cultural characteristics, do not fall into this trap. Indeed, Schmitter contemptuously refers to the cultural emphasis as the "'spigot variable' which gets turned on every once in a while to produce a different system of functional representation."[30]

A criticism of corporatism that applies to both the cultural and structural variants is that it tends to overemphasize the corporatist structures and to downplay or ignore the class antagonisms that occur within or across such structures. By viewing society as organized into functional and hierarchical groups, corporatists can explain why classes do not emerge with the clarity that they do in Western Europe. However, it is clear that these corporatist structures, while masking class conflicts in some areas, have not been successful in completely eliminating them. Indeed, many corporatist institutions have been developed to extend the state's capacity to co-opt and control the lower classes—such as the peasant and worker organizations within Mexico's ruling political party. As this example also suggests, the new corporatism often emerged as a new organizational form to compete with the class organizations that the socialists, communists, and anarchists formed in the early part of this century. These corporatist organizations were new expressions of state control, not feudal traditions that had endured from an earlier period.

As with the other development theories, these criticisms allow us to strip away some of the less successful aspects of the approach, leaving a useful core for our synthetic combinations. O'Donnell effectively utilized some aspects of corporatism to describe the structure of the BA regimes—in particular their capacity to incorporate or exclude the popular classes. Although corporatism may not be a source of positive values, it nonetheless is a good description of some of the political structures and social organizations that exist in Latin America. It is necessary to account for these structures that modify, if not eliminate, class consciousness and the capacity to organize. Further, we can gain insight into the mechanisms through which the dominant classes and the state interrelate if we examine the corporatist forms of interest representation. These functional groups may be viewed as mediating institutions within a broader analysis that puts more weight on the development of class structures. Corporatist values may also mediate class conflict as enduring elements of the ideologies and cultures in Latin America.

Convergence of Theory

As we argued in the introduction, the development theories of Latin America did not occur independent of theoretical concerns in other areas of the world. Modernizationist theory emerged directly out of the postwar enthusiasm that followed the Marshall Plan's successful restoration of European economies. It was influenced by cold war efforts to establish liberal democracies and prevent the rise of competing Communist states. The liberal bias and the assumption of modernization that "all good things go together" was part of the overall optimism in sociology and political science in the United States. This sense of unilinear progress was carried even further by analysts of Europe and the United States as they projected these trends into the future and heralded the post-industrial societies.[31]

Dependency, too, emerged as part of broader theoretical concerns, particularly the early Marxist debates over the transition from feudalism to capitalism and the role of imperialism. The dependency approach, however, was perhaps the most indigenously developed theory, tracing part of its origin to the ECLA arguments over terms of trade. Nevertheless, dependency analysis soon entered the mainstream of debate for other parts of the world as Arghiri Emmanuel explored the concept of "unequal exchange" and Samir Amin and Immanuel Wallerstein developed the now fashionable "world system" approach that applied analysis similar to that of Cardoso and Faletto to the historical development of Africa and Europe.[32]

The modes of production analysis has obvious roots in the enduring Marxist tradition and is accompanied by significant debate, especially in France and England where the *New Left Review* has become the center for controversies over Marxist interpretations of the transition from feudalism to capitalism, the role of the state, and the appropriate Marxist analysis for the Third World. Some analysts, such as orthodox Marxist Bill Warren (1973), return to Marx's own argument that the expansion of capitalism beyond Europe would accelerate the process of breaking down traditional precapitalist modes of production.[33] Others, such as John Taylor (1979), a sociologist at London's Polytechnic of the South Bank, utilize the French structuralist approach of Marxist philosopher Louis Althusser (1970), applying it to an analysis of modes of production in the Third World. Taylor argues that underdevelopment in Latin America and other parts of the Third World is characterized by an enduring symbiosis of capitalist and pre-capitalist modes of production, and that this effectively blocks the full development of capitalism.[34]

Corporatism has had a long tradition in European thought as an alternative vision to liberalism and has been assimilated into Christian Democratic movements in Europe and Latin America as a theoretical foundation for political programs. It has also enjoyed some interest in the United States with analysts, such as Theodore Lowi (1969), a Cornell University political scientist, who have found enduring evidence of corporatism even in the bastion of liberal pluralism.[35] Recently, corporatism has been applied to the study of Europe by Schmitter.[36]

Bureaucratic authoritarianism also relates to broader trends in social science. As a synthetic approach, it comes out of the earlier traditions of modernization, dependency, and corporatism as they were developed in Latin American studies. The concern with linking economic structural constraints and political regimes however, has had a long tradition, exemplified by such original thinkers as Harvard economist Alexander Gerschenkron (1962) and Harvard sociologist Barrington Moore, Jr., (1966).[37] But perhaps most relevant was the tradition of analysis of authoritarianism that Yale University political scientist Juan Linz (1970) led with his study of Iberian Europe.[38] The BA model similarly has inspired scholars to apply its concepts in other parts of the world. For instance, James Kurth (1979), a political scientist at Swarthmore College, utilized the economic concerns of the BA model in an innovative analysis of industrial development in Europe, and Douglas Bennett and Kenneth Sharpe applied O'Donnell's analysis to the United States.[39]

Given the interrelatedness of theories of Latin American development and the broader social science theories, it seems pertinent to consider the current trends in social science thinking for our reflections on the future of development theory for Latin America. It is beyond the scope of this chapter to give anything but the most brief sketch of the complex state of current theory in so large an area. However, some trends of theoretical debate suggest a convergence of thought that might encourage the synthetic merging of the perspectives we see evolving in Latin American development theory. These trends are discussed in the following paragraphs.

Two central trends seem to be emerging in the general approaches toward social science theory. The first is a transcendence of the early debates that pitted behaviorist against humanist. These debates, in which methodological and epistemological issues were hotly contested, tended to divide social scientists who used quantitative data and positivistic assumptions and those who contended that social issues were too complex and bound in historical conjunctures and values to be easily quantified and subject to scientific verification. Although there is still considerable life in these old debates, most social science analysts have begun to use complex mixtures of these opposing methodologies. Quantifiers embed their analysis in broader historical contexts, and their counterparts use behavioral data, when appropriate, to complement their observations. There is a growing awareness that neither of the methodologies alone is sufficient for understanding the complex processes of social change, and analysts are expressing less strident confidence in one or the other method.

Although Latin Americanists were less wedded to these methodological debates, they nevertheless benefited from the extension of some of the behavioralist methodology without abandoning their preference for the more holistic approach. An example of this conflict is a debate between Cardoso and Packenham over the appropriate means of evaluating dependency theory. Packenham, arguing for an analytic approach in which theories of dependency are formulated in terms of hypotheses that can be tested, suggested that dependency was a condition that should be measured to determine whether and to what degree it exists.[40] Cardoso maintained that dependency was the result of complex historical conditions and that it was not a matter of degree but rather a general characteristic of Latin American countries.[41] Cardoso's holistic definition did not admit testable verification of the basic premise of historical-structural dependency. Nevertheless, Cardoso admits the importance of evaluating various aspects of the theory in terms of rigorous empirical data, and followers of his scheme distinguish between the *structural* assumptions that are not easily given to quantifiable hypothesis testing and *process* aspects that are.[42] On the other hand, Packenham rejects simplistic positivism, arguing for a methodology that examines historical contextual characteristics, values, and interrelationships among complex variables.

A second major trend in social science theory is the tendency toward convergence between the Marxist and non-Marxist approaches to social issues. Here again, old distinctions and barriers are slowly breaking down as Marxists become more eclectic, discover more variety in their own tradition, and begin to make important breakthroughs that allow for greater communication with non-Marxists. At the same time, non-Marxist scholars are also discovering useful concepts and dynamics in the Marxist perspective.

On the Marxist side of this movement, the state has become the central focus for current analysis of the capitalist system and of the transition from feudalism to capitalism. This new interest in political structures and processes has rescued Marxism from its earlier overemphasis on economic determinism and on the crude assumption that the state was simply an extension of control by the dominant class.[43] In addition, renewed interest in the views of the Italian Communist theorist Antonio Gramsci (1916–1937) has brought the importance of ideology and political legitimacy back to Marxist analysis, further enriching its approach and, at the same time, allowing for potential convergence with the liberal Weberian emphasis on value issues.[44] Finally, several Marxist scholars, including University of Wisconsin sociologist Erik Olin Wright (1978) and Swedish sociologist Göran Therborn (1978), have begun to integrate behaviorist elements of "bourgeois" social science into their Marxist conceptual framework.[45] Although not an explicit embracing of non-Marxist perspectives, these evolutions within Marxism have allowed for conceptual and empirical communication between the two ideological perspectives.

On the other side of the ideological divide, liberal social scientists, beginning with Huntington, have been willing to borrow Marxist concepts to deepen their own analysis. For instance, Huntington explicitly embraces Leninist conceptions of the role of the political party when he considers the likely options for orderly development in the Third World. Although it does not adopt Marxist definitions of class, Huntington's class analysis, even within the modernizationist perspective, is not greatly different from that of many Marxists—especially those of the Communist parties in Latin America. More recent, and more explicitly relevant to theoretical issues, is the trend among younger analysts of the emerging field of "political economy" to borrow critically from Marxism—especially the recent Marxist perspectives on the state. University of Chicago sociologist Theda Skocpol (1979), whose major reinterpretation of the role of the state in revolutions is perhaps the best known of these explicitly non-Marxist analyses, draws heavily on Marxist concepts.[46] Analyses of international political economy by Stephen Krasner (1978), a political scientist at UCLA who examines different explanations for U.S. foreign policy regarding raw materials, and James Kurth's innovative work on changes in industrial policy in Western Europe, are other recent examples.[47] In the Latin American area, this influence has been apparent for a long time—most recently in O'Donnell's use of Marxist conceptualizations of the state (see his second selection in this reader). Hirschman and Alfred Stepan also use these themes in their recent works.[48]

We cannot do justice to the complexity of the issues we have just raised, but we have used them to suggest that in general the bitterness of the social science debates of the last two decades has receded and that there is considerable tolerance for the synthesis that we see occurring in Latin American development theory. Although methodological debates continue to define quite different approaches, there is a trend toward mixing empirical evidence with holistic conceptual frameworks while recognizing the limitations of both approaches. There is also a growing convergence among Marxists and non-Marxists to refine conceptual issues such as the state, its relation to the changing economy, and the role of ideology and legitimacy—issues that are also central to Latin American analyses.

We should also note that within Latin American studies and in the broader social science fields, there has been a general abandonment of theory in favor of more micro-level empirical studies. These studies are obviously shaped by theoretical concerns but in general tend to demonstrate how weak theoretical propositions have been. The flood of research that undermined BA is but one example of a broader trend. This phase of retreat from theory will probably pass quickly. The convergence we have observed is likely to generate a more solid, complex, and satisfying set of theories, and the retreat to empiricism will provide more material on which to base and test the emerging theory.[49]

Predicting the future is risky business, but it is unlikely that the simplistic divisions generated by the early approaches of the overly optimistic modernizationists or dependency analysts will gain adherents in an academic world that has tired of simple solutions to complex problems. It is also unlikely that simple empiricist observation will replace the fascination with theory. Indeed, it is impossible for empirical research to proceed without considerable theoretical guidance to define the areas for examination and to help interpret conflicting results.

Where Do We Go from Here?

Our central argument has been similar to the old admonition of not throwing out the baby with the bath water. We think it misleading to view theoretical development in Latin America as a clash of paradigms similar to the Kuhnian analysis of scientific revolutions and suggested by the conflictual rhetoric of the theorists themselves. Rather, we see an underlying incremental growth in theory that, in keeping with our homey analogy, rescued the babies from various tubs before throwing out the soiled water. We have reviewed the criticisms of each "tub" and suggested the core issues that have emerged as the "babies" worth saving. We will now discuss current developments in Latin America in light of the core issues that we feel should remain in a new body of synthetic theory.

A new synthetic theory must account for two central developments that were not yet apparent when O'Donnell presented his model. These developments are (1) the international economic context that is currently dominated by the "debt crisis" and (2) the progressive return to formal democracy in most of Latin America. Although considerable work is being done to examine these two issues in empirical detail, little work of theoretical significance has yet emerged to provide the basis for a major breakthrough. If we are right to suggest that a convergent synthetic approach similar to, and built upon, O'Donnell's approach will provide guidance for future theoretical growth, this approach will have to be concerned with describing and explaining these two phenomena.

In future development theory, it is likely that the broad historical process of change in the international economic context will be viewed in much the same way as it was by the original modernizationists and orthodox Marxists—capitalism will penetrate and dominate the economies of Latin American nations and the development of these economies will increasingly resemble the dynamics of capitalism in the United States and Western Europe. Although there will obviously be different mixes of production in these "late, late industrializers," the general trends of growth in capitalist production in agriculture, manufacturing, and services will be the central dynamic of Latin American economies. This view rejects Frank's notion that the international economy prevents the possibility of growth, but it is fully consistent with Cardoso's associated-dependent development. Unlike the assumption of modernizationists, however, the broad, long-term trend will not be universally applicable and will not be unilinear. As the dependency analysts noted, there will be periods of growth and periods of decline within the long secular trend of capitalist expansion, and some countries will benefit from their late entry into the market while others will suffer. It is not as clear that the center countries will have a long-term advantage over some of the countries in the periphery. The rise of the new industrializing countries and the decline of such center countries as Britain and France suggest that more complex processes are occurring. It is likely, however, that the historical periodization that dependency analysts proposed for Latin American development—outward expansion, ISI, new international division of labor—will continue to be a fruitful orientation since the economies of the continent often confront similar patterns of change in relation to the international economy.

Applying this perspective to the current international context, we find the Latin American situation dominated by the debt crisis and the general world recession. This economic crisis may be interpreted as a new period in Latin American history, or it may be seen as part of the cyclical economic changes of the "new international division of labor." The international economic crisis of the 1980s—beginning with the second oil crisis in 1979 and the steep recession in the economies of the United States and Western Europe—marked a major period of contraction for most of the economies of Latin America. This cyclical decline, brought on primarily by changes in the economies of the center, was made significantly worse in Latin America by a decade of rapidly expanded lending from Western financial institutions. In the 1970s these institutions, flush with the flood of petrodollars generated by the first oil crisis, found the Latin American economies an attractive and relatively secure investment. However, when the recession hit the developed economies and interest rates soared in the 1980s, the Latin American nations were caught with a large and accelerating debt and declining markets for their goods. Without easy means of expanding exports to the depressed and increasingly protectionist world markets and with the growing reluctance of international financial institutions to make fresh loans available, the Latin American nations have been forced, usually with the active involvement of the IMF, to restrict imports and to impose austerity programs.[50]

This crisis has forced almost all Latin American economies to contract. Unlike the economic crises of the 1960s—which were so important for analyzing the BA regimes—this crisis was the result of changes in the international economy more than changes in the internal economies of Latin American nations. However, the current external crisis is not as serious as that of the depression of the 1930s. The crisis of the 1980s has not cut off the linkages in trade or investment and financing between the center and the periphery that, as dependency analysts emphasized, had been ruptured by the depression of the 1930s. Under the current conditions the potential for growth in an "inward looking" model are remote. Consistent with our synthetic model in which the expansion of capitalism will involve greater international penetration of the national economies and increasing capitalist production within each national economy, the expansion of both the international and the domestic markets must occur if the economies of Latin America are to enter a renewed growth period.

Unanticipated by dependency analysts of the 1960s, the international loans shifted the character and dimensions of the foreign financial linkages from those dominated by MNCs with direct investment and physical presence in Latin America to those dominated by financial connections between Western lending agencies and a variety of borrowers in Latin America, primarily governments and their semiautonomous agencies. Since the debt payments fall heavily on the governments, this crisis has weakened the state's capacity to influence the economy and to carry out redistributive reforms. At the same time it has strengthened the negotiating position of the IMF, MNCs, and the national bourgeoisie.

It is not clear how the current debt crisis will be resolved. Some of the costs might have to be borne by the international financial community since there appears little possibility that Latin American export economies can grow fast enough to gain control of the external debt in the near future.[51] Although there is a real possibility of a major international crisis on the scale of the depression, it is perhaps more likely that a cycle of growth will begin again and that Latin American economies will have to pursue a growth path that mixes some elements of deepening with export-oriented growth. Paying off the debt will necessarily involve generating foreign exchange through exports, and these exports will have to be competitive on the international market. Although primary products will continue to be important exports, industrial goods will become increasingly significant. This "new international division of labor" will shape economic changes in each nation, but how each nation responds will depend on domestic national factors, which we will explore later.

Another element in the international context that will continue to be an important issue for future development theories is the role of U.S. hegemony. The historic role of the United States as the major market for Latin American goods and as the major investor in the region is changing as Latin American nations seek and gain a diversified market in Europe and the Far East and attract investments from these regions. Nevertheless, in the current debt crisis it is U.S. banks that have taken a leading role in shaping the international economic context for Latin America. At the same time, the rise of a new cold war foreign policy has dictated greater U.S. aggressiveness and an attempt by the United States to reassert its historic political hegemony in the region. These events will fit neither the simplistic cold war crusading of the early modernizationists nor the crude dependency assumptions that U.S. policy follows the dictates of U.S. business. It will be more appropriate to view the U.S. role as a complex result of both U.S. strategic and economic interests and the interrelations among different U.S. government agencies, different sectors of the U.S. business community, and the dynamics of broader public opinion.

If we shift focus from the international sphere to domestic national processes, we find that the complex issues of class structure and regime character are at the center of all the perspectives we have discussed. A synthetic approach will have to examine these issues, borrowing from the successful core elements of each approach. As Cardoso suggests in his historical-structural perspective, the relationship between the external economy and the domestic economies shapes both class structure and political processes. It will not be possible to follow the early modernizationist assumption that national processes occur in relative isolation from international influences. However, contrary to Frank's assumptions, the international influences are not likely to have a uniform effect on Latin American nations. There will be, as Cardoso's analysis suggests, multiple paths to development that will be the result of both the specific character of the links between each nation and the world economy and the character of class and political dynamics within each nation. Future theory will attempt to categorize the foreign linkages and the class dynamics into groups that help explain, and perhaps predict, the relationship between these factors and the type of regime and its policies. This was, of course the central objective of O'Donnell's model.

The future approach, however, will probably also profit from further developments in the modes of production analysis. This analysis will help develop the description of the economic bases for the classes in conflict and will, in particular, focus attention on the different classes at the lower end of the scale—filling in an area that neither Cardoso nor O'Donnell developed sufficiently.

As both the modernizationists and the sophisticated dependency analysts agree, the middle sectors—themselves more clearly disaggregated into subclasses—will be important to the process of development, although they will not take the central role assigned them by the modernizationists, and their value attachments—especially their commitment to democracy—will be contingent on other factors and not inherent in their economic situation.

The state is likely to emerge as central to future analysis. As we saw with O'Donnell, theorists have attempted to relate the character of the state to particular demands of economic structures and class conflict. As the critiques of O'Donnell suggest, the causal relationship between these factors and the type of regime has not been established. Nevertheless, it is likely that theorists will continue to search for systematic explanations for regime changes. In this area, the interest in theories of the state will continue to attract Latin Americanists. The relative autonomy of the state from class forces, and the role of legitimacy that these recent theories have raised, will continue to be central issues. These characteristics of the state will probably become important variables in determining—along with the international linkages and class conflicts—which of Cardoso's multiple paths a nation will pursue.

Corporatism will contribute to this analysis, as it has to the recent analyses of European development, with its concern for "functional groups" and paternalistic relationships. These structures will be explored as mechanisms that mediate and modify the development of class-based organizations. They will also be used to examine the relationship between the state and the upper classes in situations where interest-group representation is limited by corporatist organizations. Finally, corporatist analysis of the institutions of the state itself may become an important area of inquiry.

Value issues will also be a component of the new synthetic theory. Following modernizationists, it is likely that the role of value diffusion will be reexamined in the context of the growth in capitalist structures and the rise of both entrepreneurial values and lower-class consciousness. The enduring nature of corporatist values will be studied in terms of its relations to class consciousness and to paternalistic and hierarchical institutions of the state. Although values probably will not be examined as motors of change, as they had been by early modernizationists, they will be seen as important elements that interrelate with structural changes. In this regard, the Marxist concern with hegemonic ideology and the role of legitimacy might provide a basis for theoretical convergence on value issues. Of particular concern will be the adherence of various classes—especially the middle classes—to democratic values. No simple assumptions about commitments to democracy will be made, but the contingent factors that affect adherence to democratic values will be important components of new theory.

Applying this synthetic analysis of domestic processes to the second central event of the current period in Latin America—the return to formal democracy in most Latin American countries—we confront the problem O'Donnell attempted to address in his BA approach: how to explain the formation of particular types of regimes on the basis of economic and class factors. We have already suggested that O'Donnell's economic explanation for the rise of BA—the deepening thesis—was the least successful of his concepts. What we may be seeing is a general, and perhaps too elegantly simple, process in which economic crises— whether their origins are primarily international, such as the oil and debt crises, or internal, such as the exhaustion of ISI—are destabilizing to the regime in power. The process of regime change might have less to do with how actors anticipate the new regime will solve a particular economic problem—such as O'Donnell's argument that the authoritarian regimes were perceived capable of solving the crisis of ISI exhaustion— and more to do with the loss of legitimacy by a regime that has failed to promote economic growth—as O'Donnell's second essay suggests. With this failure nations then face the demand for some change in economic policy. This demand historically has resulted in an oscillation between the orthodox monetary policies—including government auster- ity—and the Keynesian structuralist approach—involving much more active state intervention in the economy. According to Hirschman, this oscillation is probably the major dynamic of change in government policies—neither economic policy is sufficient for sustained growth, and when the economy fails the government also fails and is likely to be replaced by a government willing to adopt the alternative economic policy.

The implications for regime change then are how the government responds to economic crises and how successfully that response reduces the economic strain. There may be no clear relationship between the type of regime and its willingness to adopt a particular set of economic policies—both democracies and BA regimes have adopted both of the alternatives that Hirschman discusses. There does, however, seem to be a related process—the oscillation between military and civilian rule.[52] Throughout Latin American history there have been periods of democratic rule interrupted by usually short periods of military rule. When BA regimes appeared, they were perceived as quite different from their military predecessors since the BA military claimed the right to rule indefinitely. Although the BA militaries were generally able to rule longer periods than the earlier military regimes, with the exception of Chile, they all succumbed to the same fate: the return of power to democratic rule. Ironically and perhaps tragically these new democracies are forced by the international context to pursue the orthodox economic strategies they had resisted in the period before BA.

The current international crisis came at the end of a long period in which much of Latin America was ruled by BA regimes. When these regimes first came to power in the 1960s and 1970s, they pursued a short period of orthodox economic policies that, with the notable exception of Chile, was usually followed by active state involvement in the promotion of growth industries—especially for nontraditional exports—and infrastructure development. These policies achieved "economic miracles" that brought high levels of growth but were dependent on the flow of credit from the center countries. This credit was largely directed toward government agencies, making the state the central linkage with external capital. Unlike the direct investment of MNCs, however, the financial flows did not mean the same level of risk and involvement for the international actors in the local economy. However, it did mean that the governments became increasingly and directly dependent on external capital, and although in some cases, such as Brazil and Mexico, the size of their debt gave them some leverage over the international banks, the governments nevertheless were forced to adopt the austerity that the international banking community—usually through the IMF— insisted on for future loans. Austerity programs imposed constraints that forced the state to withdraw from its active role in the economy— opening the way for the dominant classes and MNCs to follow their own logic in making investments and producing profits. Austerity also weakened the state's ability to provide social programs to help co-opt the lower classes and moderate class conflict. This resulted in a loss of legitimacy for the regime and forced the state either to enforce greater repression—as in Chile—or to hold out the promise of a regime change toward democracy.

It is clear that even those groups that initially profited from the imposition of the BA regimes—the bourgeoisie, the MNCs, and the international banks (the groups O'Donnell thought were most threatened in the later stages of populism)—became convinced that the BA regime had run its course and was no longer effective in managing the economy and controlling the lower classes.

It was the middle sectors that played a crucial role in changing the political regimes—though not as important as Johnson might have expected. They were the original partners of the lower classes in the populist alliance, and they abandoned the lower class in the crisis that led to the creation of the BA regimes. Although they might have been hesitant to embrace populism again, when they became dissatisfied with the BA regime they were a crucial bellwether that indicated serious loss of regime legitimacy, encouraging both the bourgeoisie and the international community, each with its own reasons for dissatisfaction with BA, to seek an alternative political structure with greater potential for gaining political legitimacy among both the middle sectors and lower classes.

The lower classes, in particular the working class, bore the brunt of the repression of the BA regimes and lost the most from the economic policies—especially during the orthodox periods. Union organizations were crushed or restructured along corporatist lines, weakening the capacity of the working class to create organized bases for unity and to develop class consciousness. Nevertheless, working class organizations became important allies of the middle sectors and the members of the dominant classes who demanded a return to democracy. Since the establishment of the new democracies, unions often have been willing to moderate demands—even in the face of austerity programs—in order to avoid creating a crisis that could bring the military back to power.

The strategies of alliance-building and class conflict that are pursued by labor organizations are likely to be a central factor in determining the future paths of development for each nation. If strong alliances with middle sectors, and perhaps some of the dominant classes, are successfully formed, then structuralist economic policies may replace the orthodox policies, and the democratic structures may endure. If, on the other hand, orthodox policies are not modified and labor is forced to pursue strategies of increasing conflict, then it is less likely that the democracies will survive.

An examination of the return to democracy would be incomplete without some attention to the value issues. Although it is hard to sustain Silvert's optimism that modernization would bring a growing commitment to democracy, it is nevertheless apparent that most political participants in Latin America today are committed to some form of democracy. Except for a brief period of enthusiasm for the early BA regimes, the military regimes never gained widespread acceptance. This is not to say that agreement on the formal terms of the new democracies was easily reached, or that the commitment to democracy will be held above other values. However, even in the face of continued economic crisis and government austerity policies, many of the post-BA regimes have sustained a honeymoon of support—suggesting some degree of enduring legitimacy. Unlike the military regimes that had to overcome the historic expectation that their rule would be temporary, the democracies appear to be viewed as somewhat fragile and in need of nurturing. Even if they do not deliver economic prosperity, they may yet maintain some measure of legitimacy beyond that granted to the BA regimes.

How does corporatism fit into the new democracies? It is clear that the corporatist structures embedded in most Latin American nations have not disappeared as the BA regimes are transformed into formal democracies. Many of the corporatist political parties that were important during the BA periods are still major participants in the new regimes. State structures involving corporatist control mechanisms, particularly for labor, are enduring. Furthermore, as Schmitter suggests, Western democracies are also built on corporatist structures. It is therefore not likely that corporatism and democracy are incompatible. The strength of these corporatist structures, however, may explain the enduring weakness of the lower-class groups in the new democracies.

All of these factors—the oscillation of policy and regimes, the weakening of the state, the role of the middle and lower classes, value changes, and corporatist mechanisms—could be used to define the different paths to development charted by separate groups of Latin American nations. It will take detailed empirical and theoretical work to develop the contours of the separate paths. We hope that the kind of approach outlined here can be used to point the way for a complex, multiple-path analysis that builds on a synthetic combination of modernization, dependency, modes of production, corporatism, and BA.

Conclusion

It is risky, of course, to predict the direction of theoretical development. We can be disproved so easily by the imagination of future theorists. Furthermore, we have been working at such a high level of abstraction that many of the generalizations presented here are open to considerable debate and challenge. Even the core argument that there are strong opportunities for synthetic convergence is itself a controversial proposition. We have tried to show that the efforts in the past—in particular those of Cardoso and O'Donnell—suggest strong merit in this approach and that some broad trends in social science theories beyond the fields of Latin America and development point in a similar direction. We have also tried, in a skeletal way, to show how this synthetic approach might be applied to current trends in Latin American development— in particular the current economic crisis and the return to formal democracy.

Synthetic convergence, however, is not without its own limitations. Clear guidelines have not been developed for assigning priorities to the interactions among the theories. Such priorities will have to be determined through further empirical work, as the emergence of significant multiple paths based on the combined elements of dependency, modes of production, corporatism, modernization, and BA are explored in each country.

A synthetic approach may also be criticized for a purported lack of theoretical rigor. By combining various theories that are based on different assumptions, the logical and conceptual clarity of each might be lost. This is of course a potential problem. However, it is our perception that among the sophisticated theorists the differences in assumptions are not seriously incompatible. The core elements chosen for our approach can be combined in such a way as to retain logical rigor.

We have not been able here to develop a new theory of multiple paths—such an endeavor requires combining theory and empirical work, an enterprise that is beyond the scope of this volume. However, we have tried to take the smorgasbord of possible theoretical approaches and show which dishes were unpalatable and which were most appropriate to combine in a new feast. We hope the readers of this text will join us in preparing that feast.

Notes

1. Thomas S. Kuhn, *The Structure of Scientific Revolutions* (Chicago: University of Chicago Press, 1962).

2. J. Samuel Valenzuela and Arturo Valenzuela, "Modernization and Dependency: Alternative Perspectives in the Study of Latin American Underdevelopment," *Comparative Politics* 10:4 (July 1978), pp. 535–557.

3. David Collier (ed.), *The New Authoritarianism in Latin America* (Princeton, N.J.: Princeton University Press, 1979).

4. Michael Wallerstein, "The Collapse of Democracy in Brazil: Its Economic Determinants," *Latin American Research Review* 15:3 (1980), pp. 3–40.

5. Ian Roxborough, "Unity and Diversity in Latin American History," *Journal of Latin American Studies* 16 (1984), pp. 1–26; Octavio Ianni, *La formación del estado populista en América Latina* (Mexico, D.F.: ERA, 1972); Ernesto

Laclau, *Politics and Ideology in Marxist Theory* (London: New Left Review, 1977).

6. Karen L. Remmer and Gilbert W. Merkx, "Bureaucratic-Authoritarianism Revisited," *Latin American Research Review* 17:2 (1982), pp. 3–40.

7. Roxborough, "Unity and Diversity," pp. 22–26.

8. Guillermo O'Donnell, "Reply to Remmer and Merkx," *Latin American Research Review* 17:2 (1982), pp. 41–50.

9. Another criticism of BA is that its applicability is limited to the most industrialized countries and therefore offers little expanation of power for countries that have scant potential for going beyond the easy stage of ISI, such as the countries of Central America. Since O'Donnell was explicitly focusing on the dynamics of one group of countries, we do not view this criticism as particularly applicable. Indeed, as we develop in this chapter, it seems pertinent to view different groups of countries as following separate paths of development within general historical periods.

10. Samuel P. Huntington, "Political Development and Political Decay," *World Politics* 17:3 (April 1965), pp. 386–430.

11. Robert A. Packenham, *Liberal America and the Third World: Political Development Ideas in Foreign Aid and Social Science* (Princeton, N.J.: Princeton University Press, 1973), pp. 123–129.

12. Fernando Henrique Cardoso, "Associated-Dependent Development: Theoretical and Practical Implications," in *Authoritarian Brazil: Origins, Policies, and Future,* edited by Alfred Stepan (New Haven, Conn.: Yale University Press, 1973), pp. 142–178.

13. Maurice Zeitlin and Richard Ratcliff, "Research Methods for the Analysis of the Internal Structure of Dominant Classes," *Latin American Research Review* 10:3 (1975), pp. 5–62; Zeitlin, W. Laurence Neuman and Richard Earl Ratcliff, "Class Segments—Agrarian Property and Political Leadership in the Capitalist Class of Chile," *American Sociological Review* 41:6 (1976), pp. 1006–1029.

14. Sanjaya Lall, "Is 'Dependence' a Useful Concept in Analyzing Underdevelopment?" *World Development* 3:11-12 (Nov.-Dec. 1975), pp. 799–810.

15. Michael B. Dolan and Brian W. Tomlin, "First World–Third World Linkages: External Relations and Economic Development," *International Organization* 34:1 (Winter 1980), pp. 41–63.

16. Cardoso, "Associated-Dependent Development," p. 149.

17. David Ray, "The Dependency Model of Latin American Underdevelopment: Three Basic Fallacies," *Journal of Inter-American Studies and World Affairs* 15:1 (Feb. 1973), pp. 4–20.

18. See Gary Gereffi, *The Pharmaceutical Industry and Dependency in the Third World* (Princeton, N.J.: Princeton University Press, 1983).

19. See, for example, Ronald H. Chilcote and Joel C. Edelstein (eds.), *Latin America: The Struggle with Dependency and Beyond* (New York: John Wiley & Sons, 1974).

20. Morris Blachman, William LeoGrande, and Kenneth Sharpe (eds.), *Confronting Revolution: Security Through Diplomacy in Central America* (New York: Pantheon, 1986).

21. C. Richard Bath and Dilmus D. James, "Dependency Analysis of Latin America," *Latin American Research Review* 11:3 (1976), pp. 3–54.

22. Peter B. Evans, *Dependent Development: The Alliance of Multinational, State, and Local Capital in Brazil* (Princeton, N.J.: Princeton University Press, 1979).

23. Nora Hamilton, *The Limits of State Autonomy: Post-Revolutionary Mexico* (Princeton, N.J.: Princeton University Press, 1982).

24. Douglas C. Bennett and Kenneth E. Sharpe, *Transnational Corporation vs. the State: The Political Economy of the Mexican Auto Industry* (Princeton, N.J.: Princeton University Press, 1985).

25. Roxborough, "Unity and Diversity," pp. 1–26.

26. Colin Henfrey, "Dependency, Modes of Production, and the Class Analysis of Latin America," *Latin American Perspectives* 8:3-4 (Summer-Fall 1981), pp. 17–54.

27. Roxborough, "The Analysis of Labour Movements in Latin America," *Bulletin of Latin American Research* 1:1 (Oct. 1981), pp. 81–95.

28. See issues 1, 4, 11, 21, and 30-1 of *Latin American Perspectives*; Philip J. O'Brien, "A Critique of Latin American Theories of Dependency," in *Beyond the Sociology of Development: Economy and Society in Latin America and Africa,* edited by Ivan Oxaal, Tony Barnett, and David Booth (London: Routledge & Kegan Paul, 1975), pp. 7–27.

29. Valenzuela and Valenzuela, "Modernization and Dependency," pp. 542–543.

30. Philippe C. Schmitter, "Still the Century of Corporatism?" in *The New Corporatism: Social-Political Structures in the Iberian World,* edited by Frederick B. Pike and Thomas Stritch (Notre Dame, Ind.: University of Notre Dame Press, 1974), p. 90.

31. Alain Touraine, *The Post-Industrial Society* (New York: Random House, 1971); Daniel Bell, *The Coming of Post-Industrial Society: A Venture in Social Forecasting* (New York: Basic Books, 1976).

32. Samir Amin, *Unequal Development: An Essay on the Social Formations of Peripheral Capitalism* (New York: Monthly Review Press, 1976); Arghiri Emmanuel, *Unequal Exchange* (New York: Monthly Review Press, 1972); Immanuel Wallerstein, *The Modern World-System: Capitalist Agriculture and the Origins of the European World-Economy in the Sixteenth Century* (New York: Academic Press, 1974).

33. Bill Warren, "Imperialism and Capitalist Industrialization," *New Left Review* 81 (Sept.-Oct. 1973), pp. 3–44.

34. John G. Taylor, *From Modernization to Modes of Production: A Critique of the Sociologies of Development and Underdevelopment* (London: Macmillan Press, 1979).

35. Theodore J. Lowi, *The End of Liberalism: Ideology, Policy, and the Crisis of Public Authority* (New York: W. W. Norton & Co., 1969).

36. Schmitter and Gerhard Lehmbruch (eds.), *Trends Toward Corporatist Intermediation* (Beverly Hills, Calif.: Sage Publications, 1979).

37. Alexander Gerschenkron, *Economic Backwardness in Historical Perspective* (Cambridge, Mass.: Harvard University Press, 1962); Barrington Moore, Jr., *Social Origins of Dictatorship and Democracy: Lord and Peasant in the Making of the Modern World* (Boston: Beacon Press, 1966).

38. Juan Linz, "An Authoritarian Regime: Spain," in *Mass Politics: Studies in Political Sociology*, edited by Erik Allardt and Stein Rokkan (New York: The Free Press, 1970), pp. 251–283.

39. James R. Kurth, "Industrial Change and Political Change: A European Perspective," in *The New Authoritarianism*, pp. 319–362; Bennett and Sharpe, "Capitalism, Bureaucratic Authoritarianism, and Prospects for Democracy in the United States," *International Organization* 36:3 (Summer 1982), pp. 633–634.

40. Packenham, "Holistic Dependency and Analytic Dependency: Two Approaches to Dependency and Dependency Reversal," *Stanford-Berkeley Occasional Papers in Latin American Studies* 6 (Winter 1984), pp. 1–12.

41. Cardoso, "The Consumption of Dependency Theory in the United States," *Latin American Research Review* 12:3 (1977), pp. 7–24.

42. Gereffi, *The Pharmaceutical Industry*, pp. 40–43.

43. Ralph Miliband, *The State in Capitalist Society* (London: Weidenfeld & Nicolson, 1969); Nicos Poulantzas, *Political Power and Social Classes* (London: New Left Books, 1973).

44. Antonio Gramsci, *Selections from Prison Notebooks* (New York: International Publishers, 1971).

45. Erik Olin Wright, *Class, Crisis and the State* (London: New Left Books, 1978); Göran Therborn, *What Does the Ruling Class Do When It Rules?* (London: New Left Books, 1978).

46. Theda Skocpol, *States and Social Revolutions: A Comparative Analysis of France, Russia, and China* (New York: Cambridge University Press, 1979).

47. Stephen D. Krasner, *Defending the National Interest: Raw Materials Investments and U.S. Foreign Policy* (Princeton, N.J.: Princeton University Press, 1978); Kurth, "Industrial Change and Political Change," pp. 319–362.

48. Albert O. Hirschman, "The Turn to Authoritarianism in Latin America and the Search for Its Economic Determinants," in *The New Authoritarianism*, pp. 61–98; Alfred Stepan, *The State and Society: Peru in Comparative Perspective* (Princeton, N.J.: Princeton University Press, 1978).

49. Other analysts of the field who argue for some sort of convergence are Joseph S. Tulchin, "Emerging Patterns of Research in the Study of Latin America," *Latin American Research Review* 18:1 (1983), pp. 85–94; Robert R. Kaufman, "Trends and Priorities for Political Science Research on Latin America," *The Wilson Center Latin American Program Working Papers* 111 (1982), pp. 37–46; Peter Evans, "After Dependency: Recent Studies of Class, State, and Industrialization," *Latin American Research Review* 20:2 (1985), pp. 149–160; Ian Roxborough, *Latin America: Class, State and Development* (London: Macmillan, forthcoming).

50. Inter-American Development Bank, *Economic and Social Progress in Latin America: External Debt, 1985 Report* (Washington, D.C.: Inter-American Development Bank, 1985), pp. 3–148; Pedro-Pablo Kuczynski, "Latin American Debt," *Foreign Affairs* 61:2 (Winter 1982-1983), pp. 344–364.

51. Richard S. Weinert, "International Finance: Banks and Bankruptcy," *Foreign Policy* 50 (Spring 1983), pp. 138–149.

52. This observation is from a personal communication with James Kurth, March 1985.

Selected Bibliography

Bath, C. Richard, and Dilmus D. James. "Dependency Analysis of Latin America," *Latin American Research Review* 11:3 (1976), pp. 3–54.

Bennett, Douglas C., and Kenneth E. Sharpe. "Capitalism, Bureaucratic Authoritarianism, and Prospects for Democracy in the United States," *International Organization* 36:3 (Summer 1982), pp. 633–664.

Blomström, Magnus, and Björn Hettne. *Development Theory in Transition, The Dependency Debate and Beyond: Third World Responses.* London: Zed Books, 1984.

Cardoso, Fernando Henrique. "Associated-Dependent Development: Theoretical and Practical Implications," in *Authoritarian Brazil: Origins, Policies, and Future,* edited by Alfred Stepan. New Haven, Conn.: Yale University Press, 1973, pp. 142–178.

Cardoso, Fernando Henrique. "The Consumption of Dependency Theory in the United States," *Latin American Research Review* 12:3 (1977), pp. 7–24.

Collier, David (ed.). *The New Authoritarianism in Latin America.* Princeton, N.J.: Princeton University Press, 1979.

Evans, Peter. "After Dependency: Recent Studies of Class, State, and Industrialization," *Latin American Research Review* 20:2 (1985), pp. 149–160.

Henfrey, Colin. "Dependency, Modes of Production, and the Class Analysis of Latin America," *Latin American Perspectives* 8:3-4 (Summer-Fall 1981), pp. 17–54.

Lall, Sanjaya. "Is 'Dependence' a Useful Concept in Analyzing Underdevelopment?" *World Development* 3:11-12 (Nov.-Dec. 1975), pp. 799–810.

O'Brien, Philip J. "A Critique of Latin American Theories of Dependency," in *Beyond the Sociology of Development: Economy and Society in Latin America and Africa,* edited by Ivar Oxaal, Tony Barnett, and David Booth. London: Routledge & Kegan Paul, 1975, pp. 7–27.

O'Donnell, Guillermo. "Reply to Remmer and Merkx," *Latin American Research Review* 17:2 (1982), pp. 41–50.

Packenham, Robert A. *Liberal America and the Third World: Political Development Ideas in Foreign Aid and Social Science.* Princeton, N.J.: Princeton University Press, 1973.

Ray, David. "The Dependency Model of Latin American Underdevelopment: Three Basic Fallacies," *Journal of Inter-American Studies and World Affairs* 15:1 (Feb. 1973), pp. 4–20.

Remmer, Karen L., and Gilbert W. Merkx, "Bureaucratic-Authoritarianism Revisited," *Latin American Research Review* 17:2 (1982), pp. 3–40.

Roxborough, Ian. *Theories of Underdevelopment.* London: Macmillan Press, 1979.

Roxborough, Ian. "Unity and Diversity in Latin American History," *Journal of Latin American Studies* 16 (1984), pp. 1–26.

Taylor, John G. *From Modernization to Modes of Production: A Critique of the Sociologies of Development and Underdevelopment.* London: Macmillan Press, 1979.

Tulchin, Joseph S. "Emerging Patterns of Research in the Study of Latin America," *Latin American Research Review* 18:1 (1983), pp. 85–94.

Valenzuela, J. Samuel, and Arturo Valenzuela. "Modernization and Dependency: Alternative Perspectives in the Study of Latin American Underdevelopment," *Comparative Politics* 10:2 (July 1978), pp. 535–557.

Wallerstein, Michael. "The Collapse of Democracy in Brazil: Its Economic Determinants," *Latin American Research Review* 15:3 (1980), pp. 3–40.

Warren, Bill. "Imperialism and Capitalist Industrialization," *New Left Review* 81 (Sept.-Oct. 1973), pp. 3–44.

Index